# Paul Lendvai

# ANTI-SEMITISM IN EASTERN EUROPE

MACDONALD · LONDON

First published in the United States of America

First published in Great Britain in 1972 by
Macdonald & Co. (Publishers) Ltd,
St Giles House, 49/50 Poland Street, London W.1

SBN 356 04016 x

Reproduced and Printed in Great Britain by
Redwood Press Limited, Trowbridge & London

# CONTENTS

## PART ONE
### Communism and the Jews

## PART TWO
### Nightmare in Poland

The Jews on the other hand with their stubbornness and fanaticism make excellent revolutionaries . . . There (in the civilized world) the eminent, universally progressive traits of the Jewish culture—its internationalism and its heedfulness to the progressive movements of the epoch—have manifested themselves distinctly. The percentage of Jews in democratic and proletarian movements is everywhere higher than the percentage of Jews in the population generally.

Lenin

They do not like collective work, group discipline . . . They are individualists . . . Jews are interested in everything, they want to probe into everything, they discuss everything and end up by having profoundly different opinions.

Khrushchev

We cannot go forward to Communism with such a heavy load as Judophobia. And here there can be neither silence nor denial.

Yevtushenko

# PART ONE
## Communism and the Jews

## 1. FROM THE CORPORATE JEW
## TO THE CORPORATE ZIONIST

*The remedy which Lenin and Trotsky have found, the suppression of democracy as such, is worse than the evil it is supposed to cure.*

Rosa Luxemburg

A quarter of a century after the deliberate murder of six million Jews in gas chambers and concentration camps, after Auschwitz and Treblinka and Majdanek, anti-Semitism, that outrage to common sense,[1] has suddenly once more become one of the main themes of political life in Poland, the very country that was the mass grave of European Jewry. In 1968 the some twenty-five thousand survivors of a prewar community of three and a half million were brutally shaken by an anti-Semitic campaign that led to an officially instigated, if not enforced exodus which may well mark the end of the thousand-year history of Polish Jewry.

It was not only the scene of the anti-Semitic crusade, but also the direction from which it came that perplexed the observer and shocked East European Jews, the fact that the instigators were the self-styled heirs of Marx and Lenin, the spokesmen of a supposedly international movement. The victims, vilified as "Zionists, cosmopolitans, Stalinists, and revisionists," were mostly Jews by force, not choice, living examples of assimilation to Polish culture, persons who had regarded themselves as Poles even when they were conscious of their Jewish background.[2]

The events in Poland refute the widespread assumption that "organized hatred of Jews cannot but be a reaction to their importance and power."[3] In 1968 Jews amounted to less than one tenth of 1 per cent of the total Polish population, and it is generally agreed that after the war, and in particular after the last mass emigration in the years 1957–58, Polish Jewry "could neither politically, economically, nor culturally be regarded as a cohesive community, conscious of its separate identity and of its distinct group interests."[4] Less than a decade ago astute foreign observers even came to the conclusion that "the possibilities for assimilation in Poland have never been so favorable as now."[5]

It will be seen later that the transition in Poland from covert unofficial prejudice to institutionalized political anti-Semitism can be fully understood only as the product of certain historical, national, and political experiences placed against a specifically Polish background. Nevertheless, since the 1967 Arab-Israeli War, political anti-Semitism, transparently disguised as "anti-Zionism," has acquired a fresh and disturbing dimension in other Eastern European countries as well. The violent, sustained anti-Israel, anti-Zionist campaign waged in the Soviet Union and Poland in particular can no longer be accepted as merely an attempt to counter a humiliating defeat suffered by Moscow's allies in the Middle East and to justify an unpopular foreign policy. Nor can the venomous attacks on Jewish history, Jewish religion, and the Jewish people be presented purely in conventional "anti-imperialist" terms, as a stand against Israel's "aggressive policies" which serve the interests of "imperialism" in the Middle East.

Stirring the murky depths of the reservoir of modern anti-Semitism, the manipulators of the Soviet "anti-Zionist" campaigns have brought to the surface the tested motif of a sinister global Jewish conspiracy. The updated versions of the "Protocols of the Elders of Zion" and of Nazi propaganda slogans have, of course, been slightly changed to correspond to the new situation. Communist propagandists do not speak about "all-powerful Jewry," let alone of a "Judeo-Bolshevik plot," but invest the essentially unchanged conspiracy theory with new forms.

Step by step over recent years Soviet ideologists have come forward with new theoretical formulations to fit the most efficient fiction of Nazi propaganda—the idea of a Jewish world conspiracy —into a "Marxist-Leninist" mold. The apparently final and officially approved theoretical line was spelled out in Yuri Ivanov's book *Beware: Zionism!* which was published in early 1969 with a first printing of seventy-five thousand copies and received "very positive" reviews in the major Soviet newspapers. Previously, Zionism was regarded as in Lenin's words a "false and reactionary idea," a variety of bourgeois nationalism. The new version is a weird mixture of old notions and Marxist trappings. Ivanov depicts "modern Zionism" as "the ideology, a complex system of organization and political activity of a big Jewish bourgeoisie which has merged with the monopolist circles of the United States and other imperialist powers." "Militant chauvinism and anti-Communism," he adds, "are the main substance of Zionism," which stemmed not from the wish of the Jews to return to Palestine but from "the aspirations of the pro-imperialist Jewish bourgeoisie to control the Jewish masses, to enrich itself and live in parasitic prosperity, and to defend and strengthen imperialism." Worse still, "the international Zionist corporation" acts as a weapon of "American imperialism's global strategy and as an instrument of psychological warfare against the socialist countries." Zionist organizations conduct "activities of ideological subversion and provocation against the Soviet Union and other socialist countries." Over the past ten or fifteen years the Zionists "took an active part in antistate, antipopular actions of the counterrevolutionary forces in Socialist Hungary, Poland and Czechoslovakia."[6]

Both Ivanov and experts on Zionism writing in the most authoritative Soviet newspapers make it abundantly clear that they are not talking about the historically interlocking themes of "Jew-Judaism-Zionism-Israel," but about the present intensified activities of Zionists against "some socialist countries." Zionists, it is claimed, want to form "fifth columns" in socialist countries, using "the exploitation of Jewish persons living in socialist countries" to benefit "the true country," the international Jewish organizations, among them the Joint,* which "under the guise of 'assistance' . . . systematically financed espionage and subversive activities of American-Israeli agents in the socialist countries." *Krasnaya Zvezda,* the organ of the Soviet Army, singled out the March 1968 demonstrations in Poland to make the "message" clear beyond any doubt: "The Polish comrades correctly emphasized that the danger of Zionism lay primarily in Polish citizens of Jewish origin who, feeling that they were the 'sons of Israel,' served Israel willingly or unwillingly."[7]

For all the differences in vocabulary, when Soviet propagandists refer to the "Zionists" they are speaking to the population in a familiar language. The Zionist is the old, mythical Jew, the faceless enemy, the cunning foe. As a Czech novelist aptly put it at the time of the "anti-Zionist" campaign in the wake of the invasion of Czechoslovakia: "Jews can be set apart and defined more easily than, for instance, the intellectuals, the opposition, or the deviationists. Neither a janitor nor a mailman can be 100 per cent certain that an attack on the intellectuals is not also aimed at him in a way; the term 'opposition' or 'those extremist forces' is even more oblique and flexible; but every Aryan knows quite definitely that he is not a Zionist."[8]

In other words, fifty years after the October Revolution and more than two decades after the Communist takeover in Eastern Europe, when the spokesmen of the ruling regimes use the euphemism "Zionists" for the Jewish citizens of socialist countries they are merely giving a new "theoretical" justification for the old stereotype, "the Jews," the agents of a closed conspiracy for world control. We are therefore dealing here not with anti-Judaic, anti-Israeli, or even anti-Zionist strictures in conventional terms, but with modern political anti-Semitism of the Communist variety.

It is no longer an orthodox believer or a shady speculator with a Jewish-sounding name who is involved, or even Judaism as a "reactionary political force" or Israel as "an aggressive outpost

* The generally used abbreviation for the American Joint Distribution Committee.

of imperialism." The Jews now appear—in the guise of "Zionists" —as the carriers of both financial conspiracy and imperialist encirclement, as the incarnation of the foreign enemy, made more powerful by their international connections: in short as a world danger. "Political anti-Semitism may be defined as the attempt to establish the corporate Jew as a general and public menace, the implication being that some official public remedy is called for."[9] In accordance with both the classic use of the scapegoat and the constant suspicion that distinguishes the totalitarian system, the corporate Jew is a symbol of external danger.

The references to the Joint, Western intelligence agencies, and political penetration into the "socialist" countries, coupled with the heavy hints about "citizens of Jewish origin," evoke the memory of Stalin's last years when the "Doctors' Plot" and the Slansky trial in Prague as well as lesser known "conspiracies" like the Kiev case and the Crimean affair[10] were regarded as a prelude to the mass deportation of Soviet and East European Jews. The "murderers in white aprons," nine professors of medicine (six of them Jews), were publicly accused on January 13, 1953, of having poisoned some of their patients among the rulers of the Kremlin and of planning further attempts on the lives of several Soviet marshals and generals, acting on behalf of the British and American security services and the "international Jewish bourgeois nationalist organization," the Joint, which had given them orders to "wipe out the leading cadres of the Soviet Union."[11]

It is important to remember that, as always, the openly anti-Jewish campaign was not an end in itself, but only a means to an end, to a last great purge "finishing off," among others, the old members of the Political Bureau of the Communist Party.[12] Equally significant, anti-Semitism had become the single most important catalytic agent for all the strains in the system. As Isaac Deutscher, a by no means unsympathetic observer of Soviet affairs, put it: "If the intrigue had been allowed to run its course, if the trial of the doctors had been held, it could have only one sequel: a nation-wide pogrom."[13]

The death of Stalin removed the nightmarish threats to which

Jews from Moscow to East Berlin, Prague to Budapest, had been exposed, threats all the more horrifying because they came so soon after the extermination of millions of Jews. One of the first moves of the new regime was to declare the "Doctors' Plot" null and void, to exonerate the doctors and to accuse "despicable adventurers" in the Ministry of State Security, who through such "fabrications" intended "to inflame feelings of national antagonisms which are profoundly alien to socialist ideology . . . in Soviet society."[14] Since then most Western Communist spokesmen and all Soviet leaders have persisted in blaming the "Doctors' Plot," like all other "shameful acts," on Stalin or Beria, his last secret police chief.

The question of how far the horrors of Stalinism were inherent in the Soviet system and how far they were influenced by the personality of Stalin is marginal to the purpose of this survey which is concerned only with the relationship between the Communist movement, in and out of power, and the Jewish Question in Eastern Europe. Though the Soviet regime tolerates and thus tacitly approves anti-Semitism, nothing would be more stupid and misleading than to identify covert discrimination in university admissions, crude anti-Judaic tracts or even cartoons depicting hook-nosed Israeli soldiers with blood dripping from their hands with the wholesale persecution and imprisonment of Jews during the notorious "Black Years" of 1948–53. There is a world of difference between not getting a particular job and being deported to Siberia, or, as in the case of many Poles and Czechs, between obtaining an exit permit and landing in jail as a "Zionist conspirator." Equally unwise and, in terms of the fight against racial prejudice, counterproductive, is the tendency to regard any criticism of individual Jews, of the State of Israel or the fall of a Communist leader of Jewish origin as anti-Semitic in character.

Yet if one looks at the more than thousand-year history of anti-Semitism and at the fundamentals of Soviet policies toward the Jews, the conclusion is inescapable: there is only a difference of degree, not of substance, among the various forms of modern political anti-Semitism. This may seem a rather outrageous way of summing up a distinction that so often meant a difference between life or death for millions of human beings. It must be borne in mind, however, that "every study of ideas—or . . . of the interaction between ideology and politics—suffers from the same weakness: it can never be more than a pale shadow of the actual historical record."[15] Even with the memory of the Holocaust fresh in mind we—Jews and non-Jews alike—have to resist the temptation of equating anti-Semitism, even subconsciously or unwittingly, with Nazi genocide, the extermination of Jews. It would indeed be a profoundly ironic posthumous triumph for Hitler if the unbelievable sufferings endured by European Jewry during World War II were to serve now as a perverse "patent of tolerance" for rabid anti-Semites in Warsaw, Prague, or Moscow. It would be almost like regarding only premeditated murder but not arson, robbery, rape, or fraud as crime in a civilized society.

## 2. MOSCOW—CENTER AND EXPORTER OF ANTI-SEMITISM

There are at least three important reasons that make Soviet anti-Semitism a matter of legitimate concern.

1. Except for the Middle East, anti-Semitism as an official policy, as a witch-hunt which cost some Jews their lives and many more their freedom has, since the fall of the Third Reich, been found exclusively in Communist countries, the Soviet Union, Poland, Czechoslovakia, and, in a more distant past, in Rumania, Hungary, and East Germany. Since the exposure of the "Doctors' Plot," no top Soviet official or any major newspaper has found occasion to condemn the specifically anti-Jewish character of the case or to mount a mass educational program against racial prejudices. At his June 1967 press conference in New York, Premier Kosygin denied that anti-Semitism had ever existed in the Soviet Union. Quite apart from the fact that he himself apparently harbors anti-Semitic feelings of a rather vulgar nature,* there is convincing evidence of a *permanent* current of hostility toward the Jews in Soviet political life, veering between tolerated covert discrimination and deliberate encouragement of latent anti-Semitic prejudices.

*At the Soviet-Czech summit meeting at Cierna on July 29, 1968, Kosygin insulted Frantisek Kriegel, a member of the Czechoslovak Party Presidium with the remark: "What is this Jew from Galicia doing here?" When Kriegel attempted to reply, Kosygin cut him short saying: "Shut your trap!" (Reported in the New York *Times* August 29 and confirmed by some Czech sources while others attributed the remark to the Ukrainian leader, Shelest.)

The question is not whether Stalin or Khrushchev or Brezhnev disliked Jews more or less, but whether they allowed the violation of one of the hallowed tenets of Marxist socialism which recognizes neither Jew, Moslem, nor Christian but only classes and class interests. While anti-Semitism in the Soviet Union as everywhere else has many and varied sources, the crucial point is that the operative logic of the Soviet system, doctrinal considerations, and, last but not least, coldly calculated "reasons of State" have led and still lead Soviet rulers to consider the Jews a security-risk group.

By its very nature, a totalitarian system cannot tolerate any form of ethnic, religious, or communal solidarity, any diversity of culture, any plurality of views or political currents. It must also create artificial outlets within the state for the dissatisfaction that inevitably develops.[16] The Jews, a unique minority with international traditions, a world-wide religion and emotional or cultural ties to their "co-religionists" beyond the borders (mainly in "hostile" countries) are a natural target.

But the troubled history of the Jews under Communism shows that the Jewish Question has never existed in a void; it must be viewed in the wider context of general policies. If it is true that the fate of Jewry has always been embedded in the structure of Soviet society, then the rekindling of latent anti-Semitism is a concomitant of the rise of social tensions in a conservative society which for a variety of reasons (loss of inner dynamism, evasion of major unsolved problems, a political vacuum at the top, the threat of China, and the growing strains in Eastern Europe) in periods of insecurity whips up party discipline and heroic traditions, nationalism and xenophobia, racialism and the hatred and fear of the alien.

It is not in spite but because of the nature of Soviet Communism that the technique of scapegoats, in this case anti-Semitism, is applied as a calculated device to release the tensions, conflicts, and struggles within the system. Recent developments in Soviet political life—the rising tide of chauvinism, militarism, and retrogression—have provided an additional stimulus to the emergence of the Soviet Union as the international center of an increasingly overt political anti-Semitism.*

2. Whether anti-Semitism as a political instrument is wielded surreptitiously with calculated moderation or openly with uncontrolled fury, under the conditions of a single-party system with a single dogma preached by Party and state, there is an important risk factor. "The fundamental reason for the superiority of totalitarian propaganda over the propaganda of other parties and move-

* Since this chapter was written, Soviet anti-Semitic and anti-Israeli propaganda has gained both in scope and intensity. In mid-1970 a new edition of Ivanov's book (*Beware: Zionism!*) was published, now with a printing of two hundred thousand copies! The author included new "evidence" of the "subversive activities of Zionist centers against the socialist countries," primarily Czechoslovakia. The Rothschilds are now accused of having financed not only "Israeli militarism" but also "the Czechosklovak counterrevolutionaries," the "West German neo-fascists," and the "Vatican." The French Rothschilds, for example, are said to have "financed directly the Czechoslovak counterrevolutionaries through a bank account in Tel Aviv."

Since the spring of 1970 almost hysterical "hate campaigns" were launched against Israel and "world Zionism" with mass meetings and the usual unanimous resolutions passed. There followed the arrests of dozens of Jews, the Leningrad trials causing worldwide protests and an "anti-Zionist" campaign unparalleled since Stalin's death in its ominous implications. Though the "sit-ins" and demonstrations of many Jews, demanding exit permits, and the pressure of international public opinion forced the Soviet government to allow a considerably larger number of Jews to emigrate to Israel, long-term prospects for Soviet Jewry are gloomy. After several long attacks of Pravda, Jews *as such* and not just those wanting to emigrate are now officially regarded as a potential "fifth column." It would be however a serious error to regard the freedom to emigrate as the *only* issue. (No Soviet citizen enjoys the "privilege" of freedom of movement!) The real issue is as before equality between Jews and non-Jews. Thus in the long run, the future of Soviet Jewry depends on the direction of political and social developments in the Soviet Union itself.

ments is that its contents, for the members of the movement at any rate, is no longer an objective issue about which people may have opinions, but has become as real and untouchable an element in their lives as the rules of arithmetic."[17]

Communism is a world of manipulated myths which have often turned into deliberate policy what may have started as a casual misjudgment. The totalitarian state demands total loyalty from its citizens and excludes every other allegiance. The statements the leaders declare to be the doctrinal truth at any given moment must be accepted by their subjects. Thus the rulers must justify not only major policies, but the juggling of concepts, sudden changes in political tactics and in rhetoric (for instance, the alliance with Hitler and the carving-up of Poland, the ups and downs in the USSR's troubled relations with Yugoslavia, the switch from a pro-Israel to a pro-Arab position in the Middle East, the conflict with Communist China, etc.) in terms of sacred theory.

Both modern political anti-Semitism and Communism need an integrated belief system. This, in turn, possesses a logic of its own, leading inevitably to a conspiracy theory with absolutist trappings. Hannah Arendt has pointed out the decisive significance of the notion "objective enemy" for the functioning of totalitarian regimes: "He is never an individual whose dangerous thought must be provoked or whose past justifies suspicion, but a 'carrier of tendencies' like the carrier of a disease."[18] The entire history of the Communist movement is a line of plots, conspiracies, and treason, the ferreting out of imagined or potential enemies. Regardless of the forms of coercion and the techniques of terror (show trials and wholesale summary executions under Stalin, demotion, deportation, or imprisonment under his successors), this kind of system needs the purges, those "artificial revolutions" to release and absorb the strains within it, to preserve its inner dynamism.[19]

The need for self-preservation requires continuous self-justification since the subjects must profess unshakable faith in the infallibility of the leadership. In terms of the official state religion a Communist country cannot be imperialistic, territorial disputes cannot make enemies of two Communist countries, a Communist state

14

cannot discriminate against a national minority, and such social problems as anti-Semitism and juvenile delinquency cannot exist in a Communist country. Since all those things do in fact occur, the official ideology has become meaningless and irrelevant to the basic issues facing the Communist regimes today. But it has not lost its operational effects on practical policies. It makes compromise between Communist governments difficult and often impossible since they are by definition "brothers" and must therefore conceal differences that would be considered perfectly natural among non-Communist countries.

At the same time unconditional loyalty to the "universal" truth that in any situation and at any given moment can be defined only by the dictator or the group in power has other consequences as well. Everything in a Communist society is linked together, so there must always be a mask of political respectability for a political practice that otherwise would seem shameful or intolerable. To put it crudely, stereotypes are sometimes more influential than reality, and words become deeds. Herein lies the enormous danger of systematic lying, which with the Damocles sword of terror is at the very core of a totalitarian system. "The consistency of fiction and the strictness of organization make it possible for the generalization eventually to survive the explosion of more specific lies . . ."[20]

Take, for example, the "Doctors' Plot." The case is now officially a "frame-up" fabricated by "despicable adventurers." Similarly, the 1952 trial of the former Secretary General of the Czechoslovak Communist Party, Rudolf Slansky, and his "Trotskyite-Titoist-Zionist center" was repudiated in 1963 as an invention from beginning to end.* Yet fifteen years after the "fabrications" a strikingly similar "hate campaign" focuses attention on the espionage activities and political and ideological subversion engineered by "Zionism" against "the socialist countries." If we compare the hair-raising absurdities in the indictment at the Slansky trial or the web of inventions in connection with the "Doc-

* See also the chapter on Czechoslovakia.

tors' Plot" with the recent spate of allegations about the omnipotent "international Zionist Corporation," an "invisible but huge and mighty empire of financiers and industrialists" created by "the blackest forces of world reaction" and acting as a "motor force" of imperialist efforts at world domination, we see the same spirit and the same methods.

Thus the erstwhile "murderers in white aprons" are innocent doctors, the murdered Slansky and his co-defendants are exonerated victims "of the violation of Socialist legality," but the rope with which they were hanged is being dangled again. Even the chief villains of Stalin's last script, the charitable organization Joint as the main instrument of espionage and subversion, and Zionism in the service of American intelligence, have re-emerged, and Communist "experts" on Judaism and Zionism use almost verbatim quotes from the source material prepared for the Slansky trial and the "Doctors' Plot." To be sure, there have been some minor changes with some alleged foes now dropped and new "objective enemies" discovered according to the changed circumstances. The "Trotskyite" danger is too obsolete a notion to be credible, and the "Titoist" conspiracy is said to have been "fabricated" by "Beria and others." These "outs" of the old script have now been replaced by new "ins," such as the previous collusion between Zionists and Nazis which has culminated in the present alliance between Zionism (which is said to have "all the characteristic attributes of Fascism"!) and the German "revanchists and militarists."

Many of the updated legends about the "Zionist" world conspiracy are so remote from reality that some Western observers tend to dismiss the Soviet diatribes as crude excesses of everyday political propaganda. One may recall, however, the notorious "Protocols of the Elders of Zion" which purported to reveal the text of twenty-four lectures delivered at a secret meeting of world Jewry. This blatant forgery prepared at the turn of the century by agents of the Tsarist secret police alleged that the "Elders of Zion" sought to foment wars, discontent, and chaos, to infect people with frightful diseases and to use subway stations to blow up modern cities in order to bring about a messianic age in which Jews would rule the world.[21] Following its publication in the wake of World War I—not so very long ago—this collection of phantasmagoria became one of the most widely read books in the world.

Soviet tales of the invisible but all-powerful world Zionist conspiracy have the odor of the "Protocols" and were born in the same underworld, "where pathological fantasies disguised as ideas are churned out by crooks and half-educated fanatics for the benefit of the ignorant and superstitious."[22] Lest this comparison seem too harsh, let us glance at a typical Soviet article on the subject. The author Y. Yevseyev, a Candidate of the Historical Sciences (the second most prestigious scholarly qualification in the Soviet Union), stated flatly on October 4, 1967: "The number of Zionism's adherents in the United States alone comes to 20 to 25 million. There are Jews and non-Jews among them. They belong to the associations, organizations, and societies that play the greatest role in American economy, politics, culture, and science. Zionist lawyers comprise about 70 per cent of all the American lawyers; physicists, including those engaged in secret work on the preparation of weapons for mass destruction, 69 per cent, and industrialists more than 43 per cent. The adherents of Zionism among American Jews own 80 per cent of the local and international information agencies. In addition, about 56 per cent of the big publishing houses serve the aims of the Zionists."[23]

Thus not only all of America's six million Jews (less than 3 per cent of the total population) but also nineteen million other Americans are Zionists, and together they practically control the United States. The fact that these "statistics" were patent forgeries, borrowed from an obscure Egyptian pamphlet (published ten years earlier and probably ghost-written by a Nazi fugitive)[24] and "improved" by the Soviet author, was irrelevant for propaganda purposes. What matters is that they fit a new political situation. The fact that refurbished "classical," Nazi or Stalinist anti-Semitic myths are freely used today is politically more important than the fact that most of them are gross falsehoods. It is not within our scope to explore the details of Soviet "anti-Zionist" campaigns.* It is enough to stress that statements like Yevseyev's do not represent idiosyncratic views of individuals but rather the basic thrust of the state's entire propaganda apparatus, which constantly focuses the attention of the citizen on external dangers (American "imperialism," West German "revanchism," Chinese "great power chauvinism," etc.) and since 1967 has harked with ominous frequency on the threat of the "international Zionist conspiracy."

This is not to say that the nightmare of 1952–53 is again hovering over the three million Jews in the Soviet Union. But Arthur Koestler's perceptive insight into the Soviet system is as valid today as it was almost two decades ago: "They believe everything they can prove, and they can prove everything they believe."[25] The stubbornness with which the Soviet propaganda continues to cling to its lies about the Joint, Jewish finance, and the global Zionist plot, which were earlier repudiated by the same regime as "fabrications," compels us to reassess old assumptions about the "Black Years" of Soviet Jewry and about the temporary or incidental character of anti-Semitism as a political weapon.

We tend to forget that even in the age of spaceships totalitarian propaganda by its very nature must strive to fit selected elements of reality into another, entirely fictitious world. "Once these propaganda slogans are integrated into a 'living organization' they cannot be safely eliminated without wrecking the whole structure. The assumption of a Jewish world conspiracy was transformed by totalitarian propaganda from an objective, arguable matter into the chief element of Nazi reality; the point was that the Nazis *acted* as though the world were dominated by the Jews and needed a counterconspiracy to defend itself."[26] Similarly, the Soviet system, striving to keep itself pure of hostile contamination, manufactures dangers that become facts of life for the population.

Under these conditions, there is no effective defense or counteraction against such practices as anti-Semitism, for the ruling regimes maintain that these ills do not and cannot exist. Consequently,

---

* This is done meticulously and reliably by such periodicals as *Jews in Eastern Europe* (London) and other specialized publications.

critics are almost automatically regarded as petty-bourgeois troublemakers who have fallen prey to foreign ideological penetration. If they persist, they are treated as potential foes who "objectively" act as the accomplices of hostile external forces.

In sum, the very fact that anti-Judaism or anti-Zionism must be presented in impeccable "Marxist-Leninist" terms as something completely different from anti-Semitism forces Societ propaganda to dress up the essentially unchanged legend of a world-wide Jewish "plot" in orthodox ideology. The corporate Jew becomes a corporate "Zionist" (occasionally also a "rootless cosmopolitan") who stands for corporate imperialism. The practical and semantic difficulties involved lend an added stimulus to the independent force of ideological rhetoric, which in turn possesses a dynamism of its own. Regardless of top-level intentions, in certain historic situations the fantasies produced by systematic lying may become a political force that sweeps along a divided leadership worn out by living in a constant state of crisis. This, then, is another extremely serious risk factor. The massive and incessant "anti-Zionist" propaganda has gradually constructed a theoretical basis that is in some ways worse and more coherent than even the pathological fabrications of the Stalin era. There is more than ample evidence that the Soviet Union has bred a climate ominously propitious for institutionalized and virulent racial discrimination.

3. Finally, ever since late 1948, the Kremlin, for different reasons and to varying degrees, has engaged in the export of covert or overt anti-Semitism. In addition to the dual threat posed to the survival of Israel and the position of the Jewish community in the Soviet Union itself, there is this third dimension of Soviet policy toward the Jews. And it is this export of first anti-Zionism and later anti-Semitism that has had a major impact on the fate of Jewry in Eastern Europe with which our study is primarily concerned.

One can distinguish two major phases in Soviet influence on the Jewish Question in Eastern Europe. The first phase (1948–53) coincided with Stalin's lifetime, when a single political system with a single line and a single discipline was imposed on the entire Soviet sphere of influence. During this phase of uniformity the position of Jewish communities was intimately connected with Soviet policy toward the Jews and in particular with regard to Israel. The Soviet Union and the United States were the midwives at the birth of the State of Israel, Stalin having decided that military and political support of the Israelis would undermine British influence in the Middle East. Then, on September 21, 1948, Ilya Ehrenburg's famous anti-Zionist article in *Pravda* heralded an abrupt change of line. In accordance with the traditional Bolshevik view, Zionism became a heresy throughout the Soviet sphere of influence. It was not so much the "ingratitude" of Israel—that is, its alignment with "imperialism"—but the emotional upsurge among Soviet Jewry, raising the suspicion of a rival allegiance, that tipped the scales and convinced Stalin that the Jews were an unstable, unreliable element. The targets of the attacks were first the real Zionists, then "the people without a fatherland" or "rootless cosmopolitans," and finally the faithful but Jewish servants of the Kremlin. The campaigns culminated in the Slansky trial, and we know now from several unimpeachable sources to what extent Stalin's agents were directly responsible for the witch-hunt that subsequently threatened the life and liberty of thousands of East European Jews.*

Nothing could illustrate the irony of changing historical situations better than the fact that the same regime that had saved the life of countless Jews in the closing stages of World War II, only a few years later suddenly and seemingly inexplicably emerged as the chief foe of the survivors of the Holocaust who had set about to re-create a life for themselves.

The death of the dictator transformed uniformity to diversity all over Eastern Europe, a tortuous transition punctuated by upheavals in 1953, 1956, and 1968. The same process of differentiation has been evident in regard to both the Jewish communities in Eastern Europe and the attitude of the ruling parties to the Jewish Question and to Israel.

* For details see the chapter on Czechoslovakia.

Yet we can detect the same distressing thread in Soviet policies in moments of acute crisis: the deliberate encouragement of anti-Semitic prejudices thinly disguised as "anti-Zionism." To use an old Communist cliché, it was no accident that both in 1956 in Poland and in 1968 in Czechoslovakia the Kremlin consciously played the Jewish card. On both occasions the element of anti-Semitism was introduced into the political debates by a besieged and embattled Soviet leadership. On both occasions hatred for Soviet domination was to be channeled into hatred for an insignificant minority—the Jews.

In short, the export of anti-Semitism as a by-product of Soviet efforts to contain the drive for independence and freedom in Eastern Europe, to stir internal discord, and to drain off anti-Soviet popular discontent is by no means a spent force. If this consistent pattern of abetting racial prejudices beyond the Soviet borders is linked to other facets of Kremlin policy toward Israel and its own Jewish problem, it becomes clear that the Soviet Union exerts a negative impact—in this special context too—on the process of change going on in Eastern Europe.

## 3.  ANTI-SEMITISM WITHOUT JEWS

The Arab-Israeli War in June 1967 had unexpected and profound repercussions in the Soviet Union and Eastern Europe. The humiliating defeat inflicted on Moscow's Arab allies was a stunning setback to Soviet prestige in the world, made even worse by the conflict in Communist countries between the official pro-Arab line and popular sympathy for Israel. Some observers indeed believed the Six Day War was the catalyst that resurrected the dormant Jewish Question as East European Jews suddenly discovered their "Jewishness" in relation to Israel and the official efforts had to be made to justify the Soviet's Middle East policy.

Subsequent developments, however, have failed to bear out this interpretation. True, the issue of anti-Semitism came dramatically into the open as a crucial factor in the political struggles that broke out in Poland and Czechoslovakia. But references to the repercussions of the Middle East conflict, though surely significant, do not explain the timing, the character, and the scene of the "anti-Zionist" purges. These were the products of very complex situations, confirming the view that general trends such as the growth of anti-Semitism can hardly ever be explained in terms of one single cause.[27]

How should we interpret the fact that the Six Day War had no impact whatever on the life of the two largest East European Jewish communities (excluding Soviet Jewry), those of Rumania and Hungary, while it exposed Polish and Czechoslovak Jews to persecution? The argument that Rumania used this issue to demonstrate its independence of Moscow does not hold water. The Hungarian Government lined up behind Moscow as quickly and as unflinchingly as all other client states, yet there was no trace of open or covert anti-Semitism, although, with a population one third the size of Poland's, Hungary had almost four times as many Jews. (Now it has almost ten times as many.) Or take Yugoslavia, whose leader Marshal Tito is widely known as Nasser's oldest and staunchest East European friend. There the sharp anti-Israeli stand was not only free of any taint of racial prejudice, but the Yugoslav Communists also publicly castigated the "anti-Zionist" campaign in Poland. It might be added that the blatant exploitation of ethnic prejudices did not develop a really dangerous momentum of its own in Poland until nine months after the Middle East War and in Czechoslovakia until almost a year later.

Have racism and bigotry deeper roots in Poland and Czechoslovakia than in Hungary or Rumania? To put it bluntly, are the Poles and Czechoslovaks notorious anti-Semites while the other East European peoples have shed their prejudices? The historical record shows that such assumptions are untenable. Hungary was the first country in Europe to introduce an official "numerus clausus" (closed number), a quota system, against Jews in higher education after World War I, and in Rumania the Jews were able to get citizenship only after four decades of international pressure in the 1920s, while Czechoslovakia was a model of functioning democracy and full civil equality in the interwar period.

Does the blame then fall on those Jewish Communists who came back to their countries in the baggage trains of the Soviet Army when World War II ended and were given top positions? There is an element of plausibility in this theory. But the Slanskys, Bermans, Rakosis, and Paukers have been gone for more than a decade, and what the Jews are now being blamed for is liberalism (disguised as "Zionism"), not Stalinism. Furthermore, they were certainly more conspicuous in Hungary and at least as influential in Rumania as in Poland and Czechoslovakia.

Why then the sudden and remarkable outburst of pent-up animosity against the Jews as such? Why now? And why in Poland and to a lesser extent in Czechoslovakia and not in Hungary or Rumania?

Simplistic generalizations are clearly impossible. Neither the radiation of Soviet influence, nor the Arab-Israeli War, nor the tangled undergrowth of myth and prejudice, nor the role of the Jewish Communists can be isolated as the chief factor. Yet even at this point in our survey we may venture to make a few general suggestions about the common background:

1. Political and social crisis is still, as always, the essential breeding ground for the emergence of political anti-Semitism under a totalitarian system.

2. There is not necessarily a direct relationship between folk (or emotional) anti-Semitism and political anti-Semitism.

3. Under the conditions of a single-party system official anti-Semitism or institutional racial discrimination does not arise from the grass roots and, in contrast to the past, no intoxicated mass movement is needed for it to appear or succeed.

4. What is needed is either an embattled and enfeebled ruling group in the party or a clique of new claimants to a share in power that, for whatever reasons, are willing to use covert or open Jew-baiting as a demagogic weapon.

5. Rampant nationalism can be, but is not necessarily an important contributary cause. Nationalism has re-emerged as the central underlying theme of political life in Eastern Europe, but it plays a complex and ambiguous role in the processes of change. It must be viewed in the context of the tension-ridden relations between an imperial super-power and a host of small nations. Since the defense of national individuality is primarily anti-Soviet, and since "anti-Zionism" is often sponsored by the Kremlin, anti-Semitism cannot be simply identified with nationalism. More than once in postwar East European history anti-Semitism has been discredited as a pro-Soviet and consequently essentially anti-national device.

We must be wary of labels and of uncritical acceptance of an "ism." The attempt to define developments, which in each country have very distinctive and often contradictory features, according to the stamp these regimes and personalities are supposed to bear, is a perilous matter. Nothing would be easier and more harmful than to lump together challenging and contradictory events under such convenient labels as "eternal anti-Semitism," a struggle between "soft" liberals and "hard" Stalinists or between "native" Communists and "Muscovites."

In speaking about Jews and Communists, one must pose the question, what kind of Jew and what kind of Communist? In each of the four Communist-ruled countries we will investigate, the traditions and position of the Jews are different; and in each of the four Communist regimes, we are faced with startlingly diverse developments and with "national regimes which cloak themselves in the verbal trappings of radical Marxism and follow domestic policies influenced to one degree or another by Marxist concepts."[28]

In practical terms, the whole issue seems to be trivial since in the late 1960s there were very few Jews indeed in Eastern Europe. The Nazi massacre decimated the prewar Jewish population of over five million to some 730,000 by the end of World War II. Several waves of legal and illegal emigration have further reduced the number to about one third of the survivors. About 250,000 Jews or less than 5 per cent are all that is left. Taking into account the population increase, this means that while before World War II, roughly speaking, every eighteenth East European was a Jew, there was in 1968 only one Jew per 420 inhabitants. In other words, the Jews account for a mere 0.2 per cent of the total population.

By any normal standards it would be hard to persuade sane people that this handful of Jews could be a serious threat to anything. In the very countries (Poland and Czechoslovakia) in which the fate of the Jews has become intertwined with the political ferment, their number is truly infinitesimal: some 12,000 in 1968 in Czechoslovakia (at the time of this writing 4000 of them have already left) and around 25,000 in Poland (which by the time of the publication of this study will have been halved to 10,000 if not less).[30]

### JEWISH POPULATION STATISTICS[29]

|  | Prewar (in % of pop.) | 1945 | 1968 |
|---|---|---|---|
| Bulgaria | 48,000 (0.8%) | 49,000 | 5,000 |
| Czechoslovakia | 360,000 (2.5%) | 51,000 | 12,000 |
| Hungary | 444,000 (5.1%) | 140,000 | 100,000 |
| Poland | 3,350,000 (9.7%) | 50,000 | 25,000 |
| Rumania | 757,000 (4.2%) | 428,000 | 100,000 |
| Yugoslavia | 68,000 (0.5%) | 13,000 | 6,000 |
| Total | 5,027,000 | 731,000 | 248,000 |

(Prewar figures refer to prewar borders and postwar statistics to postwar borders. Official censuses of 1930 for Czechoslovakia, Hungary, and Rumania, of 1931 for Yugoslavia, of 1934 for Bulgaria and 1939 calculations based on the 1931 census for Poland. The 1945 figure for Poland excludes the 250,000 to 300,000 Polish Jews who survived in the Soviet Union. Some 170,000 were later repatriated to Poland and subsequently emigrated, primarily to Israel. Statistics for 1968, albeit mainly from official sources, must be regarded as only approximate. See also notes.)

It is true there has never been an automatic correspondence between the number of the Jews and the degree of anti-Semitism in a country. As Salo W. Baron, the foremost contemporary authority on Jewish history observed: "Throughout its history anti-Semitic propaganda frequently proved most virulent in areas of slight Jewish population density. What was attacked was the prevailing image of the Jew rather than any particular Jewish acquaintances whom one could regard as favorable exceptions."[31]

But we are not dealing here with medieval Jew-hatred or the rampant passions of emotional anti-Semitism directed against devout Jews, ghetto communities, or recent alien immigrants. And in the case of modern political anti-Semitism, which reached its culmination in Nazism, the corporate Jew and his implacable foes were from the very beginning on two different sides of the barricades.

The Communist variety of political anti-Semitism is in some (not all) respects an entirely new phenomenon. The most important new note is the fact that the real targets of the attack (politicians, officials, administrators, scientific and technical experts, writers and journalists, etc.) and their persecutors claim to subscribe to the identical ideology, to belong on the same side of the barricade (whatever this notion may have come to mean during the past two decades). The overwhelming majority of those labeled "Zionists" regard themselves and seem to have been accepted by their environment as fully assimilated nationals of their respective countries.

There is a three-way split among the East European Jews. In a provocative and highly controversial essay written after the creation of the State of Israel, Arthur Koestler (himself an erstwhile Zionist) stated that "the ultimate distinguishing mark of the Jew is not his race, language, or culture but his religion." He added that the Jew has to make "the choice between either becoming a citizen of Israel or ceasing to be a Jew in the national, religious, or any other meaning of the word."[32] Regardless of whether or not one accepts Koestler's central point,* a very considerable proportion of the Jews in Hungary, Poland, Czechoslovakia, and to a lesser extent in Rumania, out of either conviction or opportunism, belong to this more or less "de-Judaized" category. Another substantial group (particularly those of the older generation) would like to remain "Jews at home" and citizens outside without being discriminated against. They see themselves as patriots and believers, as Hungarians or Czechs or Rumanians, who from religious conviction but increasingly only for reasons of heritage and family ties participate in varying degrees in Jewish religious life. The Jews in Eastern Europe have shared a world-wide process of secularization, although it is obvious that official antireligious doc-

---

* The problem of Jewish identity is beyond the scope of this work; but the last twenty years and the echo of the Six Day War appear to contradict Koestler's either-or solution.

trine, practice, and the evident disadvantages in professional advancement beyond a certain level (which affect not only Jewish but all practicing believers) have driven secularization much further than it would have gone under a democratic regime.

Two world-shaking events in their own lifetimes—the Nazi massacre and the birth of the first Jewish state in two thousand years, coupled with its permanent struggle for survival in a relentlessly hostile environment—have, of course, also influenced East European Jews' sense of continuity with a Jewish past, but in the absence of any polls or surveys, it is impossible to say to what extent they have affected their links with Judaism or their inner sense of solidarity with the Jewish people as a whole. Similarly, to define the rough proportions of the completely "de-Judaized" or "non-Jewish" Jews,[33] of the nonreligious Jews with some feeling of group identity, and of the practicing believers (not necessarily synagogue members), we would have to have access to a great deal of statistical and ethnographic information such as, for example, data on intermarriage, name changes, domestic habits, or intensity of religious practices. We do not, however, possess such information apart from estimates of dubious reliability haphazardly divulged by this or that Communist-sponsored Jewish community organization.

It is even more difficult to assess with any degree of assurance the percentage of real Zionists, that is, those East European Jews whose first and overriding loyalty is to Israel and who are restrained from going there only by travel restrictions. The size of this group varies from country to country and is significantly influenced by the degree of anti-Semitism within the country.

All we have to go by is the information gleaned from Jewish emigrants and refugees during the past decade. These figures are of limited significance, but nonetheless surprising. It is estimated, for example, that about half of the four thousand Czechoslovak Jews who left the country after the 1968 invasion and 35 to 40 per cent of the some eight thousand Polish emigrants who passed through Vienna in 1968–69 had made a mixed marriage. The fairly exact data about the proportion of those going to Israel are also highly revealing. Out of the eighteen thousand Jewish refugees from Hungary after the 1956 October uprising, a mere 10 per cent opted for Israel, and out of the Czechoslovak refugees of 1968 an estimated 15 per cent. Even among the Polish emigrants in 1968–69 the majority, an estimated 60 per cent at the time of this writing, have not gone to Israel but to a variety of other countries in Europe and overseas.[34] An official of an international Jewish charitable organization recalled the witticism credited to the established Jewish settlers in Palestine of the mid-1930s who greeted new arrivals with the question "Did you come from conviction—or from Germany?"

Clearly, there are different motives behind the departures and decisions concerning the new place of residence. The vast majority of recent Hungarian, Polish, and Czechoslovak legal emigrants or refugees left either because (along with 160,000 non-Jewish Hungarian refugees in 1956) they had had enough of a Communist regime or because they were impelled by fear or by pressure to seek safety beyond the borders. It is equally difficult to make distinctions between those who chose Israel out of a deeply felt religious or political commitment, and those who went simply out of necessity, an entry permit to any other country being automatically refused. Neat breakdowns are often misleading, and we must remember the case of the Rumanian Jews. For religious, traditional, and family reasons, 90 per cent of the emigrants from Rumania between 1958 and 1964 went straight to Israel.[35]

Had there been a democratic Eastern Europe instead of an area exposed to the twin assaults of Communism and Soviet domination, East European Jews would probably have behaved like their Western co-religionists toward Judaism and Israel. Those still living in their native countries in the 1960s (excepting perhaps a certain segment of Rumanian Jewry) made a conscious choice between their countries and Israel, opting for full assimilation or a certain degree of religious affirmation without, of course, losing all feeling and sympathy for the Israeli cause. Thus regardless of the countless factors molding the general changes affecting the special position of Jews in each Communist-ruled country, a process of differentiation has also been going on among the Jews themselves.

Even if the Jews—for a variety of reasons which will be discussed later—were and are far more visible than their number suggests, one may legitimately question the importance and propriety of a book dealing with such a seemingly trivial question. There were more Jews in Warsaw or Budapest alone before World War II than there are now in the whole of Eastern Europe. In the Soviet Union the situation is different. There, the some three million Jews, because of their dual status in religion and nationality, do represent a real issue in the context of the unsolved national problem. But how could the "Jewish Question," the quarter of a million, mainly assimilated Jews in Eastern Europe, have any possible connection with the great issues facing these nations—the pressure for freedom and independence, the drive for social justice and efficiency? Is there not a truly grotesque disparity between this minority of 0.2 per cent and a total population of 105 million? Might this seemingly small and unimportant issue not gravely threaten "our sense of proportion and our hope for sanity"?[36]

"The Jews played so important a role in modern history not because they had a mission to carry out (though this aspect should not be belittled), but because it was their fate to serve as a testimony, a living witness, a touchstone, a whipping block and symbol —all in one."[37] While this statement by the Israeli scholar J. L. Talmon may be regarded by some as "emotionally colored," no one who believes in democracy can seriously dispute the opinion that "anti-Semitism invariably reflects or foreshadows a diseased condition in European civilization. Its rise and fall is perhaps the most sensitive index of Europe's moral and political sanity."[38] Or as Jean-Paul Sartre's much maligned (but in regard to the fate of the assimilated Jews of Eastern Europe highly prophetic) essay put it: "Anti-Semitism is not a Jewish problem, it is *our* problem."

The issue transcends statistical figures. The very fact that what we are witnessing is essentially an anti-Semitism without Jews is an all the more alarming symptom of moral pollution and political disintegration. It was often thought that the use of this tool in Moscow, Warsaw, or elsewhere in the Communist orbit was possible only because individual Communist leaders were anti-Semitic in the first place. Some observers speculated over the personal motivations that impelled a Stalin or a Gomulka to don an anti-Semitic garb. While personal or emotional impulses are of some significance, one must begin with the oft-proven truth that one does not have to be an anti-Semite in the conventional sense in order to engage in or support anti-Semitic behavior. Sartre's definition is more than a witty epigram. The Jewish problem is embedded in the fabric of the society. The improvement or deterioration in the status of Jews as citizens with equal rights and duties has been and is closely tied to society's progress and decline, to the rising or ebbing tide of political reforms within the framework of even a single-party political system. The fewer Jews there are, the more the fight against racial hatred becomes primarily, almost exclusively in the interest of non-Jews.

Thus a study dealing with one particular chapter of recent East European history—the position of the Jews under the special conditions of Communist rule—cannot be concerned with the internal developments of Jewish community organizations and religious issues. That is Jewish history. Specifically Jewish problems will not, of course, be overlooked, but they will be mentioned only in so far as they have a bearing on political anti-Semitism.

To judge the East European regimes on their own terms we must focus on their behavior toward those assimilated Jews who live, feel, speak, and act as Poles and Hungarians and Czechs, even if they are conscious of their Jewish background or maintain some religious loyalty. Are these people—within the limits imposed by a dictatorship—fully equal members of the society devoted to "the building of socialism"? Or are they subject to covert discrimination, official anti-Semitism, or institutionalized racial discrimination? In short, do they suffer more or reap fewer benefits because they are men "whom others regard as a Jew"?[39]

More than once since the Communist takeover, the position of the tiny Jewish minorities has been caught up in the general conflicts of the time. If anti-Semitism has been introduced on a relatively large scale into the political debates in different countries at different times, the previous history of the relationship between Jews and the East European states and specifically the role of Jews in the Communist movement both before and after the seizure of power must contain some important clues to the continuing seriousness of the Jewish Question. To see the problem in all its complexity we must go back to the origins of the forces that are still at least partially operative.

## 4.  USURERS, MIDDLEMEN, AND ALIENS

We cannot understand the reasons for different developments to-day without at least a minimal acquaintance with the changes in the position of Jews in the Eastern European states, which them-selves lived for centuries under foreign rule and are in their pres-ent form products of various accidents of Great Power diplomacy.

Contrary to popular belief, there is convincing evidence that Jews have lived uninterruptedly for almost a thousand years in Poland, Hungary, the Czech lands (Bohemia and Moravia), and Dalmatia and Macedonia (now parts of Yugoslavia). The Jewish communities of Prague and Gniezno were mentioned in the elev-enth century and those of Hungary in the decrees of the Hungarian Kings Laszlo (1092) and Kalman (1102).[40] The bulk of the Jews, however, came to Eastern and Southeastern Europe as the result of two great waves of migration, first from Germany and then in 1492 and 1497 from Spain and Portugal. Poland especially became a haven of refuge, since Prince Boleslaw the Pious had granted Jews their first charter in 1246. For a time during the Mid-dle Ages, about four fifths of world Jewry lived in Poland.[41] As Salo W. Baron concludes in his monumental work *A Social and Religious History of the Jews:* "The Jewish people would in-deed have been in a very sad state in the sixteenth century had it not been for the expansion of the two large multinational states of Poland-Lithuania and the Ottoman Empire."[42]

The Jews were first split into two distinct groups according to their recent national origins: the Ashkenazim, who spoke a distinct Jewish vernacular, Yiddish, which became the everyday language of Central and East European Jewry, and the Sephardim who came from the Iberian Peninsula, spoke and wrote in Spanish, and settled almost exclusively in Serbia, Macedonia, Bulgaria, and Greece, where their future development was closely linked with the profound transformations going on in those regions.

The source of Jew-hatred everywhere was the Christian myth of the Jews as the crucifiers of Christ, which was taught and upheld from the fourth century on by both the Roman Catholic and the Greek Orthodox Church. It is most important to recognize that the medieval teachings about the Christ-killers who deserved their exile and misfortunes have persisted into the modern age, often coloring the feelings even of those revolutionaries who later rejected the Christian faith.[43]

The prejudice and hatred inculcated into the minds of people over the centuries were powerfully reinforced by the persistent influence of Jew-baiting folk literature which added such pagan notions as the accusation of ritual murder. Though always repudiated by the Popes and the Vatican, the charge that Jews used Christian blood for ritual purposes was revived as late as the nineteenth century. It is hardly known—or forgotten—that even in countries with highly assimilated Jewish communities like Hungary and Czechoslovakia Jews were indicted and tried on charges of blood libel. Celebrated cases such as the "great trial" in connection with the Tiszaeszlar case in Hungary (1882) and the Hilsner trial fifteen years later in Bohemia divided the Hungarian and Czech nations almost as the Dreyfus Affair divided France, with the great liberals Karoly Eotvos and Thomas G. Masaryk taking up the cudgels for justice. The enormous power of these persistent anti-Jewish legends was dramatically confirmed as recently as 1946–47 when rumors of ritual murders and poisoning by Jews found fervent believers who helped spark the bloody pogroms and anti-Semitic riots in Topolcany in Slovakia, Kunmadaras in Hungary, and Kielce in Poland.*

* It is a significant fact that a Soviet newspaper, the official organ of the local Communist organization in Buinaksk in the Soviet Autonomous Republic Dagestan provided "scholarly" evidence for the blood libel accusing

After the resolution of the Fourth Lateran Council of 1215, the Roman Catholic Church played a key role in fostering political discrimination, "particularly in barring Jews from positions of trust and confidence in the administration and armed forces of Western states and cities."[44] In Eastern Europe the deeply rooted clerical hatred of the Jew as "Christ's enemy" has had a profound impact on the modern anti-Semitic movements. Despite significant exceptions among both bishops and lower clergy, Catholic clericalism in Poland, Slovakia, Croatia, and Hungary between the two world wars and in the immediate postwar years served more often than commonly realized partly as pacemaker and partly as silent supporter of rampant anti-Semitism.

Forbidden to acquire land, barred from almost all professions, wearing distinctive badges and treated as foreigners, Jews everywhere were forced by circumstances to engage in peddling, pawnbroking, and trading. Whether they were small traders or cobblers, tavernkeepers or bankers, Jews as the result of a long historical development became symbols of money-making in the popular mind. Though the great majority of them led a miserable existence, they were exposed to the hatred of the native rural population and later of their competitors in the guilds. While in the West the French Revolution brought emancipation and with it the assimilation and entry of Jews into other occupations, in most East European countries Jews remained precariously poised first as middlemen between the nobility and peasantry, later as a peculiar middle class connecting the feudal system and the peasant subsistence economy to the market, the towns, and the developing industrial, commercial, and banking structures.

Because most East European countries remained backward agri-

---

the Jews of drinking Moslem blood for ritual purposes "at least once a year" (*Kommunist,* August 9, 1960). The article was later repudiated as a "political error" by the same paper. While this appears to be the last public allegation concerning the blood libel, there were also blood-libel disorders against Jewish communities in Margelan and Tashkent, two cities in Uzbekistan (the latter is the capital of the Uzbek Soviet Republic) in 1961 and 1962. For details and Soviet denials see *Jews in Eastern Europe,* May 1963, pp. 34–39.

cultural and feudal societies for a much longer period than the Western states, lacking a real urban middle class and, until the end of World War I, even statehood, social rather than political causes provided the first main reasons for the violent popular hatred of Jews in the most backward areas—Rumania, Poland (since 1795 partitioned between Russia, Prussia, and Austria), and Slovakia. Against the background of the unsolved agrarian question (even after the abolition of serfdom) and living in the midst of poor rural populations and impoverished gentry, Jewish retailers and innkeepers, land contractors and bankers were incomparably more visible than their counterparts in the West. The people resented them as aliens, as obtrusive links in their exploitation, and as symbols of usury.

Yet, in a longer view, the Jews accomplished a necessary but thankless task in economic development. They did not create what was in effect the product of historical forces and national catastrophes. They were rather the beneficiaries of a historic situation and subsequently of the new trends. It is surprising that even so perceptive a historian as Hannah Arendt accepts the cliché about the nefarious role of the Jew as a nonindigenous entrepreneur, an element "that stood in the way of industrialization and capitalization" in Eastern Europe.[45] A penetrating comparative study, written by Professor Nicholas Spulber about the economic role of the alien Jewish entrepreneur in Rumania (from the mid-nineteenth century until World War II) and of the alien Chinese tradesmen in Indonesia (from last quarter of the nineteenth century into the early 1960s), convincingly shows how untenable such assertions are. After presenting a wealth of evidence, he concludes: "Truly enough, the nonindigenous entrepreneur may and does resort to cruel, petty, or 'illicit' methods for amassing wealth in the early phase of development. In turn, however, he discharges complex functions which are indispensable for accelerating the process of change and development: he pries open the tightly closed subsistence economy, shifts its tastes, expands its ties to the market, forces it to diversify, and increases its dependence on trade, industry, and the towns."[46]

36

With a history punctuated by pogroms, persecutions, and expulsions, the Jews from time immemorial were dependent on local or imperial rulers for protection against the population or other powers. As a result of many political and socioeconomic developments the Jews as a corporate group of "protected subjects" were to varying degrees allied to the imperial or royal power. Though conditions differed from country to country and from period to period, the Jews "had somehow drawn the conclusion that authority and especially high authority was favorable to them and that lower officials and especially the common people were dangerous . . . Each class of society which came into conflict with the state as such became anti-Semitic because the only social group which seemed to represent the state were the Jews . . . Because of their close relationship to state sources of power, the Jews were invariably identified with power, and because of their aloofness from society and concentration upon the closed circle of the family, they were invariably suspected of working for the destruction of all social structures."[47]

Nowhere was this alliance between the Jews, an international element without a territory and government of its own, and the remote monarchial authorities such a lasting phenomenon as in Eastern Europe. The belt of nations from the Baltic to the Black, Aegean, and Adriatic seas was for long periods ruled by three empires—Austria (later Austria-Hungary), Turkey, and Russia. Historical evidence shows that the status of the Jews from the Middle Ages well into the twentieth century was always most favorable in multinational states. In contrast to another important alien group, the German settlers in Eastern Europe (whose number ultimately totaled almost five million at the end of World War I), the Jews were not only outside the political body of the nations and later nation-states, but also outside the pale of Christian society and civilization. The power possibilities and risks of their abnormal position have had a fateful influence on the recent history of Jewish communities.

Jews were living in the midst of a dozen or more "historic" and "disinherited" nations which, after having enjoyed longer or

briefer periods of independence, were subjected to German, Turkish, or Russian domination and often were divided between two or
three empires (Rumanians, Poles, and Serbs). By the beginning
of the twentieth century three distinct types of Jewish communities could be distinguished. In the western part of the Austro-
Hungarian monarchy—the Czech lands (Bohemia and Moravia),
western and central Hungary, and of course in neighboring
Austria—the Jewish communities profited from the political emancipation after the revolution of 1848. Engaging in large-scale
commerce and industry but also in the professions and arts and sciences, relatively prosperous, liberal Jewish communities gradually
emerged, speaking the local language and playing an increasingly
important role in economic, political, and cultural life. In the East
—Poland, Slovakia, Carpathian Ruthenia (now renamed Carpathian Ukraine), the northeastern border regions of Hungary
proper, Moldavia, and Bukovina, and neighboring Bessarabia,
Ukraine, and Lithuania—millions of Jews lived in compact Yiddish-
speaking communities, completely separate from the non-Jewish
environment, often wearing distinctive clothes, beards, and side-
locks. With often a less than rudimentary knowledge of Polish,
Rumanian, Czech, Slovak, Hungarian (or Russian), most of them
formed a separate Jewish nationality. This was equally true of the
eastern regions of the Austro-Hungarian monarchy (Galicia,
Bukovina, Carpathian Ruthenia) and of the pale of settlement
outside Russia proper but under Tsarist rule, including so-called
"Congress Poland."

In the Southeastern Balkan countries—Serbia, Bulgaria, and
Greece—were the Spanish-speaking Sephardic communities, who
like the Greeks and Armenians had found under Turkish rule a
haven similar to that in medieval Poland. Maintaining their group
identity patterns throughout the centuries, they lived apart from
the overwhelmingly rural population and rarely came into conflict with their environment.*

The growing nationalism of the hundred million people living

* See also the chapters on Poland, Czechoslovakia, Hungary, and Rumania.

in the so-called "Middle Zone" between Germany and Russia propelled the various Jewish communities into the center of the great conflicts of the time. Living among mixed populations and almost always on the borderline of different national cultures and civilization, the Jews, whether businessmen, intellectuals, or revolutionaries, consciously or instinctively upheld the universal as against the particularist, the internationalist as against the nationalist ideas of their time. When assimilating to their environment, they were invariably attracted by the culture of the dominant nations or center. As the prevailing culture was German, the Jews formed part of the urban German "language islands" in the sea of native peasantry.[48] This was particularly apparent in the Czech lands of the Austro-Hungarian Monarchy, especially in Prague, Croatia, Bukovina, Silesia, and, until the mid-nineteenth century, Hungary.

At this point we must emphasize the crucial, often overlooked impact of Hungarian history on the fate of Central and East European Jewry. The Hungarians, ethnically and linguistically separate from all other European nations, came to Central Europe at the end of the ninth century and enjoyed one thousand years of political rule and cultural supremacy over the Middle Danubian basin. Ever since, this "historical" nation has cut the Slav bloc in two and put up a national opposition to foreign—Turkish and Austrian —rule too strong ever to be entirely broken.[49] Though the 1848 national revolution was suppressed through the combined pressure of Austria and Russia, soon afterward Hungary achieved virtual internal autonomy and independence by the Compromise of 1867 with Emperor Francis Joseph. Under the new Dual Monarchy, the Hungarians were the privileged ruling nation within the borders of historic Hungary. But half of the population belonged to minority nationalities, Rumanians and Slavs, who had an inferior status.

Within this special system the Jews, whose number registered a tenfold increase from 1785 to over 900,000 in 1910, had a unique destiny. To counter the growing weight of the restive national minorities, the Hungarian Government was prepared to give them all rights and career possibilities provided they became completely Magyarized. This did in fact happen in less than two generations. Apart from opening a Golden Age for the second largest Jewish community (after Poland) in Eastern Europe, the process had far-reaching consequences in the regions inhabited by the Slavs and Rumanians. As even the orthodox groups became Magyarized to a large degree and the Jewish middle class and intellectuals used Hungarian as their main language, the bulk of the Jews came to be regarded by the national minorities not only as "alien usurers" but also as agents of the Hungarian oppressor.

The price on the Jewish "ticket of admission" into society under the Dual Monarchy was therefore not conversion[50] but cultural assimilation to the dominant groups—to the Germans, the Hungarians, and to some extent in Bohemia by the end of the nineteenth century to the Czechs. Apart from what Dubnow called the "stateless nation" of the Polish Jews and the traditional Yiddish- and Spanish-speaking closed communities in the border regions of the Monarchy and in the Balkans, urban Jewish groups everywhere were looking either to Vienna or to Budapest. Thus, much more than in the late Middle Ages, the disintegration of the empires and the rise of romantic nationalism served as evil auguries for the future of East European Jewry. Whether fully assimilated to the prevailing culture or remaining in ghetto communities, the Jews found their fate was inextricably linked with nationalism, the single most powerful force in modern East European history.

Nationalism in Eastern Europe has always been a much more extreme, violent, and explosive force than in the West. All these nations concentrated into a comparatively small space have endured long periods of foreign rule, and most of them achieved statehood only in the twentieth century. In contrast to the long-established nation-states in Western Europe, they saw nation and state, nationality and citizenship as two different notions. In these areas with their mixed populations the fight for survival and the defense of national individuality has always meant a struggle against "foreigners." And the rise of this nationalism involved not only aspirations for territorial statehood but also growing awareness of ethnic-cultural identity.

A number of states emerged from the ruins of World War I, all of them created under the promising banner of national self-determination, democracy, protection of minority rights, and agrarian reform. The restoration of Poland, the birth of a new Czechoslovak state, and the creation of an immensely enlarged Rumania and Yugoslavia at the expense of truncated Hungary drastically changed the political map of Central and Eastern Europe. The dreams of progress and equality (except for Czechoslovakia and there only for the Czechs) were cruelly disappointed in the interwar period under the dual impact of misrule by intensely nationalistic, inefficient, and irresponsible ruling classes and such crucial external factors as the Great Depression and the rise of Italian Fascism and German Nazism.

Instead of mitigating the strains and stresses between the nations and their minorities, the disastrous political frontier-making after World War I only proved that the nation-state principle could not be introduced into Eastern Europe without creating in some cases even more glaring injustices and almost everywhere new hotbeds of nationalist friction. The geographic distribution of ethnic groups and traditional loyalties in these regions is so tangled that no clear-cut and wholly satisfactory demarcations are possible. In addition to such vexed territorial issues as Transylvania, Bessarabia, Kosovo, Eastern Galicia, Carpathian Ruthenia, and countless other contested regions all over the area, Eastern Europe bristled with many-sided minority problems. In 1939, out of a population of 110 million, some 22 million belonged to minorities. In spite of the Minority Treaties, which were signed by all the governments, the rights guaranteed remained almost everywhere dead letters. Czechoslovakia and Yugoslavia faced even more serious problems in the conflicts between majority and minority "state nations," in the first case between Czechs and Slovaks, and in the second Serbs versus Croats and Slovenes.

All Successor States were permeated with the spirit of violent nationalism with regard to both their respective unreliable minorities and their small-power imperialism against neighboring states.

For a variety of reasons, the Jews became (except in the Czech lands and Bulgaria) the targets of nationalist fury and social protest. Not surprisingly, in the three countries that had the largest Jewish communities, Poland, Rumania, and Hungary, fascist mass parties were born in the 1930s. What came as a shock, however, immediately after the First World War was that the most assimilated and most "nationalized" Jewish community, Hungarian Jewry, became the victim of rampant anti-Semitism and terroristic outrages.

It must be said that Hungary was the great loser in the war, deprived of two thirds of its former territory and population. Neither Germany nor Austria suffered a comparable national catastrophe. Some 3.3 million Hungarians, well over one third of the nation, many of them living in large compact groups just beyond the new frontiers, were incorporated into the new Successor States. It is impossible to examine closely here the roots of the Hungarian tragedy and the political turbulence following the defeat, which led first to the proclamation of the Republic and then, under the combined pressure of Rumanian-Czech attacks and the incredible political blunders of the Allies, to the peaceful takeover by a small group of Communist agitators who proclaimed Hungary a Soviet Republic.

The 133 days of the disastrous Communist experiment in a mutilated and disarmed country surrounded by strong and hostile neighbors shattered what only a few years earlier seemed to have been a Golden Age of security. The strong Jewish element in the leadership of the Communist regime and the pent-up animosity against the prominence of Jews in so many fields made Jews easy targets for the "White Terror" unleashed by the counterrevolutionaries. To make things worse, tens of thousands of Hungarian refugees from the lost territories, mainly bureaucrats who had been the "masters" in Transylvania and Slovakia, now flocked into the towns of the truncated country. There they found the Jews. Inevitably the whole fury of national frustration and emotional reaction was directed against what was now the only alien body in a mutilated but completely homogenous nation-state.

The demagogic reactionary regime of Admiral Horthy, though permeated with the spirit of militant Catholicism, was the first government to anticipate Hitler's highly successful propaganda, the cry of a secret alliance between the Jewish capitalist and the Jewish socialist. The outbursts of savage anti-Jewish terrorism were, however, only a passing phase, and the decorous anti-Semitism in the following period of consolidation did not seriously affect the position of the Jewish community, with the important exception of the quota system in university admissions. In fact the situation of the Hungarian Jews until the late 1930s was almost idyllic in comparison with that in other East European countries and with what followed. There is a peculiar tragedy in the fate of Hungarian Jewry: it survived intact until the middle of 1944 and was then annihilated in less than eight weeks, when even the perpetrators knew that the war was lost.

There has been another unfortunate paradox in the history of Hungarian Jewry. After the Treaty of Trianon in 1920, 51 per cent became citizens of Rumania, Czechoslovakia, and to a lesser extent of Yugoslavia. Those who remained in Hungary, however assimilated and patriotic, were regarded by the middle class and the state bureaucracy as well as by the prevailing clerical-national ideology of the authoritarian regime as a menace to the purity of the Hungarian nation. Those who became Rumanian, Czechoslovak, or Yugoslav citizens were intensely resented by their fellow citizens as Jews who, in addition to being "irretrievably alien," insisted on calling themselves Hungarian. Loyalty to Hungary became an involved personal problem for every individual Jew among the almost half a million incorporated into the neighboring countries. For over two decades they were crushed between Hungarian "revisionism" (meaning here the revision of the Treaty of Trianon) and Rumanian, Slovak, and Serbian nationalism, each accusing them in turn of "treason."

The fate of the Hungarian Jews vividly demonstrated that the degree of cultural assimilation to the ruling nation could not defuse the Jewish problem, and under the new conditions after World War I it even became the source of additional problems. Yet lack of assimilation was usually regarded as constituting not only the main line of division among the Jews but also the perhaps most important reason for the endemic anti-Semitism in Poland and

Rumania. As Isaac Deutscher noted: "Polish nationalism, anti-Semitism, and Catholic clericalism on the one hand, and Jewish separatism, orthodoxy, and Zionism on the other, worked against a lasting and a fruitful symbiosis."[51] As the overwhelming majority of Polish Jews lived in ghettos, with 87 per cent giving Yiddish or Hebrew as their mother tongue at the 1931 census, and were at the same time, both in actual numbers and in proportion of the total population, numerically the strongest Jewish community in Europe, their presence constituted an exceptionally difficult problem.

It is not unimportant that the same regimes that thundered against the unassimilable aliens also did their best to retard the assimilation process for very obvious reasons. In view of the shaky balance between "state nations" and national minorities in Czechoslovakia and Rumania, the ruling nations in both countries preferred "Jewish Jews" to "Hungarian Jews" or "German Jews." It was better to record a higher number of "Jewish nationality" at the census than to tolerate the swelling of the ranks of the already large "separatist" minorities such as the Hungarians, Germans, or Ukrainians. Thus it happened that Rumanian census-takers in Transylvania, the most bitterly contested area with mixed population, insisted that Hungarian-speaking Jews should declare Yiddish as their mother tongue, and succeeded in producing at the 1932 census the staggering number of 111,000 Yiddish-speaking citizens out of 192,000 Jews the overwhelming majority of whom had for decades been Hungarian in language and culture. To a lesser extent the same practices were reported from Czechoslovakia and Yugoslavia. For good reasons intensely chauvinistic regimes either tolerated or actually encouraged Hebrew education and the Zionist movement.[52]

Even under the rule of dictatorial monarchs or military cliques, in the 1930s the East European regimes were conventional autocracies in different trappings. They vacillated between right center and extreme right, but their leaders never went as far as their bombastic speeches suggested. Though the Communist Parties everywhere, except in Czechoslovakia, were driven underground, genuine opposition parties (liberal, labor, and agrarian) and opposition newspapers were generally able to carry on even if their activities were severely limited and their members, particularly in rural areas, often persecuted.

A deep antagonism between city and village, between the interests of the ruling group (business, bureaucratic, and military) and the majority of the population, social hatred and deep national differences were the fundamental reasons for the dismal failure of the experiment in parliamentary democracy in Poland and Hungary, Rumania and Yugoslavia, Bulgaria and Greece. Functioning parliamentary democracy survived only in Czechoslovakia, more precisely in the Czech provinces of the new state. Nothing would be less fair than to paint a rosy picture of prewar conditions simply because the Communist regimes have failed to solve some of the basic problems and even created new ones. But it should also be kept in mind that these regimes were by no means fascist or totalitarian.

Everywhere, however, except in the western regions of Czechoslovakia and in Bulgaria, anti-Semitism was widespread and in the 1930s, under the combined impact of economic crisis and Nazi influence, increasingly virulent. It embodied a variety of motives and moods—national, economic, political, and religious. "Which group of people would turn anti-Semite, in a given country at a given historical moment, depended exclusively on general circumstances . . . But the remarkable similarity of arguments and images which time and again were spontaneously reproduced have an intimate relationship with the truth they distort. We find the Jews always represented as an international trading organization, a world-wide family concern with interests everywhere, a secret force behind the throne which degrades all visible governments into mere façade or into marionettes whose strings are manipulated from behind the scenes."[53]

Whether Jews were hated as representatives of liberal individualism or of cosmopolitan finance capitalism or, worse still, as carriers of international Communism, they were invariably regarded as actual or potential agents of internationalism and universalism.

But nationalism, not internationalism, was the new reality. The

"Hungarian-Jews" in Transylvania and Slovakia, the "German-Jews" in Bohemia and Moravia (the Czech regions), Silesia and Croatia, the "Russian-Jews" in Bessarabia and eastern Poland were in a double sense outside the pale of the dominant society and nation. The neurotic nationalism in interwar Eastern Europe saw the Jews as a menace whatever their national origin, social status, or political creed: "a foreign body when cultivating their own identity; a menace to the purity and integrity of the national creative genius when attempting to participate in the spiritual life of the nation."[54] The native brands of romantic nationalism, later increasingly infected by the germs of Nazi racism, provided the single most important and permanent background against which the fortunes of the assimilated, foreign, and "Jewish Jews" must be seen.

Though crude anti-Semitic propaganda always singled out the orthodox ("the Galician type") Jews with their traditional dress and habits as the easiest targets, the real social wrath and jealousy were primarily directed against the urban Jewish middle class, the rivals and competitors of the underdeveloped native bourgeoisie and intelligentsia. Concentrated in the few urban centers, faced with meager prospects of jobs in the civil service, the free professions, or the army, seething with discontent, students and graduates tended to split into extreme nationalist, later fascist, or (to a much lesser extent) into extreme left groupings. It was certainly no accident that university students or unemployed "intellectuals" produced the leaders and organizers of fascist mass movements: the National Radicals and Falanga in Poland, the "Iron Guard" in Rumania, and the "Arrow Cross" in Hungary.

The urban petty bourgeoisie, the lower middle class, was one of the main props of economic anti-Semitism, which was incessantly reinforced by the deeply rooted clerical hatred of the Jew as "Christ's enemy." In Poland, Slovakia, Croatia, and parts of Hungary and Rumania religious prejudice was also mixed with denunciations of Jewish atheists, liberals, and socialists.

## 5. THE "ENTRANCE TICKET" OF REVOLUTION

The most potent weapon of interwar official anti-Semitism, however, was the cry of the Jewish Communist Conspiracy, the identification of the corporate Jew with not only that new abomination, international Communism, but also with the service of the hereditary foe, Russia. In short, the Jew was even worse than an alien usurper, he was a traitor and an enemy of the state. As always, there was an element of plausibility in this new Jewish stereotype.

The new states between Germany and Russia were driven by both fierce nationalism and intense anti-Communism. Political power was safely in the hands of bourgeois democratic or right-wing parties. In Hungary, the short-lived democratic venture in the midst of postwar chaos was strangled for good by the political blindness of the Allies, the subversion of Communists, and the massive steamroller of an extreme-right counterrevolution. In Bulgaria, Stamboliski's radical-populist venture was overthrown by a military coup. After their abortive uprising in September 1923 in Bulgaria and assassinations and bomb outrages in Yugoslavia, the Communists in both countries were banned from public life.

It was, however, above all the fear and hatred of Russia, the traditional oppressor of these small nations and now also the standard-bearer of world revolution, that made Communism public enemy number one. Did not the Communists themselves boast of their unconditional loyalty to the Comintern in Moscow? Did they not issue slogans urging the secession of separate nationalities? What the Communists advocated amounted to the dismemberment of the new young states—Rumania, Yugoslavia, and Poland—and the conquest of such contested regions as Eastern Poland, Bessarabia, and Carpathian Ruthenia by Soviet Russia. Regardless of their motives, they were by any normal standards mortal enemies of their own countries, a real menace to the territorial integrity of the Successor States. They were regarded as antinational groups, and they were often led by elements from the national minorities. It is therefore not surprising that in no East European country (except perhaps in certain periods in Bulgaria and parts of Yugoslavia) did they ever represent a serious political force. Even the one legal Communist Party, the Czechoslovak Communist Party, which was completely free in its activities, could, at the peak of its success, poll only 13 per cent of the popular vote.

What, then, was the attitude of the Jewish communities toward the political environment and especially to the Communist movement? While it is true that the main dividing line among the Jews of Eastern Europe was the degree of assimilation, there were many intermediate positions. Those who believed or hoped that assimilation was the answer to the Jewish problem tended to espouse liberal and radical causes. During the interwar period, until the tide of anti-Semitism reached dangerously high levels, the official Jewish organizations generally supported the government in power. Jews individually favored liberal, democratic, Social Democratic, and also Communist Parties. Their voting preferences naturally also depended on their social structure. It is important to remember, however, that the great majority of the Jews were, until the outbreak of World War II, opposed to Zionism as an ideology and a political movement. Even within the "ghetto nation" in Poland, where most of the 3.3 million Jews were clinging to their faith and living on the verge of starvation, Zionists were only a significant minority who never won over the majority of their co-religionists. At the last elections of the leadership of the Jewish community in Poland in 1939, the anti-Zionist "Bund," the Jewish workers' party, polled the great majority of votes.[55] The Zionists, tolerated and to some extent supported by the governments, especially in Poland, believed in the existence of a Jewish people independent of citizenship, mistrusted the Gentile environment, and therefore advocated an exodus and the creation of a Jewish state. But the Jews, regardless of their political creed and social origin, were understandably reluctant to leave countries in which their ancestors had lived for centuries. Exodus appeared to them as a surrender to anti-Semitism, an abdication of their rights and their beliefs in the rationality of man. That this opposition bore within it the seeds of catastrophe, that, in the words of Deutscher, "in this controversy Zionism has scored a horrible victory—six million Jews had to perish in order that Israel should come alive,"[56] was the great tragedy of modern Jewish history. But neither piety nor the subsequent growth of Jewish national consciousness after the Nazi conquest must make the historian forget that most of the time most of the Jews were not Zionists.*

The first major Jewish efforts toward complete integration into society were led, both in the West and in the East, by the middle class and the early liberals. The rise of secular anti-Semitism in the late nineteenth century gave an irresistible impetus to leftist currents, primarily to Marxist socialism, which did not regard Jewish emancipation as an independent issue but as part of the universal emancipation of alienated man—Jew and non-Jew alike—from the bourgeois order. As anti-Semitism was merely a by-product of capitalism, the coming socialist revolution would not only overthrow the bourgeois system but also uproot anti-Semitism for good.

This is not the place to dwell on Marx's youthful essay on the Jewish Question and his unreserved rejection of Jewry and Judaism for which he has so often been accused (in our opinion unjustifiably) of anti-Semitism. More important for our study, although it

---

* The picture was of course different at different times in each community. The British immigration policy in Palestine was also an extremely important factor. As we are not concerned here with Zionism as such, our brief references must necessarily be oversimplified.

revolves around a later epoch, is the frequently overlooked fact that Marx himself was seen by his contemporaries and above all by his bitter critics among the socialists and anarchists as a German Jew. This hostility to Marx as a Jew, combined with general anti-Semitism, was a strong element in the makeup of radical movements in France and Russia. A number of distinguished historians have traced back these aspects of European socialism to their origins and investigated the previously forgotten or ignored vitriolic anti-Jewish outbursts of Fourier, Proudhon, and Bakunin.[57] "The phenomenon of socialist anti-Semitism was in its origin the poisoned root of a tree planted—alongside the more familiar tree of liberty—in the decades following the French Revolution. The anticapitalist and the anti-Jewish themes were intertwined and it took considerable time and trouble before they could be disentangled."[58]

In particular we should not forget the so-called "Populists," the revolutionary terrorists in Russia, who in 1881 blessed the pogroms sweeping through the Jewish regions, known as the Pale of Settlement. Their largest organization, the *Narodnaya Volya* (People's Will), issued appeals for further violence against the "nobles, the Tsar of the Jews, and the Jews." The appeal was later condemned by Plekhanov, the founder of Russian Marxism, as a "base flattery of national prejudices" and by Lenin as that "infamous proclamation." By the turn of the century both Russian and West European socialists were implacably hostile, both in theory and in daily practice, to what August Bebel once called "the socialism of the fools."

Although leftist or socialist anti-Semitism is not as such part of our survey, I would like to make one point absolutely clear: the political anti-Semitism of Stalin and his successors cannot be regarded as an offshoot of anti-Jewish currents in the early and genuinely leftist or socialist movements. I agree with Arthur Koestler who many years ago described the confusion of Left and East as a semantic fallacy: "The Left Babbitt assumed that there is a continuous spectrum stretching from the pale pink liberals to the deeper red socialists and so on to purple Communists. It is time that he got into his head that Moscow is not to his left but to his east. The Soviet Union is not a socialist country and Cominform* policy is not socialist policy. So let us bear in mind that 'East is east and Left is left' and if the twain sometimes still meet, the meeting is purely coincidental."[59] Whether we call it "postcapitalism," "State capitalism," or, as the Yugoslavs do, "etatism," the Soviet system since the early 1930s has completely broken with the ideals of internationalism and the humanistic core of Marxist socialism. This petrified bureaucratic dictatorship has nothing in common with democratic socialism or the genuine Left of any variety. Thus its anti-Semitism (in whatever "ideological" disguise) is rooted not in the radical but in the peculiarly Russian traditions of prejudice and chauvinism as embodied in *Narodnaya Volya* and also in the "Black Hundreds" and pogroms of Tsarism. "Scratch a Russian Communist and you will find a Great Russian chauvinist," Lenin warned as early as the Eighth Party Congress in March 1919.

In spite of many eminent socialist leaders of Jewish origin such as Marx, Lassalle, Martov, Trotsky, and Rosa Luxemburg, neither the Marxist-Socialist nor the Russian Bolshevik movement was ever specifically Jewish. Nevertheless both could be seen and represented as being in some way particularly favorable to the Jews. The nationalist or conservative right found it easy and almost inevitable to fasten upon international Jewry its fear and dislike of international revolution. Similarly, leftist revolutionary movements offered the only true possibilities for escaping the peculiar Jewish predicament. As Talmon put it: "His lack of roots in a concrete tradition . . . combines with the absence of experience of practical government to turn many a Jew into a doctrinaire and impatient addict of social redemption. Suspended between heaven and earth, rejected and excluded, tormented by humiliations, complexities, and ambiguities of his situation, many a young Jew threw himself with the deepest yearning and passion into the arms

---

* The Cominform as a replacement of the Comintern (dissolved in 1943) was founded by the Soviet and six other Communist Parties in 1947 and dissolved in 1956.

of the religion of revolution."[60] The Jew sought solace in Communist Messianism both in the Russia of the Tsar and in interwar Eastern Europe.

If in the early days the October Revolution appeared to the extreme right to be the product of a "Judeo-Communist" conspiracy, it also seemed to embody the first real chance of "solving the Jewish problem." Western Marxism as well as all currents of Russian socialism advocated the same approach to the problem: assimilation instead of separation. Even before the October Revolution, however, the Jewish problem vastly complicated the activities of the faction-ridden Social Democrats and played an indirect but profound role in the great split in 1903. It is not a generally known fact that the first social democratic parties in the Russian Empire were founded by Poles and Jews. The first broadly based workers' party in Russia (in 1897) was the "General Jewish Workers' Union in Lithuania, Poland, and Russia" known as the "Bund." On the eve of the first Russian revolution in 1904 it numbered three times as many members as the combined total of all Russian party committees.[61] We cannot go into the details here of the intimate and troubled relationship between the "Bund" and the rival Russian party factions. Suffice it to say that matters came to a head at the crucial second congress in 1903 in London. The Bundists were anti-Zionist (at any rate initially) but wanted an autonomous position within the party and the exclusive claim to represent the—overwhelmingly Yiddish-speaking—Jewish workers. This, of course, would have spelled the end of a single centralized revolutionary body since other nationalities—Poles, Latvians, Georgians, etc.—would soon demand the same. Accordingly, out of fifty-one mandates at the congress, forty-one voted against the Bund's claim, while five abstained. The five Bundists (and two other delegates) left the meeting in an uproar. This exodus tipped the scales in favor of Lenin's blueprint of the organizational setup of the party as against the looser rules presented by Martov, and from that time Lenin's followers were called Bolsheviks ("Majoritarians") and their opponents Mensheviks ("Minoritarians").

The point of the matter was that, on the issue of the Jewish separateness as demanded by the "Bund," the Russian Bolshevik Lenin, the Menshevik Jew Martov, and the Jew Trotsky (who until 1917 oscillated between the two groups) were of one mind.[62] The whole issue of the "Bund" was a question of principle, politics, and organization and not of any kind of anti-Semitic bias, since in fact about half of the delegates were Jewish and Lenin himself was certainly singularly free from national and racial intolerance.

The "non-Jewish" Russified Jews who were against Jewish parochialism or Zionism were once described by Lenin as "Marxists . . . who continue the best traditions of Jewry." It was Lenin himself who often stressed that "the Jews provided a particularly high percentage (compared with the total Jewish population) of leaders of the revolutionary movement."[63] In reality, the Jews were more heavily represented among the Mensheviks than in Lenin's group. This fact was duly noted by Stalin (a nonvoting delegate) at the Fifth Congress in 1907. In the small underground paper he then edited at Baku, Stalin mentioned in his report: "Somebody among the Bolsheviks (I believe Comrade Alexinski) remarked jokingly that since the Mensheviks were a faction of the Jews and the Bolsheviks that of the native Russians, it would be a good thing to have a pogrom in the party." Even more instructive is the fact that this anti-Semitic joke was republished by Stalin in his *Collected Works* forty years later! "Comrade Alexinski" incidentally later broke with the Bolsheviks, fought with the White Army in the Civil War, and subsequently emigrated.[64]

Jews were overrepresented in the entire Russian revolutionary movement, not only and not particularly among the Bolsheviks. At the same time new research[65] has convincingly proved that not only Jews, but for obvious reasons certain other ethnic or national groups also showed a high susceptibility to Communism. The Bolshevik movement was heavily staffed in key positions by Georgians, Latvians, Poles, and Armenians. The Jews were, of course, far more visible than even their undoubtedly considerable proportion in the top echelons of decision-making suggests. For a group with urban traditions and a higher educational level than that of the Russian population, the revolution was their "entrance ticket" to the party and state bureaucracy, scientific and academic world.[66]

Their prominence was particularly eye-catching between the October Revolution and 1926, the year Stalin began his open bid for supreme power. Both Soviet and Communist postwar history in Eastern Europe tends to repeat the contrasts noted between the status of the "court Jew" and the Jewish masses in the seventeenth and eighteenth centuries. ". . . The very fact of being born a Jew would either mean that one was overprivileged—under special protection of the government—or underprivileged, lacking certain rights and opportunities . . ."[67] In Lenin's lifetime the first head of state (until his death in 1919) was the Jew Jacob Sverdlov. The War Commissar and creator of the Red Army, Leon Trotsky, the first President of the Comintern, G. Zinoviev, and the leader of the powerful Leningrad party organization, L. Kamenev, were all Jews, and all three were members of the ruling Politburo to which five to seven supreme leaders belonged. Actually, at one point in 1921–22 they constituted the majority. After Lenin's death they were at loggerheads, and Stalin, after first isolating Trotsky, with two swift blows purged the other two from the top leadership in 1926. It was during his long struggle with the Opposition that he first began to stir up through his agents anti-Semitic prejudices at the meetings of the party cells. In the 1920s Jews formed 5 per cent of the total party membership. Though this was two and a half times higher than the comparative proportion of the Jews in the total population, their participation in the administration was even stronger. In 1927, 11.8 per cent and 9.4 per cent of the state employees in Moscow and Leningrad respectively were Jewish. In the Ukraine, Russians and Jews occupied a fifth each of all posts.[68]

In the 1930s came the first gradual then rapid transition from overrepresentation to underrepresentation in the Party and state administration but not in the percentage of Jews in total Party membership. In addition to the Great Terror, which decimated the many "Old Bolsheviks" of Jewish origin, Soviet Jews for over three decades now have had limited access to political and military careers and have been virtually excluded from leadership positions (with the important exception of science and the free professions). As a result, at the time of this writing there are only five Jewish deputies in the Supreme Soviet, that is, only 0.35 per cent of its membership, while Jews (officially) constitute 1.1 per cent of Soviet population. Nothing could better illustrate the results of the deliberate "numerus nullus" policy launched by Stalin and continued under his successors than the fact that there is only one Jew (Deputy Premier V. E. Dymshits) in the broader political leadership, the 360-strong Central Committee. Since 1926, when Stalin's loyal henchman L. M. Kaganovich became a candidate member of the Politburo (he was purged in 1957), no Jew has been allowed access to the center of real political power in the Soviet Union.

What Hitler revealed in 1939 has been fully borne out by later events: "Stalin made no secret before Ribbentrop that he was waiting only for the moment of maturation of a sufficiently large indigenous intelligentsia to make short shrift of Jews as a leadership stratum which he still needs today."[69] Yet the extent of Jewish participation in the Party bodies has had little if any effect on the fortunes of Soviet Jewry as such. In the 1920s, for example, the most fanatical tormentors of religious Judaism and Zionist "suspects" were the Jewish sections of the Party (the notorious Yevsektsii). True, the October Revolution freed Jews from the danger of pogroms, and anti-Semitism in those days was truly a punishable offense. But at the same time Soviet Russia declared a veritable war on religion, thus also on Judaism, while even in anti-Semitic Poland and Rumania there was at least no interference with religious practices. The October Revolution also wiped out many thousands of Jewish middlemen, peddlers, and shopkeepers, and the halfhearted attempts to settle them on the land in remote regions failed disastrously. Russian Jews found themselves trapped in what Deutscher aptly called "a tragic impasse." While uprooted Jews were being persecuted in towns as "rootless cosmopolitans" opposing the building of "socialism in one country" or as "relics of capitalism," the many Jews still active in Soviet bureaucracy were hated by the tormented peasants and petty bureaucrats. The strains and tensions of an isolated, poor, and primitive society, staggering under Stalin's brutal collectivization and industrialization campaigns and shaken by successive waves of bloody purges, hit the various segments of Jewry more sharply and more cruelly than any other ethnic or national group in the country. The cruel logic of all these trends, later sharpened by World War II, the Cold War, and the creation of the state of Israel, have combined to bring about in the USSR the suppression of all Jewish cultural institutions and the resurgence of official anti-Semitism. This has produced a unique situation in which the regime tries to destroy the Jews as a group while discriminating against them as individuals. Thus what fifty years ago seemed to so many to be a "Jewish message" has become the gravest menace to Judaism, Israel, and the Russian Jews, preventing them from living either as Jews or as non-Jews.[70]

Regardless of what happened later, the early prominence of Jews in leadership positions in Soviet Russia left an indelible mark on world opinion, and especially on the population in Eastern Europe, where the spirit of nationalism has remained central to political life. Henceforth, the corporate Jew was identified with international Communism as such, which in turn was seen—and with good reason—as a mere tool of old-fashioned Russian imperialism. We are faced here with a double and tragic paradox. In the country of the October Revolution the pendulum began to swing as early as the 1930s from special favor of to special discrimination against the Jews, and the Jewish Question, far from being solved, has become much more acute during the five decades of bureaucratic degeneration. East European Jews both before and after World War II paid heavily in terms of popular hate and social insult for the political glory of those Jewish "world revolutionaries" who were hated either as "homeless traitors" or as ruthless "commissars" acting in the service of their Russian masters.

No one in interwar Eastern Europe cared for or probably even knew about Stalin's surreptitious exploitation of anti-Jewish emotions in liquidating his potential or imagined foes. This covert anti-Semitism earned his regime fresh popularity at home but failed to make any dent in anti-Communist propaganda. Was not the Jew

Kaganovich, whose sister was rumored to be Stalin's mistress, one of his closest collaborators in the Politburo?* Did not Maxim Litvinov, another Jew, stand for over a decade (until three months before the conclusion of the Hitler-Stalin pact) at the helm of Soviet foreign policy? Was not the Comintern, the heart and soul of the "Judeo-Bolshevik world plot," heavily staffed not only by Russian but also by Polish and Hungarian, Rumanian and German Jews? That most of these people sooner or later perished on the gallows and in Arctic camps, that after the Nazi-Soviet pact hundreds of German Communists, including many Jews, were handed over by the NKVD to the Gestapo, from the prisons of "socialism" to the hell of Nazism, could no longer dent the deeply rooted image of the Jew as a Communist conspirator and a Soviet agent.

The prejudice Jew = Communism = Russia, while less and less corresponding to the new situation in Russia, expressed a definite historical truth in prewar and postwar Eastern Europe, even though active Communists were only a tiny fraction of the Jewish communities in each country. In Poland, for example, Jews accounted for 26 per cent of the Party membership. As this however hardly ever exceeded twenty thousand, we can reckon with five thousand or so Jewish Communists in a total Jewish population of 3.3 million![71] Yet in contemporary public opinion the Jews fitted the stereotype attached to them, and stereotype became more influential than reality.

In addition to the enormous influence of the conspicuous presence of Jews in key positions in the young Soviet regime, two other factors, especially in Hungary and Poland, gave an enormous fillip to the view that Communism was a "Jewish conspiracy." No one could deny that the short-lived "dictatorship of the proletariat," the Soviet regime in the spring of 1919 in Hungary, was primarily run by Jews. Out of forty-nine Commissars no less than thirty-one were of Jewish origin.[72] The leader, Bela Kun, and his associates later occupied influential posts in the international apparat of the Comintern. In that period of postwar chaos when even Lenin was

---

* For this myth and Stalin's violent anti-Semitism see S. Alliluyeva, *Only One Year* (New York, 1969).

said to be a Jew, the Soviet Republic in Hungary, the then most westward expansion of the "Bolshevik plague," provided an ominous proof of the sinister alliance between Jews and Bolshevism.

Barely a year later the Soviet Red Army, after repelling a Polish attack, invaded newly independent Poland. But the Polish nation, including the workers, responded to the call of patriotism, and instead of an uprising of the proletariat which the leaders in the Kremlin had hoped for, there was a military disaster. The revolutionary committees the Russian invaders installed as the local government were often made up of Jews; two of the four members of the would-be Soviet Government, the Provisional Revolutionary Committee, were Jews, Jozef Unszlicht, later acting chief of the GPU, and Feliks Kon; and many others played important roles in the Russian Party.[73]

The October Revolution, the Soviet regime in Hungary, the invasion of Poland, and the world-wide activities of the Moscow Comintern all reflected in different ways the Jews' sudden and dramatic rise to political significance as an international element in the service of an international movement and ideology. In view of their role in every East European Communist Party except the Yugoslav, the Bulgarian, and the Albanian, the Jews came to be regarded throughout the entire area as the group to profit most by revolutionary upheavals.

This view, though correct as a description of the surface phenomenon, overlooked some essential facts which explain the relative strength and weakness, triumphs and failures of the Communists in this part of the world. As the following chapters will be devoted exclusively to the relationship between Jews and Communism (underground and in power), it is important to understand the general background in order to avoid the impression of an enormously exaggerated, specifically Jewish factor. The American scholar R. V. Burks has broken new ground in investigating the motivating forces of the Communist movement in Eastern Europe.[74] On the basis of a careful statistical analysis of prewar election returns, depth interviews with Greek Communists, and an examination of the social composition of the Communist Parties,

Burks convincingly shows the importance of the ethnic factor and national consciousness in the motivations of Communist activists, Party members, and voters.

The seizure of power by the Yugoslav and Albanian Communist Parties during the war as well as the relative strength of the Bulgarian Communists (all countries with very small Jewish minorities) show the close connection between nationalism and Communist ideology when the latter becomes a vehicle for unfulfilled national aspirations.

Burks' study sheds light on two important aspects: social class and ethnic origin. A wealth of information supports the conclusion that "Communism in Eastern Europe has not been, in any significant sense of the term, a proletarian movement. In fact, all social classes are involved and the single most important element, at least numerically, is not the proletariat but the peasantry . . . Communist guerrillas and insurgents were overwhelmingly peasant and mountaineer in their composition. Communist voters were located largely in rural constituencies and industrial workers voted for the extreme right as well as for the center and the left. In an industrialized area like Bohemia-Moravia, the workers voted primarily for the Socialists . . . Both the middle class and the city workers are overrepresented among activists, while at the leading cadre level middle-class professionals squeeze out the peasants altogether and leave only a small minority representation to the proletariat."[75]

In which country which group of cash-croppers, tobacco workers, or professionals would turn Communist depended to a much larger degree than commonly realized on the ethnic factor. It is certainly true that in Eastern Europe "numerically weak ethnic groups produce above-average numbers of Communists, providing these groups have a traditional or an ethnic tie to Russia. Other factors being equal, the weaker the ethnic group, the greater the proclivity."[76] By the same token traditional enmity toward Russia can offset even an ethnic bond. Without overlooking social and economic factors or the cultural impact of the developed West, particularly on students from backward regions, one can say that it is rather the national environment and the ethnic factor that explain who in interwar Eastern Europe was a Communist and who was not.

Analyses of the election returns in the 1920s in the countries in which Communist Parties or their front organizations participated at the parliamentary elections yielded the following revealing facts. In Yugoslavia the Communists in 1920 received 12.3 per cent of the vote cast. But in Macedonia, where the Macedonians were not allowed to present a national electoral list, the Communists, the fervent opponents of the Serb-dominated new kingdom, polled 33 per cent, and in the district of Bitolj, directly across the frontier from their Macedonian brothers in Greek Macedonia, 51.1 per cent. At the semifree elections of 1928 the various front organizations of the Communists together polled 7.9 per cent in Poland. In the cities of Brest and Nowogrodek, however, which had been seized by Poland in the 1920 war and were inhabited mainly by Ukrainians and White Russians (Belorussians), the Communist vote reached 37.2 per cent and 29.5 per cent respectively. We find the same contrasts in Czechoslovakia. There the Communist Party in 1925 picked up 13.2 per cent of the total vote. But in the easternmost province of Ruthenia, the poorest district in the new country, mainly inhabited by Ukrainians, the Party polled 42 per cent. Here the Czechoslovak Party, under instructions from the Comintern, worked for the transfer of Ruthenia to the Soviet Ukraine in the same way that their comrades in other countries propagandized for the breaking-up of enlarged Yugoslavia and Rumania.

It would be dangerous however to link sympathy for Communism to "transcendental" ethnic factors drawing a line between Slavic people on the one hand and Hungarians and Rumanians on the other. It is the situation and not the race that provides the clue to the successes or failures of the Communist movement. Thus Poles and Ukrainians, though of Slavic stock, have always had below-average Communist Parties because of their traditional conflicts with Russia. Yet the Ukrainians and Belorussians in Poland produced the highest percentages of Communist votes and the strongest Party organizations in the late 1920s. The Communist club in the Polish Parliament in 1928 included eight representatives of the Ukrainian front organizations, five of Belorussian, and only seven of Polish.[77]

The behavior of the Hungarians is perhaps even more interesting. As the Communist Party was forced underground in 1919, no election returns for the interwar period are available. Evidence from many sources, including Communist historians, shows however that the Communists represented an utterly insignificant clandestine movement. Emerging after the liberation of Budapest in February 1945, the Party claimed 1270 registered members in the capital, that "citadel of the Hungarian proletariat" with a population of well over a million![78] Yet the Hungarians in Slovakia and Transylvania played an outstanding role in the Communist movement, producing several top functionaries of the postwar Communist regime in Hungary proper. The Communist vote at the 1929 elections in the primarily Hungarian-inhabited districts in Slovakia was 22.5 per cent of the total, twice as high as the country-wide average. Using statistical techniques of comparative analysis, Burks reveals that in the Slovakia of 1929 the ethnic factor alone produced twice as much change in the Communist vote as all the social and economic factors put together.[79]

What separated the Hungarians living in Czechoslovakia and Rumania from their fellow Hungarians in Hungary proper was their special situation as a suspect minority in the same regions in which they had been for almost a thousand years the master. They were attracted to a movement that—for whatever reasons—fought for the breakup of the Successor States and therefore also for their liberation from the "foreign yoke."*

---

* The interregional character of the German minorities, scattered all over Eastern Europe, presented special problems which are outside the scope of this survey. Though represented in all Successor States, like the Jews, the Germans were in every other respect in a different position and looked to the mother country for political protection if and when they needed it. After 1933 they drew political and ideological inspiration primarily from the Nazi Reich. Available although meager evidence seems to indicate however that until the mid-thirties ethnic Germans were also overrepresented (in relative terns) in some of the weak East European Communist Parties.

Even these few selected figures indicate that Jews were only one of the "Communist-producing social and ethnic groups." Their conspicuousness can be explained by their geographical distribution and occupational pattern. Jews were the only truly inter-regional minority (apart from the Germans) that was represented in every East European country, and as such their role in the Communist movements was clearly visible. A Macedonian Communist in South Serbia or a Ukrainian or Belorussian Communist in Poland was a local or regional case. Whether working in the Moscow Comintern, the Budapest underground, the Prague Parliament, or a small Galician town, the Jewish Communists were seen as an interregional, inter-European group whose members everywhere shared two attributes—those of being Jewish and Communist.

Jewish Communists were not only ubiquitous, but coming from an urban group with a higher level of education they were often able to get to the top faster than non-Jewish comrades of the same or different social origin. As in both the interwar and immediate postwar period, the majority (in some cases three fourths) of the Party leaders were of middle-class origin, mainly professionals in countries that had little real native middle class, the prominence of Jews in leadership positions was virtually inevitable. If we add to this the spiritual legacy, the facts of history and social psychology, the fearful environmental pressures that forced assimilated Jews to distinguish themselves in whatever avenue of power was open to them, the special position of the Jewish activists in the Communist movement appears even less surprising.

A certain set of historic, national, social, and cultural circumstances produced weak Communist Parties with excessively strong Jewish representation, especially at the command level. Just how great the extent of Jewish participation among the so-called apparatchiks, that is the full-time salaried functionaries, was we shall see in the detailed surveys of Poland, Czechoslovakia, Hungary, and Rumania. It is important to keep in mind however that it was visible and proportional, not absolute strength. The trials of Jewish Communists in interwar Budapest, Warsaw, and Bucharest were a deepening source of fear, pain, and shame among the great majority of Jews. The rising tide of anti-Semitism made them aware of the potential consequences of the Communist label which implied treachery to their "host nations."

The situation was fraught with even more ominous dangers when a Jewish Communist in a given country happened to have also belonged to another national minority. A case in point is the number of Communists in interwar Greater Rumania who were Hungarians of Jewish origin. They were subjected to a three-pronged resentment as Communists, as Jews, and as Hungarians. It was not the absence of grave social and economic ills that accounts for the weakness of the Rumanian Party (which before King Michael's coup in August 1944 had less than a thousand members), but rather the fact that it was impossible to identify the interests of ethnic Rumanians with Soviet Communism. For three decades the Rumanian Communist Party was discredited as un-Rumanian because its founders were a Bulgarian and a Russian Jew, its principal leaders either Jews or Hungarians, Bulgarians, or Ukrainians. The Jewish Communists of Ukrainian and Russian origin in Rumania, those of German origin in Czechoslovakia and of Russian or German origin in Poland belonged to the same detested category of doubly alien Jewish subversives.

These, then, were the factors that shaped the long and always troubled relationship between the Jews and the many nations of Eastern Europe. We must not assume, as Baron noted about the late Middle Ages, that "Judeo-Christian relations present only a picture of unmitigated gloom and hostility. Unlike law or theology or even economics, the daily life of the Jewish people found little reflection in the existing documentation. We can infer of course some underlying hostility from occasional violent anti-Jewish riots and massacres. But we must not forget that between these violent outbursts there were long intervals of peaceful cooperation when mutual suspicions alternated with deeds of actual friendliness."[80] It is enough to recall the peaceful life of many successive generations in medieval Poland or in nineteenth-century Hungary and the startling contrasts in the fate of Jewish communities in different countries during the same period, to doubt the notion of eternal anti-Semitism.

It was not the Jews' fault that their collective existence and their lives as individuals were so often willingly or forcibly linked to the powers that were. Whether as Christ-killers or usurers, peddlers or bankers, liberals or Communists, contemporary public opinion saw them basically as wanderers, outsiders, and never wholly assimilable aliens who appeared to be powerful out of all proportion to their actual numbers. Similarly, it was not the fault of the East European nations that they "formed a buffer zone between the West and Asia, allowing the Western nations to develop in comparative security, their own civilization while the fury of the Asian whirlwind spent itself on their backs,"[81] that their culture, individuality, and past has been—and to some extent still is—threatened by extinction under assaults of rapacious imperialist intruders. Both, the Jews and the nations, were alternatively victims and beneficiaries of definite historical situations. With the collapse of the old empires, the situation changed dramatically, but the underlying conflict inherent in the position of the Jews as a group beyond nations in a nationalized Eastern Europe became more acute than ever before.[82]

It was at this point that the birth of the Soviet Union and international Communism emerged as direct threats to the territorial integrity and social order of the new, increasingly authoritarian nation-states of Eastern Europe. Jewish Communists comprised numerically no more than perhaps ten to fifteen thousand persons in the whole of the area[83] (including the Balkans but excluding of course Russia). But since the Communist Parties were so weak and the proportion of Jewish top functionaries so excessive, the Jewish people as a whole came to be regarded as particularly prone to Communism. And from the prominence of Jews in the Communist movement came the conclusion, unconsciously shared by many Jews and accepted by many Gentiles, that socialism as such, not only the Social Democratic Party but also the Communists, were, regardless of their less attractive traits, consistent defenders of Jewish equality against anti-Semitism.

Clerical and traditional Jew-hatred, economic jealousy, social protest, and nationalist resentment all help to explain the powerful current of indifference and the absence of any appreciable reaction when Hitler embarked on the "final solution" of the Jewish Question in Eastern Europe. By the spring of 1941 the entire area was under Nazi domination. Czechoslovakia, Yugoslavia, and Poland were dismembered, while Hungary, Bulgaria, and Rumania became German vassals, partly under compulsion, partly driven by the fervent desire to regain their "lost territories." Hitler divided the spoils in a way that best served the exploitation of age-old rivalries. Hungary was allotted first Southern Slovakia, then Northern Transylvania, and finally those parts of historic Hungary that after World War I were lost to Yugoslavia. Bulgaria got Southern Dobruja from Rumania, and Macedonia and Thrace from Yugoslavia and Greece. The Rumanians, the great losers in 1940, enthusiastically joined the German side after the invasion of Russia, fired by the opportunity of reoccupying Bessarabia and Northern Bukovina, the contested regions which Soviet Russia had annexed in June 1940 when the Nazi-Soviet pact was still in force. Finally there were two new puppet client states, Slovakia and Croatia, whose fascist rulers were among the earliest and most eager supporters of the Nazi-sponsored expropriation and deportation of Jews.

Over three million Polish Jews, six hundred thousand Hungarian Jews,* and hundreds of thousands of Jews in Czechoslovakia, Rumania, Yugoslavia, and the occupied territories in Soviet Russia were the victims of Hitler's genocide campaign. There were two exceptional cases. The first was Bulgaria, which never declared war on the Soviet Union despite its status as a German client state. The fact that the Bulgarians had in the end to yield to incessant German demands with regard to the deportation of Jews from former Yugoslav and Greek Macedonia was entirely due to the Nazi pressure, as shown in the latest war crimes trials.[84] Nevertheless one of the noblest chapters of European history is the sus-

---

* Including those from former Rumanian, Czechoslovak, and Yugoslav regions which in 1944 belonged to Hungary.

tained resistance the small Bulgarian nation put up to German ultimatums concerning the deportation of Jews from Bulgaria proper, so that in the end the entire community of some fifty thousand survived intact. This case, unique in occupied Europe, was due primarily to the long tradition of peaceful coexistence of Sephardic Jews and Bulgarians in the multinational Turkish empire, to the social structure of an egalitarian society, and above all to the united front of public opinion from King Boris to the high dignitaries of the Orthodox Church.

The second exception was Yugoslavia. By the time the partisan movement began in earnest, more than 80 per cent (sixty thousand) of the Jewish population, particularly in Serbia, was in concentration camps or already killed. The rest, however, especially in Croatia and Bosnia, took up arms and fought against the Nazis and their collaborators. There were twelve national heroes and many high-ranking partisan officers of Jewish origin, and in 1943 a Jewish battalion of former inmates of the concentration camp on the island of Rab fought in the ranks of the 6th partisan division in Croatia.[85]

The picture was entirely different in the rest of Eastern Europe. Poland produced not a Quisling, but an impressive resistance movement. But neither the Home Army nor the small Communist partisan bands were free from anti-Semitic prejudices. The fight against the Germans did not exclude the denunciation or even occasional killing of Jewish refugees. To be sure there were examples of heroic sacrifices made to help Jews but—as in the whole of Eastern Europe—they remained exceptions. At the height of the massacre a Polish underground paper wrote: "The Nazis are solving the Jewish problem in our favor in a way in which we could never have solved it."[86] Everywhere the Germans were the perpetrators, organizers, and sponsors of the killings, but local fascist elements in Slovakia and Poland, Hungary and Croatia, Rumania and Ruthenia helped them enthusiastically.

To put it bluntly, there were many cases of attempts to help (particularly in Bohemia, Budapest, and parts of Rumania proper) but the majority of the population in all the countries remained passive. This was as true of the Poles, who themselves suffered unspeakably under the Nazi yoke, as of the Hungarians and Rumanians who hardly suffered at all during the war.

The war was very different for nations that were enemies of the Nazi Reich and those that were regarded as allies, however unreliable. But anyone who lived through the inferno of the war and the Holocaust finds it difficult to dispute Isaac Deutscher's conclusions: "It is an indubitable fact that the Nazi massacre of six million European Jews has not made any deep impression on the nations of Europe. It has not truly shocked their conscience. It has left them almost cold."[87]

Just how strong the accumulated resentments against this unpopular minority were became painfully evident in the years following World War II. The genocide did not "solve" the Jewish Question in Eastern Europe. Jewry was decimated in gas chambers and concentration camps. There emerged however the new Communist "court Jews." Though six out of seven had been killed, the Jews appeared more prominent, more conspicuous, and more powerful than ever before in the history of Eastern Europe. Not only did the Holocaust leave the nations "almost cold"; the greatest tragedy of the Jewish people was followed by a new eruption of pent-up resentment. Jews entered the top ranks of the new regimes at the very time when the East European nations were engulfed in a national catastrophe.

## 6. RULERS AND SCAPEGOATS

The destitute, sick, and starved survivors of the Nazi massacres, the widowers, widows, and orphans emerging from the ghetto in Budapest, the bunkers and caves of destroyed Warsaw and the forests and mountains of Poland, Slovakia, and Rumania greeted the Soviet troops as saviors. The defeat of Nazism came too late to save the bulk of East European Jewry, but it came in time to prevent the extermination of hundreds of thousands in Rumania and Hungary, and tens of thousands in Poland and Czechoslovakia.

Expecting sympathy and understanding from their countrymen, the survivors—about seven hundred thousand out of a prewar community numbering over five million—set out to build a new life on the ruins of the old. Many found their flats occupied by strangers, their property lost, their relatives killed. Many encountered not only indifference, but hatred mixed with a sense of guilt and complicity. It is often overlooked that everywhere in Eastern Europe, as in Nazi Germany and Austria, a new social class had been born: the "custodians" of Jewish property. The Slovak peasants holding former Jewish farms, the Hungarians living in vacated Jewish apartments, the Polish and Rumanian artisans and merchants using former Jewish premises, those hiding the furniture and clothing, jewels and money of their Jewish neighbors shared one common trait. They had all become accustomed to the disappearance of the Jews. They had come to regard the "aryanized" property as their own. As an astute observer in

1946 noted: "The grave of the Jewish middle class became the cradle of a new Gentile middle class in East Europe . . . These profiteers were the most demoralized, greedy, and unscrupulous elements in those nations (Poland, Rumania, and Hungary), a lumpenproletariat which turned overnight into a lumpenbourgeoisie. The death certificates of the murdered Jews were their only valid trade licenses. They look tensely and anxiously into the faces of the few Jews who now seek to return home. Has the rightful owner of the shop come back? Or his child or relative? The greater the destitution in East Europe, the wilder the scramble for material goods, the more desperate and unscrupulous the determination of this horrible 'middle class' to remain in possession."[88]

Wartime violence and its manifold repercussions had everywhere a disastrous effect on the moral life and traditional standards of the nations of Eastern Europe. There were many people who in one form or another had benefited from the massacre of millions of Jews. The beneficiaries felt and often openly stated that there were still too many Jews around. While large enterprises and factories were without exception nationalized by the postwar East European governments, all recognized the legal claims of Jewish survivors for restitution.

The first wave of postwar anti-Semitism was generated by the passions and conflicts aroused by this restitution. Even in Czechoslovakia, let alone in Poland and Hungary, the return of the Jewish owners revived the old and created a new anti-Semitic mood. Pogroms and threats, the sabotage of hostile petty bureaucrats often terrorized the claimants into abandoning their claims—and even into leaving the country.

Meanwhile the seizure of power by the Soviet-sponsored Communist Parties created an entirely new situation with unlimited possibilities and grave risks for the Jews. For the first time in East European history a relatively large number of Jews rose to leadership positions in Hungary and Poland, Rumania and Czechoslovakia. After having lived for centuries as middlemen and in the interwar years as homeless underground revolutionaries, they suddenly appeared as rulers, members of a special clique secretly manipulating the political destiny of nations.

Writing during the war about the position and future of the Jewish minorities, before the full dimensions of the massacre had been revealed, Hugh Seton-Watson forecast: "It is difficult to believe that the Eastern European Jews can have much confidence in the prospect of peaceful coexistence with their Rumanian, Polish, and Hungarian neighbors . . . At the same time, it is doubtful whether the young nations of Eastern Europe, whatever their political, economic, and social regime, will for long tolerate in the most prominent places of their economic and intellectual life people whom they cannot help regarding as strangers, or whether the Jews will be able sufficiently quickly to adapt themselves to new occupations to be able to avert a recurrence of the danger."[89]

The situation became much worse during the first postwar decade. Jews were now prime ministers and secretary generals, ministers and police chiefs in the same countries where their fathers and relatives had been barely tolerated aliens and where only a few years earlier they had been deported or killed amid the general indifference of the population. The people now hated and despised them even more intensely than they had their ancestors. Nations that had always been particularly sensitive to questions affecting their independence and national prestige were subjected soon after the war to the twin assault of Communism and Sovietization. Insult was added to injury when aliens imposed an alien system in the service of an alien power.

Meanwhile "normal" Jews were trapped in the same tragic impasse as their co-religionists in the Soviet Union one or two decades earlier. Apart from the conflicts about restitution, the Jewish artisans and shopkeepers, lawyers and commercial middlemen were soon caught between the hammer of the virulent "old" anti-Semitism from below and the anvil of Communization which destroyed the basis of their existence. Expropriated middle-class Jews were special targets for general wrath—either as "black-marketeers" and "unproductive parasites," or as "Jewish bureaucrats" if they found white-collar positions in factories or state enterprises.

The waves of nationalization, the forced collectivization of peasants and reckless industrialization coupled with the brazen exploitation of the national wealth by the Soviet Union put an abrupt stop to postwar economic recovery and hit the standard of living of the entire population drastically. The Communists answered the rising social tensions with naked terror. The real fascists in the prisons and forced labor camps were soon joined by non-Communist democratic and peasant politicians. Judges and prosecutors who immediately after the war had sentenced the native fascist leaders found themselves sharing cells with the very people they had condemned. One of the most tragic cases was that of the Hungarian Minister of Justice, Dr. Istvan Riesz, a lifelong Social Democrat. In 1948 while he was inspecting the notorious prison at Vac, near Budapest, he encountered the populist-turned-fascist historian Odon Malnasi, imprisoned for having acted as the ideologist and spiritual leader of the "Arrow Cross" movement. Riesz recalled their erstwhile friendship in the early 1930s and made a remark about the vagaries of history which had so drastically changed their respective fates. Only a few months later Riesz himself fell from grace and before long occupied another cell in the same prison but isolated from the other prisoners. Malnasi and most of the fascist war criminals or small fry were later released under the 1953 amnesty, or freed during the 1956 October uprising. Riesz was beaten to death by his Communist captors in 1950.

The intensification of the Cold War and the consolidation of Communist power soon swelled the number of political prisoners to many thousands in each East European country. Political opponents, actual or potential, were almost lost among the mass of independent peasants defying collectivization ("kulaks"), members of suspect ethnic minorities (after Tito's break with Stalin, the Yugoslav settlers in Hungary and Rumania, also the Turks in Bulgaria), recalcitrant workers ("saboteurs of socialist discipline"), and the intellectuals and white-collar workers accused alternatively of "bourgeois nationalism" or "cosmopolitanism." When the witch-hunts began in earnest against "Titoists," "nationalists," and later "Zionists" among the Communists themselves, there came the "purge of the purgers." Now it was the turn of the same men—Rajk in Hungary, Gomulka in Poland, Kostov in Bulgaria, and Slansky in Czechoslovakia—who, in the early postwar years, were responsible for wholesale terror against real or imagined foes, to die on the gallows or to be tortured in solitary confinement by their comrades.

At the height of the Stalinist nightmare, a Western observer stated succinctly: "As in other things so here the Jews suffered like all others, only more so."[90] Anyone who has spent some time behind bars under a Communist regime is hesitant to make such a sweeping generalization. In the prisons and concentration camps of Hungary in the early 1950s the author encountered the microcosmos of the entire Hungarian society. He shared cells and barracks with counts and simple peasants, generals of the Horthy regime and of the new democratic "People's Army," engineers and chess masters, doctors and writers, Catholics, Protestants, and Jews, devout believers and agnostic intellectuals.

The vast majority of prisoners and camp inmates—how could it have been otherwise—were non-Jews. One friend, a colonel of the General Staff, who was executed in 1953, thought he detected a certain extra dose of animosity in one of his interrogators, which he ascribed to the man's Jewish origin. The writer of these lines on the other hand got the impression of a covert anti-Jewish bias on one or two occasions during confrontations with his interrogator.

It was certainly true that in the prisons of Hungary, and elsewhere, long-term fascist criminals belonged, if only by virtue of tenure, to the top layers of prison hierarchy, while socialists and Communists were generally subjected to special vituperation as "particularly dangerous enemies."[91]

But let us go back to the original question—did the Jews suffer more than the others? In overall terms, the answer must be a clear no. On the other hand, they certainly constituted a disproportionately high percentage of the "unproductive" or "unreliable" elements among the former middle-class elements deported from Hungarian and Rumanian cities in 1951, and also of the political prisoners and the executed or imprisoned victims of the great purge trials of the Stalin era.

This, indeed, is the crux of the Jewish tragedy in postwar Eastern Europe. The Jews were seen as people who derived a glaringly disproportionate advantage from the birth of the new regimes. This was certainly true. Yet because they were an urban middle-class group with an excessive proportion of "Westerners" or "cosmopolitans," they were also hit harder than others by the destruction of the middle class and by the purges of the Communist "new class." The crucial point was that the prominence of Jews among both the victims and the rulers gave impetus to the resurgence of old anti-Semitism among the destitute former middle class and petty bourgeoisie and simultaneously to the emergence of a "new" anti-Semitism in the ranks of the Party apparatus and government bureaucracy.

From the very beginning these Communist states were in a paradoxical situation. Everywhere small elites of prewar tested functionaries, with a strong proportion of Jews among them, were ruling nations by means of a thoroughly anti-Semitic state bureaucracy. Once put in power by the Red Army, the minuscule Communist groups were faced with two enormously difficult tasks: to conjure up in no time at all mass parties competing for supreme power with the Social Democrats and other democratic parties, and to staff thousands of key posts in their spheres of influence: police, army, foreign service, and local Party and administrative bodies. Communist leaders began massive recruiting drives. The majority of the newcomers consisted everywhere of former members of the local fascist parties and hundreds of thousands of floating careerists and opportunists. In Rumania, Party ranks swelled from one thousand old-timers to over one million by 1948; in Hungary from a few thousands to 880,000, and after the merger with the Social Democrats to over one million. In Bulgaria the Party numbered (even according to official figures) twenty-five thousand in September 1944; four years later it was half a million. The record increase was scored by the Czechoslovak Communists. Their prewar Party numbered at its strongest some fifty thousand members. By 1948 they boasted of 2.5 million, one in every three adults belonging to this "revolutionary vanguard."[92]

It is inconceivable that the hundreds of thousands flooding into the Parties on the eve of or after the seizure of power were Communists by conviction. Nicolae Ceausescu, at present Secretary General of the Rumanian Communist Party, in 1961 shifted the blame for the welcomed entry of so many fascist Iron Guardists into the Party onto the shoulders of the "Pauker group." He revealed that after 1948, over three hundred thousand "alien, careerist elements, including Iron Guardists and hostile persons," were weeded out of the ranks.[93] It was indeed the Jewish Ana Pauker in Rumania, the Jewish Matyas Rakosi in Hungary, and the Jewish Rudolf Slansky in Czechoslovakia, together with their non-Jewish comrades, who were responsible for this deliberate recruiting policy among the ex-fascists and opportunists which discredited the Communists among the genuine socialists and democrats. True, during the purges of the 1950s, an average of one out of every four Party members was purged in each of the East European parties,[94] but many of the purged "alien" elements were former Social Democrats, people of the "wrong" origin or underground native Communists, while many of the ex-collaborators and opportunists kept their Party cards.

Communist leaders in Hungary and Rumania, Czechoslovakia and Poland were willing to tolerate anti-Semitic outbursts at election meetings, to compromise with anti-Jewish moods among their followers and to play down riots and pogroms in order to gain fresh popularity. Not surprisingly, Jewish Communist functionaries leaned even farther back than their Gentile colleagues in all matters involving Jews. After the Communist takeover, the vexed issue of anti-Semitism became taboo. Instead of launching a large-scale mass education program to demolish old prejudices, foibles, and fictions, the Communist cure, as with many other social ills, consisted of not speaking about the subject. As, however, Jewry as such was generally identified with the Communist dictatorship and the service of the Soviet masters, the old prejudices and the new roots of hatred combined to make covert anti-Semitism more virulent than perhaps ever before in East European history.

The Communists wanted to have their cake and eat it, to make a bid for popular backing, if need be through the evasion of the anti-Semitic problem, and to gain the cooperation of the Jewish survivors, who were certainly reliable and could provide badly needed trained personnel. The Hungarian writer and thinker Istvan Bibo at a very early date described the essence of this double-edged Communist strategy. "The great majority of the middle-class Jews joining the Communist Party refused to turn Communist; they had even less reason to follow the Communist Party after the different anticapitalist actions; it is only that they considered any regime in Hungary which would restore capitalism would have to be counterrevolutionary, necessarily resulting in anti-Semitic action . . ."[95] The Communists incited or tolerated the incitement of the mob against the "Jewish capitalist," while accusing all non-Communist political forces of being reactionary and anti-Semitic. All this yielded not only propaganda benefits in the gullible West of 1946–47, but also succeeded in persuading many Jews that their security depended on perpetuating Communist power.[96]

Driven by the memory of their exterminated families, the revulsion of experiencing new anti-Semitic outbreaks so soon after the Holocaust, and the fear of war and pogroms, almost three hundred thousand Jews from Poland, (many refugees from Soviet exile), Rumania, Czechoslovakia, Bulgaria, Hungary, and Yugoslavia had migrated to Israel by 1952. Those who remained, for whatever reasons, were undoubtedly responsive to the new seemingly democratic governments. Even after the Communists dropped their masks, many Jews (more than is commonly realized in the West) tended to cling to the conviction that the maintenance of the dictatorial regime rather than liberalization was the best protection against what they regarded as a basically anti-

Semitic population. This was one of the often overlooked features of the October 1956 uprising and its repercussions in Hungary.*

It must be stressed that, along with the floating careerists and opportunists, a substantial number of people, mainly of the younger generation, became socialists or Communists out of pure, unselfish motives. Having seen and experienced a devastating war and the moral gangrene of the old society, they were open to new ideas and attracted by those who claimed to stand for a world free from want, intolerance, oppression, and human injustice. In all East European countries there was a youth movement—peasant children, who for the first time had access to higher education, young workers participating in evening courses, and the sons of lawyers and government officials, doctors, and merchants—that was eager to throw its pent-up energies into building a new society. The grandeur of these early postwar years should not be forgotten because of the cynicism of the rulers and the crimes of the future.

This generation in its twenties, unprejudiced, romantic, and bursting with energy, was perhaps the last large group of young people east of the Elbe who truly believed in the Marxist-socialist vision of history and the future. They failed, but not without some measure of honor. Those who "made it," then or later, subsequently split into three categories: those who turned into rebels against the devious "socialist" mask of a degenerated system; those who survived by acrobatic exercises in make-believe, "candid self-criticism," and silence at the right time; and those who climbed to and stayed at the top, learning that everything was true, and that the opposite was also true.

Faced with the immense task of running the complex machinery of government in war-ravaged countries, the Communist leaders, for purely arithmetical reasons, could not make do with the few tested underground "old comrades." This was the exhilarating time of a "bold cadres policy." Thousands of key positions were filled

* See also chapter on Hungary.

with men in their early twenties. The Party provided everything: "an exact and perfect method to explain and change the world; a theory which, when translated into practice, righted all the wrongs";[97] recognition, power, and high salaries. The young provincials and the petty-bourgeois Jewish youth, the students and proletarian teenagers saw the growing strength of the Communists and believed that "the sky was the limit."

At the age of twenty or twenty-five, young Communists were placed in important positions as editors-in-chief, directors of publishing houses, police colonels and departmental chiefs commanding old and experienced professionals. There were success stories which would have been impossible under the former regime. Take, for example, Andras Hegedüs in Hungary. Of peasant stock, at the age of twenty-six he was in charge of agricultural matters as departmental head of the Central Committee of the Hungarian Communist Party. At twenty-eight he was a member of the ruling Politburo and three years later First Deputy Premier. After the death of Stalin in 1955 Hegedüs, then thirty-three years old, became the youngest Prime Minister in the world.

Political reliability and not age or experience mattered in the late 1940s. And who were more reliable than the Jews? Particularly the young Jews who after the horrors of the Nazi persecution received the Soviet soldiers as "emissaries from a Promised Land," who believed in the slogan "There is no freedom for the enemies of the freedom."[98] Under the changed circumstances, that part of the Jewish youth that had not embraced Zionism once again provided a disproportionate number of top and medium echelon personnel for Communism. After the enforced merger of the Communist and Social Democratic parties, their ranks were again swelled by Social Democrats of Jewish origin (although all former Socialists, regardless of their origin, were for a long time regarded as "second-class" Party members).

If their Jewish origin played some part in their revolutionary resolve, most of these young people were not conscious of the fact. Their distaste for Jewish parochialism was consciously, or more often subconsciously, submerged in their faith in a new brave world ridding the old society of its cancerous spots, including anti-Semitism. When the Party singled them out for important tasks, they "never felt that they were doing their jobs for money. They considered their advance as the well-deserved recognition of their talents and their loyalty to the Party and to the people— and as a sign of changing times."[99]

These factors—the historic past of the nations, the importation of Communism by Soviet tanks, and the special position of Jews— had, particularly in Hungary, Poland, and Rumania, and to a lesser extent also in Czechoslovakia, identical results. The Jews tended to be concentrated in certain fields and functions: the security police because they were the most reliable and the most fanatically anti-fascist; the Ministries of Foreign Affairs and Foreign Trade because they were almost the only ones the Party trusted who could also speak foreign languages; in the press and radio because of their urban traditions and often higher educational level.

The prewar stereotypes of the "Jewish capitalist" and the "Jewish Communist" were turned upside down, the "capitalist" becoming a "profiteer" or "speculator"—that is, a "subversive enemy of the people"—and the "revolutionary" a representative of the ruling power.[100] The essence, however, remained unchanged: the "alien," "rootless," "antinational" traits imputed to the Jew even if he regarded himself as a Hungarian or Pole, Czech or Rumanian.

In a sense, the fate of the "normal" and "overprivileged" Jews resembled that of their brothers in the Soviet Union. But there was one vital difference which made their situation even more ambiguous and dangerous. The corporate Jew was not only detested as corporate Communist, but also as a colonial ruler in the service of Soviet power. To make matters worse, the hated Jews appeared to grow more powerful and conspicuous in inverse proportion to their vastly dimished number. It was the political prominence of the Jews more than anything else that bred the enormous power of anti-Semitic resentment among the humiliated and suppressed East European nations.

Since the fateful identification of Jews with power reached unprecedented dimensions after the Communist takeover, it was inevitable that popular dislike should fasten first of all upon the "court Jews" of Stalin's postwar empire, the Rakosis and Slanskys, Bermans and Paukers, and a handful of others who had risen out of deep obscurity into the limelight of supreme power. They all belonged to the respected and dreaded group of the "comrades from the Soviet Union," commonly called "Muscovites." Of course not all Muscovites or top leaders were Jews. Hungary indeed was ruled for a decade by Muscovite Jews. But the Number One man in Czechoslovakia, Klement Gottwald, and his Polish counterpart Boleslaw Bierut, the nominal leader of the Rumanian Party, Gheorghe Gheorghiu-Dej and the gray eminence of his regime, Emil Bodnaras, as well as the rulers of Bulgaria (Georgi Dimitrov, Trajcho Kostov, and Vlko Chervenkov) and many other Soviet-trained functionaries were Gentiles.

Whether Jews or non-Jews, all Muscovite leaders in all Eastern European countries shared certain traits. To the knowledge of this author, the most devastatingly true picture of their personalities was drawn by two Hungarian writers, Tamas Aczel and Tibor Meray (both erstwhile Stalinists and later fearless rebels against the dictatorship): "There have been political refugees in the history of every nation, and many have, after shorter or longer periods abroad, returned to their native country. In this fact, the Muscovite emigration had not differed from other emigrations. And yet, this had been the only similarity, for these Muscovite men had spent the last ten to thirty years of their lives in the Soviet Union—and these years had left an indelible imprint on all their thoughts and actions. Thus, the chief characteristic of the Muscovite emigrants was their sense of mission, for they did not simply return to their native country at the end of the war. Instead, they were sent back with a specific task to fulfill. Now, their basic attitude had become unconditional loyalty to the Soviet Union—an unwavering fidelity to the country that had given them shelter for many years . . . The true aim of the Muscovite mission was this, upon their return to Hungary: they were the outposts and the representatives of a foreign power's interests in their own fatherland."

"But, public or private, his life was by no means enviable. Its leitmotiv was fear. A Muscovite's life was never safe, wherever he went—and least of all in the Soviet Union. He knew that neither his age nor his long Party membership would protect him. He knew that he did not even have to commit a mistake in order to be relieved of his job, or to be arrested and tried. To him nothing was impossible. After all, he had seen it all in the Soviet Union. His smile, his loyalty, and his zeal served but one purpose: to survive . . . There was only one single thing the Muscovites cared about: that they should, after long years of fear and danger, be left in peace. They cared about their beautiful homes (of a type they never had in Moscow or Novosibirsk), about nice furniture and about "protocol" boxes at the opera house. The passionate search for truth and justice, the flaming desire to right social injustices, the emotions that had once made them join the Party and face the dangers of illegality and/or of the Spanish Civil War—all these had long been extinct in their souls. There was nothing left in these souls except the dream of a life of success without financial worries . . . Life in the Soviet Union had killed that which had been their greatest virtue at the time of their emigration: their faith."[101]

When Stalin unleashed the whirlwind of the show trials and great purges in Eastern Europe, the Muscovites knew that their fate depended on luck, on the whims of the Georgian master in the Kremlin. They knew that the accusations were false since together with Soviet "advisers" they had invented the tissue of lies and nonsense, and the indictments had been written from the first word to the last by the top ideologists themselves (for example against the Hungarian Rajk by Jozsef Revai, against Slansky by Vaclav Kopecky).

The chief villains in the great purges of the late 1940s—in strict accordance with the basic Soviet script—were the underground Communist leaders who fitted the role of "Titoist and nationalist" traitors: Rajk in Hungary, Kostov in Bulgaria, Patrascanu in Rumania, and Gomulka in Poland. But in Hungary and Rumania there were many Communist old-timers of Jewish origin among the victims. Though the motif of "Zionist-imperialist" conspiracy first appeared at the Rajk trial in September 1949, the Jewish defendants were persecuted solely on account of their exile in the West, their activities in the home underground, and their participation in the Spanish Civil War. As Jews constituted a very considerable portion of the "Westerners" and "Spaniards" as well as of the native underground movements, an excessive proportion of the victims in 1948–49 consisted of Communists of Jewish origin.

The public at large, however, was indifferent to or ignorant of this aspect. What it could not fail to note was that the most prominent scapegoats were native sons while their tormentors were very often Jews. In those early years, the Muscovites, still trusted and needed by Stalin, were falling over themselves to prove their revolutionary vigilance, missionary zeal, and eager subservience to Moscow. But when they were alone, they too were trembling with fear. Some were more worried than others. They had a special handicap: they were Jews.

It was not the accumulated hatred of the embittered population, but the ominous change of line in Moscow that made them sense danger. Each of Stalin's purges had a dynamism of its own. The Soviet-sponsored anti-Zionist, anti-cosmopolitan campaigns could easily affect not only the Jews in general (they could not care less about those) but also Jewish holders of office and finally the leaders themselves.

The Communist dictatorship has never eliminated competition for jobs, status, and favor. It is the purges and screening campaigns that serve as the main instruments for the promotion and circulation of the elite. By the 1950s the "nationalization of the cadres," the replacement of the old intelligentsia by personnel trained since the war, began to make itself felt. This "proletarization" of the Party and state apparatus was an important social phenomenon that led to a reduction of the Jewish element, which was more strongly represented among the postwar Communist "establishment" than in the ranks of students leaving the universities and Party high schools.[102]

Social mobility within the totalitarian system is primarily

achieved by transfers, demotions, and dismissals. The campaigns waged against the various "isms" have always had a profound impact on the chances of competitors within this closed system which excludes freedom of choice. As most Jewish officials and intellectuals were of "wrong," that is bourgeois or petty-bourgeois, origin, the anti-Zionist drives launched by the Kremlin had a profound impact on the policy of personnel promotion. The vituperative attacks against the Zionists and "rootless cosmopolitans" in turn further animated the anti-Semitism from below since, in the eyes of the population at large, there has never been a difference between anti-Zionism and anti-Semitism.

The dynamism of the purge reached the Jewish Muscovites in 1951–53. The arrest of Rudolf Slansky in the autumn of 1951, the fall from grace of Ana Pauker in May 1952, and the subsequent Slansky trial announced first to the initiated, then to the world that Stalin felt he could and should now dispense with his Jewish tools in the "people's democracies." The dictator decided to "replace the Moscow-trained revolutionaries with equally pliable but more palatable administrators and rulers . . . who must be able to direct the local population and derive a maximum of effort. The Slanskys and Paukers were unable to do this and hence became expendable."[103] Stalin's "court Jews" were caught in a crossfire between the hatred of the population and the policy change in Moscow. Some, like Rakosi in Hungary, tried to ward off the danger by themselves initiating a vicious purge of their Jewish subordinates.

Stalin's policy spelled destruction not only for the Jewish tormentors of non-Jews and Jews but also for the collective existence of the Jewish communities in general. The old and new roots of anti-Semitism, the social resentment of the expropriated urban elements, and the nationally motivated Jew-hatred of the "new class" of Party officials and government bureaucrats had turned into an explosive political force. And Stalin for coldly calculated reasons was willing to remove the lid from the boiling pot.

As always, the Jews as such—the artisans and doctors, scientists and managers of state-owned stores, bookkeepers and engineers—were going to pay the price for the glamorous careers of the "court Jews." For different reasons, the corporate Jew was considered by the population, the non-Jewish majority of the new ruling class, and the Kremlin as a danger or a nuisance whatever his social status or political creed.

Stalin's successors continued to regard the Jews of Eastern Europe as actual or potential troublemakers because of their ties to Israel and the Diaspora.* At the same time the transition from total Soviet domination to growing internal autonomy and national affirmation also produced what might be called a polycentrism in anti-Semitism, a process of differentiation with regard to the different Jewish communities in each Communist country. It was no longer the "Israel complex" of the Soviet regime alone that shaped the status and role of the Jews. Many often conflicting factors in the individual countries began to exert a growing influence on the position of the Jews. In some cases, the changes in the Communist world affected them favorably—as in Hungary and Rumania, countries with the largest Jewish communities. Elsewhere other special factors in periods of acute political crisis placed assimilated Jews, Communists and non-Communists alike, in grave jeopardy.

Meanwhile the Jewish Communists—officials and intellectuals —never really formed a united and closely knit group, even though the population at large always regarded them as members of a special clique. Even the Muscovites of Jewish origin did not actually constitute a "family concern." There were deep ideological differences and personal hatred among them—a chasm that would be revealed only many years later. Shattering events in 1956 and 1968 must have taught us that it is impossible to speak about "Communist Jews" in general terms.

The crux of the problem is that Jews have been both authors of evils and innocent victims, rulers and scapegoats. Most of them were victims, but many of them acted as ruthless persecutors of the East European nations. Some felt genuine remorse and

* A word from the Greek (scattering) which refers to the Jews living outside Palestine since the Babylonian captivity.

changed their attitude at an early date. Others remained at the helm up to the last minute and turned overnight from "court Jews" into scapegoats. As Hannah Arendt noted in her perceptive study of totalitarianism: "The theory that the Jews are always the scapegoat, implies that the scapegoat might have been anyone else as well. It upholds the perfect innocence of the victim, an innocence which insinuates not only that no evil was done but that nothing at all was done which might possibly have a connection with the issue at stake. Whenever, however, its adherents painstakingly try to explain why a specific scapegoat was so well suited to his role, they show that they have left the theory behind them and have got themselves involved in the usual historical research—where nothing is ever discovered except that history is made by many groups and that for certain reasons one group was singled out. The so-called scapegoat necessarily ceases to be the innocent victim whom the world blames for all its sins and through whom it wishes to escape punishment; it becomes one group of people among other groups, all of which are involved in the business of this world. And it does not simply cease to be co-responsible because it became the victim of the world's injustice and cruelty."[104]

The Czech Jew Rudolf Slansky was undoubtedly an innocent victim of the Soviet-sponsored purge in 1951–52 since the specific charges against him were patently untrue. But was he not co-responsible for the horrors that enveloped his country prior to his arrest? The Polish Jew Roman Zambrowski had nothing to do with the eruption of student riots in the spring of 1968 and was singled out as a convenient scapegoat for popular wrath. But was he not co-responsible for the dark years of Stalinism and the humiliation of Polish national dignity? At the same time, many victims of the current campaign in Poland—young students and artisans, surgeons and salesmen—are "objectively innocent . . . are chosen regardless of what they may or may not have done." If one recalls the fate of the Jews during the last years of Stalin's lifetime or in today's Poland, the evidence seems to confirm the impression that "the victim of modern terror does show all the characteristics of the scapegoat: he is objectively and absolutely innocent, because nothing he did or omitted to do matters or has any connection with his fate."[105]

Not all victims, however, can be discharged of their responsibility. And when we ask the question: Why the Jews again? we must answer that they have shared the responsibility for producing parties and systems that despite their doctrine are as capable of resorting to the calculated device of anti-Semitism as their predecessors. Those Jews who were willing to pay the price of full assimilation for truly equal status in a new socialist world were more shaken by this breach of faith on the part of a movement in which they had placed all their hopes than were their dead fathers and brothers by the Jewish catastrophe under Hitler.[106]

> Ignorance or misunderstanding of their own past were partly responsible for their fatal underestimation of the actual and unprecedented dangers which lay ahead. But one should also bear in mind that lack of political ability and judgment have been caused by the very nature of Jewish history, the history of a people without a government, without a country, and without a language . . . The result was that the political history of the Jewish people became even more dependent upon unforeseen accidental factors than the history of other nations, so that the Jews stumbled from one role to the other and accepted responsibility for none.[107]

This has happened to the East European Jews repeatedly in their history, and they have never been chosen as scapegoats completely arbitrarily.

What common denominator was there between middle-class Jews and their Communist persecutors of Jewish origin? What link existed between the Hungarian dictator Rakosi and those Jewish intellectuals (Tibor Dery, Gyula Hay, and many others) who wanted to restore "a human face to socialism"? Before, during, and after the Hungarian revolution of October 1956, there were Jews on both sides of the barricades. Rakosi and Gero who wanted to throw the rebellious intellectuals, many of them Jewish, into prison and ordered the security police to open fire on the demonstrators were Jews. There were Jews in the entourage of Janos Kadar who came to power in November 1956. What indeed joined Miklos Gimes, the erudite and courageous intellectual executed along with Imre Nagy, to Rakosi, or Ervin Hollos, the chief of the secret police after the suppression of the "counterrevolution"? The only factor they shared was that they all were in one way or another involved in the business of politics and intellectual ferment and thus shared the occupational hazards of a totalitarian system. We must resist the temptation to regard all criticism of individual Jews or their fall from grace in a Communist country as anti-Semitic in character. No sane person could have viewed the toppling of Rakosi in Hungary, Berman in Poland, or Kaganovich in Soviet Russia as "a blow against the Jews."

Political actions acquire an anti-Semitic tinge only when people are harassed, dismissed, or arrested solely or mainly because of their Jewish origin. Political campaigns are anti-Semitic only when they give all Jews a joint responsibility and proclaim guilt by association. It is this anti-Semitism that—to paraphrase Sartre's famous conclusion—establishes a solidarity, not of action or interest, but of situation between the Jewish Politburo member and his Jewish reformist opponent, a Jewish security police colonel and a former Jewish prison inmate, a pro-Soviet Stalinist and an anti-Soviet revisionist. "If those who are called Jews have one common bond, it is that they find themselves in the common situation of the Jew, that is they live in a community which regards them as Jews . . . He can choose between being courageous or cowardly, sad or gay . . . But he cannot choose not to be a Jew . . . To be a Jew is being thrown into, *abandoned* in the Jewish situation, and at the same time being responsible in and by his person for the destiny and even the nature of the Jewish people."[108]

What has turned the disparate groups of assimilated, religious, or "non-Jewish" Jews who rejected religious traditions into a distinct community even in Communist countries has been not the memory of the Holocaust alone but the periodical outbursts of organized official anti-Semitism against the background of a permanently hostile Gentile environment.

Fifty years of Communist history stand as evidence that the self-styled heirs of Marx and Lenin are not averse to having truck with racism, that the Jews, regardless of what they may or may not have done, serve time and again as lightning conductors for popular storms. But it is also true that "anti-Jewish feeling acquires political relevance only when it can combine with a major political issue or when Jewish group interests come into open conflict with those of a major class in society."[109]

Neither the scapegoat theory nor eternal anti-Semitism nor rhetorical condemnation of the "Communist evil" can explain the startling differences in the fate of the Jews in the various East European countries. It may well be that Lewis Namier was right when he once remarked about anti-Semitism: "Understand and explain the problem as much as you may, there remains a hard, insoluble core, incomprehensible and inexplicable."[110] But we are not dealing here with the immensely complex subject of historic anti-Semitism, but only with a limited but intriguing and important chapter in current East European history: the background and motives of the frightening "anti-Zionist" campaigns in Poland and Czechoslovakia, and the complete absence of similar outbursts in neighboring Hungary and Rumania.

There are interesting historical parallels with the present situation. In the Middle Ages, "clearly Charlemagne or Louis the Pious were no less Christian monarchs than Edward I of England, Philip the Fair of France, or Ferdinand the Catholic of Spain. And yet while the former went out of their way to invite Jews and to bestow upon them a number of far-reaching privileges, these latter-day medieval kings expelled them from their countries."[111] Kadar of Hungary, Ceausescu of Rumania are no less Communist than Gomulka of Poland. And yet while the former grant the Jews full equality, the latter expels them from his realm. Why? Why those ugly witch-hunts in some Communist-ruled countries and not a tremor in others? To understand the direct factors shaping the position of the Jews and to grasp the atmosphere in which the events took place, we must now review the situation in each country separately.

# PART TWO
## Nightmare in Poland

## 1. "THE ZIONIST PLOT"

We shall tell you what socialism is. But, we must tell you first of all what socialism is not. Socialism is not: a society in which a man is miserable because he is a Jew, while another man feels better because he is not a Jew . . .

Leszek Kolakowski

*In March 1968 Zionist elements mounted an open attack on the political system and its leaders in Poland. The overwhelming majority of the instigators and organizers behind the extraordinary meeting of Warsaw writers protesting the suspension of the public performances of Mickiewicz's Dziady ("The Forefathers") and the subsequent student demonstrations were Polish citizens of Jewish origin. This hostile campaign had nothing whatsoever to do with the disputed production of the play or the students' grievances. The point was to unleash a campaign against the leadership of the Polish United Workers' Party (PUWP), against the government, against the people's authority.*

*The new People's Poland was faced with a dangerous, well-prepared conspiracy. The editor-in-chief of the influential biweekly of the Lawyers' Association, Kazimierz Kakol, revealed to the public: "We have known for a long time that taking advantage of the disintegration of the international workers' movement, plans for a political earthquake in 1968 were worked out . . . A conspiratorial group connected with the Zionist center was trying*

*—under cover of patriotic and democratic slogans—to bring about demonstrations and street clashes . . . We were faced with an attempt to strike at the leadership . . . with an attempt—I believe this is the proper phrase—at a coup d'état.*[1]

It was enough to cast a glance at the ringleaders of the students' riots, the so-called "commandos" (Szlajfer, Michnik, Blumsztajn, Werfel, Lasota alias Hirszowicz, Topolski alias Toperman, etc.), to realize that most troublemakers were Zionists to whom the interests of the Polish nation are alien. Many were children of important state or Party officials. They were of course responsible regardless of their positions. But behind these young people with Zionist connections stood also a group of "Zionists, bankrupt politicians, revisionists, and Stalinists." Such Stalinist-turned-revisionists as Professors Schaff, Bauman, Brus, and their ilk, who had been for a long time neither emotionally nor nationally connected with socialist Poland, were particularly responsible since they abused academic freedom in order to sow confusion in the minds of young people.

The Polish Communists have always fought anti-Semitism, and every kind of racial prejudices is profoundly alien to their ideology. These discredited Stalinist politicians and revisionists of Jewish origin, however, enjoyed impunity for many years by resorting to the bogey of anti-Semitism. The March events finally tore off their masks. The Party could no longer be blackmailed into tolerating the activities of Zionists and other reactionary elements backed by international Zionism, West German revanchism, and American imperialism.

Zionism, as First Secretary Wladyslaw Gomulka stressed in his speech on March 19, is not a serious danger to socialism in Poland. It is only one element of the anti-Communist reaction. Nevertheless the problem of Zionism and the fight against Jewish nationalism have become particularly topical questions for two reasons. First, the Party has never fought against Jewish nationalism because all attempts were immediately decried by Zionists as a sign of anti-Semitism. Second, after the condemnation of the Israeli aggression against the Arab countries a frontal attack was *launched against People's Poland by international Zionist centers and Zionist elements in Poland.*

*For years a slander campaign has been going on against Poland. In the Western countries, especially in the United States, many books have been published by Zionist organizations and Americans of Jewish origin. These tried to whitewash the Jewish collaborators of the Nazis and, in exchange for the huge sums of reparations, also the Germans of the crimes committed against the Jews. The aim of this campaign was to straddle the Polish people with responsibility for the extermination of the Jews, to accuse the Poles of being accomplices to genocide. The Israeli aggression and the violent anti-Polish campaign in turn encouraged the Zionists and other reactionary circles in Poland which in March fomented the student unrest.*

*The protagonists of the Zionists were primarily discredited people who in 1945 returned to the country in army uniform from the Soviet Union, eliminated Gomulka and other native Polish leaders, placed their Jewish friends in important positions, and in October 1956 rapidly changed sides. These petty-bourgeois elements, always alien to Communist ideology and the Polish nation, later adopted revisionist and Zionist positions. Frustrated and embittered, the leading officials of Jewish origin, once primarily responsible for the horrors of Stalinism and now creating a revisionist climate, turned against the Party and the state. Whether in or out of power, they have always been well known for their national nihilism and cosmopolitanism.*

*It was only natural that many Poles asked the question: How was it possible for such Zionist and alien elements to remain in important posts for such a long period of time? This was the reason why, after the leadership resolutely rebuffed the hostile troublemakers, hundreds of resolutions were sent to the Central Committee and to Gomulka personally to purge the Party from the Zionists and other enemies, to call to account those responsible for employing and protecting alien elements in the Party and state apparatus.*

*The March events were a test of courage, patriotism, and loy-*

*alty, especially for Poles of Jewish origin. Those who by their behavior proved their loyalty to the Polish state must be defended against unjust accusations.[2] It is not up to the Poles, who even in the Middle Ages were acclaimed for their tolerance and who saved many thousands of Jews during the Nazi occupation, to defend themselves against the charge of anti-Semitism. It is above all the duty of Poles of Jewish origin to fight against Jewish chauvinists, to defend the good name of People's Poland, and to reject publicly the slanderous attacks of Zionist propaganda.*

*The overwhelming popular response to the subversive attempts of Zionist, reactionary, and revisionist forces generated hopes of a great turning point, of an accelerated building of socialist Poland. As Kazimierz Kakol put it on April 7: "The atmosphere of the present day is unique in its kind. It offers an enormous chance and maximal exploitation is a task of great importance."[3]\**

This, then, was the official explanation for the events in 1968. The anti-Semitic campaign, unprecedented since the "Doctors' Plot" and in many ways surpassing even Stalin's morbid inventions, was an instrument in the struggle for political power between rival claimants. It had nothing in common with any specific Jewish problems. The main issue was, and continues to be, the balance of power in the Polish leadership. The wave of the racist persecution, often fascist in style, reached its peak between March and June 1968. After the July meeting of the Central Committee, the behind-the-scene manipulators had reluctantly to drop the plan of staging large-scale Zionist show trials. Though Jews were still being dismissed from their jobs, the anti-Zionist campaign became muted and almost decorous. The invasion of Czechoslovakia gave a short-lived boost to General Moczar's faction to revive the discussion on "Zionist danger" and to take the lead in ferreting out Zionist counterrevolutionaries in neighboring Czechoslovakia. But the military intervention for a variety of rea-

---

\* Every word of this summary was taken from speeches of Polish leaders and authoritative articles in the official press. See also notes.

sons, which will be discussed later, strengthened the position of the Gomulka "Establishment."

By the time the Fifth Party Congress opened in mid-November, the issue of "Zionism" had been taken off the agenda. The lengthy congress resolution condemned only "revisionism, national nihilism, cosmopolitanism, and nationalism." At the beginning of 1969, less than ten months after the "March events," it seemed to Poles and foreign observers alike as if the political storms of 1968 had never happened, that everything had been merely a nightmarish dream.

The Communist leaders of Poland are caught in the same profound social conflicts and contradictions that erupted in March 1968, but when the next crisis arrives there are hardly any Jews left to serve as the scapegoats to "attract the whole accumulated aggressiveness and frustration of the embittered and disillusioned mass."[4] The balance sheet of the year of crisis can be summed up in a few sentences: between November and May some dozens of mainly Jewish students were sentenced to prison terms ranging from eighteen months to three and a half years; the head of state, nine ministers, and four members of the ruling Politburo were replaced, in all fifty-six persons were promoted to top positions,[5] and a few thousand people took over the posts and apartments of the Jews who, after losing their jobs, were forced to leave the country. This is more or less all that has changed in Poland. What has changed outside Poland is the prestige of the country, which will never recover from a self-inflicted moral disaster.

Yet it would be unforgivable to gloss over what is in fact a tragedy affecting both Polish Jewry and the Polish nation. What Isaac Deutscher said about Stalin's paranoiac last great purge, to which the "Doctors' Plot" was to serve as a prelude, can be applied even more fittingly to Gomulka's Poland. Like Stalin they struck "at the very roots of the idea by which the revolution, the party, and the state had lived"; they were "destroying the birth certificate and the ideological title deeds even" of their own regime.[6] Not even in the heyday of Stalinism did the world see anything like the virulent, open, and institutionalized racial discrimination practiced in the spring and summer of 1968 in "People's Poland."

True, no one was killed in Poland, if we exclude the forty known cases of suicides of Jewish and non-Jewish Poles whose lives, dreams, or futures were shattered from one day to the next. True, the Jews escaped, even if narrowly, a nation-wide pogrom. But what they have had to endure since the Arab-Israeli War and especially since the "March events" is without parallel in postwar East European history.

Within less than a year, Poland progressed from covert anti-Jewish bias to official anti-Semitism (sanctioned by Gomulka's speech about the Jewish "fifth column") after the Arab-Israeli War and after March 1968 to institutionalized racial discrimination. For the first time since the collapse of Hitler's Germany, the rulers of a nation introduced racialist criteria in the definition of what was actually meant by "Jew." The Polish version of the Nuremberg laws has never been published, but in practice not only children of mixed marriages, but even "quarter Jews" were considered suspect "Zionists."

When the organizers began to whip up the anti-Jewish hysteria, the world press and public opinion in the West inevitably and naturally focused attention on the fact that several scores of high officials and distinguished intellectuals of international repute had been expelled from the Party and dismissed from their positions. But the "anti-Zionist" campaign was not directed solely against prominent people. It was a general and indiscriminate witch-hunt against factory managers and engineers, famous surgeons and humble merchants, dental technicians and low-ranking administrators—people whose only common denominator was their Jewishness.

All this happened in the country of Auschwitz, Majdanek, Sobibor, Belzec, and Chelmno, the centers in which European Jewry was massacred. It seems incredible that anti-Semitism could be resurrected in the country that was the scene of history's most monstrous massacre, and that the targets of the hate campaign could be the survivors and their children, some twenty-five thousand people at most in a population of thirty-two million. It seems so irrational that many people refuse to believe it and regard the whole affair as the fall from grace of a handful of discredited Jewish Communists.

Yet the outbursts of racial hatred in one way or another involved tens of thousands of full Jews, half Jews, and quarter Jews, as well as their non-Jewish spouses and in-laws. Apart from causing humiliation and suffering to large numbers of innocent people, the anti-Semitic campaign polluted the moral life and standards of the whole Polish nation. Though the resurgence of racial hatred resembled the classic models of political anti-Semitism and used instruments of proven efficacy, the victims who were selected as targets, the demagogy that camouflaged the appeal to the baser instincts of the masses, the coldly calculated plans and methods of the manipulators were different from conventional anti-Semitic campaigns.

What the world has learned so far from news items and personal accounts is only the top of the iceberg. No general analysis of the political and economic situation is called for here. But before focusing our attention on the origins of the crisis for the Jews and the conditions peculiar to Polish life, we should know what really happened in Poland, who the victims and instigators of the anti-Jewish witch-hunt were. The reader must keep in mind that "all purges have their own laws: they need a propitious climate, a slogan, and the existence of heretics—who are not necessarily those denounced publicly."[7]

## 2. THE YOUNG VICTIMS

On March 8, 1968, several thousand students held a peaceful meeting in the courtyard of Warsaw University. The meeting, announced previously on posters and not authorized by the university authorities, had been called for the purpose of demanding the reinstatement of Adam Michnik and Henryk Szlajfer, two students (both Jews) who had been expelled from the university for taking part in earlier protests against the ban on the performances of Mickiewicz's great national drama *Dziady*. Over three thousand students signed a petition demanding their reinstatement.

After chanting slogans upholding the constitutional guarantees of cultural freedom and individual rights and applauding the announcement that the rector had agreed to receive their delegation, the students were ready to disperse. But before they could leave the university precincts they were attacked by several busloads of Party "activists," called reserve militiamen. When the students resisted, truncheon-swinging militia units were called in. The brutality of the militia turned an orderly demonstration into three days of student riots, which soon spread to the provinces as well. In Warsaw, street demonstrations were later replaced by sit-in strikes, and the last students did not leave the Polytechnical Institute until March 23. In the meantime, mass demonstrations and violent clashes with the police took place in every provincial university town—Cracow and Poznan, Lodz and Lublin, Wroclaw and Gdansk. At the peak of demonstrations there were five thousand students involved in Warsaw, five thousand in Cracow, and three thousand in Poznan. The temporary shutdown of eight departments in Warsaw University followed (March 30–May 10), together with mass arrests and the military conscription of an unknown number of rebellious students. By such means the regime eventually restored a semblance of order, but as late as May 1 there were still demonstrations in Wroclaw that resulted in the suspension of fifteen hundred out of the Polytechnic's sixty-three hundred students.

At no point were there anti-Soviet or anti-Communist slogans; the numerous student resolutions protested the assaults on cultural freedom and student rights and demanded the observance of the Polish constitution, the release of the arrested students, the punishment of those guilty of brutalities committed against the student youth, and correction of false press reports. To underline this last demand, Warsaw students made bonfires of the copies of the newspapers that put the blame on "Zionist" ringleaders.

The massive student demonstrations were the culmination of years of mounting bitterness among the intellectuals and politically conscious students against petty censorship and the betrayal of the ideals of the "Polish October" of 1956. The limited and self-disciplined movement of the students posed no overt challenge to the political system as such. It was police brutality that infested the demonstrations and sit-in strikes with high emotional content. Except for food baskets and occasional sympathetic remarks by onlookers, the attitude of the population appeared to be one of indifference and apathy. Though the manipulators behind the scenes deliberately fanned the flames of student unrest in order to make the situation appear desperate enough to justify a resort to severe reprisals, the demonstrations ultimately petered out in the arid deserts of political isolation without ever having posed a serious threat to the Communist regime.

What, then, was the balance sheet of the repressive measures? Gomulka, on March 19, referred to 1208 arrested persons including 367 students. He added however that more than half of them, including 194 students, had already been released. Three weeks later Premier Cyrankiewicz revealed a considerably higher figure: by April 8 some 2700 people had been taken into custody, with 1850 released within forty-eight hours for "lack of proof." High officials of the Ministry of Education subsequently confirmed the fact of disciplinary proceedings against 424 students, and the expulsion of over a hundred students each from the universities of Wroclaw and Warsaw.[8] But there are no overall, reliable statistics about the real number of students sentenced at secret trials, still under arrest, or drafted into the Army. Judging from eyewitness reports, Western correspondents and student participants who are now in the West, it is legitimate to suppose that at least 10 to 15 per cent of Poland's 270,000 students at most of the seventy-three universities and colleges were in some way involved in protest activities, ranging from the signing of petitions to participating in street demonstrations.

There is ample evidence that the incidents connected with the performances of *Dziady* and the intrusion of militia into the university precincts in Warsaw proceeded in accordance with a carefully prepared plan. Mickiewicz's play, which calls for a fight against Tsarist oppression, was performed even during the worst periods of Stalinism in the 1950s. This time however the new production of the play was banned after only thirteen performances, ostensibly because of the "anti-Soviet" reaction of the audience. In fact, it was a group of plainclothesmen from the secret police that burst into provocative applause at each anti-Russian line. The students in the audience applauded too. After the first performance the director of the National Theater and producer of the play, K. Dejmek, had expressed surprise to some friends that the militia as well as some factories were ordering whole blocks of tickets. Then something unusual happened. Under the Polish system of censorship, a censor can at any time ban a newspaper article, a cabaret sketch, or a play. He comes before opening time, informs the director about the decision, and the play is immediately closed. This time however a whispering campaign went on for several weeks that *Dziady* was going to be banned. Apparently not enough heat was built up, and performances were extended for another week. By the time the last performance was scheduled the whole of Warsaw was in suspense. Not only the plainclothesmen in the audience but even some students played the roles of paid provocateurs. As later became known, one of the speakers at the student demonstration on January 31, protesting the ban on *Dziady*, had received instructions from the police.

Though both the students and the writers knew that genuine protest had become merged with intentional provocation during the uproar over the ban, they nevertheless felt they had to use this matter of national honor for a frontal attack on the government's increasingly restrictive cultural policies. The Warsaw writers convened an extraordinary meeting on February 29 and passed a resolution demanding the lifting of the ban on *Dziady* and sharply criticizing censorship by 245 votes to 124. The debate in which the greatest names in Polish culture bitterly denounced the Party's repressive cultural policies had to be broken up at two o'clock in the morning, when the chairman of the meeting warned that "provocation is being organized outside." The figures in the dark surrounding the building were said to belong to a "worker's delegation" attempting to deliver a "counterresolution" of its own.[9]

These ominous straws in the wind were followed by the deliberate provocation of March 8, which sparked the street riots in the capital. Subsequent events, such as the arrests according to lists prepared well in advance, the thrust of the interrogations and above all the witch-hunt itself, illustrated beyond any doubt that the "showdown" in the university grounds was the final touch that enabled a rising group within the Party to launch a drive for decisive power. In conversations with the author, students, professors, and eyewitnesses unanimously agreed that during the street riots police agents did their best to fan the flames of violence without ever really losing control. The foul play was particularly evident on March 11 when the line of militiamen cordoning off the main avenue leading to the nearby Party headquarters suddenly broke, while not-so-young nonstudents were egging on the crowd to storm the building. It was not accidental that the wildest rampage took place practically in front of the Party's Central Committee building in order to frighten a besieged and embattled Gomulka.

Even before the *Dziady* affair many signs showed clearly that Gomulka, despite his outward self-assurance and the cult that surrounded him, was far from being the absolute master he had been taken for by the outside world. Since the beginning of the 1960s the political scene was dominated by a growing crisis in Party morale and public confidence. The sources of this discontent were varied, but all connected with the basic immobilism of the Gomulka regime. The Polish Government could muster up no more than a few dispirited half measures in response to such grave problems as a latent economic crisis, social anarchy, recurring tension with the Roman Catholic Church, the frustration of the intelligentsia, and alienation of the youth. In the midst of the new ferment, which gripped the Communist world from Belgrade to Bucharest, Poland became a backwater of stagnation and retreat.

The Arab-Israeli War and its repercussions, popular discontent against the steep rise in the price of meat in late 1967, the dismissals of several prominent moderates in the top echelons, and a series of political trials intensified the tensions. The triumph of the reformers in Prague infused the intellectuals and students with new hopes. Meanwhile, an incomparably more dangerous threat to the Gomulka "Establishment" and its policy of tenuous compromises came from what Poles call the "right." These were the forces of the reactionary, dogmatist hard-liners: the so-called "Partisans" grouped around General Mieczyslaw Moczar, who had been in charge of the secret police for almost twelve years; a faction of disaffected Party apparatchiks whose exponent in the top leadership was Ryszard Strzelecki, a Central Committee secretary since 1960, and a motley collection of allies ranging from certain segments of the new middle class to police agents and former fascists. In the eyes of the Polish "right," Gomulka and his closest associates had failed to produce a revolutionary élan, failed to instill the disgruntled Party apparatus with a sense of purpose, and failed to make a clean sweep of Jews and liberals.

It is tempting to present the main developments and the purges after March as the work of the sinister Moczar alone. A scrutiny of the events however will show that the picture was extremely complex all along and the result of conflicting influences. While Moczar was the main driving force behind the events directly leading up to the riots, it would be a gross oversimplification to regard the ensuing violence and riots as parts of a "master plan." It is likely that the student demonstrations, once set in motion, went further and acquired larger dimensions then the instigators themselves had bargained for.

In any case, the "March events" unleashed the offensive of those forces that had been awaiting a suitable occasion for initiating a general purge of all Jews and moderates in leading and second-level positions. To surmount the hurdles, the groups craving power needed the right arena and the right issue. They had to create an atmosphere of witch-hunting to make their opponents feel vulnerable. Whether all this would have happened if the student riots had not taken place is a moot point, but it is certain that Moczar and his allies would eventually have found an opportunity for action.

While the first reports of the official news agency blamed "small groups of unbridled and mostly well-to-do students with political ambitions joined by hooligan elements," *Trybuna Ludu,* the party organ, two days later published a list of the purported "ringleaders" —eight names culled from a roster of over twelve hundred arrested persons: A. Michnik, J. Dajczgewand, A. Smolar ("son of the editor of a paper"), W. Gorecki ("son of the director-general of the Finance Ministry"), Irena Lasota ("daughter of a retired colonel"), H. Szlajfer ("son of a censor in the Main Office of Press Control"), Ewa Zarzycka ("daughter of the former Chairman of the People's Council of Warsaw"), Katarzyna Werfel ("daughter of a former Editor of a number of central papers"). All but Ewa Zarzycka were of Jewish origin, the children of prewar Communist families.

That both the arrests and the subsequent press attacks proceeded according to previously prepared lists became almost immediately evident. One of the alleged inspirers, Ewa Zarzycka, the daughter of the former Mayor of Warsaw, a non-Jewish but reformist politician, hence automatically considered a friend of the "Zionists," had in fact been studying in Paris for almost a year. A few days later *Trybuna Ludu* published a brief correction on its last page that the girl had not taken part in the riots. The fact that she was abroad was however omitted. Another girl student was on the point of being released the day after her arrest since she had not been involved in the events at all. When however an officer checked her name again and found out that she was the daughter of a former high official, the decision was immediately revoked.

The procedure was always the same. Even the first interrogations started with the questions: Your name? Your nationality? In this context it must be stressed that Jews in postwar Poland were never treated as a national minority in the sense of a distinct and cohesive community and considered themselves Poles even when they were conscious of their Jewish background. This was particularly true of the young people. Involved in the daily life of the student youth and having grown up after the war, most of them did not feel any sense of identification with Jewry or Judaism as such. Even those secondary school and university students who attended summer camps or belonged to youth clubs organized by the Social and Cultural Association of Polish Jews regarded themselves as Poles of Jewish origin, citizens of their country.

These teenagers were therefore shocked to discover when questioned by the police that they were no longer described as students of the different faculties but as Jews.[10] Those Jewish families, Communists and intellectuals and professional people who remained in Poland after the Holocaust and even after the opening of the borders in the late 1950s, had opted consciously for being a part of the Polish nation. All of them, even those in charge of the Jewish organizations and the Yiddish weekly, had an "impeccable" record with regard to Zionism and Israel. The charge of Zionism against them was a patent absurdity. Even more nonsensical were the accusations of Zionist sympathies against the second postwar generation in their teens or early twenties.

From the very beginning, the arrested students were divided into two categories: Poles and Jews, with those "of mixed Jewish blood" constituting a fluid group somewhere midway between Poles and "aliens." An example may illustrate the atmosphere that reigned during the interrogations. A girl student when asked, "Your nationality?" replied with a smile, "Polish of course." The security officer frowned. "But your name does not sound Polish at all, it looks rather German . . ." The student shrugged her shoulders, "I can't help it." The conversation went on for a few more minutes with the girl repeating time and again that she was a Pole. The officer however kept returning to her "foreign-sounding" name. In the end, the student burst out: "I will tell you what you want to know. I am of Jewish origin, but I am a Polish citizen, feel like a Pole, and Polish is my mother tongue." When she was asked to sign the protocol of her interrogation she read the following sentence: "N.N., born 1949, Warsaw. Nationality: She first pretended to be a Pole but finally admitted that she was Jewish."

As a rule, the arrested young people were not beaten up. But the Jews especially had to endure nine to ten hours of almost uninterrupted grilling, isolated from their parents and the outside world. While their desperate parents were running from one prison to the next to find out where their children were, they were asked incessantly about their Jewish friends and first of all their parents' "Zionist connections." The interrogators were particularly curious whether they belonged to the Babel Club. This youth club, operated by the Jewish Social and Cultural Association, was popular among Warsaw youth because of its very good band. Every Saturday a few scores of young people went there to dance. They did not know a word of Yiddish, and a substantial part of the public consisted of non-Jewish students. Yet now the Babel Club was officially decried as the very heart of the "Zionist conspiracy." Most of the politically active Jewish students did not belong to the club. Nevertheless several of them were confronted with the evidence of membership cards they never possessed.

More serious were the fabricated "proofs" based on the testimonies of other students. It was soon clear that Moczar's agents had prepared their provocations with the help of paid informers among the students. Whether under the pressure of threats or lured by money, these youngsters were willing to serve as state evidence not only during the interrogations but also at the subsequent trials. They were known by their fellow students as "the five hundreds" for having received immediately on signing a declaration 500 Zloty and the promise of regular monthly payments. One of these informers announced very early in the investigations and confirmed at the trial that F. Topolski (son of the government commissioner for industrial decentralization with the rank of minister) had "willfully slandered the Polish nation in that he stated that all famous people in Poland are of Jewish origin, that only Jews are capable of governing Poland, that under the Nazi occupation Poles cooperated with Germans in exterminating the Jews." Though young Topolski was not sentenced until October (to an eighteen-month prison term "for outrages against the Polish nation"), a prominent hard-liner, H. Szafranski, had quoted his alleged statements as early as March 16 at a mass meeting.[11] At the trial held in camera, Topolski, who had come on March 8 for a short visit to the capital from his university in Lodz, denied the absurd accusations, but the court believed the "several reliable witnesses."

An even more dangerous role was played by those students-turned-police informers who purported to belong to the leading young Communist reformers. Poland has a long tradition of discussion clubs. During the turbulent year of 1956 their number passed the two hundred mark, with some like the "Club of the Crooked Circle" gaining international fame. In the early 1960s, the politically conscious teenagers also met in clubs, including one called "Seekers of Contradictions." Later, when the grip of repressive policies tightened, smaller groups also got together on such occasions as private birthday celebrations and parties.

Their idols since 1965 had been two young assistant lecturers at Warsaw University, Jacek Kuron (thirty) and Karol Modzelewski (twenty-nine), who in that year addressed an "Open Letter to the Party" calling for the replacement of the Communist bureaucracy by a "workers' democracy." Sentenced to three and three and a half years respectively in July 1965, Kuron and Modzelewski were released on parole in late 1967. Less than twenty-four hours after the first student demonstrations, both were rearrested, and those who had attended Modzelewski's birthday party a few weeks earlier were accused of belonging to his "secret organization" which was in touch with "foreign enemies" of Poland. Modzelewski is Jewish, the stepson of Poland's former Foreign Minister (between 1947–51).

The security police, it appeared, also possessed full transcripts of the conversations or discussions that took place in the circle of what is called "commando groups." That one of the most prominent student rebels, H. Szlajfer, turned state's evidence even before the trial indicated that they relied not only on listening devices but also on informers. Whether Szlajfer had acted as a provocateur at the January demonstration against the ban on *Dziady* or was blackmailed later is irrelevant. What mattered was that at the trial of Michnik, Barbara Torunczyk, W. Gorecki, and himself, he did his best to support the invented charges of the prosecution. Michnik was sentenced to three years, Szlajfer and Torunczyk to two years, and Gorecki to twenty months. Szlajfer however was quietly released two days after the trial.[12] Twenty-year-old Barbara Torunczyk is the daughter of a Party hero who commanded the Polish Dabrowski brigade during the Spanish Civil War. He died a few years ago and was buried in the pantheon devoted to the heroes of Polish history in the central cemetery. After the trial, one of General Moczar's henchmen, his deputy at ZBOWiD, the veterans' organization, and Vice-Minister for Culture, Kazimierz Rusinek, came forward at a Party conference with the breath-taking suggestion that the remnants of the late Torunczyk should be removed from the heroes' memorial on account of his daughter's "anti-Polish behavior."

Nothing could illustrate the nauseating atmosphere of the Jew-baiting better than the case of young Gorecki's mother. In her desperation to whitewash her son from the odium of "Zionism," this non-Jewish woman began to bombard Gomulka, Moczar, and the supreme prosecutor with letters in which she stated that during the war she had had an affair with J.A., a non-Jewish member of the Central Committee and that he and not her present husband, Gorecki, the Jew, was Wiktor's real father. Whether because of his full "Aryan" origin or of his mother's pleading, young Gorecki was released soon after his trial.

In their attempts to pick out the Jewish children of former or present prominent officeholders, the investigators were particularly outspoken when dealing with non-Jewish troublemakers. Jacek Kuron, who with Modzelewski was sentenced again in January 1969 to a second—three-and-a-half-year—prison term, stated at his trial that both the prosecutor and several police officials repeatedly told him, "If only you could break away from that Kike crowd. You are a Pole; no one would bother you . . ." Similar remarks such as, "Why do you get involved with those dirty Jews?" were reported by many other non-Jewish students. Polish girls or boys engaged to or dating Jews were subjected to humiliating insults—"A Polish woman has no business sleeping with dirty Jews," or "Why do you stay with that Jewish pig?"[13]

One of the most horrifying stories concerns Irena Grudzinska, the twenty-year-old daughter of the Undersecretary of State at the Ministry of Forestry. Irena was engaged to a non-Jewish student. Expecting a child, she was going to marry him. Her friend however apparently broke down during his interrogation. He turned state's evidence against his own fiancée, denouncing her "subversive" views. After a difficult abortion, which almost killed her, Irena was put on trial in April 1969 and sentenced to eighteen months' imprisonment with two other girls. Her former fiancé had been released a year earlier immediately after signing his deposition.

Non-Jewish students were of course also sentenced, particularly if they behaved bravely. This happened to S. Kretkowski who was tried with J. Dajczgewand in November 1968. Both were severely beaten up during the interrogations. Kretkowski received an eighteen-month sentence and his fellow defendant two and a half years. Both were in such a state at their closed trial that Kretkowski fainted while being led out of the courtroom. The guards left him lying there, unconscious and handcuffed on the concrete stairs, despite the protests of his lawyer and family.

Good lawyers were on occasion able to save their non-Jewish and less defiant clients. Thus in one case when the prosecutor demanded a one-year sentence for a student with a German-sounding name, the defending lawyer made a point of questioning his client about his origin. It turned out that the student was the scion of an old-established Catholic family from the town of Grudziadz. He was acquitted.*

It must be said that Irena's boy friend was one of the exceptions. Most students behaved in a dignified way and indignantly rejected the anti-Jewish insults of the police officials. A case in point is an incident that happened after the purge had long passed its peak, in late 1968 on the eve of the Party Congress. The son of the well-known and, ironically, strictly conformist literary critic Arthur Sandauer, together with two non-Jewish friends, left a birthday party just before midnight. In an exuberant mood, they were throwing snowballs at each other in one of the main squares in downtown Warsaw when two militiamen arrested them on the charge of having deliberately aimed at the red banners hailing the forthcoming Party Congress. While waiting in the cell of the local police station for the appearance of the duty officer, another young man in custody offered them some bread. At this, the doors were flung open and a militiaman began to shout: "Don't give this dirty Jew Polish bread. If he does not like Poland, he should not eat Polish bread." Though the boys protested their innocence, the officer immediately singled out young Sandauer. He slapped his face and called him a "filthy Kike who should get out of Poland if he does not like it here." Another student, however, stood up for the honor of Poland "which should not be soiled by such anti-Semitic insults." They were eventually released. The students lodged a complaint at the central police station against the duty officer for violating Polish law, which forbids any form of physical violence against de-

* Most of the students and faculty members sentenced to prison after the March 1968 riots (except Kuron and Modzelewski) were released under the terms of the July 21, 1969, amnesty.

tainees and prisoners. As a result, the militia wanted to initiate new proceedings against the three students, accusing them this time of throwing stones at Party posters but in the end dropped the case.

There were also many unsuccessful attempts to blackmail or lure students into becoming police informers on a regular basis. With a special department of the Ministry of Interior, led by Colonel Tadeusz Walichnowski, working for years on the "ancestor charts" of Jews and suspect-Jews, the interrogators were generally extremely well informed about the family trees of students. Those of "mixed Jewish blood" were put under particularly strong pressure to help Poland, which was "after all also" their fatherland. A half-Jewish student of biology who had a "good" appearance was told by one officer that it would be a pity if such a good-looking Polish boy had to be expelled from the university along with the Zionists. "No one would imagine that you have any alien blood; you should go on studying." Half-revolted and half-amused, the student snapped back: "In other words, you are willing to aryanize me if I am willing to collaborate with the police!"

On another occasion, two security officials made a tremendous effort to enlist a shy, quiet, totally apolitical Jewish girl student at the faculty of law. They grilled her for seven hours without interruption. She was told that no Jewish undergraduates would be allowed to continue their studies. They would guarantee that she however could continue her studies undisturbed and even get a regular retainer if she were willing to make a monthly report about the political attitude of her fellow students. Bewildered and frightened, the girl, after some hesitation, refused the offer.

The harrowing experiences in March shattered the very basis of the lives of the Jewish youth. Even when not arrested or tried, the events left an indelible mark on their relations with their non-Jewish contemporaries. As a Polish writer put it, "Even our new generation lost its innocence." Both Jews and non-Jews were affected by the frightening resurgence of racial hatred. Consciously or unconsciously, both became aware of their being Jewish or not. Previously, intermarriage was extremely frequent, especially among intellectuals and professional people. After March however engagements were broken off and friendships polluted. As a Gentile girl undergraduate confided in tears to her Jewish girl friend: "When going out with a boy, I have never thought about his origin. Now I catch myself thinking, is he Jewish or not?" Some parents forbade their children to play with their Jewish schoolmates or their daughters to go out with a Jewish boy.

Some of the young Jews could not bear the prospect of living in an invisible ghetto after having been educated and raised as Polish patriots. Steeped in Polish culture, they rejected both emigration and living out their lives as second-class citizens or "honorary" Poles. Among them was Irina Meller, the twenty-two-year-old daughter of Adam Meller, a lifelong Communist and veteran of the Spanish Civil War, who on April 3, 1968, was summarily dismissed as Assistant Secretary of State in the Foreign Ministry and expelled from the Party on the charge of "Zionism." A few days later, the girl committed suicide. Her tragic decision may also have been influenced by the experience of her brother, who had been engaged to the daughter of Zenon Kliszko. Always the first to detect a trend, Kliszko, a member of the Politburo and Gomulka's closest collaborator, after the Arab-Israeli War had forced his daughter to break off the engagement and forbade her to have anything to do with young people of Jewish origin.

There were other tragic cases. Elzbieta Szaniawska, a young journalist, became the youngest staff member of a weekly after her graduation. Soon after the beginning of the "anti-Zionist" campaign she was told by her chief that her services were no longer needed. Until further notice all she had to do was to pick up her salary on the first of every month. She should however on no account enter the editorial offices. Elzbieta broke under the shame and humiliation and took her life.

A group of perhaps thirty or so students, whose fathers were important state or Party officials, had to run the whole gamut of vicious insults and absurd accusations. Whether at liberty or behind bars, they were depicted as Zionists and parasites who grew up in prosperity and with the conviction that they would take over power from their fathers. "When in March their masks were torn off," their real nature came to light: "hatred of socialism and anti-Polish chauvinism going hand in hand with untrammeled personal ambition." These spiritual and political leaders of the student unrest "rejected October 1956 and the return of Wladyslaw Gomulka."[14] The sinister conspirators were in 1956 on the average eight or nine years old! Such trifles did not however disturb the pacemakers of the campaigns. The party propagandists, sent to the secondary schools where the culprits had studied, explained that these were gilded youths of Jewish origin posing outwardly as defenders of Polish traditions and culture. In reality such notions as patriotism and nation were completely alien to them. The papers published whole "human interest" articles about selected young people with suitable family connections. In a profile of a dangerous troublemaker, it was related with relish that she was an active revisionist as early as 1962, drove a Peugeot, and was a woman of "loose morals." In fact, she was a biology student in her first year, the family did not possess a car, and in 1962 she was exactly twelve years old.

It is useful to remember that from the very beginning, the anti-Semitic campaign was not an abstract political conflict between dyed-in-the-wool Communists. It started with attacks on human dignity and often also on the personal freedom of young people just emerging from their teens. In their allegedly socialist country of birth, they awoke for the first time to the ominous consequences of a disregarded label which implied adherence to a cult of which they were almost totally ignorant.

## 3. THE WITCH-HUNT BEGINS

Within three days of the first clashes in the Warsaw University grounds, the "anti-Zionist" campaign erupted at full strength. The alleged "Zionist" organizers were already in custody, yet during the following days and weeks the demonstrations involved tens of thousands of students all over the country. The accusation that a handful of "Zionist" students could incite a substantial part of the student youth to protests and riots affecting every provincial university was so absurd that nobody could take it seriously, especially since there were in all only a few hundred Jewish undergraduates among the 270,000 students and some important universities had no Jewish students at all.

But statistics and rational arguments have never inhibited classical anti-Semitic propaganda which operates with time-honored stereotypes. "Whatever their origins and whatever their destination, the function of these stereotypes is always the same. They are used as justification for destructive thinking, they are employed as excuses for destructive action."[15] There were some startling parallels between Nazi propaganda attempts to justify the liquidation of the Jews and the statements of Polish Communist propagandists as to why Jews had to be purged as security risks. If the reader replaces the word "Zionist" by "Jew" and Poland by Germany, many Polish anti-Zionist outbursts may appear to be almost verbatim quotes from the *Völkische Beobachter* or the speeches of Hitler and Goebbels.

The blueprint for gradual escalation drawn up by the manipulators of the campaign was simple: take two dozen or so Jewish students with appropriate family backgrounds, apply the Nazi methods of collective responsibility of the parents, link the young people with both the sinister Babel Club and their revisionist Jewish professors, feed fabricated evidence from police files to selected mass media, imply clandestine contacts with discredited Jewish politicians and international Zionism, and you have all the ingredients of a dangerous plot, the long-awaited opportunity to get rid of your political and personal enemies, real or suspected opponents.

The hunt for the guilty immediately became a pretext for settling political scores. While *Trybuna Ludu* on March 11, publishing the list of the eight "ringleaders," merely expressed "surprise" that they were the children of responsible state and Party officials, the ostensibly non-Communist paper *Slowo Powszechne* (the daily of PAX, the pseudo-Catholic organization headed by the prewar fascist Boleslaw Piasecki) the same day fired the opening salvo: "Zionists in Poland want to turn the intellectuals and the youth against their primary responsibility to People's Poland . . . Zionist circles in Israel and West German revanchists have combined to inspire Polish Zionist circles to sow trouble in Poland." To make the identity of the "Zionists" completely clear the paper listed almost exactly the same names as the Party organ, adding one Blumsztajn and one Rubinsztajn for better effect.

On the same day two other ominous events took place. The Party secretary of the city of Warsaw,* Jozef Kepa, publicly launched the purge against the Jews. Declaring that the troublemakers were primarily of Jewish origin and associated with the Babel Club, he went on to announce that "we will not allow ourselves to be blackmailed by the bogey of anti-Semitism" and that

---

* Warsaw and four other large cities have the status of region. Thus there are in these cases two Party committees and two leading secretaries, one for the entire Warsaw region and one for the city or the metropolitan area. The country is divided into nineteen voivodships (administrative regions) with Warsaw, Lodz, Cracow, Wroclaw, and Poznan having the same status. In turn, the voivodships are divided into 397 counties. The Party's organizational structure corresponds to this territorial division.

the students' parents were responsible "regardless of their position." Moreover, he denounced as the real "inspirers" two "bankrupt politicians," former Politburo member Roman Zambrowski and former Warsaw Party chief Stefan Staszewski, both of whom were, of course, Jews, and both of whom had been living in public disgrace for four and ten years respectively.

In the evening the local Party organization in the large Zeran car factory on the outskirts of the capital convened what was the first of many thousands of "spontaneous" workers' meetings. After an inflammatory speech by Party secretary Pietrzak, the participants enthusiastically endorsed a resolution demanding the "exemplary punishment of Zionists and other enemies of People's Poland." Next morning *Trybuna Ludu* reproduced on its title page a large poster from the meeting: "Purge the Party of Zionists!" Ironically, the same Zeran plant served during the "Polish October" of 1956 as a driving force in the democratization and Gomulka's return to power. Then, its Party secretary, Gozdzik, had been a flamboyant reformer, and the factory's cars served as an essential means of transportation for alerting the capital against the danger of a possible Soviet military intervention. The author remembers vividly his visits to Zeran in those exhilarating days, when for once genuinely elected representatives of genuine workers were leading the country in introducing workers' councils and industrial democracy. Today, Zeran is a citadel of the so-called "Partisans" headed by General Moczar. Its Party secretary, Pietrzak, can claim the credit for setting the pace of the vicious campaign which soon inundated the entire country.

His eagerness was hardly surprising since his brother is none other than the notorious General Pietrzak, the chairman of the Warsaw branch of ZBOWiD (Union of Fighters for Freedom and Democracy), the veterans' organization, and one of the closest collaborators of Moczar, who since 1964 has headed the nationwide veterans' organization. Under his leadership, this association of three hundred thousand members, comprising many non-Communist resistance fighters and soldiers of the formerly vilified Home Army, became a symbol of national unity and above all a powerful pressure group. As a television commentator remarked when presenting a newsreel about its leaders, "ZBOWiD was the first to disclose the antistate character of the March events."[16]

ZBOWiD indeed led in creating the atmosphere of a witch-hunt. Barely twenty hours after his brother's call for a purge of the "Zionists," General Pietrzak's organization attacked in a strongly worded statement "the same people, who were known years ago for their national nihilism, as responsible for instigating the students" and demanded that they "should be punished appropriately regardless of their positions." It also warned that "international Zionism and its agencies are particularly active in this slanderous campaign against People's Poland and socialism." On the same day, March 12, *Kurier Polski,* ostensibly the organ of the "Democratic Party" (one of the two politically insignificant parties embellishing the parliamentary façade of the Communist regime) launched an assault with obvious anti-Semitic undertones on seven writers and several scholars such as Professors Bauman, Brus, Schaff, and Kolakowski (only the last is not Jewish), accusing them of being "enemies of People's Poland." They were all said to belong "to circles devoted to Israeli and West German propaganda." The Babel Club was castigated for "educating young people in the spirit of Jewish chauvinism."

These were the main themes of the opening phase of the struggle against first "Zionists, bankrupt politicians, revisionists, and Stalinists" and later all those who protected them. On the same day that the ZBOWiD resolution and the purge call from Zeran were published, that is within four days of the initial events, three high officials were summarily dismissed from their posts by Premier Cyrankiewicz because of their children's role in the student demonstrations: J. Gorecki, Director General in the Finance Ministry, J. Grudzinski, Undersecretary of State at the Ministry of Forestry, and F. Topolski, Government Commissioner for industrial decentralization. Five days later Roman Zambrowski, who had been ousted from the Politburo in 1963, was sacked from his relatively minor post as Vice-President of the State Control Commission and expelled from the Party which he had joined forty-three years earlier as a sixteen-year-old.

In the meantime, as a prominent non-Jewish intellectual told the author: "Overnight and everywhere, small groups of people who had hitherto remained in the background suddenly took off their masks, demanded a purge of Zionists, and intimidated all of us." The intimidation proceeded by means of carefully staged mass rallies which resulted in a flood of letters and telegrams to Gomulka. Typical of these "spontaneous" resolutions was the one issued by the ZBOWiD branch organization in the Motokow district of Warsaw; it demanded "a complete removal of Zionist elements and other enemies of our socialist reality from the political, state administrative, educational, and cultural apparatus and also from social organizations . . . Those who in their nihilism and cosmopolitanism poison the spirit and heart of the youth should lose their influence on it."[17] On March 14 *Trybuna Ludu*, the central Party organ, officially sanctioned the Zionist fable by flatly stating that "among the instigators of recent events an essential role was played by young people with Zionist connections."

But there were some serious semantic problems to be solved. Zionist organizations had after all been officially dissolved two decades before. What was the meaning of the term "Zionism"? How could a patriotic Pole identify a Zionist? The Party activitists were faced with the same problems as the Party secretary Stepanov of the Mavrino political prison, one of the unforgettable figures in Alexander Solzhenitsyn's *The First Circle*. At the end of 1949 he was called to a highly placed official in the Political Section of the Ministry of State Security (in Moscow). This official asked in a lazy, mellow voice:

"Tell me, Stepanov, what's happening about your Hebrews?"

"About my what?" Stepanov asked, straining to hear properly the second time.

"Your Hebrews," but seeing the blank look on Stepanov's face, he explained: "Your Yids, I mean."

Quite taken off his guard and fearing to repeat this tricky word, the use of which had until recently been punishable by ten years' imprisonment, Stepanov mumbled vaguely:

"Er, yes, we have a few . . ."

"I know, but what are you doing about them?"

But at this moment the phone rang, the official lifted the receiver and never got back to his conversation with Stepanov.

Feeling quite at sea, Stepanov had reread a great pile of Party directives, circulars, and instructions, but they were all insidiously reticent on the Jewish question . . . He must be getting rather slow on the uptake in his old age! But how could he have known? During all his years of Party work he had always taken it for granted that the Jewish comrades were particularly devoted. What a disgrace that a Party worker of his experience had failed to notice the beginning of an important new drive . . .[18]

Twenty years later the Polish Stepanovs were at a similar loss as to what they should do to save and screen their "healthy collectives" from the nefarious influence of the "Zionists." If it had not been for the human tragedies of the people involved, the hunt for the Zionists at Party meetings could have been described as hilarious comedies where the leading actors did not know their scripts. Even such a highly placed Party man as Jerzy Solecki, the editor-in-chief of Interpress (news agency and publishing house), made himself the laughingstock of Warsaw when soon after the Arab-Israeli War he initiated a purge of "Zionists." At one meeting, six well-known journalists, including one non-Jew who had dared to defend his colleagues, were expelled from the Party as "Zionists."

After his opening attack against Zionism, a woman journalist and respected prewar Party member challenged Solecki with the question: "What exactly do you mean by 'Zionism'? Before the war we fought the Zionists. Those who survived have gone long ago. There is now a State of Israel, a state like any other, with a Communist Party, left-wing, right-wing, and center parties. Thus fighting against 'Zionism' in socialist Poland of 1967 is an obsolete and irrelevant phrase from prewar times."

Blushing and embarrassed, Solecki, who emerged less than a year later as one of the most vituperative anti-Semitic propagandists, could only stammer that he "had not had time to look up the details in the encyclopedia" and added that a Zionist is a person whose father and mother are Jews.

In March 1968 with a massive propaganda campaign against "Zionism" in full swing, many desperate activists wrote or telephoned *Trybuna Ludu* to ask for a thorough explanation of what Zionism was. The Party paper graciously obliged and informed its readers that "Zionism is the ideology of Jewish nationalist bourgeoisie, which aims at preventing assimilation and at persuading Jewish communities all over the world to render economic and political assistance as well as intelligence information to international Zionist organizations." Needless to say, Zionism also supports American imperialism and West German revanchism, which wants to reconquer the Polish territories lost after World War II.[19]

Yet practical hurdles still remained to be overcome. A certain Banaszcyk hit the nail on the head when, speaking at the congress of Warsaw journalists, he referred to the posters demanding a cleansing of the Party from the Zionists: "One cannot exclude the possibility that as a result of unsatisfactory information the people do not know what Zionism means and exactly whom one should remove."[20] This indeed was a tricky problem. Where is there a "Jewish nationalist bourgeoisie" in Poland? How can you pinpoint Zionists when there are no Zionist organizations with meetings to be attended, dues to be paid? How can you prove that someone is a Zionist?

The campaign soon took care of this trifling problem. It is not up to the accusers to prove who is but to the suspects to prove that they are not Zionists! Television did its best to identify those who in the words of Kazimierz Kakol, the editor of the lawyers' association's fortnightly, *Prawo i Zycie,* "for years sucked the blood of the nation and the state." Every evening it began to show banners and posters at "spontaneous workers' meetings" depicting long-nosed hunchbacks identified as Zionists, or the star of David inscribed with the word "No" or bearing such inscriptions as "Zionists out of Poland."

The crucial role of television in the hate campaign must be underlined. This was the first anti-Semitic witch-hunt in history to utilize fully the enormous potentialities of the visual media. Evening after evening, over three million television sets, reaching more than one in every three families, conveyed the message in such a way that even the simplest Pole could easily grasp who the "Zionists" were. Naturally, no self-respecting newscaster, commentator, or Party activist would dream of calling for a crusade against the Jews, let alone the "Yids," in "socialist" Poland. They spoke only about elements "basically alien to the nation and socialism," or "people with two fatherlands," or simply about "cosmopolitans" and "Zionists." As however the "Zionist" or "revisionist" troublemakers often had Polish names, the television and the printed media took the greatest possible care to add their prewar Jewish-sounding surnames or—if the original name of their ancestors could not be traced—to allude to their Jewish origin. In the initial phase of the campaign, roundabout ways were also used. Thus in a case of a certain J. Nowicki, accused of treating a state enterprise as his kingdom, of treating people arrogantly and insolently exploiting them, *Trybuna Ludu* comforted its readers lest they think that Nowicki's case involved an authentic Pole: "We attach no importance to the matter of his origin, because we know that the manifestation of economic misuses and of autocracy appears independently of nationality . . ."[21]

Above all the "Zionists" were painted as dangerous foes of Poland working hand in glove with its traditional enemies, the West Germans and other nefarious imperalists. Raul Hilberg notes in his penetrating study of *The Destruction of the European Jews:* "First of all, the Germans drew a picture of an international Jewry ruling the world and plotting the destruction of Germany and German life. The theory of world Jewish rule and of incessant Jewish plots against the German people penetrated into all offices. It became interwoven with foreign policy and sometimes led to preposterous results. Thus the conviction grew that foreign statesmen who were not very friendly toward Germany were Jews, part-Jews, married to Jews, or somehow dominated by the Jews."[22] The manipulators of the anti-Semitic campaign in Poland, pretending to speak on behalf of socialism, had a more complicated task: that of vilifying the Jews while indignantly rejecting the "vile lies" accusing them of anti-Semitism.

Replacing "all-powerful Jewry" with all-powerful "world Zionism" and using a fashionable anti-imperialist phraseology to veil a familiar language, the Polish propagandists proved capable of solving the semantic difficulties. The most fervent and perhaps ablest spokesmen of the Moczar faction, Kakol, particularly distinguished himself in resorting to the classical Communist ploy of "amalgam," that is, combining completely different, even contradictory components into a seemingly credible whole. Soon after the "March events," Kakol initiated a new TV program—"Questions and Answers"—in which he enlightened the viewers about the sinister forces behind the domestic "Zionists." Some extracts may illustrate his insidious method:

"Our public has not been informed fully and properly of the activities and threat of Zionism, although signals of its ominous machinations have been plain enough for quite some time, if only in the form of data concerning the intensity of vulgar anti-Polish propaganda, inspired and conducted by Zionist circles in close collaboration with West German revanchists.* One of the links in that mechanism is Julius Klein, an American general of Jewish origin, a resident of West Germany." (An ideal culprit indeed: Jew, American, of German origin and a general to boot. Kakol omitted to mention of course that Mr. Klein was merely an officially registered public relations man for the Federal Republic of Germany in the United States during the time of the late Chancellor Adenauer's government, and that he had absolutely nothing to do with Poland or Zionism. What mattered was that Kakol had pro-

---

* Kakol's, like all other statements, usually refer to the Polish abbreviation of the Federal Republic of Germany but I have used West Germany or West Germans.

duced out of his hat a "link"—the indisputable existence of an American Jewish public relations man of German origin.)

Then came the usual hypocritical twist: "Zionism counted on our fundamental Marxist attitude which restrains us from disclosing certain facts, if only in order not to give rise to anti-Semitic attitudes. They were quite right. It was finally the disturbances inspired and organized by Zionists that forced us to put our cards on the table." After agreeing with Gomulka that Zionism is not a "serious threat," Kakol added the warning: ". . . but it can certainly cause a lot of trouble and difficulties . . . Zionism is acting in alliance with international reactionary political forces and with the revanchist forces in West Germany. The more we talk about Zionism with open honesty, the less dangerous it becomes."[23]

Kakol's "Questions and Answers" on the TV screen were so highly regarded that by the end of April they were brought out in book form. While at the time of this writing, no less than twenty-eight novels, poems, and anthologies have not been given a publication permit by the censors (some of the manuscripts having been submitted two years ago!) ostensibly because of "lack of paper," Kakol's booklet was published at the end of April 1968—and in a first printing of fifty thousand copies.

While the mass media were whipping up the "anti-Zionist" hysteria, the secret police were busily collecting the evidence to support Kakol's warning about an "attempt at a coup d'état." In addition to interrogating the "Zionist" rabble-rousers among the arrested students, Moczar's apparatus was working day and night on the preparation of the great "Zionist trial." After *Trybuna Ludu*'s report on March 14 that the students chanted, "We want Zambrowski!" (a call no one present heard, since most of the students had not the slightest idea who Zambrowski was), rumors about the impending arrest of Zambrowski and Staszewski swept the capital. These were not unfounded inventions. Moczar really went to Gomulka with a warrant for the arrest of the "Stalinist" turned-"Zionist" Staszewski.

Staszewski, a prewar Party member, spent several years in a Siberian concentration camp after 1938, the year Stalin dissolved the Polish Communist Party. A member of the Central Committee and secretary of the Warsaw Party committee, he played a key role in the events of October 1956, mobilizing public opinion and distributing weapons among the young workers and students in anticipation of a Soviet intervention. He was the first to lose power among the "men of October," when in the spring of 1957 he refused to support Gomulka's drive against the "revisionists." Later he worked as one of the editors of the "Great General Encyclopedia" whose eighth volume with an entry on the Nazi concentration camps became a favorite target of the "anti-Zionist" campaign. In addition to being blamed for "disparaging the national honor of Poland," Staszewski also committed the unpardonable sin of regularly visiting a café, the favorite haunt of Warsaw intellectual circles. Here he met occasionally, as so many did, some of the "Zionist" students, including Adam Michnik. Though long deprived of any political influence, Staszewski was almost overnight singled out as a powerful and sinister plotter. In a full-page profile, the Party paper reviled him as the man who was responsible (in the fifties) for persecuting the peasants who were reluctant to sell their grain to the state, who went the whole hog from ardent Stalinism to turncoat revisionism and ended up as a servant of Zionist centers in slandering the Polish people.

It was in this atmosphere that Moczar, the Minister of Interior, at last asked Gomulka's permission for the arrest of this cunning enemy. The Party leader however tore up the warrant with the remark: "Staszewski has already sat long enough. Don't forget that he is a strong man whom not even Stalin could break. And I do not want another Beilis trial."*

Moczar and his collaborators in the secret police had other irons in the fire however. Twelve years before, on January 22, 1957, Bogdan Piasecki, a sixteen-year-old high school student, had been kidnaped in broad daylight on one of the main streets in downtown Warsaw and murdered. He was the son of Boleslaw

---

* Shortly before World War I, Mendel Beilis was tried in Kiev and acquitted on a charge of ritual murder of a child in one of the most notorious court cases in Tsarist Russia.

Piasecki, the leader of the prewar fascist falanga group and now the chief of the powerful PAX, the organization set up after the war by the Communists to split the Catholic Church. An old Soviet agent, Piasecki had done his best to save the crumbling Stalinist regime in 1956.* The kidnaping of his son was clearly an act of political revenge.

At that time the police took a cab driver into custody, friends of the murdered youth having reported that young Piasecki and two other men had got in his cab. The driver did not deny this and even provided the name of the street where he had dropped his passengers. After spending a year in custody, he was finally released. But during the upheaval following the Arab-Israeli War in the summer of 1967, Moczar had him arrested again. The cab driver is Jewish. Friends of Piasecki began to make suggestions about a ritual murder. From the beginning of 1968 and especially after the student riots, an estimated two hundred witnesses are said to have been interrogated. Some of these who are now in the West got the impression that the questioning was aimed at establishing contacts between the Israeli Embassy and the arrested Jewish cab driver, the young Polish writer Marek Hlasko* who had left Poland for Israel in 1958, and other "Zionists." At the time of this writing both Staszewski and Zambrowski are free, and no indictment has been issued turning the kidnaping into a "Zionist trial." But knowing the cautious and devious way in which Moczar's machine works, both cases must be regarded as "plots in reserve" with a prepared script and candidates for the role of "Zionist adventurers."

Other provocations, politically less significant but perhaps even more revealing, were perpetrated publicly by Polish agents abroad. Soon after the student riots, Dr. Zofia Majewska, a Jewish woman doctor living in the city of Gdansk, received a letter from Austria. Written in rather clumsy German, the letter was sent by a Professor Helmut Bauer in Vienna, who gave his exact address. Professor

* For Piasecki and the role of the PAX see also the chapter on "The Manipulators."
* Hlasko died suddenly at the age of thirty-five in June 1969.

Bauer told Dr. Majewska that her life, as indeed the life of all Jews in Poland, was one of humiliation. She should go and settle in "the invincible and rich Israel." He also assured her that the Zionist world organization immediately provides each person who crosses the border with a gift of five thousand dollars. Dr. Majewska took the letter to the local Communist paper, which published it the next day together with Dr. Majewska's public reply, in which she indignantly rejected Bauer's insinuations and stated that her only fatherland was beloved Poland and not Israel, which cooperates with imperialism and West German revanchism (*Glos Wybreza*, March 16–17, 1968). Two days later the letter and her reply were reprinted in *Trybuna Ludu*, and subsequently commented upon in other central dailies and weeklies. There was only one minor hitch. Reading about the heroic Polish doctor's experience with Professor Bauer, an Austrian reporter called on him at the address given in his letter. Both the name and the address were correct. But Helmut Bauer told the reporter that he was neither a professor, a doctor, nor a Jew. Moreover, he had a cosmetic shop, had never written such a letter, or ever heard of Dr. Majewska before. After reading the translation of the Polish press reports, Mr. Bauer asked the Austrian Foreign Ministry to lodge a protest in Warsaw against the abuse of his name.[24]*

Subsequently it was learned that dozens of other Polish Jews received similar letters. Though most of them destroyed the crude forgeries, Dr. Majewska, naïvely or deliberately, chose to challenge those who lured her. But the provocateurs achieved their twofold purpose: to frighten the Jews and instigate their emigration on the one hand and to stimulate anti-Semitic moods on the other. Wladyslaw Kmitowski, the author of the most rabid anti-Semitic tract ever published in Poland (or in any other Communist country), highly commended her in April 1968: ". . . one can count on the fingers of one hand those 'Polish citizens of Jewish origin' who in this difficult time for the Polish community have found it possible to protest against Zionist slanders. Among them are certainly Professor Zofia Majewska of Gdansk Medical Acad-

* For the use of forged letters see also the chapter on Czechoslovakia.

emy and a few other persons who managed to protest heatedly in the press against the Zionist campaign slandering the Polish people. In our eyes, they have grown to the stature of heroes."[25]

Any hopes that the liberal-minded intellectuals, students, and above all the bewildered Jews had that the campaign would peter out since none of the top leaders had endorsed it, suffered a severe shock when, on March 14, Edward Gierek, the Party secretary of Upper Silesia, who was considered a moderate, became the first Politburo member to jump on the band wagon of the hard-liner faction. In a sharply worded speech addressed to one hundred thousand people in Katowice, Gierek repeated the roll call of the "bankrupt politicians," revisionist and Zionist intellectuals (all Jews), and threateningly announced: "The dirty scum which floated on the vortex of the October events eleven years ago has not completely been removed from the tide of our life."[26]

Bombarded by "anti-Zionist" outbursts from the television screen, the radio, the newspapers and the ZBOWiD functionaries, the public and especially the Party and state bureaucracy awaited a final word from Wladislaw Gomulka. It was announced that on March 19, eleven days after the first riots, Gomulka would make a televised address. Meanwhile the anti-Semitic campaign was rapidly approaching a climax.

It was during those days that this joke circulated in Warsaw:

"Is that you, Jaworski?" a tense voice on the telephone asks. "This is Kowalski."

"But which Kowalski? I know dozens of them."

"Israel Kowalski, the one you hid in the closet during the Occupation."

"Oh yes, how are you? Haven't heard from you in twenty years."

"Let's cut things short. Do you still have that closet?"

The joke reflected real fears and real anxiety. Those who remembered the Jew-baiting in prewar Poland were prepared for pogroms despite the fact that there were no Jewish industrialists, street peddlers, or Jewish quarters. Dispersed in the urban centers, Polish Jews in 1968 were indistinguishable from the rest of the population in profession, language, habits, and attire. Yet it was not this that protected the Jews of Poland from physical violence but rather a combination of two other factors: the young people in the population, two thirds of whom were under forty, and the ingrained skepticism toward the official anti-Zionist propaganda of a regime that over the years had lost the trust of the population. Even the Poles permeated with racial prejudices became almost instinctively less anti-Semitic because their dictators appeared to have become, for whatever reason, so much more so. Another popular joke of the time went:

What is the difference between present and prewar anti-Semitism? Before the war anti-Semitism was not obligatory.

The threat of a pogrom did not come from below. The "anti-Zionist" campaign had been carefully planned, prepared, and led from above, and the basic Party cells, who took matters into their own hands "without waiting for directions from the top,"[27] were in reality acting in full accord with the backstage manipulators. And there is evidence that some groups at least in the police and Party apparatus, with or without Moczar's knowledge, intended to resort to physical violence against Jews living in Warsaw.

Originally, some sources maintain, the rally Gomulka addressed was to have been held outdoors. The posters and banners bearing the inscriptions "Purge the Party from the Zionists" and "Act quickly—no half measures, Comrade Wieslaw" (Gomulka's underground pseudonym during the war) were too large for the hall of the Cultural Palace in which the meeting actually took place. While this supposition is open to question, there is ample evidence from unimpeachable sources that the dissident factions counted on staging a decisive showdown with the Jews, thereby producing an atmosphere in which the leadership could be reshuffled without further ado.

An army colonel on his way to the meeting in the Palace overheard two young thugs loudly boasting, "Let's go and slaughter the Jews." He immediately called a militiaman and asked him to detain and question them since they were obviously preparing acts against the Constitution and the law. "What did they say?"

the policeman asked. "They reviled the Jews and were going to attack them," the colonel said. "That is not anti-Constitutional," the policeman replied with a grin. The colonel curtly ordered him to show his identification card. Finally the militiaman stopped the two young men, only to release them a few minutes later after consultation with a police officer.

This may have been an isolated incident, but the fact remains that there had been a "Jewish department" in the Ministry of Interior since 1966, compiling massive files on all Jews with Nazi-type "ancestor charts" (*Ahnentafeln*) which listed parents, grandparents, and often even great-grandparents. Under the leadership of Colonel Walichnowski, author of the anti-Zionist bestseller, *Israel and the Federal Republic of Germany,* this section had been closely concerned with the action against Jews and international Zionism and employed over one hundred agents, officials, and "family researchers" (*Sippenforscher* in Hitler's time).

Walichnowski's department, which could produce in a matter of minutes real—or if necessary forged—proofs of a Jewish grandmother, could easily provide Jewish addresses. One might mention in this connection a minor but nonetheless revealing piece of evidence. Even after the exodus of thousands of Jews and the departure of its director, the famous actress Ida Kaminska, the heavily subsidized Jewish State Theater continues to play, albeit often to virtually empty houses. Its function is to provide proof of the flowering Jewish-Yiddish culture for foreign consumption. In the spring of 1969 a Jewish woman engineer received a mimeographed letter from the Theater appealing to fellow Jews to visit and support the continued existence of this Jewish institution. But the engineer was puzzled. She had never belonged to the Jewish community organization, was married to a Pole, and had luckily even kept her job. It turned out that in the large block of apartments two "Polonized" Jews received the same invitation. No one else in the house did. It became frighteningly clear to the three of them that the police department division of Jewish affairs must have supplied the Theater with a list of potential Jewish theatergoers.

In any case, on the eve of Gomulka's March 1968 speech, selected lists had been issued to plainclothesmen and agents provocateurs. At least five Jewish families known to the author, prominent intellectuals or former office-holders in the Party, were told by different friends from the Ministry of Interior not to sleep at home on March 19. One of them actually went to the country and stayed for several days with the same family that had hidden them during the war. This is not hearsay. The fugitives were real people, belonging to the family of a wartime Communist resistance hero, and not the "Israel Kowalski" of the political joke related earlier.[28]

There is no way of knowing why the pogroms were at the last moment called off, but, like the entire "anti-Zionist" hysteria, they would have been only a means to an end—the bid for supreme power. In settling political scores, Communist politicians act like all other politicians: they improvise; they shift their allegiances from day to day; and they are frequently swept along by the stream of circumstances. Even within the "anti-Zionist" coalition there must have been differences over the tactics and the timing of specific actions. The wavering and seesawing became increasingly evident even in the first round of the power struggle.

As Isaac Deutscher has observed, "It would be a serious mistake to treat totalitarianism metaphysically as a state of society's utter immobility, history's absolute freezing, which excludes any political movement in the form of action from below or reform from above." In his opinion the critical moment is when the crisis in leadership coincides with deep changes in the society.[29] The intensity of the crisis is in turn related to the position of the man "at the head of the Party." The fact that his authority is taken for granted inevitably leads to his glorification. The degree of the idolatry is different in each Communist country. But the "monolithic" principle, the familiar image of the Party "closely knit around its Leninist leadership," makes it mandatory to extol the wisdom of its decision and therefore that of its chief.[30]

In eleven days, the calls for a "scrupulous and uncompromising analysis" of the "Zionist"-led student unrest mounted on all sides, raising such questions as, "who has been paralyzing the processes of positive changes in many fields of our life and in what way; who has been backing incompetent, discredited people" in important jobs.[31] Nobody could seriously think of attacking Gomulka directly, but the barrage of criticism was aimed more and more overtly at the shortcomings of the Gomulka system. The house organs of the "Partisans" and their allies castigated the "false slogan of small stabilization,* the half measures of a permanently existing semisocialism and mutilated programs."[32] For the first time since Gomulka's return to power in 1956, the issue of his personal leadership was raised. The television coverage of his speech on March 19 gave the population a dramatic indication that major shifts in the balance of power were, or might be, taking place. The public build-up of Gierek as an alternative to Gomulka was evident before he began his speech, when three thousand Party activists chanted, "Gierek-Wieslaw." Somewhat later, millions of TV viewers and radio listeners could hear shouts from the audience interrupting and encouraging the First Secretary to act "more boldly." All this and the ambivalence of the speech itself seemed to imply that the image of his "autocratic rule not subject to any control" was suffering an irreparable blow.

In retrospect, his speech must be seen as the curtain raiser to his tortuous search for time to parry the challenge to his supremacy. To many, the then sixty-three-year-old Party professional seemed destined to become a figurehead, an elder statesman, and a front man for Moczar and his followers. No one in Poland (in contrast to some naïve observers abroad) ever believed that Gomulka would meet the challenge head on by enlisting popular support and mobilizing the very liberals whom he had always intensely disliked. Instead of submission or a fight, Gomulka chose a third option. To avoid an immediate confrontation and to reassert his control over the Party, he and his associates (particularly Premier Cyrankiewicz, and the ideologue Kliszko three weeks later in Parliament) decided to preempt some of the dynamism of the offensive launched by the hard-liners by virtually adopting

* "Small stabilization," referring to the system of tenuous compromises, was coined by writer Tadeusz Rozewicz in 1962.

their program. But these maneuvers, offensives and counteroffensives had nothing at all to do with the roots of the social and economic ills plaguing the country, let alone with a Jewish problem.

Anti-Semitism however provided an almost ideal battleground for the settling of scores within the bureaucratic elite. The main issue that divided Moczar's "Partisans" from the "Gomulkaites" was all along that of power and never the attitude toward the Jews. Moczar, Strzelecki, and their allies were deliberately playing on anti-Jewish emotions to buy mass support. But Gomulka, who has come to be viewed in some Western circles as a "patron of the Jews" on account of his Jewish wife,* was as willing as his rivals to exploit anti-Semitic tendencies when it suited his convenience and they helped to drain off the dissatisfactions of the new bureaucratic bourgeoisie. His speech marked a turning point in the crisis and closed the initial phase of the "anti-Zionist" campaign. The ambivalent position he took on March 19 served notice to the Jews that they could choose only between the devil and the deep blue sea, that the outcome of the power struggle would in no meaningful way affect their lives.

* Without wishing to draw exact parallels, it is important to recall that even some Cabinet members in the puppet "Kingdom of Croatia" (1941–44) under Nazi rule had Jewish wives. This, however, did not in any way improve the fate of the persecuted Jews. (Hilberg, pp. 453–58) See also the chapter on "The Manipulators."

## 4. IN THE CHINESE WAY

What did Gomulka actually say when he broke his long silence? In a lengthy (and naturally biased) account of the events leading up to the *Dziady* affair, he sharply castigated the writers and students for unleashing a campaign against "the leadership of the Party, against the Government, against the people's authority." He singled out by name some of the main culprits, such as Antonin Slonimski, one of the greatest living Polish poets, and among the "shady politicos holding academic degrees" Professors Brus, Bauman, Kolakowski, and Baczko, scholars of international repute. He appealed for calm and moderation and placed the blame for the "March events" mainly on the anti-Soviet "reactionaries and revisionists." In connection with the "active part played by a number of students of Jewish origin or nationality," he defined Zionism as a part of the anti-Communist front, and went so far as to say that "it would be a misunderstanding to see in Zionism a danger to socialism in Poland, to its social and political system." But there was what Gomulka elegantly called "the problem of self-definition on the part of some Jews—citizens of our country."

The First Secretary thereupon proceeded to enrich the Communist theory of the Jewish question by dividing Polish Jews into three categories. The first consisted of those Jews who considered Israel their homeland and were, in fact, free to go there. The second, of those who felt themselves neither Poles nor Jews. Such people should not be blamed, but because of their cosmopolitan feelings they should avoid fields of work necessitating national affirmation. To illustrate this point, Gomulka quoted from an essay written by the poet Slonimski forty-four years earlier about his ambivalent feelings toward Poles and Jews. That in the meantime he had become the foremost poet of Poland, a former president of the Writers Union and a pacemaker in the forces that brought Gomulka back to power apparently still did not make him fit for "national affirmation." (Surprisingly, Gomulka does not seem to harbor any doubts about the prominent prewar fascists in high government posts and in Parliament.) Lastly, Gomulka paid warm tribute to "the most numerous group of Polish citizens of Jewish origin" for whom Poland was the only fatherland, who "had sunk all their roots deep into the soil on which they were born," and who had rendered great services to the country and to socialism, concluding: "We are combating Zionism as a political program, as Jewish nationalism, and this is right. This is something quite different from anti-Semitism. It is anti-Semitism when somebody comes out against the Jews just because they are Jews."[33]

Unfortunately, the response to the speech provided stunning proof of the hatred many Communists feel for Jews "just because they are Jews." When Gomulka first uttered the word "Jew," wild shouts from one corner of the hall drowned his voice, and he was repeatedly prevented from talking by near-hysterical outbursts reminiscent of Nazi rallies at Nuremberg. Actually, only a part of the crowd participated in these disturbances, but those who watched the proceedings on television got a different impression. Skillful editing and camera work made it seem that the whole audience of the three thousand activists was pressing a hesitant Gomulka to act more energetically against the "Zionist enemy."

The ambiguity of Gomulka's formulations helped to create a somewhat distorted image of his speech abroad. Government circles in Israel and genuine Zionists were gratified that he was giving a green light to emigration. Some in the West called his speech "moderate" since he seemed to disassociate himself from an all-out purge. Yet in reality when he spoke about the three-way division of Polish Jews, he was quoting Roman Dmowski, the father of modern Polish nationalism and the ancestor of the prewar fascist groups. The Poland of today, with its frontiers shifted a hundred and fifty miles to the west on the Oder-Neisse line, with a homogenous population without national minorities, without Jews in particular, allied to Russia, ruled by an authoritarian government while the Catholic Church enjoys great prestige is—as K. A. Jelenski aptly noted—"a paradoxical realization of the dream of Roman Dmowski."[34]

Dmowski (1864–1939) believed that the reasons of state dictated an alliance with Russia, and his brand of nationalism hoped to divert anti-Russian resentments into anti-German and anti-Semitic channels. He also founded the National Democratic Party (Endecja; its followers known as "Endeks") that became the bulwark of anti-Semitic political demagogy.

The novelty of Gomulka's address was the fact that he combined the traditional appeal of the Polish right to "reasons of state" with cynical concessions to the baser instincts of the new bureaucratic middle class, which regards intellectuals and the Jews as equally suspect and often synonymous.[35] The three categories of Jews were borrowed—almost verbatim—from Dmowski's party program of seventy-one years before, which distinguished between Jews who have their own national aspirations; those who are neither Jews nor Poles; and Jews who are part of the Polish nation. The first were to be fought as a hostile element, an economic crusade proclaimed against the second to destroy their commercial and industrial domination, and the last accepted within the Polish community on an equal basis with the Poles.

In the interwar period, particularly after the death of Marshal Pilsudski, the fine distinctions were submerged under the rising tide of anti-Semitic agitation accentuated by widespread unemployment and the influence of Nazi Germany. There were only differences of degree between the Endeks, the frankly fascist groups of the younger elements (the National Radicals, known as ONR, and Piasecki's Falanga) on the one hand and the official Government bloc called the "Camp of National Unity" on the other. The various groups seeking political support vied with each other in anti-Jewish agitation. The avowed aim was the expulsion of *all* Jews. The Government in 1938 even sent a mission to Madagascar to explore the possibility of setting up Jewish settlements. Miedzinski, the deputy chairman of Parliament and editor of the government newspaper, candidly declared that "Poland has room only for fifty thousand Jews and the remaining three million must emigrate."[36]

And now, in 1968, there appeared to be no room for even those twenty-five thousand or so Jews who had survived Hitler's Final Solution and refused to emigrate in the late 1950s. Given the size of the Jewish population, Gomulka's decision to turn to the theories of the prewar anti-Semitic party was obviously a matter of tactics, not dogma.

The results however were exactly the same. At no point did Gomulka disassociate himself publicly from the purge or disavow the "anti-Zionist" campaign. He merely wanted to limit and channel it for his own purposes.[37] The March 19 speech thus provided grist for the demogogues' mill. The anti-Semitic campaign now surged ahead under its own steam, hitting indiscriminately all three categories—the "Jewish" Jews, the "cosmopolitan" Jews, and "Polish" Jews alike.

The day after Gomulka's speech was published a series of public mass meetings was held in each of the nineteen voivodships (administrative regions), giving the signal for similar meetings during the following weeks in the seventy thousand primary organizations of the Party. This meant in effect a campaign penetrating the entire political and cultural, social and economic life of Poland, since the Communist Party (officially called since 1948 the Polish United Workers' Party) counted in its ranks over two million members—that is, 10 per cent of the adult population— one in every five employees of the nationalized sector and three fourths of the regular officers.

As might have been expected, the main point of the speeches was not Gomulka's warning against exaggerating the "Zionist" threat and leveling indiscriminate charges against individuals "without the prior approval of appropriate bodies." The dominant theme was the call for the "self-identification" of the Jews. On March 21 alone, for example, three rallies were staged in the cities of Lodz, Lublin, and Rzeszow. Speaking to one hundred and fifty thousand people in Lodz, the second largest Polish city, Jozef Spychalski (not to be confused with Marshal Marian Spychalski, the present head of state), the first secretary of the city Party committee, challenged "the people who are either without a fatherland or those who have not yet made their choice to declare and identify themselves." His comrade W. Kozdra in Lublin, also addressing an impressive rally, reviled the "Zionist" and "revisionist" intellectuals by name and demanded "self-identification of these Jews, citizens of our state, who thus far have not declared themselves." To make clear that any opposition was useless, the Party secretary in Rzeszow warned his audience: "We shall not permit elements of Jewish nationality using provocative and demagogic slogans of anti-Semitism to prevent us from calling things by their name."[38] This man, who had been terrorizing the region for two decades, was famous in Party circles for his candid way of talking. When Yehudi Menuhin in the mid-sixties gave a celebrated concert in Warsaw, he remarked indignantly at a Central Committee meeting that he could not understand why Poland should spend money on inviting Jewish violinists: "We have enough Polish violinists—even in the city of Rzeszow alone."

At the meetings and in the mass media the calls for "vigilance" and an "uncompromising" fight against the "Zionists" and the candidates for "guilt by association" reached a crescendo. A dispatch by a Yugoslav (and of course Communist) correspondent for *Vjesnik*, the leading Zagreb paper, described the political climate on the basis of his talks with Warsaw Party officials: "The greatest problem for the Party was Zionism, the members of the city committee stated. Precisely this and nothing else. They described Zionism as a mixture of American imperialism, Israeli imperialism, and West German revanchism. It seems that for some people in Poland, Zionism has become a real obsession. No political official with whom I talked accepted the remark that it is unimportant and that it might be superfluous to add to the names of incriminated persons the attribute: a Pole of Jewish origin."[39] But the same atmosphere was described in glowing terms by the spokesman of the hard-liners as being "unique of its kind . . . Letters, telegrams, resolutions from factories, state farms, cities, and the most remote villages are constantly arriving at the Central Committee. All express best wishes for Comrade Gomulka and pledge full support for the Party policy. All demand strong actions against the people who, having advanced to important posts, have failed the trust of the working class; all call for purging our life from reactionary and Zionist elements to which the interests of our nation are alien."[40]

As if following the baton of an invisible conductor, dozens of key officials and commentators began to exhort the state executives and Party officials to the "maximal exploitation of the enormous chance."[41] To the older generation they spoke in a strikingly familiar language. Thirty years earlier the supreme council of the fascist-style "Camp of National Unity" (OZON—the government party) issued a manifesto calling the Jews "an element weakening the state. It is necessary to defend the centers of Polish cultural and social life such as the press, theater, libraries, music, and radio against their influence."[42] Now *Kierunki,* the weekly organ of the notorious PAX organization, exhorts: "We must remember that to a very large extent these shortcomings and delays were a result of the conscious, active presence in many important areas such as learning, culture, and administration of people basically alien to Poland and socialism."[43] And the resolution of the Party activists in the Foreign Trade Ministry on March 25 stated: "We feel responsible for the selection of the representatives of People's Poland and its interests abroad. There can be no place for people who do not feel any links with the fatherland, for the agents of international imperialism and its Zionist lackeys." Their comrades in the Foreign Ministry published within three days two resolutions, the first expressing "full solidarity with the general demands for an unconditional purge of Zionists from the Party ranks and particularly from our foreign service"; the second warning that "there can be no compromise with cosmopolitans and chauvinists," and that it was "impossible to tolerate their activity in any responsible position."[44]

The resemblance to the prewar social-fascist movement did not stop with rhetoric. The most vociferous newspapers were under the control of the former fascist leader Boleslaw Piasecki; C. Pilichowski, the man specializing in defaming even the memory of the three million dead Jews, in his capacity as "director of the Commission for Investigating Hitlerite Crimes" was an active member of the fascist ONR group before the war and expelled from the Party for denying it; the deputy Minister of Justice, Zawadzki, had as prewar state attorney prosecuted many left-wingers, including Communists; and several prominent editors and writers of central newspapers and weeklies had a similarly chequered past, some even having fought in fascist underground bands during the war, killing Jews and later Russian soldiers rather than the Nazis.[45]

In the midst of the general "anti-Zionist" campaign, certain institutions, and by implication the Party leaders in charge of them, appeared as specific targets of attack: the Academy of Science, the Institute of Nuclear Research, the Committee for Science and Technology, the faculties of the departments of sociology and philosophy at Warsaw University, book publishers (especially the State Scientific Publishing House PWN), the film industry, parts of the mass media, and the Ministries of Foreign Affairs, Foreign Trade, Finance, Culture, and Health. In general, the attacks centered on those sectors of Polish life that had hitherto resisted control by the right, that had employed a sprinkling of high-ranking Jewish officials or specialists, and that were led by the political and personal enemies of the Moczar-Strzelecki faction and their allies.

The signal for the beginning of the second and decisive phase of the post-"March events" purge was given on March 25 by the summary dismissal of Professors Baczko, Bauman, Brus, Morawski, Kolakowski, and Maria Hirszowicz from their university positions. This was the first time in Polish history that senior faculty members with tenure were sacked from one day to the next.

Scores of articles vilified them for protecting student troublemakers and using their positions to maintain links between students and old-line Stalinist politicians who had been ousted from power. Obscure assistant lecturers and Party hack writers questioned the professional qualifications of people whose massive studies had been translated into many languages and put on the reading lists of university courses from Prague to Berkeley. In its explanation of the reasons, *Trybuna Ludu* hastened to point out the next day the relevant fact that the dismissed professors were "mainly of Jewish origin" (four out of six to be exact).

When thirty years ago fascist students (including some of the earlier mentioned dignitaries of "socialist" Poland) staged anti-Jewish outrages in the universities, the then rector of Lodz University proclaimed in an open letter: "It is easy to see that under the lofty slogans of national solidarity and defense of the Polish character of our culture, the dignity of the autonomous authorities is brutally challenged, and the freedom of science without which science cannot exist is being undermined."[46] His letter was printed in many papers, and no minister would have dreamed of sacking professors.

In the Poland of 1968 the sacred autonomy of the ancient universities was reduced overnight by the stroke of a pen. No paper printed the resolution adopted at a protest meeting of two thousand students on March 28 demanding the reinstatement of their teachers or their slogans: "There can be no studies without freedom!", "There can be no Polish economics without Brus—no Polish philosophy without Kolakowski!" The only answer was the closing of eight departments and the suspension of sixteen hundred students. With three months' severance pay, the scholars were left as it were on the street. They could get no jobs remotely in keeping with their qualifications; publishers and editors refused to accept their manuscripts; and in no time their wives also lost their posts. As a correspondent of *Politika*, the foremost Belgrade daily, concluded nine months later: "Nobody knows how these Polish intellectuals are able to live, to buy books, or to pay their rent."[47]

Here again the Communist regime was only following the prescriptions of the prewar anti-Semites: "depriving the Jews of earning money means that they will be forced to leave Poland." Only the solidarity of their (non-Jewish) colleagues and above all students who sent not only flowers, but also gifts and parcels, and who organized collections, helped to keep these first prominent victims afloat. One must also stress that standing up publicly in defense of maligned colleagues and friends involved serious risks. The writer Pawel Jasienica, who was the first at the Warsaw writers' meeting to reveal that "disgusting anti-Semitic leaflets, coming from outside, were distributed by individuals in civilian clothes at the university as a provocation," became the target of the most vituperative attacks and received countless threatening phone calls.* The valiant Catholic author and member of Parliament until 1965, Stefan Kisielewski, another non-Jewish scapegoat (he seems to represent the "link to German revanchists"), was severely beaten up one night in March and had to be hospitalized for several days. Nor did it help the Polish Jews in Gomulka's "third category" to protest their fate. At a party meeting S. Jaszunski, an assistant editor on the staff of a large Warsaw paper, rejected the charge of Zionism as an outrageous lie and insisted that he was a Pole "with all his roots." The following evening a gang of Piasecki's (or Moczar's?) thugs attacked him as he was on his way home. With razor blades and switch knives they administered several deep cuts to his face; he also had to be hospitalized.

But physical violence was rare. The organizers preferred what they called among themselves "the Chinese way," an allusion to the Cultural Revolution in China where Mao Tse-tung, by mobilizing the Red Guards and resorting to mass demonstrations, wall newspapers, and a variety of unorthodox organizational methods, destroyed the opposition and revamped the Party.

A typical example of the Polish "Chinese way" in practice was the handling of the Foreign Ministry, one of the foremost targets

* He died in August 1970; the large crowd at his funeral was a symbolic protest against the regime which had silenced one of the country's most popular authors.

of the hard-liners' offensive. Its head since 1956, the former Social Democrat Adam Rapacki, was the exact opposite of Premier Cyrankiewicz. The latter had survived all the upheavals since 1947 by the judicious use of opportunism. Rapacki, on the other hand, was a man of absolute integrity. At the first Politburo meeting after the student riots, he condemned the "anti-Zionist" campaign in the strongest possible terms, and after Gomulka's March speech he boycotted both the Ministry and all sessions of the Politburo.*

This served the purposes of the Partisans and their allies perfectly. Three times in a week, the Party activists, the trade union cell, and the local organization issued calls for a purge of "Zionists, cosmopolitans, and other alien elements." Under the leadership of Ambassador Sidor, Moczar's candidate for the post of Foreign Minister, the extremists soon took matters into their own hands. Sidor, the former ambassador to Cairo, was an expert on Zionism, and the moment he started the purge in the Foreign Ministry, the Army paper *Zolnierz Wolnosci* began to publish a series of extracts from his new book "on the aggressive policy of Tel Aviv and the international Zionist organizations." After sharply attacking the absent Rapacki for tolerating "Zionists and other reactionaries" in the Foreign Service, Sidor called for a loyalty oath from the Jewish officials and diplomats.

During a marathon meeting, which lasted into the early morning hours of April 3, the "activists" expelled almost forty diplomats, mainly (but not exclusively) of Jewish origin in addition to several "unreliable" clerks and typists. There were several men present who did not belong to the Ministry who appeared to be extremely well informed about the private life of the prospective victims. When a woman employee attempted to defend a distinguished Jewish diplomat, she was silenced by the remark, "You are a friend of the Zionists; we know you have a Jewish lover," and was subsequently expelled too. In addition to such "Zionist suspects" as the two Assistant Secretaries of State, A. Meller and M. Wajda, both veterans of the Spanish Civil War, a number of lesser officials were summarily ousted from the Party and thus automatically from

*Rapacki died in October 1970.

their jobs. The Ministry's best translator, a forty-two-year-old woman, was also dismissed without any pension rights.

One of the most tragic incidents involved Counsellor S., a life-long diplomat. Challenged to identify himself and accused of "anti-Party" behavior, he became so upset emotionally that he lost his self-control. Denying the accusations, he related his life story, including his ordeals during the war with a small partisan group of Jewish fugitives. He described how, near the city of Lublin, they had encountered a Communist partisan band whose commander ordered the shooting of all forty Jews; he alone had survived by pretending to be dead. He named the commander and then fainted. Though the case was known to many people, it was an extremely delicate matter to mention publicly. The commander was General G. Korczynski, the chief of the military intelligence and now Deputy Minister of Defense. He had been arrested in the late forties, but was never sentenced (or officially rehabilitated). Gomulka, after his return to power, ordered his release and promoted him to a key post. (Korczynski today ranks as one of Moczar's most powerful allies, though some maintain that he has in the meantime switched sides.)

At the same meeting, Maria Wierna, a non-Jewish departmental chief, was dismissed for "Zionist sympathies." Her husband was a Jewish journalist. Her sister was also sacked from her white-collar job in Lodz. But perhaps the most revealing example of "the Chinese way" was the ouster of two high officials. One was Marian Naszkowski (who, contrary to Western press reports, is not of Jewish origin). A veteran Communist, he was First Deputy Foreign Minister for almost fifteen years and, in Rapacki's absence, was supposed to be in charge of the entire Foreign Ministry. The "activists" not only dismissed him at once, they forbade him to enter his office. The other was the Polish ambassador in London, Jerzy Morawski, a noted reformer and a member of the Politburo until 1959. He was summarily dismissed by the Party cell at his embassy. There, as in many Polish diplomatic missions, the agents of the military intelligence and the secret police were the real masters rather than the ambassador, éven if he happened to belong to the Central Committee.*

While the purifying storm was raging in the Foreign Ministry and in the embassies, selected articles presented to the public the names and case histories of Jewish defectors or emigrants, implying that all Jews were spies or at least security risks. Here again the parallels with prewar stereotypes were startling. In December 1938 a Colonel Wenda, then chief of the general staff, had warned that the departure of the Jews was necessary for national defense: "The economic structure of the country should be placed in the hands of patriotic elements which in case of crisis would support the national cause."[48] Thirty years later, on the same day that forty people were ousted from the Foreign Ministry, *Zolnierz Wolnosci,* the Army daily, published a two-piece article on "Zionist Spies in the Service of Imperialism." Digging out four cases of Jewish defectors dating back to 1953, 1956, 1959, and 1965 respectively, the paper wrote: "The basic aim of the Western intelligence service is to recruit agents among the disguised enemies of People's Poland, those who have access to the most secret sources of information. This was proved among other things by the betrayal of the interests of our state by Jozef Swiatlo alias Isaac Fleischfarb, Wladislaw Tykocinski alias Tikhotiner, Seweryn Bialer, Pawel Monat, and many others." The paper then proceeded to explain how the "small state of Israel should have great success in espionage" by quoting alleged texts

---

* The attacks on Rapacki, the treatment of Naszkowski, and the sacking of Morawski provoked an outburst of rage from Gomulka against Ambassador Sidor, the organizer of the purge. He was suspended from his post for three years. But none of the dismissals was revoked, although Gomulka prevented the public disgrace of Naszkowski and Morawski. The first was sent on extended leave and subsequently appointed editor-in-chief of the Party monthly, while the latter returned to London to leave his post a year later under somewhat more decorous circumstances. Minister Rapacki continued to boycott both the Politburo and the Ministry, though his formal resignation from the government and Party leadership was not announced until November 1968. It was not a hard-liner who replaced him, however, but Stefan Jedrychowski, the former chief planner and a member of the Gomulka "center."

from Western newspapers about "Israel's fantastic network throughout the world. In Washington, Moscow, Paris, London, Warsaw, etc. there are people, first and foremost Jews everywhere . . . who seek to supply the Israeli security service with all the information relating to the security of Israel. Zionist organizations and Jewish nationalists dispersed all over the world are thus the source of the might of the espionage services directed from Tel Aviv."

After the customary references to intelligence outfits operating under the cloak of charitable Jewish organizations like Hias and Joint, the paper went to the heart of the matter: "Until diplomatic relations with Israel were severed (in June 1967), the Israeli diplomatic mission was an unusually active espionage center in Poland. We know of many cases of Polish citizens of Jewish origin having been induced to give information constituting state secrets during their visits to the Israeli Legation in Warsaw. They were reminded that 'every Jew must serve his country.' This argument . . . unfortunately proved to be very effective in many cases." After making it abundantly clear that the four defectors, even those with Polish names, were Zionists and had astonishing careers "with the help of secret forces of which we now have some idea," *Zolnierz Wolnosci* concluded: "These revolting people were not and are not traitors to our people's homeland. Poland has never been their fatherland. Their aim was to serve foreign interests, to serve imperialism and anti-Polish and anti-socialist subversion. Their homeland is the American dollar regardless of whether they receive it from Tel Aviv, Bonn, or Washington."[49]

This implied frontal attack on the loyalty of all Jews whether they defected, emigrated, or stayed in the country was reproduced the next day in scores of other papers and several times summarized on television and radio. It served to justify the whole witch-hunt as a war against the all-powerful Zionist enemy. The Warsaw daily with the largest circulation, *Zycie Warszawy*, underlined the thesis of the Jews as security risks and disloyal to Poland by publishing lengthy statistics about the occupational structure of the forty thousand Jews who in 1956–58 emigrated from the country. According to the paper's statistics (the reliability of which cannot be verified) 18 high Army officers, 55 journalists, 180 economists, 530 doctors, and 620 engineers turned their back on "People's Poland." Why did they leave their "well-paid positions and higher than average standard of living"? In those days the same Polish papers, although the writers were different, accused the pro-Soviet Stalinists of having launched a carefully orchestrated campaign to stir up anti-Jewish feelings. In 1957 the Polish press did not castigate the "dual loyalty" of Polish Jews but placed the blame squarely upon the regime itself: "The majority of Jews who survived the Nazi massacres have reached the conclusion that under the present conditions where anti-Semitism has revived after twelve years of people's power, they cannot work, breathe, and live . . . Their exodus is a terrible indictment against our people's power, our Party, and all of us."[50]

By 1968, however, the times when Polish newspapers could publish such candid statements were gone. The torrent of abuse and hatred directed at "Zionist" defectors, emigrants, and ungrateful Jews created the right atmosphere for making it appear a patriotic task to see that government institutions were *"judenrein"* ("clean of Jews"). Leaflets were distributed at Party meetings by the Warsaw Party committee with lists of all the Jews who had defected during the past twenty years. The speakers never failed to refer to the proofs that those with no fatherland or people of Jewish origin sold military and industrial secrets to the West, Israel, and West Germany. A Polish name was never mentioned though it was common knowledge that countless non-Jewish Poles had also defected, including pilots who had flown their fighter planes to the West, high officials of the Central Committee department in charge of military and security affairs, and staff officers of the Ministry of Defense.

It also happened that the same people who accused their Jewish colleagues of disloyalty soon afterward asked for political asylum in the West. A case in point occurred at the important Institute of Nuclear Research. Its chief, Wilhelm Billig, a candidate member of the Central Committee, was sacked in early

April. This was followed by a mass cleansing of Jews who were strongly represented on the staff. At Party meetings the speakers remarked ironically that at the Institute "even the lectures had to be held in Hebrew," and pointed out that vast funds were spent on research in desalting sea water, an urgent need in Israel. As Billig candidly remarked at the July meeting of the Central Committee, the dismissals were the result of a "falsely understood fight against Zionism," and "had nothing to do with science or professional qualifications, had no moral or political reasons, and also affected several prewar Party members."[51] None of the sacked nuclear scientists was reinstated. But one of those who had railed most sharply against the harmful activities of the Institute's leadership, a certain Professor Cichy, went on a trip to the West two months later and informed the "de-Judaized" rump Institute on a postcard that he was not going to return to Poland.

But such cases did not dent the prevailing image of the Jews as a security-risk group. Accusations were assiduously spread for several years before the "March events." Gomulka's closest colleague, Zenon Kliszko, had had in his desk since the mid-sixties a list of one hundred Jewish officials who defected to the West, and he produced it on every occasion when personnel changes were discussed. Embezzlement and corruption scandals in which Jews were involved enjoyed the special attention of mass media. As late as May 20, 1968, when the "anti-Zionist" campaign showed signs of ebbing, Warsaw Radio, reporting the trial of a state official accused of fraud, not only referred to his Jewish origin, but also announced that the state prosecutor had demanded the annulment of the defendant's officially approved change of name from Icek Abram Kierbiel to Marian Kargul.

The length to which the manipulators of the anti-Semitic campaign were willing to go became evident in 1966 when copies of the notorious "Protocols of the Elders of Zion" suddenly began to circulate. A Polish edition of this infamous forgery, marked "for internal use only," was received by students at the Military Academies, regular Army officers, and some Party activists. There was no indication of the printing plant or the publisher, but the quality of the paper and the print made clear that it could not have been produced by some small clandestine press. It was later revealed that the booklet had been printed on the premises of MON, the publishing house of the Ministry of Defense. One man was fired, but after some troubles he found shelter at Moczar's Ministry of Interior, more precisely on the staff of the Department for Jewish Affairs. Soon after the Arab-Israeli War, a second edition was brought out, again of course unofficially, but this time probably produced in the printing plant of the secret police.

The rekindling of the tested motif of a sinister Jewish world conspiracy paid handsome dividends after the Arab-Israeli War. It is hardly known abroad that it was in the 275,000 strong[52] Polish Army that the purge was first launched. Such hard-liners as Generals Korczynski (Deputy Minister of Defense), Pietrzak of the veterans' organization, and Czapla (Deputy Chief of the Main Political Administration of the Army), helped of course by Moczar's agents, lost no time in using the Middle East conflict to purge their political and personal enemies in the high command and some hundred regular officers.

Gomulka's speech to the Trade Union Congress on June 19, 1967, in which he went beyond the general Communist line against "Israeli aggression," made anti-Semitism, thinly disguised as anti-Zionism, legitimate in Poland for the first time since 1956. His outbursts against a Jewish "fifth column" and his references to the alleged "drinking parties" celebrating the Israeli victory were sparked off by Moczar's reports about Jews rejoicing over the Arab defeat. Moczar is said to have given the Party leader a list of ninety-four young Jews who allegedly went to the Israeli Legation to volunteer for the Israeli Army. There is no way of checking such statements, and it is unlikely that this figure was correct. But there was, as indeed everywhere in Eastern Europe, an evident upsurge of *Polish* popular support for Israel, an upsurge prompted by glee over a major Soviet setback rather than a sudden burst of philo-Semitism among the Poles. The much quoted saying, *"Our* Jews have beaten *their* Arabs,"* reflected a phenomenon already in evidence during the "Polish October" of 1956: in Poland anti-

Russian feelings are a stronger force than traditional anti-Semitism.

The fable of the "drinking parties" served as an extremely useful instrument in removing General Mankiewicz, the chief of the air defense, and two other generals, as well as scores of high-ranking officers, either because of their candid remarks about the military aspects of the Arab débâcle, or simply because of their Jewish origin. The main target was General Mankiewicz, who was a close friend of Marshal Spychalski, the Minister of Defense. The concomitant drive was directed against the opponents of the hard-liners in the Army and indirectly against Marshal Spychalski, who was originally an architect and whose lack of qualifications in military matters had always been a fruitful subject for malicious stories.

On the day the Middle East War ended, a birthday party was held in the editorial offices of *Przyjaciolka,* a popular woman's weekly in the capital. As always on such occasions in Poland, vodka flowed and the ladies, quite a few of them Jewish, were in an exuberant mood. Next afternoon, Moczar, who almost daily briefs Gomulka on security matters, put several reports on the desk of his chief containing lurid details about orgies and celebrations among Jews. One referred to the fact that General Mankiewicz's wife also participated in the celebrations "marking the Israeli successes." The same day the general was retired from active service. After his dismissal it turned out that his wife had not even been in the capital on the day the alleged "orgy" took place. This, however, did not have the slightest effect on the decision already made.

Meanwhile a concerted underground campaign of vilification began against Minister Spychalski. The manipulators exploited the fact that Spychalski happened to have a "bad" appearance, lending credence to rumors that he was Jewish. He in fact is not, nor is his wife. But there was another factor providing grist for the mills. A certain Kazimierz Mijal, an old-style Stalinist and former minister and Central Committee member, fled Poland in 1965 with a forged passport to Albania where he set up what he called a "Marxist-Leninist Polish Communist Party." Using the powerful radio transmitters of Radio Tirana and clandestine pamphlets, he attacked Gomulka as a "Zionist agent" and the Jewish Communists as "disguised Zionists and old Trotskyites." After the Middle East War, his broadcast reported that Spychalski's wife had been in Israel visiting relatives at the moment the war broke out. Whereupon Moczar's agents immediately spread this story.

On his return from an extended Middle East trip Ambassador Sidor was asked several times after his public lectures whether it was true that Mrs. Spychalski had come back to Poland on the last airplane from Israel on the eve of the hostilities. While the questions may well have been asked by agent provocateurs, Sidor's answer was invariably effective: "I do not know; she was not on my plane . . ." This remark was made at meetings in the Foreign Ministry and the Military Academy about the wife of a senior member of the Politburo and Marshal of Poland!

The campaign soon demanded a victim: not Spychalski (who was saved by his Party chief) but Lieutenant Colonel Ostrowski, the scion of a revolutionary worker's family and a non-Jew, who stood up for his minister's honor. At a Party meeting of a military unit in Babicze, chaired by the chief of the political department of the Army, several speakers attacked Marshal Spychalski by name. The story of his wife's stay in Israel, her alleged contacts with Dayan, and other fantastic rumors were mentioned. Premier Cyrankiewicz was called "Zimmermann" and the two remaining top Jewish functionaries (Politburo member, E. Szyr and Central Committee secretary A. Starewicz) were sharply criticized.

Lieutenant Colonel Ostrowski, representing the commander of the base who was on leave, tried to counter the slanders but could not stop the meeting since it was chaired by the political officer. However, he reported everything to the minister's chief of cabinet. The next day Ostrowski, who had spent three years in prison before the war as a young Communist, was arrested together with the secretary of the Party cell and several of the demagogues. He spent eight days in the same cell of the investigating prison on Rakowiecka Street where he had been kept in custody before the war. After his release, several officers visited his home and warned him that the time of bloody reckoning, of the general attack against Israeli spies and the fifth column to which he and Spychalski belonged, was coming. Ostrowski again reported everything to Spychalski and also to friends, who alerted several Politburo members including Ochab and Kliszko. But nobody was willing to receive him. Meanwhile the Ministry of Defense had set up a tribunal to investigate the alleged material showing his activity for the Israeli intelligence service. Colonel A.K., now in the West, who related Ostrowski's case to the author, summed up the outcome in the following words: "As he was not defended by anyone and no one supported him, Zygmunt Ostrowski, fifty, shot himself on the night of September 5, 1967. He received a funeral complete with military band and a guard of honor. At his grave all those who had caused his death gave speeches. His widow demanded that a rehabilitation commission be set up. She received no answer. But rumors were circulated among the officers that Ostrowski was after all an Israeli spy."

Other victims gave up without fighting. The Orlinskis, a married couple, both doctors, were fired on the same day in December 1967. At the clinic of the Military Medical Academy, at which they had worked for many years, both were accused of "pro-Israeli sympathies," and Mrs. Orlinski of having falsified her doctor's diploma. (The method of doubting the credentials of prospective victims was used on a much wider scale after March 1968.) Mrs. Orlinski could easily have refuted the accusation, especially since she had treated the children of Minister Spychalski. But the childless couple chose a different response. Next evening they had dinner at home, offered a glass of cognac to their maid, and subsequently went to a piano recital. After the concert they returned to the apartment and took poison. She died; her husband survived, but lost his eyesight. While still in the hospital, he was accused of a "Zionist-motivated murder" of his wife and threatened with arrest. In the meantime the idea of prosecuting the blind doctor has apparently been dropped.

There were also tragicomic cases like that of Colonel Stanislaw

Nadzin, a military historian of Jewish origin. He was sitting on a jury which was awarding prizes to sports reporters. It so happened that the jury completed its deliberations on the day the Six Day War ended. As usual, the whole jury went to a restaurant and then to a bar where they drank a fair amount of vodka. This was yet another "drinking party celebrating the victory," at any rate in the police report. Nadzin was expelled from the Party and dismissed from the Army. A film director at the Army studios, Adam Forbert, suffered the same fate when a guard reported that he had grinned on the day the Arab-Israeli War ended.

Thus the witch-hunt after March 1968 did not come out of a void. Scores of people had been ousted from the Army, the newspapers, the Party high school, and several ministries in 1967, and by the autumn of the same year a quiet but systematic purge not only of Jewish officials, but of moderate politicians was in full swing. The roll call of purged functionaries within a few months included the liberal (and non-Jewish) Mayor of Warsaw; J. Zarzycki, a hero of the anti-Nazi underground and until 1964 Chairman of ZBOWiD, the veterans' union; Leon Kasman, the editor of *Trybuna Ludu* and his deputy, and the managing editor of *Zycie Warszawy* (all Jews). Colonel Walichnowski's book about Nazi-Zionist complicity before the war, which made the Jewish ghetto police the main culprit in the massacre of the Jews and emphasized the "Zionist-German collusion directed against People's Poland," was going into its second printing.

ZBOWiD and its leaders emerged even then as the manipulators of the whole anti-Zionist campaign. General Pietrzak, the Chairman of the Warsaw branch organization, gave notice that "we shall not remain indifferent toward people who in the face of a threat to world peace, hence also to the security of Poland and to the peaceful work of our people, support the aggressor and imperialism."[53] The statement broadcast by Kazimierz Rusinek, Moczar's deputy at ZBOWiD and Vice-Minister for Culture, was characteristic of the absurd length to which the instigators went in "proving" the joint complicity of Zionists and Nazis. He flatly stated: "It is no secret that many Hitlerite criminals are in the service of the Israeli Government. They live on the territory of the State of Israel. I estimate that there are over one thousand experts of the former Hitlerite Wehrmacht who have become advisers to the Israeli army."[54] Two days later, Simon Wiesenthal, the director of the Jewish Documentation Center in Vienna (who was with Rusinek in the Mauthausen concentration camp during the war), challenged his former fellow inmate to name one single Nazi criminal living or working in Israel. At the time of this writing he is still waiting for an answer . . .

Nevertheless it was the student riots of March 1968 that flashed the green light for the all-out anti-Semitic campaign and the final reckoning, not only with the Jews but with all liberals in the Party and state apparatus. Once again the Armed Forces and their publications were among the most fervent backers of the campaign. The handful of remaining officers of Jewish origin were swiftly discharged. *Zolnierz Wolnosci* announced triumphantly that Colonel Nadzin, who in the meantime had successfully appealed against his earlier expulsion for "toasting to the Israeli victory," was found guilty of "pro-Israeli agitation" after all. The proof? The military calendar for 1968, edited by him, described Jerusalem as the capital of Israel. As the paper explained, "Nadzin was readmitted but at that time the Party had not yet known about the lie concerning Jerusalem."[55]

Even those officers already dishonorably discharged were now singled out for further harassment. In July 1968 several former regular officers, including Colonel A. Kornecki, one of the most highly decorated partisan heroes, Colonels Liberman, Groniewicz, and others, were called to the military administration and ordered to vacate their apartments immediately. When they asked whether retired (non-Jewish) Polish officers also had to leave their living quarters, they were curtly told, "That is not your business." Kornecki's wife, a secretary at the Journalists' Association, was admonished at a meeting for living with a Jew and told to divorce her husband in order to save her two sons for Poland.

The purge in "the Chinese way" produced many absurd case histories. An officer (veteran of the Spanish Civil War) was attacked by several speakers at a Party meeting for having allowed his children to be brought up in the Jewish religion and teaching them Hebrew as their mother tongue. He remained silent until they were finished and then announced tersely that he had no children. Nevertheless he was expelled: by his "provocative silence he had deliberately tried to make the Party ridiculous."[56] Irena Windholz, an editor of a cultural radio program, was accused at a meeting of employees of having been the mistress of a Gestapo officer during the war. For twenty-five years no one had heard about this. The chief of the State Council's chancellery, Henryk Holder, was attacked for having been a Jewish policeman in the ghetto, thus aiding the extermination of Jews. The man had in fact spent the entire war in Moscow, but Moczar's "Red Guards" did not allow him to open his mouth until the decision about his dismissal had been made.

Often strangers at the meetings interfered in the questioning of prospective victims. At a stormy Party assembly in the Ministry of Foreign Trade, Jozef Kutin, the deputy minister, a Party veteran and former "Spaniard," was taken to task sharply by several men. He opened his defense by saying: "I have belonged to this Party organization for many years. But I have never seen you here, comrades. On what ground are you participating in the meeting at all?" He was told by the secretary of the basic cell that his critics "were comrades from the central Party activists . . ."

Many cases illustrated the remark of the Polish satirist Lec: "Yes is simultaneously No—the difference lies in the question." An engineer in a steel plant was accused by two witnesses of having expressed joy after the Six Day War. That he was at the time under an oxygen tent in the hospital could not save him from dismissal. A nurse in a Lodz hospital lost her post because of one outspoken remark. Her dark hair and "bad" appearance made her a "Zionist suspect." To silence her detractors, she produced a certificate of baptism two generations back, but also remarked that she had nothing against the Jews since they were human beings like everyone else. A slightly different mistake was made by another woman white-collar worker in a Warsaw office. After one of the usual anti-Zionist meetings, one of her colleagues walking back to work sighed, "A pity that Hitler did not gas all the Jews. Then we would have been spared all these problems." The other woman retorted sharply, "How can you make such a statement? As a Pole, I am ashamed to listen to you." It was the ashamed Pole who was ousted from her job next day.

Possessing files on the past record and current behavior of hundreds of thousands of people, police agents and informers had a variety of methods of punishing those Poles who stood up for their colleagues. There was, for example, the case of an assistant professor who was driving back to Warsaw with friends. Slightly drunk, she hit a telegraph pole. No one was hurt, and when the police appeared a friend said he had been driving because he could pass the alcohol test. This incident happened in 1964, and apart from paying a fine there were no consequences whatsoever. In the spring of 1968, the professor spoke out on behalf of the imprisoned students and her faculty colleagues. Within three weeks she was notified of her impending trial for having caused a grave car accident and, worse still, for having committed perjury.

Those Jews who dared to question the appropriateness of a campaign in a "socialist" country aimed at "verifying loyalty" according to racial criteria fared even worse. The newspapers in the provinces dropped all "anti-Zionist" pretense in reporting such cases. Thus *Glos Koszalinski,* a local daily in the town of Koszalin, reported on April 19: "The basic Party organization of the garment industry gauged the attitude of Polish citizens of Jewish origin . . . In the lively discussion Polish citizens of Jewish origin were accused of not having taken part in the meeting which had condemned the organizers of the March excesses and of having failed clearly to define their attitude following the Israeli aggression. J. Wajsbart, U. Szlyt, T. Plauner, and A. Zigler were ousted from the Party by unanimous vote." At a factory meeting in Lodz, according to an item in *Glos Robotniczy,* "Poles of Jewish extraction were blamed for not attending a meeting during which the organizers of the March excesses were condemned and also for not having openly declared their attitude during the Middle East War."

Six days later *Glos Olsztynski* made clear what was meant: "Comrade Goldyx, member of the control commission of Olsztyn, at a conference of veterans took no critical attitude against the instigators of the student demonstrations and the policy of international Zionism. She disputed the necessity that comrades of Jewish origin give an unambiguous declaration about their attitude toward Israeli aggression and the Zionist campaign against Poland."[57]

## 5. LODZ BECOMES "JUDENREIN"

The second largest city of Poland, Lodz, possibly surpassed even the capital in the intensity, scope, and excesses of the "anti-Zionist" campaign. Before the war, Lodz was the most "Jewish" city in the country, with Jews accounting for one third of the population. It was also the traditional center of the Polish textile industry. While many Jews owned factories or small-scale businesses, about half of the manual labor force in the single most important industry also consisted of Jews.[58] In 1968 the population of Lodz passed the seven hundred thousand mark. But there were only some thirty-five hundred to four thousand Jews left out of a prewar Jewish population of two hundred thousand.

This however did not dampen the ardor of the Communist city committee. With the full approval of Jozef Spychalski (no relation to the Marshal), the first secretary of the Party organization in Lodz, Hieronim Reniak, Party secretary of the municipal committee in charge of Agitation and Propaganda (Agit-Prop), in 1968 worked out a crash program to counter the threat of "Lodz becoming a second Warsaw"[59] and formed an anti-Zionist brain trust with five other paid professionals of Agit-Prop.

The press hastened to publish nine selected Jewish names out of the many students who were arrested because of their participation in demonstrations. Simultaneously Reniak organized a counterdemonstration of young people carrying placards against "Israeli aggression" or demanding "Zionists out of Poland!" The fact that the vast majority of the demonstrators were blacks or Vietnamese studying at the local university on state scholarships did not deter the Polish press from calling this "a demonstration of the healthy part of the student youth."

Reniak also commissioned two pamphlets to provide the local functionaries with Marxist-Leninist arguments against and proofs of the Zionist conspiracy. The first bore the title "The Policy of the Party and the Government, and Its Opponents," while the second was devoted to "Zionism—Its Origin, Its Political Character and Its Anti-Polish Countenance." Both were published in April 1968, officially by the Polish United Workers' Party of Lodz, the Party propaganda center, and marked "for internal use only." Thousands of copies were distributed at the university, the Polytechnic Institute, to Army units and at the basic Party cells in important institutions and businesses.

The first pamphlet presented what later became the semiofficial line. It blamed former leaders of Jewish origin for the reign of terror prior to 1956. It stressed that the "excessive concentration of Polish citizens of Jewish origin" in decisive political, military, security, and propaganda sectors was not accidental: "It is not impossible that two factors were at work: the awareness of carrying out a definite process on the part of persons in key positions in given departments, and the practical continuation of it on the basis of trust, ties, and solidarity." In other words, there was a "Jewish plot." The reign of terror "must have created among a great number of Polish Jews a pattern of breaking the law, abuse of power, and the use of provocation. Not all Jews were direct executioners, but the majority consciously aided the perpetuation and strengthening of the system of intimidation and reprisals in their departments." In other words, the Jewish power elite bore the exclusive responsibility for the years of terror. In 1956, according to the pamphlet, the Jewish Stalinists saved their skins by tactical concessions and successfully used the "bogey of anti-Semitism." Many retained their positions by changing into "revisionists." After the Arab-Israeli War these ex-Stalinists-turned-revisionists "were increasingly attracted to international Zionism and mounted a new attack, using subversion and provocation to effect a general re-shuffling of the leading state and Party posts."

While this pamphlet took some pains to clothe anti-Jewish propaganda in Communist phraseology, the second pamphlet on Zionism must surely be the crudest anti-Semitic tract ever released by a Communist Party "propaganda center." A few brief extracts will indicate its style and contents: "While millions of less wealthy Jews were put to death, the richest ones in all bourgeois states climbed to the top of the social and especially the financial ladder. The economic ruin of many capitalist states placed the finance of the capitalist world in the hands of Zionists to a degree heretofore unknown . . . Zionism today demands that all Jews be conscious of their Jewish nationality, while at the same time it proclaims that only some of them may become citizens of Israel. A much larger part must remain in other countries, not because there is no room for them in Palestine, but in order vigilantly to watch over the Jews' financial domination of the world."

Then the pamphlet raises the question "How can one reconcile service to Israel with holding leading positions in other countries?" The Zionist solution, it replies, is that the Jews must have "a feeling of their inner, exclusive union with Israel, but on the outside they are to have the right to belong not to one but to two nations." It then expresses surprise that "this sociologically absurd and politically dangerous national theory has thus far met with no opposition in bourgeois scholarship." Why not? The Polish Communist ideologist knows the answer: "Because the degree of Zionist domination over bourgeois scholarship is almost absolute."

As the Jews dominate both world capitalism and bourgeois scholarship, they inevitably also act as agents of a closed conspiracy for the control of the world. By distorting a statement of Nahum Goldmann, who at the World Congress of Jewish Youth (August 5, 1963) said that "the main struggle of Jews in future should not be aimed at equality, which has already been achieved, but at the right to be different," the pamphlet concludes that "this is obviously a program of world domination. It is openly proclaimed, and, as we saw at the time of the recent Israeli aggression, at decisive moments it is efficiently put into practice. Is it possible that the time has come in the capitalist world when, as predicted in the 'Protocols of the Elders of Zion,' the goyim themselves will meekly put their heads under the yoke and will beg the Jews to rule over them?"

Proceeding to the Polish situation, the pamphlet declares that Jews with double loyalty are capitalist-imperialist residents in Poland. After repeating the usual arguments about Jewish defectors and the Joint, it states flatly that the student demonstrations in March were "part of a long-prepared plan world-wide in scope," and demands "a testing of the real national awareness of people who claim to be Poles of Jewish origin. We can no longer be satisfied with verbal declarations, just as, after the bitter experiences of 1939 and the period of occupation, such declarations were no longer sufficient when the Germans were expelled after World War II."

In other words, the surviving Jews, except for those who praise the Poles for saving them during the war and refute the slanderous accusations of anti-Semitism against the present regime, should be expelled from the country. It is particularly important "to check and evaluate a large group of several thousand who thus far have not held any particularly important jobs, and perhaps for this very reason have been unable to take a stand in the case of Zionist attacks on the good names of Poles and Poland. It should be a civic duty and requirement of conscience for Polish Jews to refute the Zionist anti-Polish campaign, since almost every one of them owed his life to the fact that some Pole risked his life to hide him. If such an eyewitness holds his peace under these circumstances, he thereby joins our enemies, the enemies of our country, and offers proof of the Talmudic principle: 'The best of goyim—kill him!' "

After this excursion into the field of ritual blood legends, the pamphlet observed that "one can count on the fingers of one hand" the "heroes" who publicly protested the slanderous Zionist campaign. "And we address the others—speak up, bear witness! Why are you silent?" The message was clear: the "Polish citizens of Jewish origin" can prove that they are "truly Poles" only if they publicly and "heatedly" praise the policy of their present persecutors. Should they fail to do so, they should be banished. Even Jews in unimportant jobs should take the loyalty test and, if necessary, be unmasked.[60]

I have summarized the pamphlet at some length for two reasons. First, because it is a unique combination of anti-Semitism and hypocrisy. Not even the Tsarist forgers of the "Protocols" or the Nazi ideologists went so far as to demand praise and thanks from their Jewish victims. Second, it shows that anti-Semitism at its worst came from above, and that the anti-Jewish invectives so often reported in oral discussions were the rule rather than the exception. Considering the anonymous pamphlets "illegally" circulated, it does not seem so surprising that Police Agent Kolasinski who tried to organize a group on the Polish ship *Sandomierz* in the port of Tripoli to take part in a pogrom on June 7, 1967, was promoted to third mechanic after the ship returned to Gdansk, or that at a Party meeting in Warsaw a member could propose that all Jews be sent to Israel in sealed wagons.

Reniak's payoff came with the mass dismissal of Jews from all businesses and institutions in the city of Lodz. Within twenty-four hours, all Jewish journalists on the staffs of the two main papers, *Glos Robotniczy* and *Dziennik Lodzki,* were summarily fired and members of Jewish origin were refused entry to the journalists' club. The editor-in-chief of *Dziennik Lodzki,* Stanislaw Januszewski, a former underground partisan in occupied Poland whose wife had been killed in the fighting, was recovering from a heart attack in a hospital when the "anti-Zionist" campaign started. On the day that he was expelled from the Party and dismissed from his post, he was also thrown out of the hospital.

Typical of the way the mass media conducted the campaign in Lodz was the lead article in *Glos Robotniczy* on "Zionists demonstrating for Dayan." The editor-in-chief, S. Klaczkow, castigating the brazen insolence of the Zionists, described a fancy-dress ball at the students' club that spring at which two Jewish students, whom he named, appeared as Moshe Dayan with a black patch over one eye. As it turned out, there was no student with one of the names, and the other had been in the Army at that time. He managed to get a written certificate from the student organization that he had not been at the ball. The vice-president and secretary of the student body were subsequently fired for having signed the statement. Meanwhile two non-Jewish students who had come dressed as pirates with black eye-patches went to the editorial office and admitted that they were the alleged "Dayans." The editor refused to see them.[61]

An "Open Letter" to Mrs. Golda Meir (before she became Israel's Prime Minister) by Piotr Goszcynski in *Glos Robotniczy* (May 12, 1968) gives an inkling of the level at which hack writers were trying to persuade their readers about the sinister designs of the Zionists. Answering Mrs. Meir's concern about the situation of Polish citizens of Jewish origin, he wrote: "Please answer my last worry: is it true, as one hears, that your supreme commander, Moshe Dayan, is not Dayan at all but Otto Skorzeny, the well-known specialist in murder and kidnaping from Uncle Adolf's SS, hiding under the name of Dayan and concealing one of his eyes under an eye patch? Furthermore, Mrs. Meir, I have heard that— for a lot of money—you are hiding in your closet Hitler's deputy, Martin Bormann. Is this true?"

This nonsense was printed in a paper with a circulation of 250,000, and the author received a prize for "outstanding journalistic work." Why not? Did not the cultural weekly *Kultura* write that the novelist Yael Dayan, the daughter of the Minister of Defense, "reminds us of the image of the notorious Ilse Koch," a Nazi war criminal who had lampshades made of the skin of murdered Jews.[62]

The witch-hunt in Lodz was certainly one of the best-reported in Poland. On one single day, *Dziennik Lodzki* announced the expulsion of ten members of Jewish extraction from the Party (which meant of course automatic loss of job) and added that "some of them accused the party of conducting an anti-Semitic campaign."[63]

One of the chief targets was the doctors. A number of prominent physicians were not merely expelled from the Party, the

Ministry of Health was asked to dismiss them from their jobs. The film industry was also badly hit. The accusations were always the same: sympathy with Zionism and West Germany, a tendency to obscure the dedication of Poles in saving Jews and the heroic struggle of the nation against the invaders. The production chiefs of all eight film studios were dismissed, and Alexander Ford became the target of particularly vicious attacks for having been a co-producer with the "ardent West German and Zionist" Artur Brauner. That all the joint projects had been officially approved by the Ministry of Culture and that the Polish Government was also "guilty of collusion" with the German Krupp concern were of course irrelevant.

There are countless case histories of professors and textile workers, directors and doctors, pensioners and civil servants whose existence was crushed under Rejniak's steam roller. The charges ranged from "Zionist leanings" to neglecting Party duties; from "lighting candles on Friday night" to the "abduction of a peasant girl in order to kidnap her to Israel." Managing Director M. Srebnik from the association of the rubber industry was put on trial for having forged his high school matriculation certificate. When he vehemently denied the charge, *Dziennik Lodzki* remarked, "The defendant behaved impertinently, a characteristic often found in persons of Jewish origin."[64] The purge proceeded smoothly since the municipal administration had been supplying prepared lists of Jews singled out for dismissal. At the eye clinic of the Medical Academy, the administration demanded certificates of baptism from the doctors on the staff.

Within two months Lodz became practically "judenrein." Secretary Rejniak unhappily had some difficulties over the two anti-Semitic pamphlets; he was transferred to a less prestigious job. But Lodz Party chief Spychalski was "re-elected" after the Party Congress in November 1968.

Aside from the blunder of quoting the notorious "Protocols" and using a fascist rather than a "Marxist-Leninist" phraseology in the two pamphlets, there was indeed no valid reason to reproach the comrades in Lodz. With the exception of the area of Katowice, where regional Party chief Gierek soft-pedaled the "anti-Zionist" campaign and protected "his" Jews, the witch-hunt was basically the same everywhere. There were merely differences of intensity.

The oral instructions and written circulars about the removal of "Zionists" from leading positions were taken to heart by each municipal and regional administration. In the port of Szczecin, for example, the only two "Zionists" were a man in charge of a nursery and a gardener who could not prove their Aryan origin. Both lost their "important" jobs. In the Central Planning Office in Warsaw, a petty official was sacked for the following charges: four years before, his then sixteen-year-old daughter had demoralized the other girls in a vacation camp, often returning to the camp after 10 P.M.; she had also visited her aunt in Israel three years ago; and he himself in a private conversation had criticized Walichnowski's book about the Israel-West German axis.[65]

Much depended of course on the local situation, and sometimes on the courage and decency of the superiors. One of the Polish writers who had handed in his Party card in 1966 in protest against Kolakowski's expulsion from the Party was editing a specialized monthly trade magazine. One day the director called him to his office for a chat. During the conversation, the writer noticed that the man was beating about the bush, apparently reluctant to come to the point. Finally he asked him directly: "What's the matter, Comrade N.? Have I made some mistake?" The director blushed. "Not at all. On the contrary, I am very pleased with your work, Comrade K. But I hope you will excuse me. I must ask you a very embarrassing question. Are you Jewish?" The writer dryly remarked: "No, I am not, and I can prove it." "Oh, wonderful. I am so glad. You see, I have my orders. Ours is an important institution, and all Jews should be fired."

## 6. LOSERS AND WINNERS

Despite Moczar's special department for ferreting out Jews, half Jews, and quarter Jews, there are certainly many crypto-Jews or Marranos* in Poland. Those who survived the Nazi occupation had to have a "suitable" appearance, perfect command of Polish, and, often, forged documents. Walichnowski's whispering campaign about three hundred thousand Jews and part Jews was of course a patent absurdity. But there is no way of knowing just how many of those Jews—living "in disguise," learning Catholic customs, and taken for genuine Poles by their neighbors during the war—are still in the country.

Two case histories point up the special problems faced by the Polish Marranos. During the purge of the film industry, a young director, K.J., was attacked for having hobnobbed with a CIA agent visiting Poland in the guise of film expert. The truth was that J. had been asked by the authorities to welcome the American guest at a film showing. He had had little to do with him (whether or not he was indeed a CIA agent) and the real reason for the

---

* Marranos were those Jews in fifteenth-century Spain and Portugal who, called New Christians, converted in order to escape the persecution of the Inquisition. These crypto-Jews lived outwardly as devout Catholics, but among themselves carried on the traditions of their forebears. Marranos long continued to exist as an identifiable group and it took three hundred years until emigration and assimilation (initially also killing) of the New Christians led to the complete disappearance of crypto-Judaism. The word Marrano originally meant "swine" in Spanish, and it was coined by the enemies of the converted Jews.

attack was clearly his liberal attitude in general. As his professional career was gravely threatened, several noted film producers called on the Ministry of Culture to point out the absurdity of the press attacks against their young and talented colleague. They were tactfully informed that J.'s case was delicate. His susceptibility to "revisionist and Zionist" arguments could not be separated from the fact that he was of "mixed Jewish blood." His grandmother on his mother's side had been Jewish. K.J. with a "wonderful" appearance had grown up as a "true Pole," never suspecting that he was a "quarter Jew." His mother had skillfully concealed the fact during the occupation and subsequently kept her son in ignorance in order to save him from future trouble. (On learning about this, his non-Jewish wife was overjoyed: "So you are a Jew! Wonderful! Now at last we can emigrate." They did.)

The second story is a tragic one. A Jewish couple spent the years of occupation partly in Eastern Poland and later in Russia. Both having a "perfect" appearance, they survived, came back to Poland, and lived outwardly more or less in accordance with the precepts of Catholicism. They retained their Polonized surnames and sent their children to religious instruction. One day they were called to the school and informed by the teacher that their sons were doing well in their studies. There was only one problem; and it was up to the parents to do something about it: the two boys were not only insulting the two Jewish pupils in their class, they were regularly beating them up. "None of us is particularly fond of Jews, but your sons must behave in a civilized way in order not to disturb the class schedule," the teacher said. The couple's whole fictitious life suddenly collapsed. They applied for emigration.

The "professional Jews" found themselves in a slightly different but equally tragic situation. These were Jewish Communists and fellow travelers who in the late 1940s drove all other Jewish groups (Zionists, Bund, the Orthodox, etc.) out of the leadership of the Central Jewish Committee and during the Communist takeover applied the same methods as their comrades in all walks of political life. The organization, later called Social-Cultural Association of Polish Jews, in 1966 had a membership of seventy-five hundred, fifteen hundred of whom were pensioners. It published a Yiddish-language paper—*Folksshtimme*—four times a week, operated five Jewish schools, three lycées, a museum, a Yiddish theater of world renown, and a publishing house that issued both Yiddish classics and recent works by local authors.[66] In April 1956 *Folksshtimme* was the first Communist paper to release details about the massacre of the Jewish-Yiddish intellectuals between 1948–52 by Stalin and to protest against the suppression of Jewish culture in the Soviet Union. After the political change in October 1956, the material position of needy Jews improved considerably. The Joint Distribution Committee, which between 1945 and 1949 provided twenty-one million dollars' worth of aid, was invited by the Polish Government to resume its activities after a seven-year hiatus. It provided relief payments to eight thousand poor Jews and vocational courses for trainees, who then joined one of the sixteen cooperatives employing in the late 1960s over two thousand workers.[67]

The Six Day War and its aftermath destroyed with one swift blow the elaborate and effective network of charitable, social, and cultural activities. Once again the government in Warsaw banned the activities of Joint. Its letter to the head office was nevertheless courteous and referred to the fact that Polish Jews no longer needed assistance. With the outbreak of the "anti-Zionist" campaign in 1968, Joint and the Jewish community organization, especially its Babel Club, were immediately propelled into the center of the accusations. The leaders of the Jewish Association were called to the Ministry of Interior and ordered to issue an "anti-Zionist" declaration couched in humiliatingly vitriolic language. After having been threatened seven times, with among other things the dissolution of the cooperatives, the Jewish officials finally succumbed and published the desired statement condemning the "Zionist slander campaign against Poland" and "Israeli aggression." The cooperatives were nevertheless liquidated, owing to the loss of Joint subsidies and foreign raw materials.

These men, who wanted to combine the fostering of Yiddish culture with loyalty to Poland and staunch opposition to Zionism,

were unceremoniously thrown overboard the moment their useful-
ness was exhausted. Leopold Domb, the erstwhile legendary chief
of the most successful Soviet spy network during World War II,
was given the sinecure of the Chairmanship of the Jewish Association in 1962 after having spent many years after the war in the
dreaded Lubyanka prison in Moscow. The "anti-Zionist" campaign ruined his old age, just as it did the life of Grzegorz Smolar,
his predecessor and editor of the Yiddish paper. Smolar had declared as early as November 1948 that the Zionist-nationalist
ideology was an enemy and that Jews should be educated in the
patriotic spirit of Poland. At his organization's conference in
October 1949, he thundered against "abstract Judaism," "cultural
particularism," and "cosmopolitan self-abasement before his maj-
esty the dollar"; defined Jewish nationalism (like Gomulka twenty
years later) as "anti-Semitism in reverse" and called on all Jews
to be united with "Poland, the Polish soil, and their socialist fatherland."[68] In March 1968 he was expelled from the Party and relieved of his post as editor for professing the Zionist ideology.

There were many cases in which officials and white-collar workers of Jewish origin vigorously condemned Zionism and Israel and
signed whatever declaration of loyalty was presented to them, only
to fall victim nonetheless to the "anti-Zionist" campaign. A university professor of Jewish origin, a prewar Communist who spent the
years of occupation in the Soviet Union, was accused by a Party
tribunal of being a Zionist. He responded that before the war he
had spent six weeks in prison for breaking up a Zionist meeting, and
that as a Communist and an internationalist he was willing to sign a
personal declaration condemning the "aggressive and expansionist"
policy of Israel. Two weeks later, he was again called before the
Party control commission and accused of lying. The Party had
proof that he was in correspondence with Israel. The professor
did in fact have a cousin in Israel with whom he exchanged New
Year's greeting cards. The commission confronted him with photo-
graphic copies of the anti-Israel declaration he had signed and of a
postcard from the Israeli cousin. He was unreliable and unfit to

educate Polish youth, the tribunal decided. He was deprived of his Party membership, of his appointment, and even of his flat.[69]

Many more Jews did not have to sign an "anti-Zionist" statement—they were kicked out unceremoniously. Some—as during Stalin's drive against "rootless cosmopolitans"—tried to save themselves by discriminating against other Jews subordinate to them. Others refused to sign anything. There was for instance a simple Jew, a skilled worker in a Lodz textile plant, who had never noticed any overt anti-Jewish bias in his environment. In the spring of 1968 he made a casual remark to his fellow workers: "It is very cold here today." Somebody snapped at him, "Go to Sinai if you don't like it here." Others grinned. The worker was shattered. Having never previously contemplated emigration he went next morning to the Dutch Embassy in Warsaw (which represents the Israeli interests since the breakoff of diplomatic relations) and applied for a visa to Israel.

This incident raises the question: What was the popular reaction to the "anti-Zionist" campaign after the initial shock of the student riots wore off? Though the ingrained suspicion of official propaganda remained as vivid as ever, though the gap between political authority and real society, between "them" and "us" broadened rather than narrowed, we must not overlook the impact of modern totalitarian propaganda. It was not merely a matter of vicious cartoons or long-winded political arguments. Television, radio, and the press produced absurd stories, historical arguments, and living proofs to convince the Poles that the corporate Jew was the incarnation of evil and a sworn enemy of Poland.

To show that Jews and Zionists (both terms were used) had been all along the enemies of the Poland reborn after World War I, several articles contained sweeping statements (without any source given of course) to the effect that the Zionists did whatever they could after the First World War to prevent the creation of the Polish State and attempted to persuade President Wilson and British Prime Minister Lloyd George that Silesia should not be returned (from Germany) to Poland. During the Silesian plebiscite and the early years of interwar statehood "they joined forces with

German nationalists even in the ranks of brown-shirted thugs fighting for the great Reich." None of the authors shed light on the mystery of why the Zionists should have been interested in the fate of contested Silesia. As a keen foreign observer aptly noted: "Reading these (articles) one gets the impression that Zionism did not arise in order to create a national home for Jews in Palestine— as it is officially stated—but in order to fight against Poland and the Poles."[70] It was precisely this impression that the pseudo-scientific "documentary" pieces intended to create among their readers.

Television in May 1968 featured at prime viewing time a program about Israel, "Intolerance," which was warmly praised for exposing the racist atmosphere "permeated with cruelty and hate. This is created both by the fanatically religious element . . . and by the spirit of imitation . . . of the military State machine created by Hitler in the Third Reich, with its storm troopers, its racist laws (including 'separate tramways' for Jewish and Arab children), and with its powerful psychological terror directed against its own population." This general "introduction" to Israel, a country ruled by an elite "which is fascinated by Hitler's theory of the *Herrenvolk*," was embellished by special programs featuring a handful of Polish wives of Jews, who for one or another reason had returned to Poland. The papers published their stories under the title "Documents From Hell." In front of the TV cameras they related their martyrdom; how they were tyrannized by rabbis and their Jewish husbands, whose anti-Polish fanaticism burst out in the racist climate of Israel.[71]

Finally *Trybuna Ludu*, the Party's central mouthpiece, published what may have been the most bloodcurdling story of all, the account of a trial three years before of a forty-eight-year-old Warsaw woman, Maria W., who had been involved in illegal foreign exchange transactions, remitting money orders from abroad to Polish residents. But she was also accused (according to *Trybuna Ludu*) of searching out Jewish children saved during the Nazi occupation and brought up by Polish families. This she did for payment and on behalf of "various citizens of Jewish nationality residing in Israel and the U.S. They were sought cut in order

to persuade them, or to force them, to emigrate to Israel." Maria
W. found and took care of Zofia, a young girl who had
been brought up from infancy by a Polish family and was now
sought by an uncle in Israel. According to the long and involved
story, she was finally induced by Mrs. W. to leave Poland. When
after two months she wanted to return, her uncle took away the
gifts he had given her and an official of the Israeli Foreign Ministry
slapped her face. Giving evidence, Zofia told the court her letters
were intercepted, she was threatened, and men were sent to her
with proposals of marriage. One of these men confessed to Zofia
that he had been told (by her uncle and aunt) to rape her in order to
compel her to stay. She said she was also sent anonymous letters
from Poland, written by one of Maria W.'s "wards," which said:
"We all breathe with relief now that you are no longer among us,
for you polluted our Christian air, you dirty Yid." Nevertheless
she returned.

According to her, the pressure from Israel continued, and she
got a letter "from a certain Fleischer": "Why have you returned
from Israel to this Goy woman? You won't stay there anyway . . .
I give you a week to make up your mind. If you don't agree,
you are going to die . . . I will catch you and kill you anyway."

But this was only one case, the Party paper warned, and
inadvertently revealed its source of information by stating: "Our
security agencies found out that young Polish citizens of Jewish
nationality, adopted by Poles under the occupation, were illegally
forced to leave Poland by Zionist organizations in the U.S." American rabbis, physicians, and others, helped by Jewish nationalists
in Poland, were said to have kidnaped several young Polish citizens. After this absurd story, the paper concluded: "This is the
true face of rabid Jewish chauvinism which—allegedly in the name
of fighting anti-Semitism—has recently, with the help of international Zionism, unleashed a repulsive campaign of slander
against the Polish nation throughout the world. The vileness and
perfidy of these activities are beyond imagination and can arouse
but one feeling—that of disgust."[72]

By reproducing allegedly abusive letters from Jews exuding

fanatical hatred for the Polish "goyim," hack writers and police agents (the two often being the same person) deliberately fanned the embers of latent folk anti-Semitism. In view of this incessant whipping-up of racial hatred, it is both a wonder and a tribute to the Poles that no reported cases of physical violence (as distinct from the deliberate assaults on Kisielewski and Jaszunski mentioned earlier) occurred.

Professor Bauman was surely right when he stressed that "the anti-Semitic exhortations of the Polish leadership are directed in the first place, if not exclusively, at one specific class of contemporary Polish society. It is the new middle class, consisting of officials of state and local administration, party officials, regular officers of the armed forces, and executives of the academic enterprises. Thus the final settling of accounts with the remnants of Polish Jewry is to give vent to the frustrations of that new middle class, as well as to provide it with a target for its disappointed hopes and ambitions, and a semblance of fulfillment for its problems and anxieties."[73]

But it was economic corruption rather than Stalinist-type terror that shaped the response in the Poland of 1968. In contrast to the hate meetings in the 1950s in Eastern Europe, nobody believes in anything today. What the state bureaucrats, Party officials and officers hanker for is a well-paid position, a voucher for an imported car, a more spacious flat, the possibility of trips abroad. The political demagogy and ideological acrobatics should not deceive us: the blind faith of the Stalinist cadres in "the best of all possible worlds" has been replaced by careerism and cynicism on the part of the young second- or third-tier officials, academics, and technocrats.

What did the "small stabilization" of the decade from 1957 to 1967 mean concretely for the man in the street? As a Pole succinctly put it: if he keeps silent, is hard-working and thrifty, in ten years he can afford a new flat and after another decade even a car. The frustrated and dissatisfied bureaucratic bourgeoisie was now offered not only a scapegoat in the persons of the surviving Jews, but also a chance of advancement, since the mass dismissals gave a push to upward mobility. The number of Jews sacked or expelled could not have totaled more than five or six thousand at the most. Many, but by far not all, of them held posts in the middle and upper-middle echelons of the administration and in the scientific and cultural world. Thus a vacancy in one hitherto "Jewish" job often meant that a dozen officials could move up one rung on the ladder.

In the horribly overcrowded urban centers, the eviction of a Jewish official from his living quarters and, more often, the emigration of Jewish families benefited not only the man to whom the local authorities allotted the flat, but many more families who in turn were able to get the apartments of those officials moving into the "Aryanized" flats. In other words, the dismissal of some five thousand Jews had a beneficial impact on the standard of living of some thirty to fifty thousand members of the new middle class.

As far as the workers and peasants went, however, anti-Jewish demagogy soon proved to be a boomerang. As a worker at a factory conference in the Zeran car plant put it: "We were told that the departure of the Zionists would improve the economic situation. Thousands of Jews left, but meat prices are as high as ever. I for one do not see any change in the food supply." Warsaw Party secretary Kepa, the man who had launched the anti-Zionist campaign in the capital and who later attempted to dissociate himself from "extremism" and "excesses," complained on April 17: "Among other things, the misleading thesis has been spread that some of our justified economic and price decisions, as for instance the rise in the price of meat and meat products, were the work of Zionism and its agents."[74]

The population at large was not at all affected by the power struggle at the top and the concomitant witch-hunt; it could not have been otherwise when two traditional elements of society, the Church and the peasantry, were deliberately left in peace. In a country where sixteen million people—half of the population— live in the countryside and 85 per cent of the land is held by private farmers, only renewed attempts at collectivization could have shaken the peasantry out of its apathy. But the regime that came to terms with the peasants by tolerating the collapse of collective farms in October 1956 had not the slightest intention of disturbing the truce. On the contrary, Party propagandists and plainclothes-men on several occasions informed the suspicious villagers that it was the "Zionist" gang that had wanted to take away their farms and the truly Polish leaders who had foiled these sinister plans. So it happened that a young writer returned to Warsaw from a tour of the provinces with the puzzling impression that there was intense anti-Semitism in areas where nobody had seen a Jew for at least twenty-five years.

As for the Church, it remained scrupulously silent during the year of political storms. Cardinal Wyszynski, the combative Primate of Poland, who in 1966 raised the sharpest public protests when the transport of a Madonna painting was hindered by the police, who issued pastoral letters against abortion and the use of contraceptive devices, did not deem it necessary to voice any criticism of anti-Semitism. Even the scurrilous attacks on the five Catholic deputies of the genuinely progressive "Znak" group in Parliament for their courageous stand on behalf of the students could not induce the Cardinal to break his judicious silence.

A well-informed Yugoslav correspondent interpreted the conspicuous reserve of the Catholic dignitaries in these words: "Cardinal Wyszynski, it is believed here, started from the premise that there is a quarrel going on among the Communists, and so much the better. Besides, Wyszynski is said to be a well-known anti-Semite so that the general assault on Zionists and certain persons of Jewish origin suited him well . . . He is known as a fanatic nationalist, and he had expected that the so-called national or nationalist current as opposed to the international one would prevail in political life."[75]

Whatever one may think of this interpretation, the fact was that the acknowledged standard-bearer of the "real country" (as opposed to the "legal country") in a profoundly Catholic country with millions of churchgoers refrained from any public stance whatsoever in a delicate political situation.

In sum, certain segments of officialdom reaped benefits from the "anti-Zionist" purge. Many were willing to support the nationalist rhetoric of what the resident correspondent of the Paris *Le Monde* likes to call "rising forces" for reasons other than primitive anti-Semitism. The conclusion that "it is possible to be anti-Semitic without being an anti-Semite—at least any more of an anti-Semite than anyone else,"[76] applied very well to the manipulators and supporters of the campaign. The public reaction was by and large one of deep indifference and to some extent of cynicism, although many people, especially among the intellectuals and professionals, stood by their vilified friends, gave money and advice, and appeared at the station in tears and with flowers at seven each night when the Chopin Express set out on its twelve-hour trip to Vienna, with friends and former colleagues huddling in its second-class carriages.

## 7. EXODUS

During a period of about four weeks after the March demonstrations—and even according to official figures—eighty Jews lost their
jobs and ninety-seven were expelled from the Party in Warsaw
alone. By June the number of those expelled from one district
organization in downtown Warsaw, where many government and
academic institutions are located, reached 281. In October the
rector of Warsaw University revealed that ninety-nine faculty
members had been dismissed (his statement was later withdrawn
by the official news agency).[77] The authorities were understandably reluctant to divulge exact figures; a Yugoslav correspondent
of the Belgrade *Politika* on December 2, 1968, revealed that he
had been told by his colleagues at *Trybuna Ludu* of the dismissal
of seven hundred Jews from central institutions in the capital and
added: "It is said that in Lodz this number has been surpassed."
And these figures clearly do not include the gardener and nursery
administrator from Szczecin, the textile workers from Lodz, the
foremen from Cracow, and the nurse from Warsaw—the many
hundreds of people in medium, low-level, and manual posts and
institutions not regarded as "central."

Most of the dismissed civil servants, journalists, academicians,
economists, doctors, and engineers sought in vain for another job.
Some were forced to live on the usually meager earnings of their
non-Jewish wives. The former editor-in-chief of the best monthly
for foreign consumption, *Polish Perspectives,* Emanuel Planer, a

frail fifty-year-old war veteran, was "offered" only manual jobs in factories and, with the ebbing of the campaign, it took eighteen months before he managed to get a clerical post. A prominent scientist working in a mathematics institute was told, after her dismissal, to work as a ticket collector in the tramway. Dozens of old and ailing war and Party veterans were divested of part or all of their pensions. According to several sources, there were oral instructions that transferred or demoted Jews should not receive more than 3000 zlotys as monthly salary. Average earnings in Poland are between 2000 and 2500 zlotys, but a poor-quality suit costs 2000 (tailor-made, between 4000 and 5000), a pair of men's shoes 400 to 500, a television set between 10,000 and 12,000, and the smallest Polish-made car (Syrena) no less than 71,000.

As the great majority of the Polish Jews did not register with the Jewish Social and Cultural Association and regarded themselves as Poles, there are no data on age, educational qualifications, professions or income concerning Jews as a distinct community. The last statistics from the end of 1948 showed that out of thirty-seven thousand gainfully employed persons, 19 per cent were active in civil service, 10 per cent in health and social work, and 5 per cent in educational and cultural fields.[78] Though these figures reflected great changes in the occupational structure compared to before the war and gave an inkling of how many people had poured into the ranks of the bureaucracy, they are today largely meaningless. Migration movements, particularly between 1956 and 1958, and the continuous influx of repatriates from the Soviet Union profoundly changed the social and demographic character of Polish Jewry. There are no comprehensive figures available for a sociological analysis of the approximately 25,000-strong Jewish community in 1968. But the Jewish Association's membership statistics may serve as pointers. As of 1966, it had only 7500 members, 1500 of whom were pensioners and half manual workers. There was a staggering gap between the age groups. Thus only 1500 members belonged to the 25–40 group. Intellectuals and professional people were on the whole reluctant to show any sign of national separateness by becoming members of the Association. In the fourth largest city, Wroclaw, there were an estimated 4000 Jews in 1966, but only thirty intellectuals were registered among the Association's 1070 members.[79]

Professor Zygmunt Bauman, the noted Polish sociologist (now in Israel), holds that the criteria for the classification of Polish Jewry in the new situation is the attitude toward emigration. He distinguishes between five main categories: 1. Old Communists who, regardless of the differences in their positions and the degree of their Jewish consciousness, are too old to undertake the effort of building a new life. Many of them are determined to retain their pride and for ideological and moral reasons refuse to give in, even though the Party to which they have devoted their entire lives has ousted them. 2. Members of the older generation whose qualifications are solely clerical and administrative but who were not Party professionals. They know that there is no place for Jews in Poland. But their decisions are influenced by such practical considerations as lack of relatives abroad and the fear of starting afresh without the necessary qualifications. 3. Intellectuals, i.e. scientists, writers, and journalists, members of the older and to a lesser extent of the middle generation, who belong to the Polish culture. To break their links with that culture and the conditions for their own creativity is difficult, and Bauman predicts that some time will have to pass before they can make up their minds. 4. People with a clearly defined, exportable profession, either intellectual or manual. These are the people who are trying to obtain exit permits and who will probably leave Poland within a comparatively short time. 5. Finally, the well-educated, politically and socially conscious young people who experienced a real crisis and a turning point after the student demonstrations and the use of the Zionist bogey.[80]

What Bauman fails to mention are the high proportion of mixed marriages, which enormously complicate the situation of countless Jewish families, and the many Jews who, in addition to having little money after they lost their jobs, were waiting, particularly after the July 1968 Central Committee Plenum, which stopped the most glaring excesses, to see if they might not be quietly rehabilitated or at least offered suitable jobs.

In point of fact, though the fight against "Zionism" was taken off the agenda, and definitely so after the November Party Congress, hardly any Jews have been reinstated in their former or equivalent positions. Some have received small pensions which guarantee minimum living standards, but except in a few cases their situation has remained as intolerable morally and as unsatisfactory materially as it was. Did not Kliszko, the Party ideologist, say at the plenum that "the extent of these phenomena ('excesses' against Jews) is not great"?[81] The case of the Scientific Publishing House (PWN) might serve as a yardstick to gauge the mellowing of the climate. There, on a single day in April 1968, no less than thirty-four Jewish employees were sacked. At the time of this writing one of the thirty-four has been reinstated.

With their savings exhausted, their children mostly expelled from the universities and no sign of a decent job, the purged Jews were left with no alternative but to apply to the emigration office. This in turn was the beginning of a new ordeal. Countless Polish Jews applied for a passport to Britain, the United States, or some other West European country. Many of them did not want to renounce their Polish citizenship. The answer was invariably the same: you can emigrate if you wish, but you have to repudiate your citizenship, and exit permits are valid only for Israel. The reason was apparently twofold. As a customs inspector remarked, "If you could travel to countries other than Israel, all Poles would ask for permission to emigrate or to travel to the West, and half of the country would not return." The real reason, however, was more simple: by linking the exit to the renunciation of citizenship, the way back was blocked. In other words, this was a forced expulsion. The emigrants became legal uncitizens with their exit permit merely stating that they are not of Polish nationality. The authorities do not care whether they really go to Israel or manage to get a residence permit in some other country. What matters is that the regime can produce irrefutable proof that these persons, as the first official statement about emigration (June 10, 1969) indeed stated, "do not feel bound to People's Poland but to the State of Israel."

What better proof could there be that the Jews are not "truly Poles," even if most of them do not speak any other language and leave bearing in their hearts attachment to Polish culture and history? The official Polish Government statement referred to 5264 Jews who had left the country from July 1, 1967, to the end of May 1969. In fact, the overwhelming majority emigrated only after the witch-hunt started in March 1968. Even after the Six Day War, the figure for the whole of 1967 reached less than five hundred. Emigration started in earnest in April and by September had reached an average monthly total of five hundred. Between May 1968 and May 1969 the number of emigrants was ten times larger than the year before. The warning that as of September 1, 1969, the "temporary conditions" with regard to the issue of exit permits "for persons expressing their desire to settle permanently in Israel" would be replaced by "standard [that is, tightened] procedures" gave, as they were probably intended to, a renewed push to the exodus. By the end of 1969 the number of emigrants reached about 12,000, that is doubled in six months.[82]

The Deputy Minister of Interior, Moczar's right hand in Jewish affairs, Franciszek Szlachcic, predicted in several lectures held in the summer of 1968 that if the present trend continued, only some ten thousand Jews would remain. But these too, he continued, were likely to depart by the end of 1970 with the exception of some two thousand old people and invalids. This "hard core" would be removed from the great urban centers, and the problem "will find a natural solution." In other words, what not even the Nazis could accomplish, the Communist regime seems likely to achieve: an irrevocable end to the thousand-year history of Polish Jewry.

The Poles admittedly apply less violent methods than the Nazi occupiers. Yet the devices of expropriation, flight tax, and other regulations designed to take advantage of emigration are very similar to those of the forced emigration of the German Jews in the mid-1930s.[83] At the outset, the would-be emigrant must pay 5000 zlotys—equivalent to two months' salary—for his exit visa. His apartment (which is state property) has to be put back into perfect order at his expense for the benefit of the next tenant according to the assessment the state inspector may make about the extent of the "damage." To this must be added the cost of the crates in which personal belongings other than hand luggage must be packed, the transportation fee and the rail tickets. Initially, he could not even take his diplomas, certificates of employment, or other essential personal papers. Later this was permitted provided the migrant had them certified at the Foreign Ministry, a time-consuming procedure involving additional stamp fees. In all, each emigrant must reckon with a per head expenditure of 15,000 zlotys. Children mean extra complications; if they have completed higher education, their parents must repay the government the cost of schooling, and this could well raise total costs to two or three times the average annual income.

After payment of all these levies and taxes, there are stringent controls at the customs before the emigrants are allowed to leave. (The crates of books and larger objects are of course sent separately weeks after the departure of the owners, and Moczar's police agents on occasion use this hiatus to take special precautions. Thus they filmed the entire contents of the crates belonging to N.T., a well-known film director. By skillful editing and visual tricks, the pictures can be made to give the impression that T. took extremely valuable possessions out of the country. Should he make a statement against the Polish regime, it would take no time to show on television "the true face of the Zionist parasite attacking the very country in which he collected treasures and lived much better than many decent Poles.") After having surmounted all the hurdles, emigrants at last reach the Vienna East Station at seven in the morning—with no money and no valid passport. All they have is five dollars in cash and a piece of paper stating that they have no nationality.

Nothing could illustrate the ludicrous character of the official procedures better than the case of the wife of a Jewish television producer. At the time the "anti-Zionist" campaign began in earnest, her husband was in France on business. He decided to remain in Paris and wrote to his French-born wife, who was employed by the foreign broadcasting section of Radio Warsaw, that she should apply for a visa for herself and their daughter for France. Her application was however refused. This "full-blooded Aryan" woman was told to apply for an exit permit to Israel. This she finally did, and the permit was granted in a matter of days.

The July plenum of the Central Committee and the Fifth Party Congress in November, important as they were in the power struggle, had no appreciable effect upon the fate of the Jews. It was only after the Party Congress at the end of 1968 that Gomulka ordered a stop to all discussion of the Jewish problem and a Party reprimand to the two pacemakers of the anti-Semitic campaign, the hack writer Ryszard Gontarz and Colonel Walichnowski, author of the "anti-Zionist" bestseller. (They were reprimanded however for their criticism of the congress at a cell meeting in the Ministry of Interior; Gontarz specifically mentioned among the "revisionists still sitting in high places" two men close to Gomulka, Central Committee secretaries Kliszko and Starewicz.)

At no point did Gomulka, Kliszko, or any other top leader publicly condemn the "anti-Zionist" campaign. While deploring some "excesses," they in fact endorsed it. Gomulka made only one attempt to limit the purge two months after it had erupted when two women personally complained to him. One was Mrs. Koszutska, a prewar Communist who had hidden Gomulka's wife during the occupation. She was one of the ten staff members of the women's weekly *Przyjaciolka* who were fired from both the Party and their jobs on a single day. He was also warned by Mrs. Roloefs, the widow of the Party hero Janek Krasicki (killed in the war) who had been instructed to compile a list of all Jews employed in the institutions belonging to the Committee on Science and Technology. Gomulka also received a full list of purged Jewish journalists and protest letters from several prominent non-Jewish public figures, including M. Rakowski, the editor of the only Polish paper that refused to join the campaign, the influential weekly *Polityka,* which was attacked by General Moczar personally for "deliberately ignoring the strengthening of pride, national dignity, and patriotism" and "showing a disrespect for heroism."[84]

Following these warnings Gomulka made a speech against anti-Semitism at a closed meeting of the Warsaw Party committee. The text of this has never been published, but he is said to have ordered his associates to draw up a "Letter of the Central Committee" to be read in all Party organizations. The order was sabotaged, and the letter was not written until months later and then in a watered-down version. Gomulka's published speech at the July plenum appealed to the Party apparatus to drop the campaign against Zionism, since "this problem has already been sufficiently clarified" and keeping the issue alive would only help "the Zionists' slanderous campaign to create a certain atmosphere in our society, to equate a Zionist and a Jew" in order to "facilitate anti-Communist attacks on the one hand and to increase the number of emigrants to Israel, even among non-Zionists, on the other" and thus to obtain "cannon fodder."[85] Far from denouncing anti-Semitism, Gomulka merely implied that the issue of Zionism should be shelved after having already accomplished its purpose.

By the time Gomulka really halted the anti-Zionist campaign, most of the primary targets of the witch-hunt had been removed. It was this factor—and this alone—that induced the majority of the apparatchiks to heed his appeal for moderation. The new Party line changed the priorities: Zionism should not be treated as the main danger; the Party must fight against reactionary, revisionist, and nationalist elements. Whether and how Zionism was added to the list of evils was merely an indication of whether a given Party dignitary was a "Gomulkaite," a fence-sitter, or a declared ally of Moczar's group.

The new attitude toward the Jews was aptly formulated after the July plenum by Stanislaw Tomaszewski, the first Party secretary of the Olsztyn region: "The idea of differentiating among citizens according to national criteria is completely alien to the Party. If such cases occurred here and there, they were a distortion of the Party's policy and must be set straight . . . Such cadre changes as have been accomplished are justified and correct. The

Party leadership believes that, as Comrade Gomulka put it, 'there is no need to devote as much attention to this matter (Zionism) as before.' The point is that the main danger must not be seen solely in Zionism while disregarding the truly dangerous enemies of socialism and the nation."[86]

At the plenum, twelve speakers out of a total of thirty-six admitted that there had been "unjustified dismissals" during the purge. But the prevalent mood in the apparat was reflected by the first secretary of the Rzeszow Party committee, Kruczek, who lightheartedly referred to the cases of unjust firings by the remark, "where wood is chopped, chips fly." Even more outspoken was Secretary Kodrza from Lublin: "We can hardly speak of excesses. We have been treating all too leniently and humanely people who attacked and undermined the work of the Party from the positions of Zionism and revisionism."[87]

Thus there were considerable differences of emphasis, ranging from being "far too lenient" to the expressions of regret over "unjustified dismissals." But no one (apart from a few members who had been purged themselves) took an unequivocal stance against the anti-Semitic witch-hunt. Professor Bauman has related a characteristic conversation he himself overheard between two prominent Communists, one a Jew, the other a Gentile: "Both had been purged from the Party and both had lost their employment, one because he was Jewish, the other because he had dared to defend his national honor by protesting against anti-Semitism. The Jew asked the Gentile: 'Let us assume that the political situation changed radically and you were appointed to the leadership of the Party; would you be able to restore me and others like me to Party membership, would you be able to give us back our jobs, and publicly declare that the charges leveled against us were false?' After a prolonged pause the Gentile, horrified by the truth the question had uncovered, answered sadly that he could not if he wanted to stay in power . . ."[88]

This indeed is the crux of the matter. The discussion of the "national cadres policy" set irreversible forces in motion. Even though they were later brought under control, at least for the time being, the clock could not be turned back.

The foreign reaction to the witch-hunt and Gomulka's reassertion of his authority, due partly to the Czech crisis, combined to foil the "grand design" of great "Zionist" trials. How threadbare the basis of the campaign, the notorious charge of an "organized attack mounted by Zionists on People's Poland," was could be seen in an interesting episode at the Party Congress in November. The First Secretary from the province of Zielona Gora, Tadeusz Wieczorek, complained that there had been many conflicting instructions and guidelines with regard to the issue of Zionism. At the end of his speech, Wieczorek posed a question: "We have here among us Comrade Kosztyrko, our Attorney General. I would like to ask him: 'Is it true that the March events were the work of a Zionist conspiracy?'" Kosztyrko got up and declared calmly: "No, we have no proofs whatsoever for this supposition."

Today the memories of the 1968 witch-hunt are shrouded in silence, and there is a taboo on recalling the drama of combating the "Zionist" and "alien" elements. But the recent tragedy of Polish Jewry has torn the bandage from every half-healed wound—not only in Jewish, but also in Polish history.

## 8. DEAD JEWS—GOOD POLES

In the midst of the witch-hunt, on April 18, 1968, Polish authorities celebrated the twenty-fifth anniversary of the Warsaw ghetto uprising, an event that, in the words of Hilberg, the historian of the Holocaust, was "literally a revolution, for after two thousand years of a policy of submission the wheel had been turned and once again Jews were using force."[89] Aside from a handful of "professional Jews," newly installed or surviving members of the leadership of the Jewish Association, there were present mainly dignitaries of ZBOWiD, the veterans' organization, and of the ministerial bureaucracy (by then almost totally "judenrein"). The main speech in remembrance of the Jews, who after the murder of 310,000 from the ghetto rose and fought for four weeks against the Nazis and their Ukrainian collaborators, was made by Kazimierz Rusinek, the Secretary General of ZBOWiD and General Moczar's right hand.

He spoke about the magnificent assistance rendered to the Jews by the Poles during the occupation, while foreign Jewish organizations, the U. S. Department of State, and the present leaders of the State of Israel "showed a criminal indifference" to the murder of millions of Jews. He castigated Western Jews, "more concerned about their billions in bank investments than with the fate of the millions of Jews being burned in the crematoria," and finally condemned the slanderous anti-Polish campaign in Israel and in the West aimed at "diverting the attention of public opinion from the real perpetrators of the crimes committed by Hitler on the nations of Europe . . . from the crime of Israel on the Arab nations."[90]

Both the macabre ceremony, complete with a military parade, and the sordid press campaign which finally sank to the level of defaming even the memory of the three million murdered Polish Jews, recall Lec's bitter epigram: "Has a cannibal the right to speak on behalf of those whom he swallowed?"

It was the Germans, not the Poles (let alone people like Rusinek who themselves were in concentration camps), who killed the Jews of the Warsaw ghetto, of Lodz, of Cracow, of Lublin. And it was in Warsaw and Lodz and Cracow that the most heroic records of underground resistance to the Nazis were written. There were hundreds of Poles who tried and often died to save Jews. Walking along the alley of "Righteous Gentiles," lined with trees leading to Yad Vashem, the austere memorial with the eternal flame in remembrance of the Martyrs and Heroes on a hill overlooking Jerusalem, the pilgrims and tourists, Jews and Christians, invariably stop to look at the tablets under each tree. They bear the name of the man or woman who planted the tree, who rendered particularly great services to the persecuted Jews during World War II. And the majority of these tablets have "Poland" written on them.

But there were also gangs of hoodlums and fascist youth groups, the notorious "Jew-catchers," the dreaded *szmalcownicy,* roaming the streets, ferreting out fugitives and turning over to the Gestapo those who could not pay ransom. There were Communist and non-Communist resistance groups that did not admit Jewish partisans and some, like the one led by General Korczynski, that shot the Jews turning to them for help. There were tales of great heroism—and also of unspeakable treachery. Those were long years of terror and bitterness, ruins and misery for the non-Jewish Poles, three million of whom perished on the battlefield and in prisons and camps or died from hunger and sickness. He who betrayed a Jew to the Nazis pocketed a reward; he who sheltered or aided a Jew risked the death penalty.

Those who lightheartedly pass judgment on the Polish nation

for "behaving no better than the Nazis toward the Jews" cannot have even a nodding acquaintance with this tragic, strange, "schizophrenic country of great bravery and great cruelty."[91] One should remember American experiences with war and anti-Semitism: "One propaganda effort during World War II was designed to reduce anti-Semitism among Americans by linking Nazism and anti-Semitism, and then attacking Nazism. An evaluation reported that the campaign increased hostility toward Nazism without reducing hostility toward the Jews. The American public fought bitterly against Hitler during the war, without apparently altering its attitudes toward Jews."[92] Was it then so surprising that during the horrors of a Nazi occupation, breeding intense nationalism and religious fanaticism, the mass of the population hated the Nazi enemy more and more fiercely, but remained by and large indifferent to the fate of the Jews? The centuries-long isolation of the Yiddish-speaking communities from their non-Jewish environment on the one hand, and the long heritage of religious, folk, and political anti-Semitism on the other provided the dark and complex background to the tragedy of the Polish Jewry. Self-styled judges should ask themselves whether any other nation under similar circumstances would have behaved differently.

Films, novels, and penetrating studies both in Poland and abroad have probed from different angles the twisted roots of guilt and generosity, complicity and indifference in war-ravaged and occupied Poland. But A. M. Rosenthal was proved sadly right when he noted in 1965 on the occasion of the twenty-fifth anniversary of the creation of the Warsaw ghetto—that is, long before the reappearance of overt anti-Semitism—that "to the measure that the Jews of the ghetto died to save future Polish Jews from anti-Semitism in Poland, to that measure they died in vain . . . Those Jews who died in the ghetto had lived their lives amidst the heavy stench of Polish anti-Semitism. That stench is lighter, now and again perfumed with guilt, but I believe it still hangs over Poland like a miasma."[93]

Now it is the Communist government itself that has begun "to rake the ghetto's ashes to find living coals of evil." Everything has become possible again; it is permissible—even commendable —to declare that the persecuted were responsible for the persecution they suffered.

It is the cynical defamation of the memory of the dead and the ruthless forging of history as a weapon for tormenting living Jews that confers upon the "anti-Zionist" campaign a particularly distressing and morally intolerable character. The evils of yesterday have become tools in the hands of the anti-Semites of today. Their task has been facilitated by the powerful if subterranean current of sensitivity and reaction against the assumption of any Polish complicity in the Nazi extermination of Jews.

The latent tension between the confession of culpability and the rejection of guilt, along with the whole problem of postwar anti-Semitism, was deliberately brought into the open by the spokesmen of the nationalistic and anti-Semitic hard-liners as early as the beginning of 1966. It was Jerzy Kosinski's generally acclaimed novel *The Painted Bird* that sparked the first venomous attacks against "the dirty waves of anti-Polish publications." The writer left Poland in 1957 and now lives in the United States. His novel describes the wanderings and suffering of a small boy through "Eastern Europe" without naming any specific country; it is a picture of the cruelty of war as reflected in the shattering experiences of the child-hero who is either a gypsy or a Jew.

The Polish Communist press declared that the book dealt in fact with the relations between Poles and Jews during the occupation; it was attacked as a slanderous work designed to denigrate Poland and the Poles as being anti-Semitic, backward, and barbarous. Neither the novel nor excerpts from it have been published in Poland. While it is legitimate to have different opinions about this powerful novel with its visions of physical torment and sexual assaults, the point with which we are concerned here is the rapid escalation of political accusations.

It was, not surprisingly, Moczar's chief propagandist, Kazimierz Kakol (whom we have already quoted), who fired the opening salvo in his fortnightly, stating that "the dirty wave of anti-Polish publications is not accidental. It is inspired, directed, and financed

. . ."[94] Dozens of furious articles followed in other newspapers and periodicals. Though the German-language edition was published in Switzerland, the papers soon announced that "West German money financed" publication and translation of the book, because "Kosinski whitewashes the Germans." This work of fiction became "a clearly defined psychological attack at a time of great problems for NATO and Bonn's offensive for gaining access to nuclear weapons," part of the efforts "to prepare psychologically the American nation for an armed showdown with the barbarous Poles and 'Communist Eastern Europe,' to prepare the American, French, and English nations for the idea of a common crusade . . ."[95]

Finally, Kosinski's novel was described as a link in the chain of anti-Polish attacks, with the "reviewers" classifying a number of works on Jewish history or the Holocaust, written at different times about widely disparate subjects, as a conspiracy by "American imperialists" and "German revanchists." Kakol, who returned three times within a few months to the subject in his journal, which was ostensibly devoted to legal subjects, in December 1966 for the first time linked the German revenge-seekers with "the most rightist Zionist groups" as the real inspirers of *The Painted Bird* and other "slanderous works."

When the Arab-Israeli War gave the signal for the showdown with the Jews and moderates, the opinions of the critics were used as proven facts to fabricate more far-reaching theories. Walichnowski's bestseller on *Israel and the German Federal Republic* illustrated the infamous thesis about "the alliance of victims with their executioners," the collusion between Nazis and Zionists, with lengthy and skillfully doctored quotations from Kosinski's novel. On the eve of the "March events," one paper published an article under the characteristic title "The Alliance of the Black Cross with the Star of David," in which it was stated that *Exodus* (by Leon Uris), *Treblinka* (by J. F. Steiner), and *The Painted Bird* constituted "a flood of slanders of a decisively anti-Polish edge in which world Zionism pays its debts to its allies under the auspices of the Black Cross."[96]

The campaign was not an end in itself, but a means to what the manipulators described as a "counterattack against the diversion carried out by the Zionists and the inheritors of Hitlerism."[97] This was in fact a three-pronged operation aimed at próving that Zionists exaggerated the number of murdered Jews, that the Nazi occupation was the same for Jews and non-Jews, and that it was the Councils of Jewish elders (the Judenraete) and the Jewish ghetto police who were the principal accomplices of the genocide, while all Poles did their best to save the Jews. The campaign appealed to all those who were weary of hearing about Auschwitz and the martyrdom of Jews. The weekly *Stolica* had reminded its readers obliquely three years before that the Jews ("a certain part of the population") were always contriving to make the most of their sufferings, though many non-Jews also perished in the concentration camps.

It was Rusinek of ZBOWiD who with "a group of partriots" lodged a public protest with the government against the editors of the Great General Encyclopedia for distorting history, minimizing the number of the martyred Polish victims, and exaggerating the proportion of Jews among the dead. The attack concentrated on the entry "Concentration Camps" in Volume 8 of the encyclopedia. Criticism was also directed against the Scientific Publishing House (PWN) and its director, Adam Bromberg. And, as if by coincidence, one of the senior editors was none other than Stefan Staszewski, "the former Stalinist-turned-Zionist bankrupt politician."

Rusinek made clear first of all that dead Jews are good Jews; they are Polish patriots. He took the editors indignantly to account for including "Poles of Jewish origin" among the Jewish victims. "As a matter of fact this definition of the nationality of people who considered themselves Poles is not only groundless scientifically but especially harmful politically because Zionists as well as anti-Semites continue to use these criteria for the definition of nationalities." Moreover, the writers committed "grave errors" by differentiating between extermination camps and concentration camps, thereby suggesting that the policy of extermination affected the Jewish population almost exclusively. To put matters straight, Rusinek informed the public that "the so-called final solution of the Jewish question was not an exceptional action in the occupied territories of Europe. The number of people murdered in the framework of the *Endlösung* amounted to 30 per cent of the total number of victims of Hitlerism. Such is the truth and such are the facts."[98]

What were indeed the facts in this case? The Great General Encyclopedia is generally regarded as the single most important postwar achievement of Polish book publishing. The encyclopedia's Scientific Council, headed by the doyen of Polish philosophers, Dr. Tadeusz Kotarbinski (definitely not a "Zionist"), included a roll call of most illustrious Polish scholars, very few of whom were Jewish. More than two thousand scientific collaborators provided the essays and entries for the ten published volumes. The entry on the concentration camps was prepared by an editorial team of qualified experts led by the former director of the Main Commission for Investigation of Hitlerite Crimes, Janusz Gumkowski. It made the generally accepted distinction between extermination centers (created mainly for the Jews) and concentration camps, and scrupulously noted the number of all victims of all nationalities.

With the eruption of the full-blown anti-Semitic witch-hunt in the spring of 1968, the "political and journalistic scandal" of the encyclopedia's entry was described as a deliberate attempt "for the sake of Zionist and revisionist aims to minimize and to pass in silence over the martyrdom of the Polish nation."[99] Who were the main culprits? Senior editor Staszewszki who "thus gave free rein to his hatred for the Party leadership," another Jewish editor, Jerzy Baumritter, and a third Jew, Bromberg, the director of the publishing house. Day after day the campaign against the "encyclopedists" gained in volume and intensity. Finally, the Party organization demanded the dissolution of the entire editorial team. Thirty-four Jewish employees of the PWN were summarily dismissed, and the Attorney General launched an investigation to track down reported "illegal business practices." Bromberg—"the father was a well-to-do Jewish merchant"[100]—was vilified, dismissed, kept under arrest for several months, expelled from the Party; his last known job was that of a librarian in a Warsaw factory with a monthly salary of 2000 zlotys.

The new government commissioner in charge of PWN promised the correction of the mistakes and falsifications. Volume 11 of the encyclopedia, now in print, will contain a four-page supplement about the concentration camps which subscribers can insert in the place of the "erroneous entry" in Volume 8. (Such practices recall the Stalin era, during which subscribers to the Great Soviet Encyclopedia learned about the fall from grace of public figures by receiving substitute pages for the entry on them. Thus after his arrest in 1953, former police chief Beria was "expelled" from the encyclopedia and the subscribers received a substitute article about the Bering Strait . . .)

Moczar's faction had already taken over such key institutions dealing with World War II and the Holocaust as the International Auschwitz Committee whose headquarters are in Warsaw* and the Main Commission for the Investigation of Hitlerite Crimes. After the "March events," his agents quickly moved to the second stage in rewriting the history of Poles and Jews. The new director of the Main Commission, Czeslaw Pilichowski, published a three-part series in *Trybuna Ludu*[101] stating that "only" three million Jews had been killed by the Nazis and the figure of six million dead was "a basic Zionist lie." Pilichowski, an active member of the prewar fascist ONR group,[102] went on to glorify Polish help to the persecuted Jews, while the blame for collaboration was placed exclusively on Jews—Zionists, camp inmates of Jewish origin, Jewish collaborators with the Gestapo, the Judenraete, etc.—leading him to the conclusion that "the forces of international Zionism, capitalism, and imperialism took part in the liquidation of the Jewish proletariat in Europe." Simultaneously, other dailies published articles about the Jewish blame for the Holocaust.

---

* Moczar's men controlled the apparatus and publications of the "de-Judaized" Committee to such an extent that its French president, Professor Weitz, resigned in protest.

That dead Jews were good Jews and truly Poles enabled the Polish Government to dangle the figures of six million Polish victims in its vituperative campaign against West Germany (Communist East Germany having per se no share in past Nazi crimes, its population consisting solely of decent Germans).

At this point it is appropriate to recall that there were many Jews who did in fact cooperate—willingly or by force—with the Germans. Their role and the rationalizations of the Jewish office-holders amid an unprecedented tragedy is a hotly debated issue in Jewish history. As Hilberg puts it: "The Jewish councils . . . continued until the end to make desperate attempts to alleviate the sufferings and to stop mass dying in the ghettos. But at the same time the councils responded to German demands with automatic compliance and invoked German authority to compel the community's obedience. Thus the Jewish leadership both saved and destroyed its people—saving some Jews and destroying others, saving the Jews at one moment and destroying them at the next."[103]

The Jewish leaders were held personally responsible for the execution of German instructions in the same way that the death penalty was imposed upon Poles who helped Jews, and this became a tool in the hands of cynical operators. Prewar fascists and nationalists in Communist disguise denied the existence of past and present Polish anti-Semitism in order to eradicate the ineluctable sense of guilt and complicity by the ingenious device of blaming the persecuted for their suffering. Rusinek attacked living Jews in remembrance of dead Jews, that is, good Poles, and his associates eagerly organized exhibitions in honor of Poles who saved Jews, published collections of documents and books and made films about "Polish aid to Jews." By stretching these efforts to absurd lengths, however, they have defeated their purpose. The blanket denial that any Pole ever delivered Jews to the hands of their murderers must seem to any sober observer as ludicrous as the allegation that the Polish people since the time of Casimir the Great has never been anti-Semitic.

The eagerness of the anti-Semitic propagandists to pose as

saviors of the Jews raised doubts about even genuine cases of truly heroic deeds or generosity shown by the Polish people toward a persecuted minority. But the dynamism of an almost Orwellian rewriting of history was feeding itself at an unbelievable pace. Within a few weeks the number of Jews whose life was said to have been saved by Poles rose from "several thousand" to "many thousands," finally reaching the "official" figure of "more than 100,000," with provincial Party dailies stating that "Poles at the risk of their lives saved several hundreds of thousands of Jews."[104]

But the Jewish complicity and Polish heroism in the face of Nazi massacres could be shown only after unmasking those who by "a reign of terror" imposed a silence on the discussion of this subject. As *Zolnierz Wolnosci,* the army organ, revealed: "Behind this activity [Jewish complicity] there were reactionary forces, including Zionists and various political bankrupts for whom patriotism was the opposite of the harmful cosmopolitanism and Zionism they represent."[105] And "after the removal of all sorts of Zionists, people who falsify the picture of Polish culture and history," the truth had finally prevailed. The government commissioner of the Scientific Publishing House hastened to announce new publications about Nazi crimes and the resistance which "will be prepared in close collaboration with the historical commission of ZBOWiD."[106] The director of another large publishing concern, S. Wronski, "the well-known ZBOWiD activist," revealed an ambitious project to cope with the lack of information about recent Polish history, the partisan underground, the martyrdom of the nation, and the aid given by Poles to the Jewish population. There will be many volumes about this last topic; in all, twenty titles will be brought out.[107]

The film industry was also accused of denigrating the national honor. The same producers—Alexander Ford, Jan Rybkowski, Andrzej Wajda, etc.—who were highly praised as recently as August 1967 in the most authoritative Party organs were singled out as the chief culprits. Here again ZBOWiD took the initiative. On March 20, 1968, it protested against Rybkowski's (who incidentally is not Jewish) new film, *When Love Is a Crime,* asking that it be suppressed on the grounds that it "insulted the Poles and painted an untrue picture of the occupation." The movie tells the story of the love affair of a Polish slave laborer and a German girl during World War II in Germany. Within twelve days ZBOWiD's call was heeded, and the film was recalled. Soon afterwards the distribution of another film was stopped because it showed a Jew in danger of being denounced by Poles during the occupation. Production of Rybkowski's newest film, *The Ascension,* was halted. Based on Adolf Rudnicki's novel, it dealt with the occupation and Polish aid to Jews but, according to the accusation, "tended to obscure the dedication of Poles in saving Jews as well as the heroic struggle of the nation against the invaders." The same fate befell the movie based on the true story of the Jewish doctor Korczak who chose death in a concentration camp with the orphans in his care instead of escaping. Kakol's fortnightly *Prawo i Zycie,* the supposedly legal journal, devoted no less than three vitriolic articles to the "tendentious overemphasizing of Jewish martydom" and the "deliberate neglect of heroic traditions."[108]

Those Jews who happened to have written recollections of the war years at the time of the witch-hunt fared even worse. Journalist M. Martula, for example, had kept a diary of the occupation, which he had tried for a long time to have published, submitting it to several publishing houses. Suddenly he was arrested and sentenced in February 1969 to three years imprisonment for "slinging mud at the national honor of Poland." The prosecutor stated he could not imagine that any Pole could have done such things as Martula described in his manuscript. Associate Professor Szapiro (the brother of the surgeon sacked in Lodz) also received a three-year sentence for a similar offense.[109]

The daily diet of tales of national heroism and bravery in saving Jews which the mass media fed to the population had one slight flaw. If the Poles were without exception valiant friends of the persecuted Jews, how was one to explain the simultaneous campaign against students, scholars, writers, and officials invariably described as being "of Jewish origin" or "mainly of Jewish origin"? The Polish propagandists had a standard answer: "The subversive campaign against Poland . . . grew in volume as the alliance between the forces of the Washington-Bonn-Tel Aviv axis developed and the campaign to rehabilitate the former Hitlerite torturers, conducted with all accessible means of mass propaganda by Washington, Bonn, and World Zionism, progressed, and as a new conspiracy of Zionism and the sworn enemies of Poland unfolded in exchange for the financial support the Federal German Republic gave to Israel—a conspiracy that, irrespective of obvious facts, was designed to saddle the Polish nation in the most glorious chapter of its struggle for existence with responsibility for the crimes of Hitlerism committed in the Polish territories."

Zionism "also seeks in alliance with Hitler's heirs in Bonn the rehabilitation of itself, the rehabilitation of the Judenräte, the Jewish policemen in the ghettos, the Jewish Gestapo brigades, thanks to whom the Zionist organization led the Jews to the crematoria. There has been almost no literature on this subject; sensitivity made it taboo . . . Zionism contrived to establish an 'intelligence' base in our country for forces hostile to Poland, which made concentrated attacks on our Party, socialism, and national goals . . . and propagandized for support of the revanchists in the German Federal Republic and its swallowing up the German Democratic Republic."[110]

This lengthy article was published by a certain Z. Soluba on April 21, 1968, in *Trybuna Ludu*. Its main gist was that Poland, which did more than any other nation for the Jews, now had to pay the bill for the conspiracy of Nazis and Zionists, each attempting to whitewash their own dirty record. And the "rehabilitation of West Germany at the cost of the Polish people, the anti-Polish demagogy, which can be compared only to Goebbels' methods, was lately intensified because of the condemnation of Zionist aggression, of the murders committed against Arabs, and of the unmasking of Zionist espionage centers in the socialist countries."[111]

Hundreds of thousands of words have been written and said on this subject in Poland. It is therefore of some importance to recall that before the breaking off of diplomatic relations between Israel and Poland on June 12, 1967, in the wake of the Six Day War, relations between the two states were cordial. In a symbolic gesture, Foreign Minister Abba Eban had in May 1966 convened the first regional conference of the heads of Israeli missions in the Communist world in the Polish capital. And before the week-long meeting, the Israeli Government, the alleged "close ally of West German revanchist forces," informed the Polish Government in an official note handed to the Polish Ambassador in Tel Aviv that it recognized the controversial Oder-Neisse line as the final and definitive frontier between Poland and Germany.[112] Moreover, Poland was, after Rumania, Israel's most important source of trade in Eastern Europe. One might add that as a result of the generous facilities for Jewish emigration from Poland in 1956–59 and the fostering of Jewish-Yiddish culture, no Communist country enjoyed friendlier relations with international Jewish organizations. Thus the charge repeatedly raised by Moczar and his associates that "Zionists and Americans of Jewish origin . . . had for years been conducting a slanderous campaign against Poland and the Polish people"[113] is a patent absurdity.

What gave the campaign a particularly nauseating flavor was that its manipulators, not satisfied with staging an anti-Semitic witch-hunt and defaming the memory of the dead, also wanted to be treated with respect as Communists and patriots to whom any thought of racial discrimination was alien. Not only that, they expected pity from both the Jews in Poland and the world at large as victims of a slanderous Zionist campaign. But there were apparently very few "good Jews" even in the Party's Central Committee to pay tribute to the leadership's courageous battle "against Zionists, revisionists, Stalinists, and bankrupt politicians." Abroad the echo was disappointing. Under the influence of "anti-Polish propaganda waged by neo-Nazi and revisionist circles in West Germany and by international Zionist organizations,"[114] Western public opinion was so "confused" that it began to lend credence to the reports about anti-Semitism.

In the midst of the "anti-Zionist" campaign therefore ambassadors and press attachés in important centers were instructed to give press conferences. Jan Druto, the Ambassador in Paris, declared on April 12, 1968 that there was no anti-Semitism in Poland, that the great majority of the small Jewish community was deeply attached to the country, and that no one was subjected to any kind of discrimination. On the same day *Trybuna Ludu* reported that seven people lost their jobs and Party membership. These included two nuclear scientists, the bookkeeper of a pharmaceutical plant, Rector Piatkowski of the University of Lodz, Vice-President Blass of the National Bank and A. Dukier, an assistant departmental chief in the Ministry of Health. On the same day in the city of Wroclaw a lecturer and two students were expelled from the university, and a retired journalist, a former hospital director, and a Party veteran lost their pensions and Party memberships. The day before, *Tribuna Mazowiecka,* the sharply "anti-Zionist" organ of the Warsaw Voivodship Party Committee, reported the expulsion of fifty people from the Party. And it is crucial to remember that the expulsion in each case also involved the loss of job.[115]

While Ambassador Druto was only doing his duty in denying undeniable facts, the special propaganda missions sent to Austria and the Netherlands were unique. The same people who at home were the ringleaders of overt anti-Semitic agitation, appeared poker-faced on foreign rostrums to dispel "the fabrications of the press and certain Western agencies as well as of the Israeli press." Those missions were usually made up of a prominent "anti-Zionist" propagandist and a preferably Jewish partisan, or a Pole who saved Jews during the occupation. Four days after Druto's briefing in Paris, a press conference was held in Vienna by the same Soluba whose absurd article about Zionist-Nazi collusion was just quoted and Colonel Bolkowiak, a Jewish partisan, one of the handful of "honorary Aryans" used by Moczar's faction. Commenting on their performance next day, *Volksstimme,* the Austrian Communist daily, remarked that "many question marks remained even after their answers," while the Social Democratic paper concluded that Soluba's and Bolkowiak's statements "confirmed rather than dampened the anxiety among Western democrats about 'anti-Zionist' moves in Poland."[116]

The Austrian journalists learned only later that their host had during the war belonged to an extreme right-wing anti-Soviet partisan band and was also known as one of the most vitriolic anti-Semitic spokesmen of the hard-liners. Three days after his return to Warsaw, Soluba produced the previously quoted piece about Zionism, which, to prove the "historical" roots of Zionist-German collusion, flatly stated: "It was not accidental that the 'Jewish-State' by Herzl, the great codification of Zionist doctrine, was written and published in Germany and was peddled in German among the Jewish communities of the world."[117]

Soluba's mission was a failure however, since on May 25 some twenty prominent Communist and leftist intellectuals sent a letter to the Polish ambassador in Vienna protesting against events in Poland. Nevertheless Soluba reaped his reward and in May replaced Leon Bielski, the highly decorated Jewish veteran of the underground who had been parachuted into occupied Poland, as editor-in-chief of the capital's largest popular daily.

The crusader against the "Zionist lies" about the number of murdered Jews, Director Pilichowski of the Commission for Investigating Nazi Crimes, held a similar series of press conferences in the Netherlands, accompanied by a resistance fighter. In early 1969 a second mission descended upon Vienna, consisting this time of Wladyslaw Machejek, the editor-in-chief of the Cracow weekly *Zycie Literackie,* which already in the mid-1960s was notorious for its anti-Semitic allusions. His escort was a man with even more impeccable credentials: W. Szewczyk, a particularly active member of the fascist-inspired ONR group, editor of a fascist weekly before the war and currently one of the leading producers of articles unmasking the Bonn-Tel Aviv axis.[118]

It is not unusual for the defenders of the Polish national honor to be prewar fascists. The same Boleslaw Piasecki who in 1937, as leader of the fascist Falanga, declared that "the Jews were to be expelled from Poland" and until their expulsion "were to be refused all civil rights, and their fortunes confiscated," who called "for a systematic and radical elimination of Jews from Poland," warned in the Polish Parliament on April 11, 1968, that the utmost vigilance was needed against the Zionists who are linked with the German revanchists.[119]

These prewar fascists and right-wing extremists who revive and propagate their old pernicious doctrines in the name of Karl Marx or of "socialist-minded Catholicism" are not men who erred and repented, but virulent anti-Semites who vent their fury upon the tiny remainder of an exterminated Jewish community as hack writers, editorialists, and members of the Jewish department in the Ministry of Interior. A certain Z. Przetakiewicz, one of the leaders of the ONR detachment and Piasecki's friend, attacked a peaceful May Day march in 1938 with his thugs who allegedly murdered two children. In 1968 he applied for membership in the journalists' club and received a standing ovation.[120] In the country that was the scene of Hitler's most monstrous crimes, his erstwhile Polish accomplices have taken up the twofold task of stirring up the reservoir of irrational hatred and of protecting Poland from the "vile accusations of anti-Semitism."

The greatest figures in contemporary Polish culture and science have raised their voices at one time or another in defense of what Jerzy Andrzejewski called "the basic rights of social, political, and moral existence." Andrzejewski, the foremost living Polish novelist, broke his long silence on the eve of "the March events" to warn the Warsaw writers' meeting: "What the nation thinks and says is not heeded and is held in total contempt . . . Every bold initiative aimed at probing our contemporary life is destroyed. Every creative work boldly dealing with our wounds and ailments is banned or subjected to destructive treatment. The present is lied about, history falsified . . . The very existence of Polish culture and Polish creativity is threatened. Where are we going?"[121]

Andrzejewski later protested publicly against the national shame incurred by Polish participation in the invasion of Czechoslovakia. Tadeusz Kotarbinski, the respected scholar; Leszek Kolakowski, the intellectual hero of the "Polish October"; Slawomir Mrozek, the best contemporary playwright, sounded the alarm. In the last two years alone over twenty prominent writers and critics have given back their Party cards in disgust. As Professor Zolkiewski, the Marxist historian, stated at the plenary meeting of the Central Committee in July 1968: "The dismissals have thrown Polish science and arts back twenty years." Zolkiewski was expelled two months later, Mrozek exiled; Kolakowski went into voluntary exile; Andrzejewski and many others were silenced. And into the moral and political vacuum moved a motley collection of forces ranging from faceless Party professionals and primitive nationalists in Communist clothing to the prewar social-fascists and rabid anti-Semites. A Kolakowski is an undesirable element in today's Poland, but a Piasecki is more indispensable than ever before. As he himself put it at a public meeting in December 1967, in the presence of Jerzy Putrament, the conformist chairman of the Writers' Union: "The Communists made mistakes; we, the ONR, also made mistakes in the past. But now we have found a common language and a common road."

## 9.  THE MANIPULATORS

Question to Radio Jerevan: "What is the most difficult thing to predict under Communism?" Answer: "The past . . ."

A Polish joke

When more than fifty years ago a Jewish friend complained to Rosa Luxemburg about the virulence of anti-Semitism, the founder of the Polish Social Democratic Party, who was by then a leader of the left-wing German socialists, replied: "Why do you care about special Jewish pains? To me, the poor victims of the rubber plantations in Putumayo, the Negroes in Africa . . . are as close"; she had "no special corner for the ghetto" in her heart: "I feel at home in the whole world where there are clouds and birds and human tears."[122]

Rosa Luxemburg was born the same year (1870) as Lenin, who once praised her as someone who "for all her errors was and remains an eagle."[123] Assassinated in Berlin in January 1919, she was the single greatest woman figure in the history of international socialism and one of its most original and dynamic thinkers. Equally at home in Polish, Russian, and German culture and a leader in the labor movements of these three countries, she "sought to inject into German socialism something of the Russian and Polish revolutionary élan and idealism . . . and occasionally she tried to transplant the Western European democratic spirit and tradition into the socialist underground movements of Eastern Europe."[124] Though she is a revolutionary hero even in the Communist pantheon, her most prophetic and timely works have been kept out of circulation by the ruling Communist Parties. Luxemburg's heritage is still a time bomb menacingly ticking in the archives of the Agit-Prop Departments from Moscow to East Berlin, none of which has ever dared to face up to her devastating and prophetically correct criticism of the single-party dictatorship Lenin founded.

Alluding to the events in Poland, Franz Marek, the ablest ideologist of the Austrian Communist Party,* stated sadly at the 1969 Party Congress: "Take for example the fact . . . that Rosa Luxemburg, were she still alive, probably could not occupy today any leading position in the workers' movement because of her Jewish origin."[125] She certainly could not. This thoroughgoing internationalist was truly the epitome of the "rootless cosmopolitan" (as indeed was Marx himself) whom not only the Moczars but also the Gomulkas want to eliminate from the Communist Party.

In his moving essay on "The Non-Jewish Jew," Isaac Deutscher wrote about the "great revolutionaries of modern thought: Spinoza, Heine, Marx, Rosa Luxemburg, Trotsky, and Freud" who "all went beyond the boundaries of Jewry . . . Each of them was in society and yet not in it, of it and yet not of it. It was this that enabled them to rise in thought above their societies, above their nations, above their times and generations, and to strike out mentally into wide new horizons and far into the future . . . Like Marx, Rosa Luxemburg and Trotsky strove, together with their non-Jewish comrades, for the universal as against the particularist, and for the internationalist, as against the nationalist, solutions to the problem of their times . . . All these great revolutionaries were extremely vulnerable. They were, as Jews, rootless, in a sense; but they were so only in some respects, for they had the deepest roots in intellectual tradition and in the noblest aspirations of their times. Yet whenever religious intolerance or nationalist emotion was on the ascendant, whenever dogmatic narrow-mindedness and fanaticism triumphed, they were the first victims."[126]

In the very long, historical view, Deutscher may be right in his

* Dismissed from the Politburo and at the last congress also from the Central Committee; certain to be expelled from the Party by the time this book is published.

cry: "But theirs is the ultimate victory." Today however, as we look at the Communist Parties and states, we can no longer doubt that Rosa Luxemburg's ideas—both in her lifetime and during the half century that has passed since her assassination—failed to achieve their purpose: to integrate the nations into an international brotherhood and infuse a democratic spirit into the victorious revolution. She, like so many of her contemporaries and disciples, ignored the overwhelming appeal of nationalism to her own peril. To understand the specific nature of the current political crisis in Poland, therefore, one has to go back to the roots of the factional divisions —to the early history of the Polish Communist movement.

Even before the turn of the century, the socialist movement was deeply split over the crucial issue of national independence. While the Polish Socialist Party (PPS) founded in 1892 proclaimed as the primary task the attainment of national independence of a Poland partitioned since the end of the eighteenth century between three empires, the internationalist left wing of the movement a year later set up the Social Democracy of the Kingdom of Poland— and in 1899 of Lithuania (SDKPiL) as well. Its founders and leaders, Rosa Luxemburg, Julian Marchlewski (Karski), Leo Jogiches, Felix Dzerzinski, and Adolf Warski, subordinated the national problem to the battle for world revolution and held that Polish socialists should not strive for their country's independence but for revolution in Russia, which, when accomplished, would allow Poland its autonomy within a free Russia. Though the Polish Social Democrats clashed in heated debates with Lenin about the nationality question, because he regarded the slogan of national self-determination as an immensely powerful weapon in the battle for power, they always had especially close relations with the Bolsheviks and were an autonomous part of the Russian Social Democratic movement. This special relationship was also partially due to the fact that the SDKPiL's activities were restricted to the Russian-controlled "Congress Poland."[127]

However, by far the strongest radical force among the Poles living in the three empires was not Rosa Luxemburg's group but the Socialists, the PPS, whose program and propaganda were openly and strongly nationalistic. The Socialist Party was also torn by factional fights between a nationalist right, a Marxist left wing, and a center wavering between the two extremes. The nationalist branch was headed by Jozef Pilsudski, who formally left the PPS in 1916, became the first head of state of independent Poland and subsequently for nine years the absolute ruler of the country. The bulk of the socialists however refused to follow him, and the PPS remained in opposition.

After the Russian Revolution, the Luxemburg wing (SDKPiL) and the left wing of the Polish Socialist Party merged and in December 1918 founded the Polish Communist Party (KPP). From the very beginning the Communists placed themselves outside the mainstream of national life. During the war with Russia (1919–21) Polish workers and peasants, instead of embarking upon the creation of a dictatorship of the proletariat, enthusiastically participated in the fight against the Soviet forces that had set out to liberate them in the name of "proletarian internationalism." The military disaster suffered by the Red Army also meant the kiss of death for the Polish Communists who had cooperated with the traditional enemy, Russia. The KPP was banned after Pilsudski's victory and remained in the underground for a quarter of a century.

Thus there was an almost institutional division between those socialists to whom liberation of the nation came first and those who were dedicated to internationalism. But the birth of the new Poland, whose survival was a function of the relations between its two powerful and rapacious neighbors, Russia and Germany, presented the vexed national question in a different form. Where the Poles themselves had been under the tutelage of the Russian, German, and Austro-Hungarian Empires before, so now five million Ukrainians, a million and a half Belorussians, and a million Germans came under Polish rule. If the more than three million Polish Jews were added to these, it could be said that about 30 per cent of the total population consisted of minorities and "alien" elements. During the entire interwar period, nationalism, heightened by the traditional hatred of Russia, proved a stronger force than social discontent.

Because it belonged to the Comintern, the instrument of old-fashioned Russian imperialism, the Polish Communist Party represented a line diametrically opposed to the country's national interest and was almost universally regarded as intrinsically "anti-Polish." Its branch organizations in the Western Ukraine and Belorussia were always much stronger than those in ethnically Polish areas, and an excessively high percentage of its key personnel and activists was Ukrainian, Belorussian, German—or Jewish. That the Party was much more influential among the minorities than among the Poles and that it held virtually no attraction for the Polish intelligentsia is openly admitted by the present-day Communist regime.

This is not the place to go into the origins of the almost permanent political and economic crisis in interwar Poland. Suffice it to say that all Poles were united in their determination to protect national independence. On everything else they were divided by the personal rivalries and scrabble for lucrative jobs between the followers of Pilsudski and Dmowski, the two men with the greatest influence on twentieth-century Polish history.[128]

The die was cast in May 1926 when Marshal Pilsudski with the help of the Army marched on Warsaw, executed a successful coup d'état, and overthrew the parliamentary democracy. Not only the Army, however, but the entire left from the PPS to the Communists placed their hopes on Pilsudski. Once installed, Pilsudski abandoned his leftist supporters, made peace with the industrialists and big landowners, and installed a regime of social conservativism and political authoritarianism. After his death in 1935 the "Government of the Colonels," the dead dictator's lieutenants, took over and tightened political repression. As the years passed, the difference between the followers of Pilsudski and Dmowski dwindled away, and it was sheer opportunism that tipped the balance in favor of one or the other rightist groups. The "Camp of National Unity" set up in 1937 became the chief bulwark of the semidictatorial regime, rallying the nation around the Army, nationalism, and Catholicism.[129]

The May coup had a shattering impact on the small clandestine

Communist Party, which had supported Pilsudski as the lesser evil. The Marshal's subsequent quick turn to the right was the spark that brought the accumulated tinder of intrigues between the different Party factions to the point of explosion, dividing the Party into a "majority" and a "minority" faction. Meanwhile, Stalin's victory over the opposition in Moscow caused a series of political earthquakes in the Comintern that spread to each of the Communist Parties, including the KPP. The factional squabbles and the liquidation of Bucharin's "right" opposition in Moscow led to the ousting in Warsaw of the "majoritarians" headed by Warski, Walecki, and Wera Kostrzewa and the installation of the leftist critics of the "May error," the "minority" led by Lenski, in the leadership.[130]

The interwar history of the Polish Communist Party had virtually no significance in terms of Polish national history. But it is important to keep in mind two facts: the Jews were vastly overrepresented in the upper and middle ranks of the Party apparatus, but they did not form a cohesive group *as Jews* in any meaningful sense of the term. They were as involved as everyone else in the factional battles. The leader of the "majoritarians," Warski, was Jewish, and so was his bitter opponent and successor as head of the Party, Lenski.* It is equally wrong to see in "Luxemburgism," that is the subordination of Polish national interests to the cause of world revolution and the vision of international brotherhood, something specifically Jewish. Such "Aryan" leaders as Marchlewski or Dzierzinski were as unbendingly doctrinaire internationalists as the Jewish Rosa Luxemburg. It was after all Dzierzinski who appealed to Lenin in 1917 to incorporate Poland into Soviet Russia, and it was Lenin who time and again warned his Polish comrades (non-Jews and Jews alike) not to overlook the national aspirations of their native country.[131] All this was amply documented in Russian and Polish Party documents at a time when no Communist historian would have dreamed of depicting the revolutionaries of interwar Poland as "petty bourgeois Jews, insensitive to the problems of Polish patriotism."[132]

When today the Communist press accuses "world Zionism" of having "fought" for the secession of Silesia from Poland, it is im-

* In the meantime I have been told by a former member of the Central Committee that, contrary to the above, Lenski was not a Jew, albeit it is true that there were many Jews in his faction.

portant to recall that this demand figured in the program of only one group in Poland—that of the Communist Party between 1928 and 1932 before Hitler's seizure of power in Germany. And these policies, emanating from the Comintern in Moscow, were the same as the respective slogans of the Yugoslav and Rumanian Communists.

This does not of course change the fact that the accusations of the Polish right against the "Judeo-communism" contained an element of truth. While only a tiny fraction of the Polish Jews participated actively in the Communist movement, the percentage of Jews in Party membership was two and a half times, and at the policy-making level five times, as high as the percentage of Jews in the total population.[133] Less is said nowadays about an equally important fact: the excessively high number of Jews among the Polish Communists massacred by Stalin during his Great Purge.

Because of the special role played by the Poles in Soviet Russia (to some degree comparable with that played by the Irish in England),[134] no other foreign Party had to suffer such heavy casualties. During the entire interwar period, the KPP could not claim that more than two or three dozen members had been executed by the Polish Government for high treason.[135] In the fatherland of the proletariat however, according to some accounts, a total of fifty thousand Poles was shot at the height of the terror. From 1937 to 1939 all twelve members of the Central Committee residing in Moscow and several hundred others were executed. The erstwhile "majoritarians" and "minoritarians," the veteran Warski and Wera Kostrzewa, Lenski and Walecki were shot.[136] As a Polish leader remarked in 1956: "Almost all the leaders and active members of the KPP then in the Soviet Union were arrested and sent to camps." In 1938 came the last blow, the dissolution of the entire KPP, an event unprecedented in the annals of international Communism. The Party was dissolved, Manuilsky, the Comintern delegate to the Eighteenth Soviet Party Congress, succinctly declared, because "agents of Polish fascism managed to gain positions of leadership" in it. While this extraordinary measure may actually have been a preliminary move to forestall opposition to the forthcoming Nazi-Soviet Pact, the circumstances surrounding it are still shrouded in secrecy.[137]

A year later Stalin and Hitler in the secret protocols of their agreement once again divided Poland. Seldom have Soviet statesmen so candidly declared themselves the heirs to Tsarist expansion as Molotov did in his statement at the session of the Supreme Soviet on October 31, 1939: ". . . one swift blow to Poland, first by the German and then by the Red Army, and nothing was left of this ugly offspring of the Versailles Treaty."[138]

Soviet participation in the destruction of the Polish state and the subsequent occupation of Eastern Poland have left an indelible imprint on Polish attitudes toward the Soviet neighbor. The country's population losses were due to both Nazi and Soviet extermination policies. It is not known how many hundreds of thousands (some estimates speak of one and a half million) of Poles were deported to the Soviet Union who never returned. And to these must be added the ten thousand Polish officers killed by the Russians at Katyn and elsewhere.[139]

The few Communist functionaries in Poland who were not important enough to be invited for "consultation"—and subsequent execution—in Moscow, or who had the luck to be kept in Polish jails like Gomulka, survived the Great Purge. After the end of the hostilities most of them moved to Soviet-occupied Eastern Poland. For twenty-six months after the destruction of Poland, the Communists did not step forward as an independent political force at all. The first Communist paper appeared five months after the beginning of the war between Germany and Soviet Russia.[140] As everywhere, it was the Nazi invasion of Russia that overnight turned the "second imperialist war" into the "great fatherland war" and opened a new chapter in the history of the Communist Parties.

In contrast to the situation prevailing in other East European Communist Parties, the division between the "home-grown" Polish Communists, those who fought on home territory, and the "Muscovites," those who spent most of World War II in the Soviet Union, was institutionalized as early as 1942. In that year the Communists who remained in occupied Poland founded the Polish

Workers' Party (PPR), now officially described as "a national
Party par excellence." By this time most of the Jewish Party members had either perished or managed to escape to the Soviet Union.
From the very beginning, Stalin always mistrusted any Communist
group that was not under his direct supervision. At the same time,
the home Communists harbored a sense of resentment against
the Muscovites, whom they regarded as little more than the stooges
of Stalin. Moreover, there were personal and tactical differences
of opinion both within the small Communist underground and
with the emissaries sent from Moscow.

As a matter of fact it was not Gomulka, but one of the emissaries from Moscow, Marcel Nowotko, who in January 1942
founded the new Party. Gomulka did not report at the new leadership until July. The early history of the PPR was marked by several mysterious events. Nowotko, the first Party chief, was
assassinated in November—not by the Germans, but by another
Soviet agent. The assassin was not tried before a "Party tribunal"
as *Trybuna Ludu* twenty years later euphemistically reported, but
shot in accordance with the general rule of Stalin's purges: killers
and dangerous witnesses must be liquidated. Pawel Finder, another
emissary from Moscow and a Jew, became the new Party leader.

In the meantime, relations between Stalin and the Polish Government in exile became progressively worse and the dictator
began to assemble the surviving Polish Communists from the
Siberian camps, Central Asia, and the foreign-language section
of Radio Moscow. In the spring of 1943, the Union of Polish
Patriots was set up. Soon afterward the discovery of the mass grave
of murdered Polish officers at Katyn led to the severance of relations between the Government in exile in London and Moscow.
Stalin immediately ordered the formation of the first Polish detachment under Communist leadership; by May the Kosciusko Division under General Berling was set up, and in June the first
congress of the Union of Polish Patriots was held.

The Katyn affair caused a complete rupture between the non-
Communist and the Communist underground in Poland. The
creation of a rival Communist organization in Moscow could only

sharpen the mutual suspicion between the two groups. Then, in that turbulent and confusing period, another mysterious event took place. In the autumn of 1943 Finder, the Party leader, and another member of the Central Committee were caught and executed by the Gestapo under circumstances that have never been fully clarified. It is generally agreed that they were the victims of an informer. During this crucial period, radio contacts with Moscow were temporarily cut off. Before the arrival of the new contact man (Boleslaw Bierut), the underground Party on its own, without prior approval of the Soviet command center, elected Gomulka Secretary General.[141]

The composition of the two groups—the PPR in occupied Poland and the Patriots' Union in Moscow—was startlingly different. The first consisted mainly of second-tier functionaries, among them very few Jews, while in the leadership of the Union, which also included left-wing socialists, and in the political apparatus of the Berling Army, there was a disproportionately strong Jewish element. Thus the deep sense of frustration among many (but by no means all) "native" Communists against the Muscovites was tinged very early with latent but powerful anti-Semitic resentments.

In all the later Communist countries, there were psychological, organizational, and tactical differences between the "native" Communists and the "Muscovites." But there were two special cases: Yugoslavia, where Tito's Partisans first instinctively and later deliberately opposed Stalin's grand design and seized power in a civil war against the advice and without the approval of Moscow; and Poland. Here Stalin had important strategic, geographic, and political interests at stake and was, not without reason, suspicious of the leaders of the new workers' Party, the PPR, who were not "professional revolutionaries" of the Stalinist school. His candidate for the supreme leadership was Boleslaw Bierut, a Moscow-trained Polish Communist and a veteran agent of the NKVD, the Soviet secret police. Bierut was dropped into occupied Poland by parachute in late 1943. It was he who founded and became president of the Communist-sponsored National Council of Poland, set up on December 31, 1943, on the eve of the Red Army's crossing the prewar Soviet-Polish border.

The tensions between the home Communists and the Muscovites were superseded, if only temporarily, in July 1944 when the PPR and the Soviet-sponsored Union of Polish Patriots combined to set up in Lublin the Polish Committee of National Liberation, the nucleus of the future Communist Government. Though it is beyond the scope of this survey to describe the road to ultimate power, which basically was the same as elsewhere in Soviet-occupied Eastern Europe, it is important to remember one very great difference between Poland and the rest of the Soviet zone of interest (with the exception of Yugoslavia)—a difference that exerted a belated but enormously significant influence on the factional struggles in the 1960s.

In contrast to the Communists in Rumania, Hungary, and Czechoslovakia, the Polish Communists could not pose as liberators and could not claim any monopoly of patriotism. In Poland all parties had joined the anti-Nazi resistance movement. It was the Home Army (usually called AK—Armia Krajowa) that, with the exception of the extreme right-wing (NSZ) and Communist groups, comprised the entire armed resistance of the nation and was subject to the Government in exile in London. By the middle of 1944, Home Army units claimed to number over three hundred thousand men. In contrast, the Communist Partisans (who called their groups first the People's Guard and later the People's Army) were all along very weak. During the Warsaw uprising in August 1944, for example, they managed to mobilize in all five hundred men, while the Home Army in the capital produced forty-six thousand fighters.[142] (These figures appear to be closer to the truth about the actual strength of the Communist Partisans than the wildly exaggerated accounts published nowadays by Moczar's "Partisans.")

Though the Soviet Army at that time held a bridgehead on the western bank of the Vistula, Stalin refused to give any assistance to the insurgents, who after six weeks of heroic fighting capitulated; he even vetoed any idea of Western planes using the Soviet bases.

It is estimated that the failure of the uprising cost Poland at least two hundred thousand victims from "among its most politically active non-Communist element, and destroyed the organizing center of the most numerous and powerful resistance movement in Europe."[143] Soviet inactivity during the Warsaw uprising may also have intensified Polish hostility to the "Soviet liberators," but Stalin doubtless never had any illusions about this. What mattered to him was the destruction of the non-Communist resistance movement, the potential basis of a future government, and the opening of the access to power for his Lublin Committee of National Liberation. And there can be no doubt whatever that his tactics yielded tangible benefits.

Nevertheless, the Communists, united in the pursuit of the seizure of power but divided on the tactical level, had to break armed resistance more prolonged and intense than in any other Soviet-occupied country. Between 1945 and 1948, the Communists lost about thirty thousand militiamen and activists in armed clashes with the anti-Communist underground.[144] At the same time the Communist rulers in Poland had to bid higher for national sentiments than elsewhere.[145] By moving the new Poland's western frontiers one hundred and fifty miles west to the Oder-Neisse line, Stalin carried out a political masterstroke of European significance: he forced all future Polish governments to remain faithful to the Russian alliance for "reasons of state." At the same time, however, the expulsion of the Germans from the west and the loss of the non-Polish population in the east (which now belonged to Soviet Russia) for the first time gave Poland ethnic homogeneity; it became "a Poland for Poles only."

This not only lent added importance to the external national trappings of a Communist dictatorship basically as subservient to Moscow as all the others, but also made the tiny remnant of the prewar Jewish community more visible than ever before. Proportionately speaking, there were more Communists and left-wingers among the fifty to eighty thousand Jews[146] in the early postwar years than among the millions of Poles. The Jews, regardless of political commitment, were grateful to the Red Army for having saved their lives, while the Poles, including many members of the Communist underground, could not forget or forgive the carving up of their country by Hitler and Stalin, the deportations, the Katyn massacre, Soviet inaction during the Warsaw uprising, and the looting, raping, and other dangerous antics of the Russians who came as "liberators" but behaved as conquerors.

The Party's membership jumped from 20,000 in mid-1944 and 30,000 in January 1945 to 235,000 by December 1945; more than doubled to 535,000 a year later and reached 954,000 in 1948 (after the merger with the socialists, in December 1948, total membership was nearly one and a half million). The key positions in the Party and state apparatus, the security police and the Army, as well as important ministries had to be staffed by reliable, trained activists. And among the Muscovite old Communists and in the ranks of the Soviet-sponsored Berling Army, there were many Jews who were now promoted to "sensitive" posts. Those assimilated Jewish intellectuals and craftsmen, workers and merchants who, for whatever reason, chose to remain in Poland, could make a living only by entering the rank of the bureaucracy. But it was all along the visibility and not the actual number of Jews in top and middle echelon positions that mattered. One should keep in mind that of sixty-four thousand government employees in prewar Warsaw less than 2 per cent were Jews,[147] and these only in minor positions.

Against the background of ruins and hunger, Russian occupation and the dismantling of factories, the sudden emergence of Jews as rulers over an ethnically united Polish nation engendered a sharp and dangerous increase in anti-Semitism. Despite the efforts to make concessions to national sentiments, the presence of three Jews in the top leadership—Jakub Berman (in charge of secret police and propaganda), Hilary Minc (the economic overlord), and Roman Zambrowski (secretary of the Central Committee), and many more in prominent or second-level posts seemed to bear out the old stereotype "of all Jews being Communist and all Communists being Jews." While it is still a hotly disputed matter as to which anti-Jewish outrage was instigated by low-ranking Communist bureaucrats and which by the anti-Communist Opposition, the pogroms of Cracow and Kielce and many other cases of violence were undeniable facts and a frightening indication of simmering hatred for the Jews. It was estimated that by April 1946, over eight hundred Jews had been killed, and the subsequent pogrom in Kielce alone took forty-one Jewish victims.[148] Regardless of the collusion of the militia and some local Communist officials with the mobs, anti-Semitism in those days was part of the political struggle against the Communists and an expression of national defiance.[149]

The Catholic Church was as silent and as "neutral" during and after the outbursts of anti-Jewish violence in the 1940s as during the "anti-Zionist" campaign in 1967–68. Cardinal Hlond had not changed his opinion expressed in his 1936 pastoral letters calling for an economic boycott of Jewish shops and defining the Jews as "freethinkers (who) constitute the vanguard of atheism, Bolshevism, and revolution."[150] In 1946 after the pogroms he refused to issue a pastoral letter condemning anti-Semitism. Finally, after the pogrom in Kielce and the repeated pleas of the United States ambassador, he published a statement which described the pogroms as a "painful event" and blamed "the Jews in the Government for creating animosities" leading to such events. The deterioration of the friendship between Poles and Jews was, he said, "to a great degree due to the Jews who today occupy leading positions in the Polish Government and endeavor to introduce a government structure that a majority of Poles do not wish." A number of other Church dignitaries and even one anti-Communist Socialist deputy in Parliament agreed that the growth of anti-Semitism was "a reaction to Jewish behavior."[151]

The argument of "Jewish behavior" was of course an ancient device to rationalize traditional Jew-baiting. Yet Cardinal Hlond and the others spoke the truth when they pointed out the political role played by the Jews as a group. That the masses vented their fury upon the poor Jewish settlers in Silesia and Jewish artisans rather than upon the "court Jews" was secondary to the chief political fact: all Jews were seen as—and many of them really were —instruments of Soviet domination.

Meanwhile the brief period from 1945 to 1948 was marked by an uneasy coexistence between the home Communists and the Muscovites. The "natives" held important positions. In addition to remaining Secretary General, Gomulka was also deputy Prime Minister; Spychalski, Vice-Minister of Defense; Kliszko, chief of the personnel department, and Wladyslaw Bienkowski, head of the educational department. In 1948 the satellite countries began to undergo a transition from tolerated diversity to enforced uniformity. In the wake of his conflict with Tito, Stalin unleashed purges against most of the native Communist leaders who had fought in the undergrounds of their countries.

It was in the context of these bloc-wide purges, that Bierut and his Muscovite collaborators finally won the struggle for power against those whom they regarded as "radishes" (that is, red only on the outside), they themselves being "beetroots" (red all the way through). At the Central Committee meeting of August 31 –September 3, 1948, Bierut in a lengthy indictment accused his rival of "rightist nationalist deviation" in his attitude to the Soviet Union. Gomulka duly exercised self-criticism and resigned as Secretary General; Bienkowski was expelled from the Central Committee, while four other home Communists, including Moczar, were demoted from full to alternate members. In contrast to the Rajk and the Kostov affairs, three years elapsed between Gomulka's public disgrace and his arrest: in November 1949 the charges were escalated, he was accused of "tolerating spies, former Trotskyites and nationalists" in the Party ranks and in the ministries and even of being responsible for the deaths of his predecessors, Nowotko and Finder. This time however Gomulka defended himself and denied the accusations. He was expelled from the Party together with Spychalski and Kliszko, and in July 1951 placed under house arrest.

While the Hungarian, Rajk, was a pure and simple scapegoat, who never represented anything remotely comparable to a national platform, the original charges against Gomulka, however twisted, were not completely invented. Even when Stalin changed the tune and demanded open and complete subservience, Gomulka, despite his attendance at long ideological courses in the mid-thirties in Moscow, was not "Bolshevized" enough to recognize the qualitative change of the general line and had insisted on dancing to the popular tune of a "Polish way to socialism." What however in the period of diversity was "correct," even obligatory, now became the serious deviation of "denying the universal significance of the Soviet experience."[152]

Gomulka was never a "revisionist" or a "Titoist." But he regarded himself as a Polish Communist with equal emphasis on both words; he wanted a close alliance with Moscow, coupled with a degree of internal autonomy in accordance with Polish conditions. The root cause of all the trouble was that Gomulka had chosen the wrong Party when in 1927 at the age of twenty-two he joined the Communists. His subsequent speeches many years later confirm the impression that his real home was the PPS to which he had belonged for five years before joining the Communist movement. It was patriotic and pragmatic socialism of the PPS brand that shaped his thinking, while he repeatedly (both in 1945 and 1948) criticized the prewar Communists for their "Luxemburgist heritage," their "national nihilism" and doctrinaire disregard of the peasant problem.[153]

It was symbolic that the same Central Committee meeting that expelled Gomulka, Spychalski, and Kliszko from its ranks in 1949, also "admitted" the Soviet Marshal Konstantin Rokossovsky as member of the CC and later of the Politburo. For seven years this Soviet officer was the Minister of Defense in formally independent Poland, directly responsible only to the Soviet High Command and independent of any Polish control. He was assisted by numerous Soviet officers, who commanded all the major branches of the armed forces. The second key lever of power, the Ministry of State Security, was also firmly in the hands of the Soviets. Stanislaw Radkiewicz, an old NKVD hand, the "Polish Beria," was a full member of the Politburo. He had Soviet officers as his personal guard, rarely reported to his colleagues in the Politburo, and was "advised" by General Lalin from the Soviet Security Ministry. In the Polish ministry itself, of twenty departments eight were headed by Soviet officers directly and three had Soviet "advisers."[154]

It is fair to say that as far as key political issues were concerned it was Stalin and not the twelve members of the Politburo who ruled Poland. Within these limits, Boleslaw Bierut was clearly the Number One man, and he added to his post as Party leader first the Presidency and (from 1952 after that office was abolished) the Premiership. His closest collaborators were Berman and Minc, both of Jewish origin. Including Zambrowski, there were thus three Jews among the twelve Politburo members. They were no more and no less zealous in executing Moscow's orders than the non-Jewish Zenon Nowak, Franciszek Mazur, Edward Ochab, or Francisek Jozwiak. The role of the last incidentally shows that the division between "natives" and "Muscovites" was never a completely clear-cut matter. Jozwiak was a genuine home Communist who had been Chief of Staff of the People's Army, yet he played a significant role in the liquidation of the Gomulka group.

Stalin always preferred multiple lines of control in each satellite country. He trusted Bierut, but had Marshal Rokossovsky to watch over the Army, General Lalin and others to control the secret police. Berman headed the Politburo commission on security, yet even as late as 1956 Politburo member Mazur was considered to be in the service of the MVD (the successor of the NKVD).[155] Even this cursory review of the direct and remote control system under the era of Stalinism shows how absurd are the charges saddling the three Jewish Politburo members and the Jewish functionaries with the sole responsibility for the horrors of Polish Stalinism.

Yet had there been no Jews in the Polish leadership, would the Stalinist terror system have been any different? "Perhaps the shape of its nose," as a Polish writer sarcastically remarked. The terror in Bulgaria (or even in Yugoslavia until 1950) was as bad, in fact even worse than in Poland. There was another significant point. It was only in Poland that "a rightist nationalist leader" charged with actions bordering on treason was not put in the dock at a show trial and executed. All students of Polish Communist history agree that the Politburo's refusal to try and execute Gomulka and his collaborators was a gesture unparalleled in other Communist countries. To the repeated proddings from Moscow, Bierut, Berman, and the other Polish leaders answered evasively that evidence was still being collected and that the trial would come in due time. It is easier to explain why the Poles resisted Stalin's pressures than to provide a clue as to how they managed to get away with sabotaging Stalin's orders. The resistance was certainly due to the traumatic memories of the dissolution of the KPP and the wholesale execution of almost all of its leaders; perhaps also to the very weakness of the "healthy core" in the Party. At any rate, even at the historic October 1956 plenum, no Central Committee member disputed Berman's account claiming credit (with the Politburo) for having saved Gomulka's life.[156]

If we add to the absence of Communist show trials such facts as the relatively slow pace of agricultural collectivization and the much later though brutal start of the persecution of the Catholic Church, then the conclusion can only be that Stalinism in Poland was "milder" than in Czechoslovakia, Hungary, or Bulgaria. But as the crisis year of 1956 revealed, this purely relative "mildness" was meager consolation for a suppressed, humiliated, and exploited nation. Next to Rumania, Poland may have suffered the most from colonial exploitation by Moscow. The losses in coal exports to the Soviet Union alone by 1956 amounted to half a billion dollars, and total Soviet gains through exploitation are estimated to have reached two billion dollars between 1945 and 1956.[157]

Even during the heyday of Stalinism, the Polish Communist Party was never a monolith but rather a web of interest groups. The multiple and often contradictory crosscurrents within the Party surfaced during the prolonged crisis of 1956, whose origins go back to 1954, when Radio Free Europe began to broadcast the sensational revelations of a former high security official, Jozef Swiatlo, who had defected to the West in December 1953. His broadcasts about the luxurious life of the new ruling class, the mechanism of the terror system and the bestiality of the secret police (to which Swiatlo himself had contributed!) forced the Party leaders to curb the police, release Gomulka quietly from prison in April 1955, abolish the Ministry of State Security, dismiss Radkiewicz, and put on trial some of the sadistic interrogators.

But it was the Twentieth Soviet Party Congress with Khrushchev's de-Stalinization campaign, the almost simultaneous death of Bierut, the subsequent fight for succession and the Poznan riots in June that combined to bring the growing tensions to the point of explosion. There has long been a legend that Gomulka's return to power in October 1956 marked the triumph of a liberal leader at the head of the "revisionists" against the bitter opposition of pro-Soviet "Stalinists." The situation however during the troubled summer and autumn of 1956 was much more complex than these deceptively simple labels would indicate.

The outward solidarity of the men who had held the stage for over a decade was split first by the struggle for power after Bierut's death and then by the impact of the Poznan riots. Division in the leadership and demoralization in the Party against the backdrop of the general disintegration of Stalinism led to the calculated stirring up of anti-Semitism from above and the resurgence of anti-Jewish resentment from below. What was before shrouded in silence now came out into the open—both at the top and among the general public.

It all started with Khrushchev, who flew personally to Warsaw to supervise the selection of Bierut's successor. He vetoed Roman Zambrowski, the Politburo's choice for the post of the First Secretary, primarily because the latter was a Jew and "you have already too many Abramoviches." Finally a compromise was reached with the election of Edward Ochab, a non-Jew, a Muscovite, and supposedly a reliable Stalinist. By the July plenum of the Central Committee, the Poznan riots and their aftermath had made the split within the Central Committee overt and institutionalized. There were two main factions—and over both hovered the shadow of Gomulka's alternate team, the former underground leaders, released but not yet fully rehabilitated and held in popular esteem for having been victimized as "nationalists" by Stalin and his Polish stooges.

Faced with growing pressure from dissatisfied workers and progressive intellectuals, the two main groups—the so-called "Pulawska" and "Natolin"—advocated different approaches. The Pulawska men (named after the street in a residential suburb where most of the Muscovites lived), out of disillusionment, opportunism, and fear for the fate of the regime, pleaded for bold reforms. At the July plenum some of them at first even dissociated themselves from Gomulka's alleged nationalism. The previous triumvirate of Bierut, Berman, and Minc, as well as Zambrowski and all the Jews belonged to this group. But it was not in any way a "Jewish group" as such. None of the "young secretaries" of the Central Committee and "Pulawska men," were for example Jews. But the fact that the rival Natolin group (Natolin is a villa near Warsaw where this faction held its meetings) was "racially pure," mainly of peasant stock and proletarian origin, meant that it could afford the luxury of anti-Semitism. These men, headed by two Muscovite Politburo members, Zenon Nowak and Franciszek Mazur, were openly pro-Soviet and wanted to restore order and discipline by a combination of strong-arm methods and demagogic devices such as a 50 per cent wage increase. At the same time they were the first to come out in favor of Gomulka's inclusion in the Politburo—as a much needed symbol, of course, rather than as supreme decision-maker.[158]

One cannot neatly divide the two factions according to their ideological positions, nor is it possible here to go into a detailed summary of the issues that divided them—and frequently caused internal dissensions within the two groups as well. It must suffice to say that the most hotly debated topics were the character of Soviet-Polish relations, the reinterpretation of the past, and Gomulka's future role. During the Stalin era, both the pro-Soviet "dogmatists" and those who later became genuine or opportunistic converts to liberalism held power; what had always divided them was the issue of anti-Semitism. It may be an indication of the level at which the factional battle for power was fought, that the

Natolinists liked to call their opponents "Yids," while the latter in turn referred to them as "boors."[159]

The death of Bierut, Khrushchev's veto against Zambrowski on account of his Jewish origin and the resignation of Berman, the "gray eminence" of the Stalin era, induced the Natolin group to play the card of anti-Semitism to gain popular support and to lay a smoke screen over its subservience to the Kremlin. In the summer of 1956 the Natolinists seized on the fact that both the main culprits in the excesses of the past (Berman and Minc) as well as some of the leading moderates among the leadership had been Jews; they launched an open campaign to channel hatred for Communism (and the Russians) into hatred for Jews. Thus at the July plenum of the Central Committee, Zenon Nowak, deputy Premier and Politburo member, proposed a "national regulation" limiting the number of Jews in responsible posts. After rattling off statistics about the proportion of Jews in prominent positions, Nowak assured his listeners that he, of course, was not an anti-Semite at all; it was only that the "Party's personnel policy has often stimulated anti-Semitism." From that time on, however, the Natolin faction used barely veiled anti-Semitic and anti-intellectual slogans—at public rallies as well as in closed meetings—to divert popular discontent and weaken the reformers.

It should not be forgotten that the very size of the Party made it rely on an apparatus that at its lower and middle echelons was permeated not only with "petty-bourgeois and nationalistic" but also with religious and traditional anti-Semitic sentiments. There was a resurgence of folk anti-Semitism reflected in the beating of children whose parents were atheists, in the desecration of Jewish cemeteries, in a flood of anti-Semitic readers' letters to the papers, and the intimidation of Jewish workers and artisans. Kolakowski and a number of prominent public figures warned against the upsurge of a deliberately instigated anti-Semitism which went beyond the threshold of the Party offices. As an article in *Nowe Drogi,* the Party's theoretical monthly for June 1956 noted: "It is not only the anti-Semitic excesses that give cause for concern but also the reaction to them, the obvious moral indifference of our central apparatus and even of some party authorities." Other papers stressed that there was a calculated plan carried out by the Stalinist center to awaken anti-Semitism.[160] At a conference of activists of the Warsaw Voivodship Party committee, several speakers demanded that persons of Jewish origin discard their Polonized family names in order to facilitate their identification. At another Party meeting in Lodz, Ochab received a piece of paper on which an anonymous participant asked, "Why are the best posts in the government and Party apparatus occupied by Jews?"[161]

Thus anti-Semitism, as Gomulka himself later confirmed, was a major and overt political issue already in 1956, before and during the October upheaval. Speaking about the divisions among the former leadership and appointments to leading posts, he remarked: "Some comrades approached this problem in a very simplified way, which could be taken for anti-Semitism."[162] Moreover, the resolution adopted at the plenum which elected Gomulka First Secretary stressed: "The Party condemns . . . manifestations of discrimination against any group of the population because of their origin which tend to foster anti-Semitism and other nationalistic trends that are alien to the Party ideology and demoralize the Party cadres."[163]

Neither the issue of anti-Semitism nor the issue of Polish nationalism was really resolved in October 1956, but both were temporarily pushed below the surface. The attempt to use anti-Semitism as the chief political weapon was a fiasco. The reason was not that racial hatred lacked appeal but that it was recognized as essentially a pro-Soviet device. It was the upsurge of anti-Russian feelings that tipped the balance in favor of the liberals and authentic revisionists. Since the Natolin group had by October become a discredited tool of the Kremlin, Gomulka, who had been approached by both factions, finally allied himself with the Pulawska group. One might add that neither Gomulka nor the Pulawska group was anti-Soviet; what they both wanted was internal autonomy in the context of a close but more equal alliance with the Soviet Union, which was, after all, the chief protector of Poland's Oder-Neisse frontier.

Notwithstanding the carefully fostered myth, Gomulka was the symbol rather than the creator of the "Polish October," and the "Polish October" was a negation rather than a product of the spirit of 1956.[164] Relying on his popularity as a victim of Stalinism and "the man who stood up to Moscow," and also on his control of the Army and the secret police, Gomulka soon began to direct blows at his former allies, to stop the purge of the Natolinists, to play off one group against the other, and thus to consolidate his hold on the Party apparat. Gomulka, born in 1905, was a professional Party apparatchik of proletarian origin. He was never a liberal, but rather a self-taught professional, deeply devoted to the Party's monopoly of power, mistrustful of intellectuals, and suspicious of any reforms that might weaken the Communist grip on Poland. Understandably enough, Gomulka never felt any loyalty, let alone friendship, for the Pulawska group, his temporary allies. After all, these were the very men who had attacked and toppled him in the 1940s with the same single-minded dedication and enthusiasm with which they praised and welcomed him in 1956.

What, then, did October bring? It produced a sense of real change, but in fact it marked the turning point from which the retreat began. The three greatest achievements of 1956 were: (1) the collapse of political terror, a profound difference in the political climate and style of life as a result of the restoration of personal security; (2) the end of agricultural collectivization; and (3) a modus vivendi with the Church. Yet all this had basically been achieved before Gomulka's return to power. The peak of liberalization and cultural ferment coincided with the greatest weakness of the political leadership as a result of discord at the very heart of the ruling group, with warring factions striving to win popular backing and thereby forced to make concessions.

As a keen Polish observer provocatively put it: "The masses endowed Gomulka with enormous trust just at the moment when his aim was to achieve maximum concentration of power in his hands and to utilize it for abolishing the reforms that had already been effected and of preventing any further reform. The masses attached great hopes to the coup, which was carried out only to disappoint these hopes . . ."[165]

As early as 1957–58, Gomulka firmly rejected institutional reforms such as the program for radical economic decentralization. He divested the workers' councils of all real power and clamped down on revisionist intellectuals and students by banning their influential organ, *Po Prostu*. Winning and retaining the confidence of Khrushchev, Gomulka gradually brought into the Politburo his fellow victims (Kliszko, the ideologist, Loga-Sowinski, the trade union leader, and Spychalski, the Minister of Defense) while eliminating one by one the genuine reformers and the most uncompromising Stalinists.

The turning point came in 1959, when he answered both the growing popular dissatisfaction in the wake of a meat crisis (just as occurred later in 1967) and the uproar caused by the defection of Pawel Monat, the chief of the military intelligence (and a Jew), with a general tightening of the reins. His old comrade-in-arms, the moderate Minister of Culture, Bienkowski, and such "liberals" as Morawski, Matwin, and Albrecht (secretaries of the Central Committee) were replaced by former Stalinists who took over the key posts in the Army, the Ministry of Interior, and the state security service. This marked the beginning of the rise of the "Partisans," the former underground fighters, who, after years in the political wilderness or behind bars, were eager to make a political comeback. The Partisans shared with the Natolin group a belief in discipline, a profound distrust of intellectuals, and, last but not least, anti-Semitic prejudices. However, in contrast to the Natolins, the Partisans had always been intensely nationalistic and therefore intrinsically anti-Soviet.

Even this simplified survey of the intricate connections among the diverse groups struggling for power in Poland should indicate how dangerously misleading the conventional distinction between "Stalinists" and the "men of October" is. In point of fact, both today's "liberals" and their opponents include former Stalinists, while the "Partisans" are made up of both hard-liners and former victims of Stalinism.

Over the years of his rule, Gomulka presented himself as the advocate of the "Party of order"—the upper and middle strata of the Party and state bureaucracies and the administrative and managerial class. Initially he presided over a strange coalition of his erstwhile adversaries from the Pulawska and Natolin group and a middle-of-the-road center composed of his personal followers. Gradually, as his rule became more autocratic, he eliminated his real and potential opponents, most of whom were moderates and ex-Stalinists-turned-liberals. Since many of these men—as well as some of the ablest and most articulate spokesmen of the genuinely reformist intelligentsia—happened also to be Jews, Gomulka's fight against the remnants of the "Polish October" was in a sense "a fight against the Jews." The net result was the almost total elimination of the former Pulawska group, whose leader, the Jewish Zambrowski, lost his seat in the Politburo in 1963.

Gomulka's system of an "enlightened absolutism," which seemingly bridged the abyss between the "real" and the "legal" country, was in fact a drift into political and economic stagnation, a patchwork of compromises without any long-term consideration of the real problems. The differences in the climate and political developments in, for example, Poland and Hungary since 1956 were to no small degree the reflection of the different personalities of the respective leaders: Gomulka and Kadar.*

Gomulka is indeed a patriot and an incorruptible man of integrity. But he is also an authoritarian orthodox Communist, whose formal education ended at the age of fourteen and whose view of the world and of what a "socialist" Poland should be has remained virtually unchanged since 1948.[166] Never tempted by luxury, he lived with his Jewish wife, Zofia, in a two-room apartment until a few years ago when they moved into a four-room house, whose construction was financed by the royalties from his book. His only son, Ryszard Strzelecki, an engineer and since 1969 Deputy Minister of Foreign Trade, lives in the house next door with his wife and two daughters. (Ryszard was hidden during the

* See also chapter on Hungary.

occupation by Strzelecki, now a secretary of the Central Committee, and therefore bears his name even today.)

Since his return to power, Gomulka has been living more and more in a self-imposed isolation from the realities of Polish life, relying increasingly on his closest colleagues, but he has become incapable of candid discussion even with them. His friend from the underground days, Wladyslaw Bienkowski, disgraced at the same time as he in 1948, became Minister of Culture in 1956. An able man of liberal views, Bienkowski tried to prevent Gomulka from sliding back into rigid dogmatism. His last face-to-face attempt in late 1959 ended with a furious Gomulka throwing a cup of tea at his head. The next day Bienkowski was dismissed as Minister (and in 1969 expelled from the Party for his sharp criticism of the "anti-Zionist" witch-hunt). When at a stormy Politburo meeting in mid-1963 Zambrowski protested against the brutal treatment of striking nurses, opposed the rise of coal prices, and warned against the increasing power of the security police, Gomulka in a fit of rage threw a chair at him. Zambrowski left the meeting, slammed the door, and never returned.

It is certain that Gomulka has never been consciously or "subjectively" an anti-Semite. But at an early date he is said to have expressed some apprehension about the "unhealthy national composition" of the Party. A former high officer of Polish intelligence told the author that the then Minister of State Security, S. Radkiewicz, in 1947, at a conference of the regional security chiefs, gave orders to open files about the Jewish officials in the secret police in order to replace them with ethnic Poles. When the officer, a hero of the underground and former associate of the Party leader, went to see Gomulka, the Secretary General said that he approved the minister's instructions and quoted Stalin who had told a Polish delegation that Poland should be ruled by Poles and not by Jews. Gomulka even added that one should take the Soviet Union, where only one Jew belonged to the Politburo, as an example.

More important however was the resentment Gomulka harbored against the Muscovites who had pushed him, the Secretary General of the underground Party, first into the background and then

226

into disgrace. By necessity he shared power after October with men like Zambrowski, who a few years earlier had signed the warrant for his arrest; Roman Werfel, who wrote a booklet against him while he was in the political wilderness; and Leon Kasman, Moscow's emissary who on Stalin's orders had rejected his repeated pleas for more weapons. That Zambrowski remained at the top until 1963 and Kasman in the chair of editor-in-chief of *Trybuna Ludu* until the end of 1967, did not mean that Gomulka had forgotten the past, but merely reflected his keen sense of political realism. Actually his closest friends all along have been his former associates from underground days, who are largely mediocrities.

Among these can be found the Number Two man of his regime, Zenon Kliszko, the so-called theorist. Kliszko, who before the war began to study law then tried his hand at poetry, is sarcastically described by Polish writers as a mediocre "quarter intellectual." His (and Gomulka's) real thoughts were expressed with startling clarity in 1966 in a speech at the Cracow meeting of Polish historians. Kliszko praised the patriotic spirit of the prewar Endeks (National Democrats), hinted at the "diabolic role" of Jewish intellectuals, and defined national integration as the gathering of patriots into one fold even if this involved for "some peoples" personal injustices or tragedies. As a Polish "Aryan" historian remarked of his lecture: "It exuded the spirit of two ghosts, one dead, the other living, Dmowski and Piasecki."*

By and large the Gomulka center wanted to build a Poland which was parochial and conservative, regular and disciplined; to mobilize support without arousing the ire of Moscow. But the Gomulka regime has never taken on the real problems. Output records in steel, power, coal, and shipbuilding can not hide the lack of sufficient incentives, the chronic shortages, proliferating absenteeism, thefts both small and enormous, the surplus of an estimated one million white-collar and manual workers,[167] and, above all, the urgent need for the modernization and moral reform of the entire state machinery. (In a country where two thirds of the

* Kliszko's lecture was so dangerously outspoken that its full text has never been published and he ordered the destruction of the tape recording.

population is under forty and the average age is twenty-seven, the members of the Politburo [before the last congress] were on the average sixty years old.) As a result, the political situation has deteriorated, and the bitter discontent of the younger bureaucrats, let alone of the masses, has increased steadily with the years.

The basic goal of the rising new groupings from the "right," which have stepped into the political arena, is to replace the decaying dynasty based on the personal dictatorship of Gomulka with a new, vigorous, and ruthlessly determined authoritarian regime. Whatever their personal and tactical differences, all hard-liners were disappointed over Gomulka's failure to carry out a drastic large-scale purge of Jews and liberals.

The most important and dynamic new factional group is the "Partisans," among whom, ironically, Gomulka and his closest friends might qualify as members, as might some of the most prominent non-Jewish victims of the "anti-Zionist" witch-hunt, who were genuine Partisans in occupied Poland. Today, however, the label is applied primarily to those second-tier functionaries and wartime subordinates of Gomulka who formed a tightly knit faction around General Moczar in the early 1960s.

A man of extraordinary drive and ambition, Mieczyslav Moczar has been called the "Polish Fouché" because of his tactical brilliance in building up a power base in the police apparatus. Born in 1913, he is (as is so often the case with rabid nationalists) not of Polish, but of Ukrainian origin and his original family name was Nikolai Demko. He joined the Communist movement in 1937, and in 1938 was arrested, accused of spying for the Russians, and kept in prison until the outbreak of the war.

In 1942 he became the commander of the Communist Partisan detachment operating in the regions of Lublin and Kielce. But despite what it says in his much publicized memoirs published in 1962, he never belonged to the general staff of the People's Army. Immediately after the war, he embarked on a professional career in the secret police. As early as January 1945, he was chief of Bezpieka, the dreaded security police in Lodz. In recognition of his services in this capacity he was promoted to Deputy Minister of State Security. During the 1948–49 purge he was degraded to candidate member of the Central Committee for "his conciliatory attitude toward rightist and nationalist deviation." The fact that his chief accuser was Zambrowski, a Muscovite and a Jew, may have injected an element of personal revenge into his anti-Semitic feelings.

Unlike Gomulka, he was never actually a victim. Throughout the worst period of Stalinism, he occupied the politically obscure but personally lucrative posts of the "voivod" (governor) of the regions of Olsztyn, Byalistok, and Warsaw respectively, and retained his candidate membership in the Central Committee. If it is true that in 1948 he defended Gomulka, then his subsequent political and personal survival is something of a mystery. Swiatlo, the defector, claimed that Moczar had been about to take over as Minister of State Security in 1951 before the arrest of Gomulka. During the period of political thaw, his slow political comeback was reflected in his appointment as Minister of State Farms (in April 1956) and his regaining full Central Committee membership at the July plenum.

During the stormy period leading to October and the return of Gomulka, Moczar prudently stayed in the background. Yet he must have enjoyed Gomulka's full confidence, since six weeks after Gomulka's election as First Secretary he was appointed Deputy Minister of Interior in charge of security matters.

By supervising Gomulka's briefing on security matters, Moczar managed to gain a growing influence over his views, and, more important, over his personal policies. The defection of Colonel Monat in 1959 and the Holland affair* in early 1962 enormously

* Henryk Holland, a Jewish intellectual and prewar Communist, was accused of espionage, when in fact he merely related Party gossip, including Khrushchev's alleged revelations about how Beria was murdered, to a French correspondent. After a forty-hour questioning by Moczar's agents, he was taken back to his house where he apparently jumped to his death. It is still a matter for conjecture whether Holland was murdered or committed suicide. But the fact that several hundred prewar Communists, including six Central Committee members, appeared at the funeral of this "suspected spy" was a stunning protest against growing police power.

strengthened his position in the police apparatus. At the end of 1964 he was promoted to the post of Minister of Interior.

During his twelve years of tenure at the Ministry of Interior, Moczar built up an almost unassailable position of power for himself and an impressive network of informers and a system of files on everybody who mattered in the country. He also managed to place trusted associates in key positions in the Army, the Foreign Service, and the mass media. Before every Party Congress rumors circulated about his becoming a member of the Politburo. But even after the removal of his hated enemy, Zambrowski, his bid was again and again thwarted.

Moczar was not initially the leader of a political faction, but a power-hungry state official. He needed a political platform and an organization to win the backing of the new middle class and to project himself as a patriot rather than a policeman. His ascension to the chairmanship of ZBOWiD, the veterans' organization, made him a political power, and under his leadership, the association of three hundred thousand members became a formidable pressure group. Its rehabilitation of non-Communist resistance fighters and the veterans who served with the Polish forces in the West—people who had been sent to prison after the war (many by Moczar!) —was an act of justice. But it also served as a launching pad for an exalted nationalism identified with the person of the Minister of Interior. ZBOWiD became a symbol of national unity and with its branch organizations all over the country a valuable political lever in the struggle for power.

The second organizational base and ideological "action program" was provided by Boleslaw Piasecki and his PAX movement. Piasecki regarded the expulsion of the Jews in 1937 as the necessary condition for building a single-party system within the framework of a new Catholicism stressing national goals and social equality. He was even then in favor of the nationalization of key industries and the maintenance of peasant ownership and small businesses.[168] During the war he was arrested first by the Gestapo, then by the NKVD, and managed to survive. Before the war he founded the green-shirt Falanga modeled on the German SA. After the war he unexpectedly emerged as the founder of the PAX society. Working simultaneously for the Russians and his own profit, Piasecki built up a strong pseudo-Catholic organization designed to split the Catholic Church and also amassed a commercial empire for himself. PAX currently publishes six dailies and periodicals, owns a publishing house which turned out twelve million books between 1959 and 1967, runs enterprises which manufacture a wide range of products from devotional articles to mustard, has a retailing outlet of fifty-six shops and can boast of over five thousand members in the movement.[169]

In 1956 Piasecki was an ally of the Natolin group and an unflinching opponent of Gomulka, but survived even this blunder because Gomulka was unwilling to divest himself of a blackmailing device for his on-and-off campaign against the Church. Piasecki and four other PAX representatives are members of the Parliament and claim to speak on behalf of "progressive Catholics committed to the building of socialist Poland." No one knows whether Piasecki still has direct lines of communication to the Soviet secret police, but it is certain that on basic issues he sees eye-to-eye with Moczar; both believe in the historic concept of organic ethnic unity, an alliance with Russia for the reasons of state, and in an authoritarian state as the protector of this unity.*

The retired colonels and young functionaries of ZBOWiD, the prewar fascists and younger men in Piasecki's PAX movement (half of whose membership is under thirty!), and the disgruntled second- and low-level Party and state bureaucrats were all united in their craving for power. From the early 1960s onward, they began a whispering campaign to evoke national emotions. At the meetings of ZBOWiD and PAX and in the circle of disaffected bureaucrats, it was more and more often proclaimed that it was the Jewish Stalinists (now revisionists) who denigrated Poland's heroic traditions and blocked upward mobility by holding

* As yet another recognition for his services, Piasecki in July 1969 received one of the highest Polish decorations—the Banner of Labor, First Class —on the occasion of the twenty-fifth anniversary of "People's Poland."

In June 1971 (that is already under the new Gierek leadership), he was even "elected" as member of the State Council, the highest state body.

tens of thousands of lucrative posts while they secretly favored Israeli interests over those of Poland.

The extent to which the secret police regained its hold on the country after the short-lived period of personal freedom was dramatically illustrated by the mechanism and escalation of the "anti-Zionist" campaign. Meanwhile, the slanted reports provided by Moczar's agents constituted the only real link between the top leadership and the population. The police chief is also said to have won the favor of Gomulka's private secretary, W. Namotkiewicz, and his administrative assistant, the Ukrainian Mrs. Reminjak. Recognizing the importance of international respectability, the "Partisans" also paid great attention to resident foreign correspondents and attained an early success, even with Yugoslav journalists who in their first reports in March 1968 painted a glowing picture of the "progressive patriots" who had removed "imported Poles," the source of all evils. The reaction of Yugoslav intellectuals to the purge of Kolakowski, Baczko, and the other respected scholars put an early end to this trend, but some Western correspondents remained sympathetic, almost completely ignoring the atmosphere of terror and witch-hunt and extolling Moczar as a kind of Polish Dubcek and Ceausescu combined.

Surprisingly, many of Moczar's opponents lend credence to his private declarations that he "personally" is not an anti-Semite (at least no more of an anti-Semite than anyone else). As a Polish writer put it, "Moczar is a man without any ideological motivation whatsoever. If philo-Semitism would serve his purposes, he would be tomorrow a declared friend of the Jews."

The point is that Moczar, Piasecki, and their associates learned from the failure of anti-Semitism as a political weapon in 1956 that it can become a potent political force only if it is joined with the much stronger anti-Russian feelings of the population. That most of the Jews had already been edged out of the top positions in 1964 had no effect whatever on the anti-Semitic whispering campaign.

The student riots in March 1968 provided the ideal breeding ground for demogogues. With the anti-Zionist witch-hunt in full swing, Moczar gave a widely reported interview on April 12 that amounted to an anti-Semitic manifesto with anti-Soviet undertones. By castigating the "politicians dressed in officers' uniforms" who arrived with the "heroic soldiers" from the Soviet Union in 1944, Moczar was not only hitting at the "Zambrowskis, the Bermans"—that is to say, the Jews—he was also, and for the first time, mounting an explicit attack on the Muscovites (and implicitly on their Soviet masters) who claimed to have "a monopoly on determining what is right for the Polish nation" and "persecuted the advocates of a broad national front."[170]

After this statement, the Kremlin, already fully occupied with rebellious Czechoslovakia, was more convinced than ever that there was no workable political alternative to Gomulka, its most vocal ally against Prague, and that Moczar's anti-Semitic campaign was merely a smoke screen for a potentially dangerous appeal to anti-Russian nationalism. Within a week, Soviet Ambassador Aristov on the anniversary of the Polish-Soviet Friendship Treaty paid a pointed tribute to Gomulka "the loyal son of the Polish people who with great care guards our friendship against all kinds of black reactionary forces which are trying to sow distrust between us."[171] But anti-Sovietism like anti-Semitism was merely a calculated device for Moczar. When the wind shifted, he was wise enough to trim his sails. He never mentioned the issue again and ardently courted the Russians, while continuing to vent his fury on Israel and the "Zionists."[172]

The stage was set in the tense days of March for the replacement of the "Gomulka Establishment" with another "Gomulka Establishment," the difference being that a weakened Gomulka would have been forced to rely on the alliance of the rising factions instead of dominating the failing coalition of old officeholders. Moczar could certainly have won power in March, but it is a matter of dispute whether he really wanted it against Gomulka's will and at the risk of a state crisis. In any case, assured of Soviet backing, Gomulka managed to gain valuable time by postponing the convening of the Central Committee while using anti-Zionism as a tactical weapon in parrying the challenge to his power. By virtually adopting the anti-Semitic program of the Partisans, he preempted the dynamism of Moczar's offensive.

By April the Partisans successfully eliminated many of their opponents in middle-level positions and enforced the dismissal of the head of state, Edward Ochab, whose daughters had been involved in the student movement. But despite the leaks planted by Moczar through his contacts among the Western correspondents, no general Cabinet reshuffle took place. Ochab was simply replaced by the slightly senile Marshal Spychalski, while a professional general, loyal to Gomulka, was put in charge of the armed forces instead of the Partisans' candidate, General Korczynski.

Though the dismissals with overt anti-Semitic overtones continued, Moczar and his allies began to lose momentum in their bid for supreme power. It is possible that they may have overestimated their own strength. In any event, from April onward the differences between the radical Young Turks among the Partisans and the hard-liners in the apparatus who were *already* in power, began to strain the cooperation between widely disparate forces. The fence-sitters, waverers, and opportunists began to shift back to the "Gomulkaites," still "the Party of order." The drive for power launched "from below in the Chinese way" and the "Red Guard" tactics began to threaten the very core of the bureaucracy, which after all had hardly any "Zionists" in its ranks.

By the time the long-awaited meeting of the Central Committee was held in July, Gomulka had already won the first round in the struggle for power. He staved off the challenge to his rule in part because the Kremlin supported him, in part because he cleverly exploited the personal rivalries and animosities among the hard-liners, and perhaps above all because so many influential politicians in Poland shared a profound distrust for Moczar and his ex-fascist advisers. In other words, Gomulka benefited from the unbridled excesses of the "purification" campaign. Nevertheless, events showed that he was not powerful enough to halt the purge single-handedly, let alone "to protect the innocent."

The Partisans also reaped some tangible benefits: the resignation of Ochab from the Politburo and the elimination of two mod-

234

erates from the Government. However, at the plenum Moczar once again failed in his bid to become a member of the Politburo. He was elected alternate member and Secretary of the Central Committee, but he had to give up formally the portfolio of the Ministry of Interior. At that moment it appeared that Gomulka was *no longer* strong enough to check the ascendancy of the Partisans, while Moczar and his allies were *not yet* powerful enough to gain full control.

That the maneuvering on all sides had nothing to do with the repudiation of the "anti-Zionist" witch-hunt was unmistakably shown by a startling historical survey of the "Jewish problem" in the Party published on the eve of the July plenum. The lengthy essay written by Andrzej Werblan, a Central Committee member and chief of the Party's Educational and Science Department (Miesiecznik Literacki, Warsaw, June 1968), deserves special attention, because of both its contents and its author. This self-styled "Contribution to the Genesis of the Conflict" put the crude anti-Semitism of the Lodz pamphlets* in "proper" Marxist terms; it provided a justification for the purge that had already solved the Jewish problem; it officially legitimized anti-Semitism and its numerus clausus in the Communist movement.

After copious references to the role of "scholars and students of Jewish origin" among the revisionist troublemakers behind the student riots, Werblan raised the question: "Why is it that in certain intellectual fields and central institutions a relatively large number of posts was occupied by people of Jewish origin (much more numerous than would be normal on the basis of the percentage of Jewish population compared to the total population)? And why can we note a special proclivity for revisionism, and for Jewish nationalism in general and Zionism in particular, in certain Jewish environments or among people of Jewish origin?"

The trouble was, the author explained, that in prewar Poland the KPP was more influential among the Jews than among the Poles. This was bad because a Polish worker or intellectual joined the Communist movement "mainly for social reasons," while in

* See Part Two, Chapter 5, "Lodz Becomes 'Judenrein.'"

the case of Jews "an important and sometimes decisive role was played by the desire to protest against national discrimination." Groups joining the leftist movement for other than social motives "as a rule have less political stability and greater proneness to leftist or rightist extremism." Thus in Werblan's model of a workers' party there would have been no place for a Jewish Marx or Lasalle, not even for a Lenin (his father was a high civil servant and hereditary noble at the end of his life; his mother, the daughter of a small landowner) since none of them entered the revolutionary movements of their time for social reasons.

These ideological "activists of Jewish origin," Werblan continued, made it more difficult to correct the Party's mistakes on the national level since they were "obviously less sensitive to the problems of Polish patriotism, the attributes of national sovereignty and independence. Under the influence of these (though not only these) factors, a certain part of the Party actif began to favor a primitive cosmopolitan approach to internationalism, failed to appreciate national aspirations . . . and mechanically subordinated these aspirations to international tasks and duties instead of seeking their mutual concordance . . ."

In other words, it was the "less stable" and "cosmopolitan" Jewish activists who were responsible for the failures and weaknesses of the past. A Comintern with a line that was binding for all Parties apparently did not exist. All this however pales in comparison to Werblan's sketch of the postwar period: the Polish Workers' Party (PPR) formed in 1942 was "par excellence a national party" since because of the "objective conditions" (a new Marxist term for the Holocaust) Party activists "of Jewish origin could not except for very rare exceptions participate in political activities in occupied Poland." He is careful to point out the contribution of the Muscovites to the liberation of the country and the fact that the great majority of the emigrants played a "positive role" after their return. But a small minority headed by Berman, Zambrowski, and Minc (all Jews) started a struggle against the patriotic home Communists, and were guilty of cosmopolitan deviations. They gave "particularly responsible positions" in key sectors "to people of Jewish origin, the majority of whom were never even connected with prewar leftist movements but frequently came from the wealthy Jewish bougeoisie who had sought refuge from Nazism in the Soviet Union."

Furthermore Werblan contradicted the previous official Party histories' explanation that the purge of Gomulka and his friends was due to external pressures, and made the amazing allegation that "the thesis of the rightist nationalist deviation arose above all upon internal foundations." Jewish "group solidarity" and "cosmopolitanism" were solely responsible for the Stalinist purges in postwar Poland. Werblan justified Nowak's demand for a numerus clausus in 1956 and the entire anti-Zionist witch-hunt in the following words: "Internal cosmopolitanism has provided a basis for the false accusation of anti-Semitism against those comrades who understood that no society can tolerate the excessive participation of a national minority in the élite of power, particularly in defense, security, propaganda, and diplomacy . . . This cadre policy . . . surrounded this ethnic group with an aura of privileged position, and any society would react with displeasure against such privileges. Only absolute thoughtlessness and clique solidarity of a nationalistic origin can explain the rapid advance of persons from the Jewish petty bourgeoisie, traditionally unconnected with Communism and frequently subject to Zionist influence. Experience has shown that the majority of them were ideologically alien, later easily sliding to revisionist positions. Many went over to Zionism, breaking with Poland altogether and emigrating."

Finally, Werblan referred to the removal "of a relatively large number of people of Jewish origin from central institutions," some of whom formed an "embittered group" based "on national solidarity and Zionism. There were even cases of open treason and crossing over to hostile positions." But there was no reason for concern: "The main ideological danger is revisionism. Jewish nationalism and Zionism have done a great deal of harm, but they have only a limited scope for being a political danger. Improving the national composition in those institutions in which it is necessary will to a large extent eliminate this problem . . . The criticism of the attitude and policies of a certain element in the Party leadership from 1949 to 1955 must not however overshadow the achievements during that period . . ."

In plain language, both the failures of the prewar Party and the purges of postwar Stalinism were due to the Jews, who are ethnically incapable of being good Communists and good Poles. Werblan's article was the first racist manifesto carrying the full authority of the Party ever published by a ranking Party ideologist in a Communist country. The application of his "Marxist" quota system in a country in which the ratio of the Jews is less than one tenth of 1 per cent meant not only the reviving of the numerus clausus, but the complete barring of Jews from all responsible positions.

It should be said that Werblan's racialist doctrine was sharply attacked by three prominent (and non-Jewish) members at the July plenum. But it was approved by Gomulka as "a good platform for discussion."[173] Neither Gomulka, Kliszko, nor any Party paper criticized him. On the contrary the article was excerpted in *Trybuna Ludu* (June 16, 1968) and widely disseminated by all media.

The truth was that Gomulka agreed with the basis of the Partisans' anti-Semitism, albeit not with the "undignified" form in which the "national ratio" was corrected. But he recognized that the nationalist and covertly anti-Soviet undertones of the "anti-Zionist" campaign involved great potential risks—the raising of the issue of past and present Soviet domination. He was willing to jettison the Jews, but his instinct for self-preservation and keen sense of political realism alerted him to the dangers inherent in playing with the fire of Polish nationalism. As Jendrychowski stated at the July plenum: "Nationalism in Poland may initially have this or that feature, but in the end it will always show its anti-Soviet claws."[174] Sooner or later the new wave of nationalist sentiment is bound to bring about a real confrontation with issues hitherto regarded as taboo: the carving up of Poland by Hitler and Stalin, the Katyn massacre, the deportations, Soviet inaction during the Warsaw uprising, and so on.

The invasion of Czechoslovakia dampened the fervor of the nationalist propagandists and compromised the "nationalist" platform of the Moczar faction. The day the Soviet tanks rolled into Prague, the hopes of Moczar and his allies were shattered. If the Partisans' offensive had lasted a few months longer instead of being cut short by the Czech crisis, it might have borne results. But the invasion of Czechoslovakia and the armed clashes with China helped Gomulka reconsolidate his hold on the Party to a surprising degree. Brezhnev's warm personal tribute to the aging Polish leader at the Party Congress in November was a clear pointer that Moscow had an interest in maintaining the status quo in Poland.

The distribution of clandestine leaflets on the eve of the congress, accusing Jedrychowski, Spychalski, and Cyrankiewicz of being Jews, the calls demanding "a fight against revisionism and Zionism to the very end,"[175] even the campaign against "Zionists" in Czechoslovakia, failed to affect the reshuffle of the leading Party bodies. Three members, including Rapacki and the only Jew, Szyr, were dropped from the Politburo. But Moczar was not promoted to full membership.* Insult was added to injury when junior functionaries, the thirty-five-year-old S. Kociolek and the forty-one-year-old J. Techma entered the highest echelon without even having been alternates.

The rejuvenation at the top was minimal. Two other newcomers, Kruczek (a former Natolinist) and the secretary from Poznan, Jan Szydlak, are hard-liners but no friends of the Partisans. But the potential threat represented by the radical "Young Turks" and dynamic hard-liners has not been removed. Gomulka halted Moczar's advance only at the price of completely destroying the coalition he had dominated. No less than twenty-nine members of the old Central Committee, mainly "liberals" (including five Jews) and ex-socialists, were removed and replaced by little-known provincial secretaries and younger activists from large factories.

There is a new balance of power with Gomulka relying on his

---

* Contrary to widespread speculation, however, he was re-elected as chairman of the veterans' organization, ZBOWiD, at its congress in September 1969.

old associates and younger men who are more docile because more dependent upon him. But the temporary stabilization may prove deceptive. The reformist wing has virtually disappeared, and Gomulka can no longer play one group against another. The underlying strength of the Partisans and their allies was evident at the elections to the new Central Committee. More than one third of the delegates crossed out the names of Jedrychowski and the two remaining Jews, Artur Starewicz and Eugenius Szyr, from the membership ballot.

In summary, Poland's "anti-Zionist" witch-hunt proved beyond any doubt that stirring up anti-Semitism against a handful of Jews long removed from really commanding positions is not only possible but can be extremely useful in a factional battle for power in a Communist country.

Confronted with the burning issues of the day, none of the warring groups had to make even the slightest allusion to a real program designed to cope with the manifold problems plaguing Poland. The outcome was the destruction of the Polish Jews and some striking but not decisive gains for one branch of the ruling bureaucracy. Those who seek radical reforms must wait for better days.

Polish Communism is today without ideology and without intellectuals. The Polish nation, in the strait jacket of an unalterable geopolitical situation and condemned to remain faithful to the Russian alliance, has lost its hope of becoming truly independent and shaping its own destiny—at least in this generation.

Given these factors, the people of Poland will judge their rulers in the long run by what they manage to do about the country's still deplorably low standard of living. The few thousand jobs and apartments vacated by the "Zionists" were only a drop in the ocean of rising expectations amid a veritable population explosion. The Jews have left or are leaving Poland, and when the profound social contradictions spark off the next crisis, there may be no one to serve as scapegoat.

*Only one year after these words were written, the eruption of popular discontent in December 1970 dramatically confirmed our sombre warnings. The whirlwind of the workers' uprising along the Baltic Sea and the successive waves of strikes in the rest of the country within a week (December 12–20) shook the Communist regime in its very foundations, overthrew the Gomulka group and brought the country to the verge of a civil war. For the fall of Gomulka and his closest associates (Kliszko, Spychalski, Strzelecki and others), the Polish working class had to pay a high price. According to an official report, 48 people were killed and 1,165 wounded; private estimates put the number of the dead even at over 100.*

*In the course of the reshuffles at the top (by February 1971 seven of the 12 members of the old Politburo had to resign), General Moczar seemed to have achieved the pinnacle of power; he was promoted to full membership in the Politburo and as secretary of the Central Committee he became responsible not only for the security service but also for the army. Moczar's friends in the press and the apparatus were pressing for a radical line: "Let us carry out the policy of March (i.e. 1968) to the very end."*

*Moczar's victory was, however, short-lived. In mid-April he lost control both over the police and the army; suffered what seems to be a "political heart attack" and by June 1971 he became President of the State Control Commission, the traditional sinecure position for demoted politicians. At the end of the month he formally resigned as secretary of the Central Committee. Scores of his influential followers in the Ministries of Defence and Interior as well as among the regional party secretaries have been dismissed.*

*The key to the sudden and seemingly inexplicable demise of Moczar can probably be found in what seems to be a policy decision in Moscow rather than in the undeniable tactical dexterity of Edward Gierek, the new party chief. As in 1968 when faced with the challenge of the "Partisans" to Gomulka, the Kremlin once again opted for the status quo and stability, that is for Gierek's cautious middle course and against Moczar's dynamic and unpredictable nationalism.*

*There is no sign however of an official or even a semi-official rehabilitation of the victims of the 1968 purge. Nor should the fact be overlooked that quite a few pacemakers of the past campaign not only against a handful of Jews but against reform, progress and humanism still occupy important positions in the administration and above all in the mass media. The Jews are gone; Gomulka and some of the main actors have vanished from the political stage—but Poland's grave problems remain. Gierek and his team live on borrowed time and the working class is more than ever conscious of its power to change things and destroy taboos—if necessary—by force.*

# PART THREE
## Czechoslovakia:
## How to Manufacture Zionists

# 1. THE GHOST OF SLANSKY

With the passage of time they changed the accusations but the anti-Semitic insults remained the same.

Eugen Loebl

On July 31, 1951, the Czechoslovak Party organ *Rude Pravo* carried on the front page a letter of the Central Committee of the Communist Party congratulating its Secretary General Rudolf Slansky on his fiftieth birthday and praising him as "an indefatigable fighter from his early youth . . . one of the most outstanding leaders" of the Party and the "closest and most faithful collaborator of President Klement Gottwald." He was awarded the highest order and on August 17 yet another factory (this one in the city of Letov) was renamed "Rudolf Slansky Plant."

Less than four months later, the same paper published a laconic communique announcing that "hitherto unknown circumstances have recently been established which prove that Rudolf Slansky has been guilty of antistate activities and has been detained for purposes of investigation."[1] Almost exactly a year later Rudolf Slansky, the Number Two man in Communist Czechoslovakia, and thirteen co-defendants went on trial as "Trotskyite-Titoist-Zionist bourgeois nationalist traitors and enemies of the Czechoslovak people," charged with having formed a subversive conspiratorial center spying for Tito's Yugoslavia, Israel, and the West, with high treason and economic sabotage. Slansky and the others accused pleaded guilty on all counts. Eleven of the fourteen were sentenced to death and three to prison for life. All voluntarily renounced every right of appeal and plea for clemency. Slansky, who had admitted having wanted to become a "Czech Tito," and the ten others sentenced to death were hanged in the early hours of December 3, 1952.

Almost eleven years later, on May 14, 1963, the Czechoslovak Supreme Court announced that no antistate Trotskyite-Titoist-Zionist conspiratorial center had existed, that the alleged criminal activities had been fabricated by the organs of the Ministry of Interior and that the confessions were forced from the defendants by means of physical violence and psychological pressure. The "Slansky plot" and seven more group trials involving more than sixty prominent politicians and officials were said to have been frame-ups. But it took a further five years until the world learned the truth—or at least part of the truth—about the background of the most horrendous show trial ever staged in an East European country.

In a sense, Slansky and the others accused were victims of the occupational hazards every Communist leader faced during the Stalin era. What distinguished the purge trial in Czechoslovakia was its openly anti-Semitic character and its scope and violence. Of the fourteen defendants, eleven were Jews. While Clementis, the Foreign Minister, and two others were described as "Slovak" or "Czech," the indictment added the words "of Jewish origin" to the name of each Jewish defendant. The anti-Semitic overtones were evident on every page of the indictment and the trial protocols. These lifelong Communists whose only link with Judaism was their Jewish birth were denounced as Zionists, parts of a world-wide Zionist plot, active agents of a conspiracy to seize power. Where the names were not obviously Jewish, the original name was added in the indictment, Ludvik Frejka (alias Ludwig Freund), Slansky (alias Salzmann), Andre Simone (alias Otto Katz), or they were described as "Zionists, cosmopolitans, Jewish bourgeois nationalists" and in some cases just as Jews.

The anti-Semitic character of the trial was not exhausted in the description of the men in the dock. Countless other Jews were mentioned as co-conspirators, including dead and living foreign statesmen ranging from "the Jewish nationalist and French Minister of Colonies, Georges Mandel" who in the 1930s "recruited" Simone as an agent to "the Jewish nationalist Supreme Court Justice Frankfurter" and Mosha Pijade, the "Titoist Jewish ideologist." The vast conspiracy penetrating every part of political and economic life, the indictment said, was the result of a secret conference that took place in Washington in 1947. The participants had been President Truman, Secretary of State Acheson, former Secretary of the Treasury Morgenthau, and the Israeli statesmen Ben Gurion and Moshe Sharett. Agreement had been reached on a Morgenthau-Acheson plan "according to which American support for Israel was promised in exchange for the use of Zionist organizations for espionage and subversion in the People's Democracies." Slansky, "by his very nature a Zionist," the great hope of the Jews in the Communist Party, "son of a rich merchant" and "old agent of the bourgeoisie" admitted placing "Zionists in important sectors of the Government, economy, and Party apparatus" and confessed that he covered their deeds by launching "vast campaigns against anti-Semitism."[2]

The objects of the vast Zionist-Titoist-Trotskyite conspiracy pursued in conjunction with the intelligence services of Israel, the United States, Yugoslavia, and France (and also with the American Jewish organization, the Joint) were the assassination of President Gottwald with the help of a "freemason" physician, the sabotage of the economy, and the restoration of capitalism in Czechoslovakia.

It was the typical Soviet show trial replete with a hate campaign calling for vigilance and ruthlessness toward the hidden enemy. During the week-long proceedings no less than 10,500 resolutions were adopted at public meetings in factories and offices demanding the ultimate punishment for the gang of traitors.[3] The "moral fracture of society" was such that the nearest relatives of the defendants wrote letters asking for exemplary punishment of their husbands and fathers. Thus the French-born wife of Artur London, former

Deputy Foreign Minister, wrote to the President of the court: "As a Communist and as a mother I am happy that the treacherous gang was unmasked and destroyed. I can only join all honest people in demanding a just punishment for the traitors." The eighteen-year-old son of Ludwik Frejka wrote: "I demand that my father be given the severest punishment—the penalty of death. I see now that this creature that cannot be called a human being because he does not possess a bit of feeling or human dignity has been my greatest and most wicked enemy."[4]

The absurd charges leveled against the accused, the abject confessions, and the entire staging and character of the trial left no doubt even in 1952 that this was a classic "Moscow trial" in everything but name. When six weeks later the "Doctors' Plot" was "unmasked" in Moscow, it became evident that the Slansky trial was a prelude to Stalin's last great purge.

But the extent to which Soviet "experts" were responsible for the anti-Jewish thrust of the purge was revealed only seventeen years later during the Prague Spring. Both the victims and Stalin's Czech henchmen, for different reasons, lifted the veil of silence and half truths. It is only now that it has become possible to understand the sudden emergence of violent political anti-Semitism in the one country in Central and Eastern Europe that had deep democratic traditions and where the "Jewish Question" was never a real problem.

As George F. Kennan noted in a report sent from Prague in 1939 after the dismemberment of Czechoslovakia: "It seems evident that if Czechoslovakia existed in a vacuum the Jews despite their considerable number would not present any problem . . . The country does not contain in itself the basis for a really serious and widespread anti-Semitic movement." Even under the Protectorate there was practically no noticeable anti-Semitism among the Czech people. Despite the latent resentment against the German-speaking Jews (by then a minority within the Jewish community) the fact remained that in Bohemia nationality was "a matter of language rather than of blood, that speech rather than origin is the distinguishing characteristic of friend or foe."[5]

The situation was different in backward Slovakia where religious and folk anti-Semitism was reinforced by resentment against the educated Jews, who were mainly Hungarian-speaking or, to a lesser extent, had German cultural orientation. After World War I the Jews who were loyal to Czechoslovakia were accused by the Slovak nationalists of having made common cause once with the Hungarians and now with the Czech "oppressors," and later the clerico-fascist government of puppet Slovakia willingly collaborated with the Germans in the destruction of the Jews. After World War II anti-Semitism in Slovakia culminated in a number of bloody pogroms, largely inspired by the fear that the Jewish survivors might get back their property, by then distributed mainly among Slovaks. With the resurgence of Slovak nationalism, the anti-Semitism of the 1950s and, especially, the 1960s in Slovakia reflected the fight between the Czech majority and Slovak minority for the redistribution of power and wealth.

As of 1951, when Zionism became public enemy Number One, there were very few Jews indeed. Of the prewar community of 360,000, only one fifth survived, and by 1950 about three quarters of the survivors had left the country. In all, the fourteen to eighteen thousand Jews formed about one fifteenth of 1 per cent of the total population. Moreover, the Jews were linguistically and culturally assimilated, considered themselves Czechs or Slovaks, and were primarily intellectuals, professional men, and administrators.[6] Most of the genuine Zionists had left, and the majority of the remaining Jewish community did not belong to the Communist-dominated "religious community" and did not profess religion, let alone "Jewish nationalism."

Was an excessively high proportion of the top Party leadership of Jewish origin? This certainly was the impression created by the list of defendants and the co-conspirators mentioned by the prosecutor, the accused, and the witnesses. Did not Slansky admit placing "Zionists in important sectors . . . These Zionists placed other Zionists in those sectors and through them I maintained contact with Zionist organizations." Yet the composition of the most important Party bodies does not indicate an excessive preponderance of Jews. There were only two Jews in the twenty-two-member Presidium, and the same two represented the "Jewish element" among the seven members of the central secretariat. Key posts were indeed held by B. Geminder, the head of the Party's international department, and O. Sling, the Party secretary of Brno, the capital of Moravia, while a number of Jewish Communists occupied second-level positions as deputy ministers and high officials, primarily in the Ministries of Foreign Affairs, Defense, Foreign Trade, and Finance and of course in the press. But most of the Jewish victims had scarcely anything to do with the leader of the "conspiratorial center," Slansky, who spent the years from 1938 to 1944 in Moscow.

The Slansky affair was not an isolated case, but, as the Czech Communist historian, K. Kaplan, put it, "the logical culmination of the five-year period of illegality. The technology of manufacturing political trials attained a classical form, was developed to the highest degree of perfection, and the machinery devoured many of those who helped to prepare the trials. Illegality is not selective: it acts as an uncontrollable, reckless force which, once unleashed, knows no boundaries."[7] The technical and political basis and the mechanism of destruction were the same in Czechoslovakia as in the Soviet Union of the 1930s and the other East European satellites. The terror in Czechoslovakia however raged with a fury unprecedented anywhere else. And in contrast to the Rajk and Kostov trials in Hungary and Bulgaria, the purge was directed primarily against not "Titoism" but "Zionism."

The character of the Czechoslovak Party and the timing of the purges provide part of the explanation. When the Communists took power in February 1948, they had a reservoir of well-trained, reliable cadres. Allowed to operate legally in the interwar period, the Communist Party at the last prewar election in 1935 received over 10 per cent of the popular vote, and in May 1946 almost 38 per cent. This enabled President Gottwald to resist the first Soviet demands, conveyed through the Hungarian dictator Rakosi, for the arrest of sixty "agents of imperialism" in September 1949.

Time and again Gottwald resisted the demand only to yield later to Stalin's iron will.[8]

The strength of the Czech Party and the fact that the purges started after the pattern had already been established in the other satellites explain the scope and intensity of the terror. After the Rajk trial and the Cominform meeting calling for the unmasking of hidden enemies and spies, the search started in earnest for a "Czech Rajk." And Slansky himself was second to none in the appeals for vigilance: "We cannot take it for granted that we have no Rajk or Kostov. There are many of them here. Every week we uncover sabotage and espionage. In nearly all cases people holding membership cards in our Party are involved. It is necessary to carry out a much more vigilant cadre policy, to investigate the past of each member, especially the dark spots in his past. We have the instructive example of Rajk and the others (Spain, Switzerland, prison, etc.). We have to discover such dark spots in the past of each member, examine his life to see that he does not lead a double life. An agent always leads a double life."[9]

The scenario for the purge was prepared from the very beginning by the Soviet "advisers." They came in October 1949 after Rakosi and the Poles as well as the Soviet "expert" in Budapest, General Bielkin, had recommended to Gottwald that he should ask for Soviet "advisers." Soviet secret police officers were convinced that Czechoslovakia was "the focal point" of the great international conspiracy of imperialist and Yugoslav enemies of socialism.[10] On their arrival, the leaders of the Soviet team, Komarov and Likhachev, were surprised "that no enemy had been discovered within the Party." As Kaplan noted: "A special position was held by the Soviet advisers in the security service. Their influence can be seen especially in the preparation of the trials, in assembling the groups, in preparing the structure of conspiracy, in preparing the accused for appearance in court, etc. Their position was quite extraordinary, their proposals and opinions were accepted by the minister as well as by other officials and their correctness was never questioned, while the leader of the advisers took part in conferences with Gottwald when security questions were involved."[11]

The two men who held the post of the Minister of State Security between 1950 and 1953, Karol Bacilek and Ladislav Kopriva, revealed that there had been twenty-six Soviet advisers in the Ministry of Security directly supervising the interrogations.[12]

The purge began in November 1949 with the arrest of Eugen Loebl, Deputy Minister of Foreign Trade, and Vilem Novy, editor-in-chief of *Rude Pravo,* both "Westerners" (men who spent the war years in the West). The Russians insisted that spies must be sought especially among the "Westerners" and the "Spaniards" (veterans of the Spanish Civil War). A special commission investigated the personnel files of no less than six thousand suspects in this category. Somewhat later the circle widened to embrace the Slovak "bourgeois nationalists." This group, headed by Vlado Clementis, the Foreign Minister, was comprised of Slovak politicians and partisans in the Slovak uprising of 1944. The first scenario selected Clementis for the role of the "Czechoslovak Rajk." By late 1950 the purge began to embrace the central Party apparatus with the arrest of the Brno Party secretary, O. Sling (a Jew), and Maria Svermova, the widow of the Party hero and martyr Jan Sverma, and Deputy Secretary General of the Party.

As during Stalin's Great Terror in the 1930s the procedure was "the reign of the lie," the extortion of confessions universally known to be false. In the beginning of 1951 the accusers themselves were accused and imprisoned. Within two weeks Clementis and over fifty leading officials (including eight departmental chiefs of the State Security service) were taken into custody. But even at this point there was no allusion to Zionism or the special role of Jews. On the contrary, the victims, who were "declared traitors, spies, and enemies without any possibility of defense," were accused of wanting "to remove Slansky and Zapotocky (the Premier) and to assassinate Gottwald and in that way tear Czechoslovakia away from the Soviet Union and socialism." One might add that the arrest of the fifty officials was suggested by the Minister of Security Kopriva and approved by Gottwald; his influential son-in-law, A. Cepicka; Foreign Minister Siroky; Premier Zapotocky and Slansky himself.[13]

The investigation soon reached a deadlock, however. For unknown reasons neither Clementis nor any of the others was any longer regarded as suitable for the role of head of the conspiracy. It was then, in the spring of 1951, that the Soviet advisers without the knowledge or approval of the Czech leadership began to change the ideological basis of the plot from "bourgeois nationalism" to "Zionism." The name of Slansky, the second most powerful man in the country, began to appear in some of the depositions of the accused. That this was done on the direct instructions of the interrogators and their Soviet masters was confirmed in detail by Eugen Loebl and others. Though Minister Kopriva had one of these interrogators arrested, they nevertheless continued to send their reports through the Soviet Embassy direct to Moscow.

It is beyond the scope of this survey to describe all the details of Stalin's intrigues to convince and force a reluctant Gottwald to sacrifice his oldest comrade-in-arms. Suffice it to say that the removal of Slansky from his Party post was decided at a meeting of the *Soviet* Politburo in Moscow where the ailing Gottwald was represented by his ambitious son-in-law, Minister of Defense Cepicka. Incriminating "evidence" was collected by the security officials even after Gottwald had given instructions to stop the investigation, and in November 1951 Anastas Mikoyan, a member of the Soviet Politburo (and in 1964–65 head of state), came to Prague to demand—on behalf of Stalin—Slansky's arrest.[14]

The climax of the intrigues resembled a cheap thriller. To overcome Gottwald's scruples, the Soviet advisers spread rumors that Slansky's flight was being prepared by Western intelligence. Their chief, Alexej Bescasnov, handed Gottwald a letter, intercepted by Soviet secret agents, which had been allegedly sent to the "Great Sweeper" (apparently a code name for Slansky), in which he was offered help to escape to the West. The letter had been delivered to a Czech citizen, Daniela Kankovska, accompanied by a request for a meeting a few days later. She however had refused to have anything to do with the affair; she did not know Slansky and never passed the letter on to him. (This did not save her from being sentenced to thirteen years for "preparing Slansky's escape abroad.") Confronted with this "evidence," Gottwald gave in and on November 23, together with Premier Zapotocky, Police Chief Kopriva, and the chief Soviet adviser, decided to arrest Slansky. The way in which the arrest was carried out reflected the total moral degradation of the Czech leadership. In the morning Zapotocky participated in the conference that passed a virtual death sentence on his lifelong friend; in the evening he was his host at a friendly dinner given in the honor of a Soviet delegation. After the Russians left, he and his wife continued to drink with Slansky and his family and two other Party leaders, reminiscing about the past until midnight. On returning home, the Slanskys entered their dark house to be surrounded by plainclothes policemen, aiming machine guns at them, who arrested the entire family, including Slansky's two-year-old daughter.[15]

Next morning the six members of the political secretariat of the Central Committee (Gottwald, Zapotocky, Cepicka, Siroky, Bacilek, and Dolansky), three of whom had spent the previous evening drinking and chatting with Slansky, approved his arrest. The decision was confirmed by the Presidium on the same day and subsequently on December 6 by the Central Committee plenum. Writing in the official Party monthly seventeen years later, the Communist historian Kaplan summed up the situation: "Thus it was that even the highest organ approved the action taken against its former Secretary General and, without hearing him, condemned him as an agent, enemy, and traitor. Although not one foolproof shred of evidence existed, Gottwald said that 'all the traitors and conspirators caught up to then were proved guilty of these dishonorable intentions and finally confessed under the burden of evidence' . . . Thus the head of the conspiracy was found. It was Slansky, former Secretary General of the Communist Party, a leading Party and state functionary for nearly a quarter of a century, the closest collaborator of Gottwald, Zapotocky, Siroky, Bacilek, and Dolansky, all of whom had decided on his arrest and about his life. In cooperation with those working in the security department, they turned him into a traitor, an enemy, and an agent of imperialism, just a few weeks after celebrating with him his fiftieth birthday, when they had rewarded him with the highest state decorations."[16]

This is not the place to describe the unbelievable tortures to which the victims, especially Slanksy, were subjected to provide the prepared confessions to substantiate the scenario worked out in Moscow; the dress rehearsal of the trial during which questions and answers were tape-recorded, the fixing of the entire staged trial to the minutest detail, including the sentences, which were decided by the then eight members of the Political Secretariat.* The point of the matter was that the switch from "bourgeois nationalism" to "Zionism" propelled the Jews among the "Westerners" and "Spaniards"—and even among the "Muscovites"—into the foreground. That Slansky, the symbol of subservience to Moscow, was linked with Clementis, the Slovak patriot, was in accord with Stalin's time-tested tactic which started from the premise that "when destroying one group of enemies it is helpful to throw in and accuse of the same plot a variety of other hostile figures in no way connected with them."[17]

This however did not change the fact that the main purpose of the Slansky trial was to imply that every Jew, whatever his political record, was a secret partner in the "Zionist plot." It is only now that the memoirs of two survivors, the Deputy Ministers London and Loebl, have made it possible to get an inkling of the rabid anti-Semitism behind the scenes of the trial.[18] The published evidence in 1951–52, the trial itself, and the hate campaign against the "cosmopolitan traitors" spoke for themselves. But London and Loebl give firsthand evidence of the virulence of anti-Jewish hatred among their tormentors.

"You and your dirty race, we shall eliminate you! You are all the same! Not everything that Hitler did was bad, because he killed the Jews and that was a good thing. Too many escaped the

---

* In December 1951, Antonin Novotny, the Prague Party chief, and the rabble-rousing demagogue V. Kopecky were promoted to the Political Secretariat. Novotny officially succeeded Gottwald as First Secretary of the Party in September 1953 and retained the supreme position until January 1968.

gas chambers. What he did not finish, we shall complete . . . Ten meters under the earth, that is where we shall bury you and your filthy sort!" This was how Prison Commander Smola greeted Artur London, Deputy Foreign Minister, before his first interrogation.

"And these words were uttered by a man who wore a Party badge in his lapel in the presence of three others in uniform who through their silence approved," London added and concluded: "And all this by a security official in a socialist country, a member of the Communist Party. Is it possible that the spirit of the 'Black Hundreds,' the spirit of the SS, revived in our ranks? It is the same spirit that animated the men who shot my brother in 1941, who deported to Auschwitz and dispatched to the gas chamber my mother, my sister, her husband, and dozens of my family."[19]

This was in January 1951. Later London wrote: "When in the beginning I was confronted with a virulent, truly Hitlerian anti-Semitism I may have thought this was merely some individuals . . . Now however I know that this spirit reflects a systematic line. Whenever a new name was mentioned, the interrogators immediately wanted to know whether he was Jewish. Then they asked: 'How was he called before? Did he not change his name in 1945?' If he was really of Jewish origin, this was put in the record under one pretext or another, even if it had nothing to do with the matter at issue. And before the name they placed the ritual qualification, 'Zionist.' The aim was to accumulate the greatest possible number of Jews . . . giving the deliberate impression that the accused was in contact only with Jews or at least with a remarkable number of Jews."

As London was also a "Spaniard," many questions revolved around the other arrested veterans of the Spanish Civil War. When he remarked that apart from himself and one other man, all the other accused were not Jews, the investigator replied seriously: "But you forget their wives. They are all Jews, and it comes to the same thing." There was even a theory about the Jewish wives as "instruments of indirect Jewish penetration." And London adds that the most outrageous anti-Semitic expressions as well as the names of a number of other suspects were not included in the stenographic record of the trial, this material being reserved for future purposes.

London, who probably owes his life to the fact that his brother-in-law was (and still is) a member of the Politburo of the French Communist Party, stated unequivocally: "It seems to me that our trial went beyond the credibility of the public. Never was there such a violent anti-Semitic tendency, such crude falsifications, such enormous lies . . ."[20] When his colleague in the Foreign Ministry, Deputy Minister Vavro Hajdu, was expelled in March 1951, the meeting of the local Party cell was attended by "strange people" who did not have the right to be there. One young woman, a lawyer, justified her presence by announcing that "she was a specialist on Jewish Questions."[21]* Eugen Loebl, one of the first victims, was initially accused of contacts with the "American double agents" Noel and Hermann Field, and with Titoism because, as Deputy Foreign Trade Minister, he had signed a trade agreement with Yugoslavia. Later he was attacked as one of the leaders of the "Slovak bourgeois nationalists." In March 1951 he "advanced" to a "cosmopolitan of Jewish-bourgeois background" and a member of Slansky's "antistate conspiratorial center." Loebl adds, "With the passage of time they changed the accusations, but the anti-Semitic insults remained the same."[22]

Richard Slansky, the chief culprit's brother and former ambassador, related the following episode: "I am convinced that any honest worker knows the name of Klara Zetkin, the leader of the German proletariat, the friend of Lenin, etc. Once when I was being questioned about my wife, I said that she had been a colleague of Comrade Zetkin. My investigator roared: 'What kind of a Jewish whore was she, this Zetkin? What did she trade in?' Unfortunately, this is not the only evidence of the moral and political character of these investigators."[23]

Neither the memoirs nor the lengthy study of the entire "plot"

* See, for the startling similarity of the purge methods, Part Two, Chapter 4 on Poland, "In the Chinese Way."

published by the Czech historian Kaplan can provide a full explanation for the anti-Semitic angle. Though Kaplan relied on what was available from the documents in the Party archives and revealed the role of Mikoyan and "the pressure from outside," he did not have access to the Soviet and Czechoslovak secret police records. While admitting that "many questions still remain to which we cannot give an answer," he saw a "certain connection" between the predominance of the "anti-Zionist" theme and the "shift of policy in the socialist camp toward the Middle East—especially the change of attitude toward Israel." Kaplan also referred to the fact that "anti-Semitism to varying degrees appeared in the persons who took part in inventing the 'conspiracy'; this applied to the security officials, the Soviet advisers, and the political functionaries. These anti-Semitic tendencies became particularly ripe in 1951. A special department was formed in the security which dealt with Zionism."[24]*

It is unlikely that considerations of Soviet foreign policy played the decisive role in the purge of Jewish Communists. As Theodore Draper has observed, "in Stalin's last years, Soviet policy was less pro-Arab than anti-Israel"[25] and while the anti-Zionist and anti-Israeli propaganda barrage could not but help Soviet foreign policy, the real reasons for it must be sought in the internal tensions and factional infighting of Stalinist Russia.

The Slansky affair was accompanied by the wholesale dismissal, if not always the imprisonment, of Jewish officials, journalists, and administrators in all walks of life. But it is important to remember that the seeming Jewish preponderance in the Slansky trial was deliberately manipulated by the Soviet advisers. In fact, the majority of the arrested officials were non-Jews, including such

* Thus the Polish "anti-Zionist" witch-hunt in 1968 copied both the organizational methods and the ideological explanations applied already in 1951! Compare, for example, the prosecutor's speech at the Slansky trial about the Zionists "having shamelessly abused the Czechoslovak people's traditional abhorrence of anti-Semitism . . . to infiltrate the Communist Party and to hide their faces behind the suffering of Jews under Nazi rule" and many similar statements with the same "arguments" used by the manipulators of the Polish anti-Semitic campaign.

outstanding Party members as Clementis and the entire Slovak leadership headed by Gustav Husak, the chairman of the provincial government, Maria Svermova, Deputy Secretary General of the Party, O. Zavodsky, chief of the security police, Josef Smrkovsky, the leader of the Prague uprising, Josef Pavel, the Deputy Minister of Interior, several Army generals, and scores of high officials.

Though Gottwald died barely a week after Stalin, the terror continued to rage. Political trials were held well into 1954. The new Party leader, Novotny, steadfastly refused to reconsider the trials even after the other satellites announced rehabilitations and the investigators themselves had described in detail the "technology of manufacturing" the trials. A new theory was produced: Slansky was transformed from a "Czech Rajk" into a "Czechoslovak Beria." Time and again, Novotny and his associates repeated and two special investigating commissions confirmed that "Slansky committed a number of criminal actions . . . he deserved his fate." As late as 1961 and 1963 Novotny emphatically stated that "Slansky and company had really set into motion the terror machine in whose coils they themselves were to be caught."[26]

The consciousness of collective guilt rather than personal loyalty forced the leadership to close its ranks. As a keen Western observer noted: "The country's tragedy lay in the lack of a Communist dissenter, all the leading Party members being almost insolubly bound together by the weight of their responsibility."[27] But the ghost of Slansky and the other executed victims kept haunting the ruling group. Some of the victims (for example, Loebl and Husak) remained in prison until 1960, and it was not until 1963 that they were all legally rehabilitated and most of them politically exonerated. Stalin's Czech accomplices maintained themselves in power until 1968. Siroky was forced out as Premier and Bacilek as Slovak Party leader in 1963, but they retained their Central Committee membership. Only at the height of the liberalization movement in Czechoslovakia did the May 1968 plenum of the Central Committee expel Novotny and three others from this body and suspend their Party membership.

The purges had a shattering moral and social impact on the

entire nation, producing an atmosphere of fear and suspicion that encouraged the rise of informers and ruthless careerists. They also caused such extensive changes in Party and state personnel that—in Kaplan's words—"it is possible to talk about the emergence of a certain social class recruited or promoted by this situation." Class origin and absolute obedience rather than experience or ability became the hallmarks of this "qualitatively new type of official."[28] From Novotny down to the local Party secretaries, the apparatus had a vested interest in maintaining the status quo and resisting a truly radical de-Stalinization. Gottwald's heirs were not only guilty of terror launched in cold blood, they were also mediocrities not only unwilling but unable to think in a wider context.

The purges raised the most profound moral issues. Slansky and his co-defendants were the victims of a Soviet-sponsored purge. But Slansky himself and quite a few of the victims, including Husak in Slovakia and Deputy Minister of Interior Pavel, had thought nothing of deporting, imprisoning, or even killing their political opponents. Slansky had committed or connived at similar acts of repression, first against non-Communists and later against leading Party figures. Still the significance of the Slansky trial went beyond the personalities of those involved and became the symbol of a system based partly on coercion, partly on systematic lying. The fight for and against rehabilitation awakened intellectuals and students to the fact that there could not be a double standard of morality, one for the loyal Party victims and another for the potential or imagined opponents of the Communist system. The death penalties meted out to the group of former Social Democrats and non-Communist politicians headed by Dr. Horakova in June 1950 and the trial against the "Vatican agents" a few months later were as appalling and fabricated as the trials of Slansky and the other "anti-Party" groups. What lent a special significance to the Slansky affair was the fact that it had involved the very core of the ruling oligarchy and created a sinister precedent for shifting the blame for blunders and failures onto "alien" elements whose true loyalty lay elsewhere.

The "Zionist plot" was fabricated in Moscow, but the campaign against the two isms, Zionism and cosmopolitanism, picked up a momentum of its own in Czechoslovakia. Although it was abandoned in the mid-1950s, it left a residue of reactivated anti-Semitic prejudices and, more important still, a Party tradition of playing upon anti-Jewish feelings whenever convenient. It was against this backcloth of guilt and shame, complicity and resistance, that the Six Day War and the disintegration of the Novotny regime combined to lead to a sudden re-emergence of the Jewish Question.

## 2.  "TWO MILLION ZIONISTS BEHIND THE CZECH COUNTERREVOLUTION"

The Arab-Israeli War in June 1967 suddenly and unexpectedly became the catalytic agent for the reform movement in Czechoslovakia that six months later toppled Party chief Antonin Novotny and embarked upon the great experiment toward "socialism with a human face." The Six Day War highlighted more than anything had before the yawning gap between the regime and public opinion, and at the same time brought the latent and increasingly serious political crisis into the open.

The war broke out at a time when the conflict within the Communist leadership and between the Party and the intellectuals was approaching a climax. The most industrialized country in the Soviet orbit, with the highest degree of democratic traditions, was in the throes of a permanent political, economic, and above all moral crisis. Faced with growing discontent among the intellectuals, the youth and the Slovaks demanding equality with the Czech ruling nation, Novotny and his clique had begun to tighten the reins to bring to an end the period of even limited thaw.

Czechoslovakia had traditionally played a key role in the Soviet political and military strategy in the Middle East. If Israel owes its existence to outside powers, it owes it to the United States, the Soviet Union, and—often forgotten—Czechoslovakia, which after the Arab invasion of Palestine and at a particularly crucial moment, supplied the Israelis with badly needed arms and ammunition, according to some accounts even with fighter planes.[29] Czechoslovakia was among the first to recognize the new State of Israel (on May 18, 1948) and with no other Communist-ruled country were Israel's relations in those early days closer and friendlier. All this was of course in accord with Soviet foreign policy, and friendship was replaced by implacable hostility as soon as Stalin's line changed.

When Stalin's successors embarked upon the political and military penetration of the Middle East, Czechoslovakia was once again given the role of spearhead. The Czechoslovak-Egyptian arms deal in September 1955 marked a historic breakthrough, upsetting the military balance and giving a decisive push to the unending arms race. Though the arms deal, rumored to be worth two hundred million dollars, and several subsequent agreements with Syria and Egypt were initially publicly attributed to Prague alone, they were in fact mainly Soviet arms shipments. But Czechoslovakia, with long traditions of arms production and the most highly developed heavy industry in the Soviet bloc, has been second to none in shouldering the burden of military and economic aid to Moscow's Arab clients.

After the outbreak of the Six Day War, the Novotny regime launched an anti-Israeli, anti-Zionist campaign more intense and more violent than in any other East European country. Czechoslovakia was the first Communist state after the Soviet Union to sever diplomatic relations with Israel, and the first to send a high-level military and political delegation to Egypt and Syria. Within a week, Novotny in three speeches sharply attacked Israel, and Party papers published a number of "spontaneous" pro-Arab, anti-Israeli resolutions from factories and mass organizations as well as a series of savage anti-Zionist, anti-Israeli articles.[30] *Rude Pravo* of June 15, 1967, linked the breakoff of diplomatic relations with the "illicit activities" of Israeli diplomats in Czechoslovakia, including their "being in touch with Jewish religious communties . . . visiting some of the officials of the Jewish religious community in their homes . . . utilizing various Jewish holidays as opportunities for exerting ideological influence and for meeting with the youth . . . organizing illegal emigration."

In addition to disclosing the arrest of at least two members of the religious community, *Rude Pravo* resorted to the methods used during the Slansky purge, publishing the former names of the Israeli diplomats who came originally from Czechoslovakia: Second Secretary Karel Yaaron, formerly Karel Gruenwald; Zwi Shamir, formerly Kurt Stein; Nahum Lavon, formerly Erik Liebman, etc. As usual (and as during the Slansky trial) the article hypocritically claimed that "there is no place whatsoever for anti-Semitism in Czechoslovakia, and it will always be suppressed without any compromise. We have proved on many occasions how much we esteem the victims of Hitlerite Nazism."

This esteem was convincingly illustrated by the fact that the sale of stamps issued in connection with the thousand-year anniversary of the first Jewish settlement in Prague and the seven hundredth anniversary of the world-famous Old-New Synagogue was banned after the Middle East conflict. In an urgent circular letter, the postal administration prohibited the further sale of stamps showing the thirteenth-century synagogue, the Jewish museum, and other religious motivs, not only in the post offices but even in the special shops for philatelists, and ordered the return of all unsold stamps. As a reader's letter in the writers' paper *Literarni Noviny* ironically remarked: "What was the connection between stamps and Israeli aggression? It would be certainly feeble-minded to imagine that the Hebrew stamps issued by the Prague postal authorities inspired Israeli aggression. And yet someone did connect these two things . . ."[31]

Other episodes also shed light on the regime's spurious claim of being anti-Israeli but not anti-Semitic. The celebrations planned to mark the millennium anniversary of Prague Jewry were abruptly canceled. Arab students were allowed to demonstrate on June 6 with placards announcing: "Israel is an imperialist base, it must be destroyed." Despite the strongly pro-Arab official line however, the Egyptian Ambassador in Prague was obviously dissatisfied with the press coverage of the crisis. At a press conference he reproached the Czechoslovak journalists for "not writing objectively" and for their support of Israel. This he attributed to the fact that "the Czechoslovak press remains infested with many Jews." This statement was passed over in silence and did not provoke any official reaction.[32]

It was the zeal of the regime's anti-Zionist and pro-Arab campaign that inflamed the feelings of shame and bitterness among Czech intellectuals to boiling point. Two outstanding (non-Jewish) Communist writers took the lead in organizing a series of protests against the official line. Jan Prochazka, a candidate member of the Party's Central Committee, the chess grand master Ludek Pachmann, and the Jewish writer Arnost Lustig sent a letter to the Party leadership protesting what they termed the immorality of the country's Middle East policy. Prochazka and two other writers also attempted to initiate a serious discussion in *Literarni Noviny*. But these attempts and other letters of protest foundered on the barrier of a rigid censorship.[33]

Matters came to a head at the meeting of the Communist writers and the subsequent Czechoslovak Writers' Congress of June 26–29, 1967. At the Party caucus, Lustig read the text of the letter sent to the Party leadership. This and the entire matter of censorship, as well as the fate of the recently arrested young writer, Jan Benes, sparked off an acrimonious debate between the writers and the Party functionaries. As Lustig revealed almost a year later, Politburo member Jiri Hendrych told him privately "that perhaps personally I am right, that he understands me but that in the fight for the strategic position in the Middle East and over the question of to whom the richest oil deposits in the world will belong there cannot be a question of morals . . ."[34]

Despite the warnings from above, the prominent playwright Pavel Kohout (also a non-Jew) made a remarkable speech at the congress, comparing Czechoslovakia in 1938 with Israel in the June crisis: "If in 1938 the Czechs instead of capitulating had fired the first shot, could they be regarded as the aggressor by just judges of this conflict? In a moral sense, hardly . . . Has the citizen of the country that went through the betrayal of Munich the right to ask whether one is allowed to juggle with the definition of aggression as one-sidedly as our press did? A loyal citizen can also have a personal standpoint—and in the twenty-second year of socialist democracy he must also have the right to publish his opinion."[35]

This was the crux of the matter. The writers merely articulated the feelings of the public at large, for the position of Israel seemed truly similar to the events leading up to the destruction of prewar Czechoslovakia. Even the official press in its attacks on both Israel and the rebellious writers admitted that "certain segments" of the public (which in Communist parlance stands for the vast majority) were impressed by a "sentimental argument" and parallels with 1938.[36]

While Party functionaries were preparing retaliatory measures against the writers and their outspoken weekly, two dramatic events in August further embarrassed the regime. The first was the trip to Israel of Ladislav Mnacko, the country's most successful writer, whose books had sold well over a million copies, as an act of protest against the Czechoslovak pro-Arab policy. In a public letter, this former Partisan and holder of several high decorations stated: "I find it impossible to support a policy, even through silence, which would lead to the extermination of a whole people." After castigating the dictatorial censorship, which imposed a silence on the critics of Czech foreign policy, Mnacko stressed that his country was facing a moral crisis that went back to the Slansky trial and had never been properly discussed. He linked the excessive zeal of the Czechoslovak policy toward Israel with the unmastered past, "the Slansky trial and its consequence, the anti-Semitic tide. People responsible for the events of those days are still around, and it might be more comfortable for them to justify themselves through a new wave of anti-Semitism. I have read recently in our press exactly the same mischief about Zionism and cosmopolitanism as I read at the time of the Slansky trial. The final straw that influenced my decision to travel to Israel as an expression of protest was a small episode rather than a big event.

In a newspaper report on the trial of Pavel Tigrid* I saw that to his name was added his former Jewish name. I know that during the war Tigrid converted to Catholicism. His name was now given as Tigrid-Schoenfeld. I cannot consider this an accident. There was a time when persecution was prepared by similar techniques . . ."[37]

The Communist regime reacted to this act of protest with impotent rage. The letter by a non-Jewish Party veteran and one of their best-known writers received world-wide publicity. Five days after its publication, Mnacko was expelled from the Party, stripped of state decorations and his title of "Meritorious Artist," and deprived of Czechoslovak citizenship. On the same day this was announced, Charles H. Jordan, the fifty-nine-year-old executive vice-president of the Joint, left the Hotel Esplanade in Prague in the evening. He told his wife he was going to buy an American newspaper. Mrs. Jordan never saw him alive again. His body was discovered in the Vltava River four days later. The circumstances of the entire affair, from the behavior of the police to the autopsy, raised widespread suspicions of foul play.

The disappearance of a high official of the same Joint that had been accused during the Slansky trial in 1952 and again in the aftermath of the Six Day War of being an "American espionage agency" should in itself have been sufficient reason for the regime to act speedily to dispel the suspicions. The Czech authorities however did exactly the reverse; despite the Joint's request that foreign doctors be present, Czech pathologists conducted a hurried autopsy without notifying the American Embassy, and by the time the doctors from Switzerland arrived the body had already

* Pavel Tigrid, a Czech Catholic politician, is the publisher of a Czech language periodical in Paris. He lived in exile during the German occupation, and again left the country after the 1948 Communist takeover. In July 1967 he was sentenced by a Prague court "in absentia" to fourteen years, while the young Czech writer Jan Benes received seven years. Benes was pardoned in March 1968 by Novotny. After the invasion in August 1968 and the campaign against "counterrevolutionaries" Tigrid has been repeatedly described as one of the chief "links" between foreign intelligence and domestic "antisocialist" forces.

been dissected and vital organs removed. Two months later Louis Brodio, chairman of the Jewish charitable organization, ruled out the possibility of accident, suicide, or criminal attack and declared: "Someone from one of the Communist or Arab countries murdered Jordan. There are only three possibilities: the Soviet Union, Czechoslovakia, or an Arab agent."[38]

The world will probably never know whether the Soviet or/and Czech secret police were involved in Jordan's death. The mystery deepened when, in December 1967, Professor Hardmeyer, the Swiss specialist who had carried out the second autopsy and was due to publish a report about the tissue samples he had received, was found dead in the snow on a hillside near the lake of Zurich. His car was parked nearby with windows and doors locked. After a long silence, some semiofficial leaks during the 1968 Prague Spring tried to clear the Prague security police of complicity accusations. The murderers were said to have been agents from "the Arab world"; the Czech Government had been unable to reveal the facts because of its relations with the Arab countries.[39] Three years after the event however, Jordan's death still remains a mystery.

In the meantime Novotny's desperate efforts to keep the ferment of the intellectuals, students, and disaffected reformers within bounds failed, and the flood could no longer be checked. It was a temporary coalition of Slovak Communists, intellectuals, and economic reformers supported by deserters from the camp of the Prague centralists, that in December–January finally rid the Party and the country of Novotny's fifteen-year rule. In the train of events leading to the triumph of the reform movement, political and economic issues soon overshadowed the repercussions of the Middle East conflict. Yet, even in retrospect and without losing a sense of proportion, it must be stressed that the popular reaction to the pro-Arab line marked the beginning of the end of Novotny's regime.

Even a cursory review of the Czech experiment, the "attempt for the first time in history to marry socialism with liberty"[40] would be far beyond the scope of this survey. What we are concerned with here is the fact that, as the reform movement gained a momentum, the vexed issues of Israel, anti-Semitism, and Zionism soon surfaced again and played an increasingly important role.

With democratization surging ahead, the re-establishment of diplomatic relations with Israel was regarded by the students and, more obliquely, by the press as a test case for a greater degree of independence in foreign policy. Several reasoned articles pointed out that the breakoff of relations was illogical since Czechoslovakia did not sever diplomatic relations with France during the war in Algeria, nor with the United States on account of the Vietnam war. Taking the example of Rumania, commentators stressed that a resumption of relations should not disturb Czechoslovak friendship with the Arab countries and that Czechoslovakia could thus actively contribute to a peaceful solution in the Middle East. At the same time, the press revealed the scope of popular protest in 1967 and condemned the anti-Semitic propaganda waged by Arab students in Prague.[41]

It was the students who took the initiative in demanding a reappraisal of their country's Middle East policy. During the May Day demonstrations a youth group carried the Israeli flag and another a placard: "Let Israel Live!" At the end of May the students of the philosophical faculty of Prague's Charles University launched an action unprecedented in postwar East European history. They issued an appeal to the population to sign a petition for the resumption of diplomatic relations with Israel: "If Czechoslovakia is to take any initiative that might lead to a solution of the conflict, it must have the same relationship to both sides . . . In view of the fact that diplomatic relations with Israel were broken off at a time when some spokesmen of the Arab states were proclaiming genocide, we consider this step to have been not only politically but also morally wrong. We demand therefore that diplomatic relations with Israel be immediately and unconditionally resumed."[42]

For three weeks the students solicited signatures in the streets of the capital. On June 21, a delegation called at the Foreign Ministry and handed in the petition with 13,662 signatures calling for a resumption of formal diplomatic relations and proposing a nation-wide referendum on the issue. The reply that relations could be resumed only if Israel accepted the UN Security Council resolution calling for an Israeli withdrawal from occupied territories failed to satisfy the public. A few days later, *Student,* the youth weekly, published an open letter to Foreign Minister Hajek by a group of historians reaffirming the plea for re-establishment of relations with Israel, and at the end of June the paper printed an interview, prominently displayed on the first page, with the chief of the East European department in the Israeli Foreign Ministry. Finally, the editors sent a protest to Foreign Minister Hajek and announced the formation of a "Union of the Friends of Israel."[43]

While the official line toward Israel remained outwardly unchanged, the rehabilitation of Mnacko was a significant straw in the wind. Before the end of April, the Ministry of Interior revoked without comment the decree depriving the writer of Czechoslovak citizenship. Even before this step, *Kulturny Zivot,* the weekly organ of the Slovak writers, had published an interview with the exiled writer who finally in mid-May returned to the country whose government only nine months earlier had branded him a traitor. In several interviews Mnacko spelled out in unequivocal terms the reasons for his trip to Israel and the moral and political reasons why he felt there should be a radical change in Czechoslovakia's Middle East policy.[44]

There was also an external factor that injected a new element into the controversy about Israel and anti-Semitism: the student riots in Warsaw and subsequent "anti-Zionist" witch-hunt there coincided with the liberalization movement in Czechoslovakia. At this point it is appropriate to stress the fact that the suppression of the student demonstrations, the purge of the professors, and the anti-Semitic undertones of the campaign provoked a storm of protest in Yugoslavia as well. No less than 160 leading Yugoslav intellectuals, including two members of the Party's Central Committee and 1520 students signed a letter of protest sent to the Polish Embassy in Belgrade and to the Rector of Warsaw University.

From *Komunist*, the central organ of the League of the Communists of Yugoslavia to the literary weeklies and scholarly quarterlies, a number of Yugoslav publications sharply attacked the anti-Semitic excesses in Poland. But since Yugoslavia was always regarded as a maverick from "true socialism," the Polish regime decided to ignore the Yugoslav protest. It was quite different when "tendentious" and "slanderous" attacks came from a neighboring "socialist" country, a full member of the Warsaw Pact. From the very beginning Gomulka was among the sharpest critics of the reform movement in Czechoslovakia.

The protests began with statements issued by the Czech and Slovak writers' unions, universities, and student bodies. The distinguished Marxist philosopher, Karel Kosik, publicly invited several of the sacked Polish professors to come as guest lecturers to Prague. Arnost Lustig, the Czech writer and a Jew, condemned on Prague television the anti-Semitic campaign in Poland and in an open letter challenged the most vitriolic "anti-Zionist" propagandist in Poland, Ryszard Gontarz, to produce proofs for his allegations that a number of Polish writers and scholars were "enemies of the people." Lustig wrote: "It is tragic if people who are the pride of Polish culture are enemies, and tragic that anyone could describe them as such arbitrarily and publicly." Instead of taking up his suggestion of publishing both his letter and Gontarz's reply, the Polish ambassador on April 27, 1968, protested verbally at the Foreign Ministry against "anti-Polish statements."[45]

Perhaps the most moving appeal to the Polish leaders was an open letter by three Czech writers—Pavel Kohout, Jan Prochazka, and Arnost Lustig. Stressing that they were born in three different environments and brought up in three different confessions, united only by their profession and convictions as writers and Communists, they asked that the natural criticism of the younger generation not be confused with hostile subversion, appealed to the Polish leaders to "put an end to the shameful anti-Semitism that stains the common fight of Poles and Jews against Nazism. The official campaign against Zionism gives reason to fear the revival of the phantom of anti-Semitism, which in our century has always signalized a catastrophe."[46]

The answer to this plea was an official Polish note on May 6 addressed to the Czechoslovak Party leadership and the government protesting an "anti-Polish campaign waged in press, radio, and recently at some public meetings." This last was an allusion to a student rally in the old town square of the capital on May 3 at which several thousand young people approved a resolution voicing full solidarity with the Polish students and condemning the anti-Semitic campaign in Poland, which was forwarded to both the Polish Embassy and the student union in Warsaw. The Polish protest failed to put an end to the "tendentious" and outspoken reporting of the Czech press. Though the Czech Government three weeks later, in a cautiously worded reply, disassociated itself from the "opinion of individuals" published in the mass media, which "can be taken as interference in Polish internal affairs,"[47] several Prague papers continued to report the truth. The weekly *Student,* for example, candidly stated that the entire "anti-Zionist" campaign was merely a trump card in a power struggle within the Polish leadership.

The Czech-Polish polemics were of course a by-product of the diametrically opposed political trends in the two countries. But they were also influenced by two special issues. On the Czech side, the revelations about the background of the Slansky trial and related purges had brought the question of moral and political rehabilitation of victims of past injustices into the foreground of debates. The resurrection of anti-Zionism in Poland could not fail to inflame passions to a pitch. As J. Brejchova put it in the Prague daily *Prace* on June 8: "The word Zionism reminds us of the six million victims and of the fact that some years ago when people were thrown into prison and hanged, a campaign against Zionism was launched here. Thus our concern is legitimate when neighbors of Czechoslovakia depict Zionism again as a bogey."

At the same time, Polish extremists began to accuse the Czech critics of Polish anti-Semitism of Zionism, hoping in this way to give a further push to the witch-hunt in Poland. This counteroffensive, actually a part of the mounting pressure from the whole Communist bloc on the reformers in Prague, began in earnest after the Polish protest note in May.

The first attack was launched on Warsaw television on May 11 by J. Barecky, deputy editor of *Trybuna Ludu,* who accused "antisocialist and Zionist forces in Czechoslovakia" of waging an anti-Polish campaign, of "demanding bourgois political parties and improved relations with West Germany and Israel." The PAX papers wrote about "cosmopolitan" elements in Czechoslovakia, while *Zolnierz Wolnosci,* the Army organ, connected the "hopes of Washington and Bonn looking for cracks" in the Communist world with "the voices of antisocialist, liberal-opportunistic, and Zionist elements heard during the developments unfolding in Czechoslovakia." Speakers at Party meetings in Poland attacked "the revisionist, counterrevolutionary, and Zionist elements in control of Czech mass media."[48] *Kultura,* the organ of the Partisan faction, sanctimoniously complained that "articles in Czech publications discredit the meaning and the moral and social merit of the changes that have taken place in our country as a result of the March events."[49] The fact that, with the exception of Lustig, all the Czechoslovak intellectuals protesting against Polish anti-Semitism were non-Jews did not of course have the slightest effect on the charges of "Zionism" leveled against them.

It would be however wrong to believe that the accusation of Zionism against the reformist intellectuals in Czechoslovakia was a purely Polish invention. The Poles simply spoke first. The invasion of Czechoslovakia opened a synchronized anti-Semitic campaign jointly organized by Moscow, Warsaw, and East Berlin in close cooperation with the pro-Soviet Stalinists in Czechoslovakia itself.

With the successful offensive of the reformists, the discredited Stalinists, driven underground, resorted to the deliberate stirring-up of anti-Jewish resentment. In February 1968, five Party veterans headed by a certain Josef Jodas drew up and circulated among various Party organizations, functionaries, and factories a fourteen-page mimeographed pamphlet that described the January plenum of the Central Committee and the fall of Novotny as a "bourgeois putsch" and pledged loyalty to Novotny.[50] What distinguished the document was the anti-Semitic undertone of its attacks against the "revisionist and treacherous group . . . our fifth column which with the support of responsible functionaries has launched an anti-Communist and anti-Soviet propaganda offensive on a broad front. Through economic measures, Zionism, falsification of the Party's and the nation's history, it proceeds to the defense of Munich, Hitler, and fascism."

After the theoretical innovation of "Zionism as a means to defend Hitler," the authors denounced the members of "an old faction which used to meet in the Institute for Party History" as the "shock troop" responsible for the January plenum. The list of the chief culprits, the "provocateurs," "liquidators," "careerists," and "agents of imperialism" read like a copy of the indictment in the Slansky trial: Goldstuecker (sentenced to life in 1953), Smrkovsky (arrested 1951, life sentence), Svermova (sentenced to life in 1954), Josefa Slanska (widow of Rudolf Slansky), Hajek-Karpeles (life term, almost blinded in prison), Josef Pavel (arrested 1951, also life sentence), etc. Of the eight names mentioned, six were victims of the 1951 frame-up and five were Jews, including the only Jewish Central Committee member, Frantisek Kriegel. Bedrich Hajek, the sixty-eight-year-old prewar activist arrested in 1952 and rehabilitated in 1963, was pointedly referred to as "Hajek-Karpeles." The last time he had been so described had been during the Slansky trial when the chief defendant was accused of "taking into the Cadre Commission of the Central Committee his people, such as Hajek-Karpeles, Jancik-Jung, and others."

Although it provoked disgust, the letter of the "Five," as the inveterate dogmatists were nicknamed, was widely regarded as unimportant within the Party. Many more Party veterans were publicly taking a stand in favor of the "January course." How indeed could anyone imagine that anti-Semitic innuendoes would carry any weight in a country with a minuscule Jewish minority and in a Party in which not a single Jew had occupied an executive position since 1951. In Prague, the heart of the reform movement, out of one million inhabitants an estimated seven thousand were Jews, more than half of whom had no contact whatever with the religious community; in Brno, the second largest city, there were some six hundred Jews among 320,000 inhabitants, and in Bratislava, the capital of Slovakia, two to three thousand in a population of a quarter million.

True, a handful of Jewish writers and newspapermen, including Professor Eduard Goldstuecker, the literary critic; Ivan Klima, the young playwright; Lustig, the novelist, and a few others were enthusiastic supporters of the new "January line"—along with the entire Czechoslovak intelligentsia. During the entire period from January to August 1968, only two Jews played an important role in the country's political and spiritual life: Professor Goldstuecker, elected Chairman of the Writers' Union in January, and Dr. Frantisek Kriegel, a physician and veteran of the Spanish Civil War, who on April 5 became a member of the eleven-member Party Presidium and Chairman of the National Front.

Nevertheless, hundreds of anonymous anti-Semitic letters flooded the leading reformist newspapers and scores of prominent intellectuals received threatening letters accusing such "full-blooded Aryans" as Pavel Kohout, Ludvik Vaculik, and Jiri Hochman of being "Zionists and revisionists, agents of imperialism."[51]

From the very beginning the threats tried to exploit the fact that many Czechs and Slovaks have German-sounding names (Liehm, Fleissig, etc.) without being Jews. The letter writers also invariably pretended to speak on behalf of the working class and used Communist phraseology. *Prace,* the trade union daily, reprinted a typical example: "You slander the Party and try to undermine the confidence of people. You call yourselves trade unionists, you who sneaked into the TU paper although you have nothing in common with the unions. Messrs. Stern, Fleissig, Kohn, Weiner, Kraus, or whatever you are called, we know that you are Jews and parasites of the nation whose destiny is no concern to you." The letter was signed "Workers of Avia works, Cakovice."[52] As with many other similar attacks, this was a fictitious name.

A month later one of the vilified editors, Josef Fleissig, summarized the readers' reactions. While many condemned the anti-Semitic insults, there were also anonymous letters endorsing them. One letter said it was obvious that the paper was full of Jews willing to sell out the republic. This letter and others "blamed the Jews for bad housing, high rents, fees for pharmaceutics, low pensions, etc." Commenting on the letters, Fleissig wrote that he had had to prove his "Aryan origin" to the Nazis during the war; now he had to do the same for a "worker from the Avia works." The only difference was that the Nazis passed him as an "Aryan" whereas the petty Czech Hitlers of today did not. The fascist anti-Semitic letters would not matter, he added, if most of the scribblers did not emphasize that they were members of the Party and "true" Communists. Such "socialism" made Fleissig wonder whether he wanted to stay in the same Party with anonymous letter-writers. He also mentioned in passing that there was only one Jew on the paper's staff.[53]

Hand in hand with the anti-Semitic letters, some foreign "friends" of Czechoslovakia prepared a clumsy provocation. At the end of May and the beginning of June several hundred people, non-Jews and Jews, in Prague received a letter ostensibly sent by the Documentation Center of the Federation of Jewish Victims of Nazism in Vienna and signed by its director, Simon Wiesenthal. The recipients, addressed as "Dear Friend," were told that the "democratic developments making such excellent progress in Czechoslovakia are also advantageous to the cause of world Jewry and our state—Israel. The Jews love the freedom because they can fulfill their historical mission, the spiritual leadership of the world, only under the conditions of freedom . . . Therefore I appeal to you as to other friends in Czechoslovakia, as courageous fighters for the cause of the Jews, to carry out further active efforts in the interests of our cause."

The letter stressed the importance of liberalization because this alone "would make possible the intensification of our efforts aimed at the re-establishment of friendly relations between Israel and Czechoslovakia and the gaining of Czechoslovak support for the just cause and·achievements of Israel. This would also allow the resumption of normal relations between Czechoslovakia and the German Federal Republic." Stressing "the special importance of the fight against anti-Semitism in the Communist countries, especially in Poland," the letter concluded with an appeal for further protests and also for the dispatch of relevant documents about anti-Semitism to the Documentation Center.

The stationery was an exact copy of that used by the Vienna center, and Wiesenthal's signature was also his. But in fact the whole letter was a forgery. Wiesenthal sent a public protest to the Czech minister in Vienna, and the Austrian Legation in Prague was informed about the provocation on June 20.[54] A comparison of the "Wiesenthal letter" with the forged letter sent to Dr. Majewska in Gdansk two months earlier* and the special reference to Poland seem to indicate that both provocations were prepared by the same people—Moczar's agents.

Initially, the Number One target of the anti-Semitic campaign was Professor Goldstuecker who, as Chairman of the Writers' Union, was one of the fervent and vocal advocates of the new model of democratic socialism. A prewar Communist, Goldstuecker had been Czech minister to Israel and Sweden before he was caught up in December 1951 in the Slansky purge. Sentenced to life imprisonment in 1953, he spent four years in prison and in the uranium mines at Jachymov. In 1963 he was appointed Professor of German Literature at Prague University and won international fame the same year when he presided at an East-West conference to commemorate the birthday of the great German writer from Prague, Franz Kafka. Despite the bitter resistance of the East German delegation, Kafka was—four decades after his death—"rehabilitated." Until the Prague Spring, Goldstuecker's role was minimal however and even after his appointment as Chairman of the Writers' Union, he held no position whatsoever in the Party itself.

But being a reformer and a Jew, he was singled out as the first

* See the Majewska case in Part Two, Chapter 3, "The Witch-Hunt Begins."

target of the counteroffensive. On June 23, 1968, *Rude Pravo* reprinted an anonymous letter sent to Goldstuecker and his reply. Even a few quotes suffice to give an idea of the style: "Mr. Goldstuecker, rascal, Zionist hyena, on your birthday we send millions of curses on behalf not only of the working class of our country but also in the name of other socialist countries. Only the last developments opened the eyes of honest Czech people, workers and Party members, to the fact that you should have been given the rope along with Slansky and not a life sentence. The honest Communists know that you are a Western agent . . . You should found another party, perhaps an Israeli party. The Communist Party is a workers' party, and we know very well with whom you were in contact in England, Israel, and elsewhere. These are the representatives of espionage centers, and we also have photocopies and other documents which we shall very soon put at the disposal of the competent authorities, first of all in the Soviet Union and then elsewhere, to undertake the necessary steps to unmask your nature . . . You can write your last will. You are the instigator of recent events, which you. and your kind had prepared a long time ago. But the working class has not yet said its last word . . . You want to rule, you Jews, not only in Israel; as a Zionist you wish to dominate the whole world. That is why we here know very well that the instigators of recent events, in Poland too, are the Zionists who do all this in context of fulfilling the expansionist plans of international Zionism. Don't worry, your time will come; your days are numbered, you filthy Jew."

Within less than two months, it became clear that Goldstuecker was right when he took this letter seriously and, instead of ignoring it, published a reply: "It may be the product of the pathological periphery of political life found in every country. But men of my generation cannot forget that it was in such a pathological atmosphere that, for example, the Nazi Party emerged. It would be an unforgivable omission to treat lightly such a well-known phenomenon. I know its vocabulary, phraseology, and stylistic principles. It is the language of my investigators from Ruzyn in 1951–53, of my guards from Pankrac, Leopoldov, and Jachymov in 1953–55, of my indictment and the speech of the prosecutor."

Goldstuecker made it clear that the letter must have been written not by a worker but by someone who might have been a worker a very long time ago but later was connected with the security service of the 1950s, "a wheel of the security machinery still turning in the same way as it was wound up at that time." He challenged the anonymous bullies to present the evidence about the "Zionist conspiracy" and concluded: "I learn from the anonymous letter that some one in our country once again dreams of staging a trial against an alleged Zionist conspiracy and that I am singled out for the role of main defendant. I know this song and the authors of its text and music very well. I know that my life is at stake. I put myself under the protection of my fellow citizens knowing that this is the best protection."

From the Federation of the Antifascist Resistance Fighters to several prominent scholars, a number of organizations and individuals took a public stand against anti-Semitism and pledged support for Goldstuecker. On July 1, *Rude Pravo* revealed that within a week it had received two hundred and eighteen letters, the majority condemning anti-Semitism, but some complaining that "Goldstuecker had not been gassed."[55] The issue of anti-Semitism remained on the agenda of articles and television roundtable discussions. It was a component of the sharpening conflict between the reformist leaders and their domestic and foreign opponents. The anonymous leaflets distributed in Prague and other urban centers, occasionally even dropped from airplanes, always connected the attacks against the "January line" with overt "anti-Zionist" outbursts.

The methods were basically the same as those used by the Polish dogmatists in 1956. However, with so few Jews around, let alone in the Party ranks, the manipulators had to resort to manufacturing Jews in order to discredit the leaders of the reform movement. Deputy Premier Ota Sik, the distinguished economist and creator of the Czech economic reform plans sabotaged by the dogmatists, was singled out as a "Zionist." Sik, a member of the Central Committee and the select Academy of Sciences, played an outstanding role at the crucial January session of the Central Committee and during the fight with the conservatives. Never before had anyone heard about his being of Jewish origin. Regardless of whether he indeed has one Jewish grandparent or a Jewish mother, even the Nazis had treated him as an "Aryan."[56]

Such men as Goldstuecker and Kriegel were of course hated because they were progressive, not because they were Jews. But they had to be discredited as Jews, and by linking people of "dubious" origin like Sik, or "pure" Czechs like Central Committee secretary Cestmir Cisar with them, they too could be made to seem Jewish by implication, or at least "Zionist stooges." Thus a typical leaflet circulating in July in the capital attacked Sik, Kriegel, and Cisar as "political adventurers striving for a kind of freedom that would allow them to slander the Communist Party and prepare the ground for the rule of Zionism, a freedom that would lead to the liquidation of the achievements of the people."[57]

When on the night of August 20, Soviet, German, Polish, Hungarian, and Bulgarian Army units invaded Czechoslovakia to "save" the country from "the counterrevolution" and the "restoration of capitalism," the Kremlin achieved a military success at the price of a political disaster. This is not the place to analyze the tangled motives of the military intervention or the phases of the slow agony of that unhappy country. What matters here is that within forty-eight hours it became evident that the anonymous authors of the clandestine anti-Semitic pamphlets and those who made threatening phone calls and dispatched intimidating letters during the tense spring and summer of 1968 were not acting on their own but in close cooperation with their Soviet masters.

The invasion also marked the beginning of a full-scale "anti-Zionist" campaign launched by Moscow, East Berlin, and Warsaw. It is no exaggeration to say that not since Stalin's death had the world witnessed such a vicious and centrally manipulated international operation to channel hatred for Soviet domination into hatred for the Jews. The evidence is overwhelming and points to the existence of a blueprint, prepared well in advance.

On August 22, that is, one day after the invasion, the Soviet Government newspaper, attacking a motley collection of "former Nazi generals, SS officers, old fascists, reactionary clergy, etc." also accused three leaders of the "Club of engaged non-Party people" bearing the distinctly non-Jewish names of Rubacek, Musil, and Klementiev of being not only "counterrevolutionaries" but also "agents of the international Zionist organization known as 'Joint.'"[58] The "anti-Zionist" propaganda campaign erupted at full strength on August 25, following the fantastic feat of the Czech reformers who, despite occupation and the kidnaping at gunpoint of their leaders, managed to convene the fourteenth extraordinary Party Congress, originally scheduled for September 9, in a Prague factory.

The congress confirmed First Secretary Alexander Dubcek and the other abducted reformers in their positions and elected a new Presidium, cleansed of collaborators and including Professor Goldstuecker and Deputy Premier Sik. Thus among the thirty-odd members of the new Presidium two were Jews—Kriegel and Goldstuecker. The "Zionist" Sik, Foreign Minister Hajek, and three other ministers happened to have been on vacation in Yugoslavia when the invasion took place. This fact unexpectedly strengthened the bargaining position of the Czechoslovak leaders who, after having been handcuffed, starved, and in the case of Kriegel allegedly even beaten, were "negotiating" with their captors in Moscow. The declaration of the Czechoslovak ministers in Belgrade, their treatment as the only legal representatives of the Czechoslovak Government by their hosts, Sik's flight to Bucharest where he was demonstratively received by the Rumanian President Ceausescu, and Foreign Minister Hajek's appearance at the United Nations Security Council debate on Czechoslovakia implied a barely veiled warning to the Kremlin: the setting-up, if necessary, of a government-in-exile harbored and supported by two Communist-ruled countries. This threat, together with the magnificent popular resistance in the country, thwarted the Russian attempt to install immediately a puppet regime.

Meanwhile in Moscow, Dr. Kriegel, who had been insulted at

the Cierna talks at the end of July by the Russians as a "Galician Jew" who should shut up, was not admitted to the conference table and was kept manacled. Kriegel refused to sign the August 26 "Moscow agreement" that accepted the forced occupation of the country by Soviet troops, and his name was not mentioned in the list of participants. When Dubcek, Svoboda, and the rest of the Czech group assembled at the airport to fly home, Kriegel was missing. Several unimpeachable sources agree that the Czechs were told by the Soviets that an anti-Zionist trial must be staged with Kriegel and Goldstuecker in the dock. Dubcek and the other Czech leaders refused to depart without Kriegel. After several hours, Kriegel, officially still a full member of the Party Presidium and chairman of the National Front, was finally taken to the airport and allowed to embark with the rest of the delegation. As a condition of his release, Kriegel immediately on his return had to resign from his political post and return to practicing medicine.[59]

The anti-Zionist propaganda barrage on August 25 was launched simultaneously in East Germany and Poland as well as Czechoslovakia. Commenting on the extraordinary Party Congress, *Neues Deutschland,* the central organ of the East German Communists, flatly announced: "Zionist forces have taken over the leadership of the Party." No names were given—admittedly it would have been difficult to produce more than two Jews. *Berliner Zeitung* (East Berlin) of the same day however carried a list of the "enemies of socialism: Sik (who was in Belgrade), Goldstuecker (also abroad at the time of the invasion), Kriegel (in a Moscow prison), and others . . ." Next day the East German Party paper implicated one of the "big four" in the Czechoslovak leadership, Josef Smrkovsky, the president of Parliament, as being in the "Zionist Plot." Announcing that patriots (that is, Soviet technicians) managed to broadcast regular television newsreels, the paper's correspondent drew attention to the "sensational news that Smrkovsky's adviser sold strictly confidential information about the (Soviet-Czechoslovak summit) meeting at Cierna-nad-Tisou to the Israeli secret service, and Cestmir Cisar used to receive British 'journalists' after internal conferences." In other words, one of the top leaders worked for the "Israelis," the other for the British espionage.

On the same day that *Neues Deutschland* revealed that "Zionist forces" had taken over the 1.7-million-member Czech Communist Party, General Jan Czapla, the deputy chief political commissar of the Polish Army, announced that "the sources of the March events in Poland and the attacks in Czechoslovakia were identical: revisionism and Zionism. Their aims were also identical—but while in Poland their attacks were effectively repelled, in Czechoslovakia these forces went so far as to effectively threaten the basis of socialism . . . They wanted to breach the southern flank of the Warsaw Pact."[60] General Czapla's article was published in *Trybuna Ludu,* reprinted next day in scores of newspapers, and summarized several times by Warsaw radio and television. The hardliners lost no time in pointing out next day that "West Germany was actively assisting counterrevolutionary and Zionist forces in Czechoslovakia." *Trybuna Ludu* described the "Zionist forces" as being "among the most important wirepullers of counterrevolution. Unfortunately in Czechoslovakia one speaks little about the powerful Zionist forces in view of the unpleasant experiences of Stalin's time, which also affected citizens of Jewish origin."[61]

The central direction was also evident in the resolution adopted by the Soviet-Ukrainian Writers' Union on August 27, the day after the Soviet-Czechoslovak Moscow "agreement." As a neighbor of Czechoslovakia, which has a two hundred thousand Ukrainian minority of the Soviet Ukraine, itself plagued by rising nationalism, was the Soviet area most susceptible to the reforms in Prague, and therefore the first to back the invasion and to describe the "so-called writers Goldstuecker, Prochazka, Vaculik, and others . . . as accomplices of world imperialism and militant Zionism."[62]*

But outside "anti-Zionist" outbursts were a trifle compared to the anti-Semitic propaganda unleashed in Czechoslovakia itself. Having failed to break popular resistance and the network of

* Apart from Goldstuecker, none of the much-maligned "counterrevolutionary" and "Zionist" writers such as Mnacko, Kohout, Prochazka, Vaculik, Liehm, etc., is Jewish.

clandestine radio broadcasts, the occupiers printed a Czech news-paper called *Zpravy* in East Germany and began to beam broad-casts from "Vltava" station, which in fact simply used the international wavelength of the East Berlin radio. The Soviet-German smear campaign was exposed as early as August 26 by the Czechoslovak Radio:

At last we have learned who is responsible for the nonexistent Czechoslovak counterrevolution. We have been told this by the official press of the occupiers, and they have done so in their cus-tomary refined and euphemistic manner. They did not say outright the Jews, they said international Zionism. Apparently on this topic our East German friends have been experts ever since the days of World War II. At that time it was the final solution of the Jewish Question, today it is the suppression of the Czech counterrevolution.

In the beginning it was asserted that there was only a handful of counterrevolutionaries or Zionists, anarchists, traitors, or antisocialist elements in Czechoslovakia, but that they had become rulers within the Party and in the country in general. Today Soviet soldiers are better instructed. Allegedly two million people are involved, and when they have been liquidated the soldiers will apparently leave our country. I lack precise data on how many Jewish inhabitants live in Czechoslovakia. Insofar as the uninvited guests from Ger-many, the Soviet Union, and the other three Warsaw Pact states divide them into Zionists and others, I doubt that with the best will in the world they can find enough to make up the aforementioned two million people. However what does not exist may exist, and from our experiences with the occupiers it actually will exist . . . Since last Wednesday morning all sorts of things have been found in our country, and a lot more are sure to be found. Why then cannot two million Zionists be found if the Soviet Army command or perhaps *Neues Deutschland* should wish it? Anyhow, the Germans are today the sole authentic experts capable of exactly distinguishing Aryans from those less developed races."[63]

That German soldiers, thirty years after the destruction of prewar Czechoslovakia, once again, this time in the guise of "fra-ternal comrades," overran the country, added insult to injury.

And the fact that the most venomous onslaughts on "counter-revolutionaries and Zionists" came from German territory did not pass unnoticed. Leaving aside the Vltava radio station, the official East Berlin mass media surpassed even the Poles in the intensity and frequency of their anti-Zionist slanders. The German Communists saw the resurrection of the Zionist bogey in Czechoslovakia as a politically welcome opportunity to capture Arab sympathies. In addition to vilifying the leading reformers day and night, the Germans, past masters in the "hate Israel campaign," hastened to link Czech "counterrevolutionaries" with Israel.

As the invasion took place in the holiday season, many Czechoslovaks were abroad, including a group of journalists on assignment in Israel. Like all Czechoslovaks abroad, including most of the diplomatic missions, these six (non-Jewish) journalists and radio commentators condemned the occupation of their country. This is how *Neues Deutschland* reported the episode under a banner headline: "The Czechoslovak counterrevolutionaries had close relations with imperialist circles in Israel. This emerges from a report according to which a group of journalists from the counterrevolutionary periodical *Literarni Listy* was surprised in Israel by the news about the supporting action of the socialist countries. The group issued a counterrevolutionary appeal from Israeli territory . . ."[64] Countless similar attacks were published in the East German press, many aimed at Goldstuecker, Kohout, and other writers who happened to have been out of the country when Moscow struck.

In a survey of former Nazis in leading positions in East German mass media, Simon Wiesenthal pointed out the startling parallels between the present and past phraseology at a press conference, stressing that if one replaces the word Zionist or Israel with Jew, and "progressive forces" with "national socialism," the articles could have stemmed from Goebbels. This was not surprising, since thirty-nine former Nazi journalists occupied prominent positions, such as chief of the Government's press office, official speaker of the Party, deputy editor of *Neues Deutschland,* and so on.[65] The Berlin-Moscow axis as the center of anti-Semitic propaganda was attacked even by *Volksstimme,* the official organ of the Austrian Communist Party, which described the anti-Zionist outbursts as "intolerable."[66] The outcry in Czechoslovakia itself, particularly after the scurrilous East German attacks on Foreign Minister Hajek, Goldstuecker, and Sik, was such that, despite the censorship imposed by the "Moscow agreement," *Politika,* the official (and now defunct) weekly of the Czechoslovak Party, in October 1968 condemned those "utter lies, fabrications, and slanders . . . Assertions and pseudo conclusions with clearly anti-Semitic undertones are among the most deplorable aspects of the current activity of the East German press. I certainly do not believe that we ought to gloss over or excuse anti-Semitism or any other racist tendencies no matter where they come from. If moreover they come from Berlin of all places, they create an even more obnoxious impression and must be all the more condemned."[67]

The invasion added one more prominent figure to the small group of purported Zionists: Jiri Hajek, former Czech ambassador to the UN, Minister of Education (from 1965 to 1968), and since April 1968 Foreign Minister. This was of course because Hajek in a cautiously worded but unequivocal speech before the UN Security Council repeated and expanded the statement issued in Prague on the night of the invasion, that the entry of Soviet and other East European armies took place "without the knowledge and agreement of the head of state, the Premier, Parliament, and the Party Presidium." Thus he became one of the prime targets of Soviet and East German attacks. *Izvestia* published on September 4 a two-column piece devoted exclusively to Hajek, who was charged with having "entered into a plot with O. Sik, known for his rightist revisionist views," in Belgrade to bring the question of Czechoslovakia before the United Nations, of working against the Warsaw Pact, of wanting to change Czechoslovak foreign policy, and specifically of intending to establish closer relations with West Germany and favoring the resumption of diplomatic relations with Israel for which "not accidentally he was praised and thanked by the Israeli press."

What received world-wide publicity was the astonishing fact that the Soviet Government's official organ connected the attack on the *"former* Czechoslovak Foreign Minister" (actually he had not resigned at that point nor was he dismissed) with the sensational revelation that this "handmaiden of the dark forces of reaction and counterrevolution" was a Jew. In a personal profile, Hajek was accused of having "collaborated with the Gestapo during the German occupation in order to save his skin. Perhaps this is the reason why he changed his name from Karpeles to Hajek." Karpeles is of course a distinctly Jewish name, and *Izvestia* went on to describe the Foreign Minister as "Hajek-Karpeles."

Even in the Communist world, the unprecedented attack on Hajek, who was still officially Foreign Minister of an ostensibly sovereign (though occupied) country, caused an uproar. *Volksstimme* protested: "One cannot reject sharply and energetically enough this filth, which was printed in the organ of the Soviet Government." After denying the political accusations against Hajek with regard to West Germany, Israel, etc., it added: "And the 'Karpeles' story reminds one of the tone of *Der Stuermer.* Bad enough that there exists a Mr. Korzhev [the author of the article] who writes such a thing. Much worse is the fact that *Izvestia* prints it."[68]

The anti-Semitic propagandists in Moscow had however committed a painful blunder, revealed by the world press the following day. As *Volksstimme* put it: "They caught the wrong Hajek. Foreign Minister Dr. Jiri Hajek was never a Jew nor ever called Karpeles. Quite apart from the intolerable style of *Izvestia* with its strong anti-Semitic under (or over) tones, the other allegations are pointless, since the attacked Hajek is not the same as the Hajek they aimed at. There is really a Hajek, not Jiri but Bedrich, who was once called Karpeles. He changed his name in 1945 to Hajek. He did not collaborate with the Gestapo because, as a Jew, he had to flee and lived during the war in Britain as an emigrant, actively participating in the Czechoslovak liberation movement. Apart from having been called once Karpeles, *Izvestia*'s allegations do not fit this Hajek either."[69]

Whether *Izvestia* (and *Neues Deutschland* which had of course immediately reprinted the article) had committed this embarrassing mistake by relying on the earlier mentioned letter of Czechoslovak Stalinists the previous February, or on the transcript of the Slansky trial, was of comparatively minor interest. What stood out was the fact that Moscow had tried to make a Czechoslovak statesman into a Jew. The Soviet leaders had revealed themselves as inheritors of the Stalinist tactic of deliberately encouraging anti-Semitism in moments of acute crisis. In an interview several weeks later Professor Hajek, who is also member of the Academy, replied to the attacks, without mentioning *Izvestia,* in the following dignified words: "These attacks were directed not only against my personal honor, they had in part a racist character, which, one must acknowledge, were without any basis whatsoever. It is not true that I am of Jewish origin. But I would not be at all ashamed if it were true, because we must judge a man on the basis of what he does and how he behaves, and because this country said farewell to racism a long time ago."[70]*

The "Hajek-Karpeles" blunder did not change the Soviet leaders' determination to use every possible means, including anti-Semitism, to force the resignation of the most prominent liberals as a prelude to the wholesale purge of the Dubcek team. *Izvestia* published no correction, and Hajek as well as Kriegel and Sik resigned in September. They remained however members of the Communist Central Committee. Though those abroad on leave of absence, Sik and Goldstuecker, kept silent, the campaign was relentlessly intensified. *Neues Deutschland* on September 27, and five days later *Literaturnaya Gazeta,* the organ of the Soviet Writers' Union, published full-page articles against Professor Goldstuecker, "the many-faced liberal," one of the main theorists of the "quiet counterrevolution," linking his nefarious role before August 1968 with his "not at all incidental" attempts "to study and to propagandize the philosophy of Franz Kafka, 'the poet of alienation.'"

Aside from the timing of the attacks in East Berlin and Moscow, the special feature of the outbursts against Goldstuecker was the revival of the accusation of Zionism. Rarely if ever before in

* *Izvestia* has never retracted its false denunciation of Hajek.

Communist history was a victim of a frame-up accused a second time of the same sins—and by the spokesman of the same power that almost killed him fifteen years earlier to boot. *Literaturnaya Gazeta*, after describing Goldstuecker as a particularly dangerous man "working always in the shadows," made the "significant" point that he had been "an active member of a Zionist youth organization in secondary school." It will be remembered that Goldstuecker with many others was tortured and compelled to testify in the Slansky trial and was sentenced to life imprisonment.

In the Soviet paper's version however the persecuted became the persecutor: in connection with the trial of a number of people "who were as it turned out groundlessly accused of criminal ties with world Zionism," Goldstuecker was a denunciator and turncoat. The paper charged that Goldstuecker published an anti-Zionist article. "This denunciation did not save him from arrest. But Goldstuecker's 'zealousness' was noted. He became one of the chief witnesses for the prosecution at the trial of the 'Slansky Affair.' Goldstuecker, who many years later would picturesquely don the toga of a fighter against anti-Semitism, saved his life even though later—in connection with a different case—he himself had been sentenced to prison."

In other words, Professor Goldstuecker, who was of course "neither a well-known literary expert nor a famous writer," was "at first a Zionist, then a Communist . . . afterwards a 'witness for the prosecution' and 'exposer of Zionism' who supported the groundless charges against certain persons. And finally (as Chairman of the Writers' Union) almost the 'father of Czechoslovak liberalism.'" The character assassination was completed by the description of the anonymous anti-Semitic letter to Goldstuecker and his reply as "a sly maneuver," a part of "the final blow to discredit the Communists and the Communist Party in general." Even though the Soviet weekly was constrained to admit that "Goldstuecker has not said one word in public since August 21" he was linked with the unnamed forces of counterrevolution in Czechoslovakia, which behind hypocritical calls for normalization were attempting to regroup themselves.

It was of course not against Goldstuecker alone, but the whole progressive leadership that the anti-Semitic campaign was directed. After the invasion failed to achieve its purpose, the Soviet tactic was to split the reformists who still tried to save the remnants of the Prague Spring. The Czechoslovak leaders and the newspapers published a series of blistering rebuttals to the continuing flood of anti-Semitic anonymous letters, but because of the secret protocols of the "Moscow agreement," they could not publicly reply to the Soviet and East German statements and had to restrict themselves to repeated warnings against the danger of an artificially fed anti-Semitism. Dubcek himself in a nation-wide speech declared that "the Party must insure that it is not blemished by anti-Semitism."[71]

Nevertheless the campaign of vilification went on at an accelerated pace. *Zpravy,* the paper distributed by the occupiers, provoked an official protest from the Presidium of the Czechoslovak Parliament when it published an anti-Semitic attack against Dr. Kriegel[72] who with three other members of Parliament voted against the October treaty legalizing the "temporary stationing of Soviet troops on Czechoslovak territory." Later *Zpravy* accused the Jews in Czechoslovakia of "being a part of a spiderweb of the Israeli aggression."[73]

Preparing for the decisive blow against the Dubcek leadership, TASS, the Soviet news agency, expressed "surprise" that "Sik, Goldstuecker, and others engaged in hostile activities against their country still remain members of the Communist Party."[74] Defying Soviet pressure, Sik and Goldstuecker returned in January 1969 for a short visit to Prague and took the oath as members of the Czech National Council, the Parliament of Czech lands under the new federal system.*

While the nation-wide mourning for the student Jan Palach, who immolated himself as a protest against his country's occupation, led to a temporary delay in the Soviet timetable, anti-Semitic outbursts against Czechoslovak politicians and intellectuals were rapidly approaching a climax. At a meeting of some five hundred

---

* Soon after Dubcek's fall both lost their positions and were subsequently expelled from the Party.

pro-Soviet dogmatists called to mark the forty-fifth anniversary of Lenin's death and (ironically) the fiftieth anniversary of the murder of Rosa Luxemburg and Karl Liebknecht, Vilem Novy, a Central Committee member, castigated "the infamous role" played by Goldstuecker, Hajek, Sik, Kriegel, and others. The meeting responded by chanting, "Down with revisionism and Zionism!" and "Drive them out, shame!"[75]

It is important to remember that the anti-Zionist drive was, as always, a means to an end—the fall of Dubcek and his associates. And along with Dubcek, Svoboda, and Smrkovsky, as late as March 1969, Sik, the father of the new economic plan now living in self-imposed exile as visiting professor at Basle, was named in a public opinion poll as one of the five most popular politicians in the country. But by then Smrkovsky had been skillfully removed as President of the Federal Parliament, and preparations were in full swing to stage the final showdown.

In early March, TASS reprinted in its foreign edition an article published in the pro-Communist Lebanese newspaper *Al Dunia*. The article subsequently appeared in a number of Soviet newspapers and was broadcast in full by Moscow Radio.[76] It was a prime example of the ancient Soviet technique of "feed-back" and "cross references."

The technique works in the following manner: *Neues Deutschland* reports the "collaboration of Bonn-Tel Aviv for the planned sterilization of Arabs." Evidence: "the Lebanese weekly *Al Hadaf* reports that eight West German doctors before the end of the year (1968) came to Tel Aviv and Jerusalem to sterilize Arab men and women. *Al Hadaf* sees a connection between the recent trip of West German Minister of the Interior Benda to Israel and this criminal project." In fact, Benda visited Israel several months earlier as President of the Israeli-West German Friendship society, and no source was given for *Al Hadaf's* information. Several months later Moscow Radio broadcast the same news item in Arabic. Or to take another example, the Poles announced in the summer of 1967 that "about a thousand Nazi officers and war criminals are training the Israeli Army," and in March 1968 that

Prime Minister Golda Meir "hid the Nazi criminal Martin Bormann in her house." Using the familiar Stalinist ploy of "as is well known," both reports were repeatedly broadcast by Radio Moscow's English and Arabic stations.[77]

This is the way that propagandists in Berlin, Warsaw, and Moscow, in collaboration with Arab experts on Zionism, produce the contemporary versions of the "Protocols of the Elders of Zion." Thus President Nasser's spokesman, M. H. Heikal, the editor of *Al Ahram*, could state on September 3, 1968: "In Czechoslovakia and the Middle East the enemy follows the same aims. The possibility of certain forces in the Czechoslovak leadership contacting foreign hostile forces, especially the United States and West Germany, cannot be overlooked." Eight months later Cairo Radio claimed that the entire reform movement had been "steered by Zionism."[78]

The *Al Dunia* report was an interesting mixture of previous charges by the Soviet and East German media and some new "facts": "A secret meeting has recently been held in London. Taking part were representatives of the biggest Zionist organizations and supporters of the so-called 'United International Organization of Czech and Slovak Politicians Inside and Outside Czechoslovakia,' the Lebanese newspaper *Al Dunia* reports in a dispatch from London." No date was given for the meeting, which must have been very secret, since it eluded the attention of the entire British and foreign press except of course the Lebanese newspaper. Neither has anyone ever heard of a Czechoslovak emigrant organization under the name given.

The paper, according to TASS, pointed out that "Israel and international Zionism had watched developments in Czechoslovakia closely since January 1968. They tried . . . to exert active influence on events in Czechoslovakia. Tel Aviv had a certain success in this. It knew about the subjects of discussion in the Czechoslovak leadership and about the talks with foreign representatives, including those between Soviet and Czechoslovak leaders at Cierna-nad-Tisou. This was possible because many of the Jews residing in Czechoslovakia maintain strong contacts with Zionism and with the Great Israel movement, the dispatch says. Many of them hold responsible posts in political, scientific, and cultural spheres and are in favor of toppling the socialist system in Czechoslovakia and the restoration there of a capitalist system that would be in keeping with Israel's interests . . . Israel as well as Zionist organizations in the United States and the West European countries have allocated huge sums to finance internal opposition in Czechoslovakia."

A reader of the TASS dispatch would hardly believe that by the spring of 1969 one in every three Jews had left, and this dangerous community numbered less than eight thousand in a population of fourteen and a half million.

But a conspiracy is meaningless without leaders, and the sting came in the last paragraph of the story, which explained that the Zionists and anti-Communist groupings outside the country were striving to create a united organization called the "People's Assembly." *Al Dunia* referred to "information received from Czechoslovak refugees that the London meeting was attended by new émigrés" and concluded: "It is also known that the meeting was attended by representatives of the Czechoslovak political opposition such as O. Sik and E. Goldstuecker who have broad international contacts with, among others, Zionist organizations all over the world. The participants at the meeting agreed to establish contacts with groups and individuals both inside and outside Czechoslovakia."

The incredible TASS dispatch forced the former Deputy Premier, who at that time was still a member of the Central Committee, to break his silence. In an open letter to Prague papers, Sik wrote: "It is somewhat awkward when a Communist is compelled to reply to a Communist news agency because of lies with racist undertones. And it is shocking if one considers that the German fascists who held me imprisoned in the Mauthausen concentration camp for four years because of illegal activity in the Communist movement did not regard me as a Jew even according to their racial laws. Apparently the epithet 'head of the counterrevolutionaries' (the way in which I have been described to date) is no longer effective and therefore new variants of a somewhat heavier caliber, appealing to the basest instincts, are resorted to—namely that I am supposed to be a Zionist."

Sik repeated that he was engaged in exclusively scientific activities in Basle to prevent his "becoming an obstacle to the 'normalization' process at home." He concluded with a warning: "However this does not concern me alone. At the present time victims of the trumped-up charges and illegal trials of the 1950s are being rehabilitated at home. Many of the arguments and tactics employed in the report quoted by TASS remind us of these recent times. Is the time of the rehabilitations in our country perhaps also to become the beginning of a new political persecution?"[79]

Nevertheless the smear campaign achieved its purpose. As a Prague radio commentator, sometime after the Soviet-Lebanese revelations, noted, a group of conservatives had distributed a pamphlet attacking four popular figures as "Zionists" in March 1968. "None of the four—Kriegel, Sik, Hajek, and Goldstuecker—holds the same position now. Sik and Goldstuecker teach abroad, Hajek lectures in Prague, and Kriegel heads the Institute of Rheumatism. What happened to these so-called Zionists? In this or that way, for these and other reasons they have simply ceased to occupy the posts they held a year ago. This terribly exact coincidence makes it impossible for me to sleep well. Not all four men are Jews, but it is the anti-Semites who decide whether a person is Jewish or not."[80]

This is indeed the point of the matter. Sik and Hajek went on official Soviet record as being "objectively" Zionists whether they had a Jewish ancestor among their grandparents or great-grandparents or not. Goldstuecker and Kriegel raised no problems since, as prosecutor Urvalek said of Slansky in 1952, they were by their "very nature Zionists." But "Zionists" have been manufactured as effortlessly by the Soviet "Marxists-Leninists" as Roosevelt and Churchill were transformed into "Jews" by the Nazis. If Governor Nelson Rockefeller can be called a "Zionist leader" by Soviet authors,[81] then there is no valid reason why the writers

Kohout and Prochazka or the politicians Sik and Hajek cannot be made into Jews or "Zionists."

Zionism was not of course the only plank in the Soviet propaganda in Czechoslovakia, but it played a much more significant role than is generally realized in the West.

Shortly after the fall of Dubcek in April 1969, Dr. Gustav Husak, his successor as First Secretary, stated at a televized public meeting that "Czechs and Slovaks are themselves sufficiently cultured and advanced not to require lessons on democracy from Sik, Kriegel, and Lederer."[82]* Husak, like most of his friends among the Slovak Communists who were imprisoned in the 1950s, is not only a Slovak patriot, but also permeated with old resentments against the "aliens" in Slovakia—the Hungarians and the Jews.[83]

In any case, after the reshuffle of the top leadership Moscow quietly liquidated both the radio station "Vltava" and the occupiers' newspaper *Zpravy*. This was not a concession to enraged public opinion but merely acknowledgment that Husak and the new strong man, Lubomir Strougal (Novotny's Minister of Interior between 1961–65), and their pro-Soviet associates would themselves impose strict censorship and carry on the purge of the reformers at all levels in the Party and state apparatus. The same considerations applied to the use of anti-Semitism.

The new leadership not only ordered the Czechoslovak press to stop the series of rebuttals to anti-Jewish prejudices but itself

* Jiri Lederer, perhaps the most prominent journalist of Jewish origin, was one of the editors of the outspoken weekly *Reporter*, which was banned in April 1969. In January 1970, Lederer was arrested and accused of having plotted with five young Polish intellectuals, then on trial in Warsaw, to distribute "subversive material" and to "overthrow socialism in Poland." The Poles initially intended to link the defendants not only with a Polish émigré organization and its Polish language monthly, *Kultura,* in Paris but also with "the international Zionist movement" and Israel, although none of the defendants was Jewish. Later, however, the "Zionist angle" was quietly shelved. Lederer, as a prominent reformist, a half-Jew with a Polish wife, was obviously regarded as an ideal culprit. The five Poles were sentenced to between three and four and a half years in prison. Lederer was provisionally set free in the late spring but at the time of this writing he is still interrogated and his fate, as indeed that of so many other prominent intellectuals, is shrouded in uncertainty.

switched to an "anti-Zionist" line. *Rude Pravo* and other Party organs began to use anti-Semitic innuendoes against the purged progressives, especially Dr. Kriegel. In a venomous article, *Rude Pravo* on July 4, 1969, tried to discredit him as a man with a dark past, an erstwhile servant and friend of former Party chief Novotny, and not a "real" Czechoslovak since he was born in Stanislav in former Polish Eastern Galicia of an Austrian father and Polish mother, and did not come to Prague until the 1920s.

Other ominous signs indicated the beginning of a wave of official anti-Semitism. Attacking Pavel Tigrid, a Czechoslovak émigré writer who has served time and again as a convenient foreign "link" with "antisocialist" or "counterrevolutionary" intellectuals, *Bratislava Pravda* resorted to the ugly trick of calling him "Tigrid-Schoenfeld."[84] With the power of the secret police restored and the Soviet agents firmly entrenched again, links were established between a plot hatched by Western intelligence agencies and the internal "right-wing and antisocialist" forces. A group of leading intellectuals, including a disproportionate number of Jews, was singled out in this connection by Minister of Interior Pelnar at both the Central Committee meeting and other conferences.[85]

The Zionist angle was explicitly mentioned by the Slovak Minister of Interior, General Pepich, who referred to no less than "thirty-two foreign centers organizing subversive activities against Czechoslovakia." Among these were, according to him, branch offices of "reactionary clerical groups directed by the Vatican" and those of "the nationalist Zionist organizations Joint, Sochnut, and Hias" in Vienna. The latter "gather information from all spheres of life, organize emigrants from Czechoslovakia, and it has been proved that their activities are being carried out on directives from Western intelligence."[86] The allegations were immediately rejected by the Austrian Minister of Interior as "completely without foundation."[87]

What matters is that the conspiracy theory linking the American CIA, the Vatican, and international Zionism has been formally resurrected. It remains to be seen how far the agony of Czechoslovakia will go and how durable the "hard line" will be. What is certain, however, is that Jewish politicians and intellectuals are bound to be among the prime scapegoats, if there are any left in the country.

Between August 1968 and February 1969 about thirty-five thousand Czechoslovaks left their country. While the proportion of the Jews in the total population was well under one tenth of 1 per cent, they accounted for more than 10 per cent of the refugees.

In the spring of 1969 on the eve of the final showdown with the reformers, *Zitrek,* the political and cultural weekly (soon to be banned), published a remarkable piece by Vilem Hejl, a young Czech novelist, about the dangers and motives of the anti-Semitic maneuvers:

> In uncertain times it is not advisable to be too certain about anything . . . The danger of anti-Semitism must be seen from this angle. The depressing developments elsewhere and certain statements made in this country are a warning sign, not only an illustration of the old truth that nothing is so stupid and barbarian that it cannot be resurrected under changed conditions. That is to say that what is involved is not only a numerically insignificant minority which is excommunicated from the nation. What is involved is any minority, whatever its type—and the principle, whose strength was tested on the first of these minorities . . . After the first minority, the turn of other minorities must inexorably come. And everyone belongs to some minority—whether by his origin, religion, profession, or by the degree to which he is committed. And the second time around, everything will go much more easily, because the apparat has had its workout in the first round; coercion belongs among well-tried and accepted methods of governing the state; moreover, its success in the solution of the Jewish problem intimidates those whose turn comes later.

After pointing to the danger that anti-Semitism "could win considerable influence for unscrupulous persons in their quest for power," Hejl warned those who might be tempted to look on passively, thinking that "all this does not concern us": "However this may be, no one has the right to complain that he did not expect this, that he was deceived, that he thought it was only the Jews who were supposed to be involved."[88]

The attacks against the "Zionists" and Moscow-produced "Jews" —Sik, Kriegel, Goldstuecker, Hajek, etc.—served as a prelude to a general settling of accounts. Within three months of Dubcek's fall came the liquidation of other "minorities"—of the reformers in the central, regional, and district Party apparatus, of the progressive ministers and high officials, of all the editors of dailies and weeklies, as well as the banning of a number of quality weeklies. Two years after the invasion hardly anything substantial remained of the Prague Spring.

The invasion and its aftermath also put an end to the hopes of the small Jewish religious organization that celebrations of the Jewish millennium in Prague, canceled after the Six Day War, might be held. For the third time, in May 1969, the Jewish organization "decided to postpone" the celebrations, which would be held "at an appropriate time."[89] There is only one rabbi, ninety-four-year-old Dr. Feder of Brno,* for the few thousand members of the religious community scattered over the country. Closed and desecrated synagogues, neglected and abandoned Jewish cemeteries mark the dying of a thousand-year-old community. The tourist showpieces in the capital—the Old-New Gothic synagogue, the Jewish town hall with the Hebrew dial, the Jewish museum, and a few other historic sites—are of course significant exceptions. What the late Jewish writer Alexander Charim observed four years ago is even more pertinent today: "Prague Jewry has become an attraction for tourists—like the Indians who live on reservations in the United States, like the bears in some Central European countries which must not be killed in order to preserve them for the next generations . . ."[90]

To sum up, the most democratic country east of the Rhine twice within a generation has become the scene and the experimental laboratory of a new kind of political anti-Semitism. And on both occasions—in 1951–52 and 1968–69—the element of anti-Semitism has been introduced from the outside. The Jewish problem was a marginal issue during the height and after the crushing of the

---

* Since this chapter was written, Rabbi Feder died.

Czechoslovak reform movement. But it showed more clearly than ever that the present Soviet leaders are as eager as Stalin was to abet anti-Jewish prejudices as a calculated weapon to consolidate Soviet hegemony.

Moscow's anti-Zionist line in the Arab world is obviously designed to further Soviet foreign policy and win Arab sympathies. Its use in Czechoslovakia, against a rebellious Communist Party and a united nation, was a by-product of efforts to stir up internal discord and drain off anti-Soviet popular discontent. Anti-Semitism never before had so little relevance to the great political and national ferment gripping the countries under Soviet domination. In their search for symbolic scapegoats, the men in the Kremlin, fighting for power and driven by fear, chose—as did their predecessors from time immemorial—the traditionally suspect and unpopular minority—the Jews. This indeed is the chief lesson the sad history of strangled freedom in Czechoslovakia holds for the Jews living in the Soviet sphere of influence.

# PART FOUR
## Where Jews Are Not Zionists

# 1. HUNGARY—A STUDY IN CONTRASTS

If the counterrevolution had not been put down within a comparatively short time, it might have spelt death for Hungarian Jewry.

*White Book, Budapest, 1957*

Zionists took part in the antistate, antipopular actions of counterrevolutionary forces in the past decade or so—in Socialist Hungary, Poland, and Czechoslovakia.

*Komsomolskaya Pravda,* Moscow, 1969

Nowhere in Eastern Europe did Communists of Jewish origin dominate the first postwar decade as much as in Hungary, yet there were no serious outbursts of anti-Semitism during the October uprising in 1956. The post-1956 Communist regime, headed by Janos Kadar, has always been as unflinchingly pro-Soviet on major issues—including the condemnation of "Israeli aggression"—as all other client states, but at no point has it shown any sign of official anti-Semitism. This may seem even more surprising in view of the fact that, with one third of the population of Poland, Hungary in 1968 had more than four times as many Jews. (Now it has ten times as many.)

It should be made clear here in analyzing the startling differences between Hungary and some other Communist-ruled countries I am not speaking about the comparative strength, prevalence, and overtness of popular anti-Semitic prejudices. The point is not whether the Hungarians are less anti-Semitic than the Poles or Czechoslovaks. Lacking data about the respective attitudes, no one can answer such basically irrelevant, albeit all too frequently asked questions. The heart of the matter is the level of resistance to anti-Semitism. Does a Communist leadership or a faction in a power struggle tolerate and if necessary instigate anti-Jewish feelings as a calculated political weapon? Are the assimilated Jews fully equal citizens? Both foreign observers and Jewish residents agree that in this respect Communist Hungary's record between 1956 and 1969 is unblemished.

Why and how has Hungary remained immune to the contagious disease of indigenous or "imported" political anti-Semitism? Since Stalin's death special factors have shaped the situation of Hungarian Jewry, with the Jews themselves playing as prominent and as contradictory a role as they did during the "Golden Age" between 1867 and 1918.

The massive entry of Jews into the ranks of the ruling bureaucracy after 1945 had its origins in both the unique structure of the old Hungarian society and the early Jewish prominence in Hungarian labor and left-wing movements. More than anywhere else in Central and Eastern Europe, the Jews in Hungary were not only fully assimilated but constituted the only middle class between a large landowning aristocracy and an impoverished gentry on the one hand, and millions of landless peasants on the other. Hungarian Jews were not merely commercial middlemen as in Poland and Rumania, but simultaneously the pacemakers of capitalism and the carriers of liberal and socialist ideas.[1]

From 1880 until 1944 the Jews accounted for one fifth of the one million population of Budapest, and emancipated and assimilated urban Jews were undoubtedly the most dynamic and most progressive element in Hungarian society. At the great liberal (non-Jewish) thinker Oszkar Jaszi put it in 1920: "Hungarian Jewry played an important role not only in Bolshevism but in every economic and ideological movement."[2] From the founding of the first labor party in 1878 and of the Social Democratic Party in 1890, Jewish intellectuals, doctors, and white-collar workers provided a considerable part of the leadership. Thus it was almost inevitable that the extreme left wing of the Social Democrats and the leaders of the short-lived Communist dictatorship were also overwhelmingly Jewish.[3]

The First World War ushered in a double tragedy—the dismemberment of the country and the lasting defeat (for twenty-five years) of social and political progress. Though the great majority of the Jewish middle class and professional people were strongly opposed to the "dictatorship of the proletariat," they paid a high price for the brief political success of Bela Kun and his mainly Jewish associates. Admiral Horthy's counterrevolution destroyed every chance of political progress and bolstered both the archaic feudal economic structure and the rural gentry. Indeed the ideological basis of the Horthy regime was a curious mixture of parochial conservatism, reactionary clericalism, intense anti-Communism, official anti-Semitism and, above all, virulent nationalism.

The interwar Danubian political order was built on the ruins of old Hungary. Neither Germany nor Austria suffered even remotely comparable losses in population, resources, and industrial capacity. Deserted by the West and encircled by suspicious new states, Hungary was virtually forced into an alliance with the forces that wanted to blow up the Versailles Treaty, Hitler's Germany and Mussolini's Italy. This was the second great tragedy in modern Hungarian history.

A humiliated, degraded, and unjustly treated small Central European nation turned to those who, for whatever reasons, were willing and able to help in the "liberation" of one in every three Hungarians from foreign rule.* A generation that grew up per-

* The reference to the glaring injustices in Hungary's dismemberment should not of course overshadow the equally intolerable suppression of the Slav and Rumanian minorities in historic Hungary. As Oszkar Jaszi put it, "in order that five and a half million people should escape from a suffocating irredenta it was necessary for four and a half million people to come under a new irredenta" (*Hungarian Calvary, Hungarian Resurrection*, Vienna, 1920, p. 164). Under the tangled distribution of ethnic groups and traditional loyalties in the Danubian basin, only a Danubian confederation

meated with the feeling of hurt national pride responded with
enthusiasm when Hungarian troops entered the Czechoslovak and
Rumanian and later, through a shameful betrayal, Yugoslav territories ceded by a victorious Hitler to his client state. This belated
satisfaction of national grievances explains (but of course does
not justify) the fact that Hungary was the last German satellite,
faithful to the end. Its incapable and shortsighted rulers missed their
chance even in the twenty-fourth hour to escape total collapse.
Horthy's amateurish attempts in October 1944 were quickly
thwarted by the Germans and three months of Arrow Cross terror
followed, the nightmarish orgy of the Hungarian Nazis.

At the same time, the population did not suffer but rather profited from the war. Aside from the eighty thousand losses of the
Hungarian units at the Battle of Voronesh in 1943, the country
until the very end regarded the war as a distant affair and lived
under the conditions of a wartime boom. Even the number of
conscripts was relatively limited compared to other European
countries. It was the massacred Jewry that accounted for three
fourths of wartime losses in life. No other Nazi satellite received
so much bounty as Hungary, which increased its territory by 85 per
cent and its population by 58 per cent from 1939 to 1941.[4] And
apart from a few insignificant actions before the Red Army reached
Budapest, there was virtually no organized resistance movement
against the German occupation.

It is against this historical background that the prominence of
Jews in the weak Communist movement must be seen. The fully
assimilated Jewish middle class provided an equally disproportionate share of the liberal intellectuals and a considerable proportion of the Social Democratic leadership in the first years after
1945. In fact, Jews were elected on the slates of almost every party
in November 1945, the only free election ever held in Hungary's
history.

---

could have satisfied the old grievances of one side without causing new injustice to the other. Fifty years after the collapse of the Austro-Hungarian
Monarchy, however, the nations are further than ever from realizing this
dream.

But it is also true that the Communist leadership was more "Jewish" than any other political group. Above all, the Moscow-trained general staff consisted almost entirely of Jews. Due to a number of special factors during the interwar period—the irredentist frenzy and shock of the Communist experiment in 1919, the strength of reactionary clericalism and the channeling of social protest and national rage against the Jews—the Communists formed an insignificant sect on the fringes of the labor movement, torn by factional infighting both in exile and at home. As a result of the predominantly Jewish leadership in 1919 and the absence of national minorities, both the top personnel in exile and the new recruits remained heavily Jewish.

The erstwhile People's Commissars and high officials of the Communist Government in 1919 became the leaders of the underground Communist Party and emissaries of the Moscow Comintern. From its foundation on November 24, 1918, for almost four decades, the top leaders of the Party were Jews: Bela Kun, Jeno Landler, Zoltan Szanto, Matyas Rakosi, and Erno Gero.[5] Of the fifteen members of the first Central Committee, at least eight can be identified as being of Jewish origin; and of the eight members elected at the first official congress in 1925 in Vienna, at least four.[6] In the 1930s the Jewish element was even stronger both in the so-called Foreign Committee (that is, in Moscow) and in the leading secretariat of the underground groups at home. This also meant that most victims of the Horthy regime such as Sandor Fürst and Imre Sallai (executed in 1932) and Zoltan Schönherz and Ferenc Rozsa (killed in 1942) were Jews. The same can be said of the Hungarian Communists who perished during Stalin's Great Terror.[7]

The survivors returned to their country in the baggage trains of the Red Army and immediately proceeded to prepare the Communist takeover. Their leader—"Stalin's best Hungarian disciple"—was Matyas Rakosi, the son of a provincial Jewish grocer and a People's Commissar in 1919. A highly cultured, extremely able but totally unscrupulous man of exceptionally ugly physical appearance, Rakosi had spent no less than sixteen years in Hungarian prisons after an international campaign had saved his life. It was only in 1940 that the Hungarian Government extradited him to Moscow in exchange for the flags of the 1848 Revolution which had been seized by the Russian Tsar almost a century earlier.

Rakosi was the uncontested leader of the famous "foursome"— himself; Erno Gero, the economic overlord; Mihaly Farkas, responsible for the Army and the security matters; and Jozsef Revai, the cultural "pope"—that led the Party and after 1947 ruled the country. All four were Jews. Of the twenty-five members of the first Communist Central Committee ("elected" in May 1945) nine were Jews.[8] The real dividing line was that between the "Muscovites" and the "home Communists" (or Westerners) and not in any sense between Jews and non-Jews. But as far as public opinion was concerned, the fact that the top Communist leadership was "Jewish" was important.

The weakness of the Hungarian Communist Party created a paradoxical situation. It was not only Jewish "overcompensation" for psychological complexes, but rather part of profoundly cynical Communist tactics in the battle for power that impelled the predominantly Jewish leadership to recruit members and make a bid for popular backing by tolerating anti-Semitic excesses. Within four months after the Red Army's entry into Budapest, Party membership rocketed from less than 2000 to 150,000;[9] and by the first Party Congress in September 1946, to 653,000. A "general staff" with a large proportion of Jews was directing a mass party whose ranks were swollen by tens of thousands of former Arrow Cross, fascist "activists." Rakosi himself gave the signal for demonstrations against black-marketeers, which predictably ended in anti-Semitic outrages, when in demagogic speeches he claimed: "There is a place in a democracy for spontaneous acts of the masses, and it is only right that the people should take justice into their own hands . . ."[10]

The Communists were not averse to playing on the anti-Jewish emotions of a population suffering from a runaway inflation, and when in summer 1946 pogroms erupted at Kunmadaras and Miskolc, their leadership remained silent. On both occasions Party members were involved in the anti-Semitic outrages that caused the death of five Jews. Twenty years after the event, a high-ranking Party functionary admitted that the local Communist organization of Diosgyoer, the industrial stronghold, was "led astray by reactionary instigators" to support what was undoubtedly the largest "spontaneous" anti-Jewish mob action in postwar Hungarian history.[11]

It was the Social Democratic Party that all along publicly and staunchly condemned anti-Semitism. In the same way, the traditions of genuine radicalism and Marxism were upheld by the Social Democratic left-wing intellectuals and youth grouped around Paul Justus, the party's outstanding ideologist. But the Communists in what they now regard as their "heroic period" between 1945 and 1948 leaned backward in all matters involving "unpopular" issues, including anti-Semitism. Thus it happened that a party run to a great extent by Jews was widely and justifiably regarded by many democrats as mainly responsible for the lack of energy in prosecuting the organizers of mob outrages. Western and primarily Jewish observers often regarded the Communist Minister of Interior, Laszlo Rajk, as an anti-Semite because he sabotaged court proceedings and criminal investigations against the perpetrators of pogroms. This is of course a patent absurdity since Rajk was simply carrying out the Party's instructions. Moreover, the political police proper was headed by the Jewish Gabor Peter, a former tailor, and was staffed at its command level mainly by Jews.

By the notorious "salami tactics" the Communists destroyed the country's largest party, the Smallholders, which had received 57 per cent of the popular vote at the free 1945 elections, and subsequently swallowed up the Social Democratic Party. In 1949 the witch-hunt began against the Communists themselves. But even in the purges that shook the Party the Jewish problem did not play any role. The proportion of Jews was as high among the purgers as it was among the purged.

The first purge began in May 1949 with the arrest of Laszlo Rajk, former Minister of Interior, at that time Foreign Minister and member of the Politburo, and over two hundred prewar

Communists.[12] Rajk's trial in September 1949 gave the signal for bloc-wide witch-hunts against "Titoists" and "imperialist agents who penetrated the Party." The trial itself was prepared on Stalin's orders with a "scenario" drawn up under the direct supervision of General Bielkin, the chief of the MVD, the Soviet security police in Southeast Europe. But Rakosi was a more eager accomplice than any other satellite leader. It was he who took the lead in the anti-Yugoslav campaign and put pressure on a reluctant Gottwald in Prague.

Rajk was obviously selected by Stalin and Rakosi as chief culprit because his participation in the Spanish Civil War, internment in a French camp, and subsequent arrest and deportation to Germany in 1944–45 provided convenient "links" to both his former Yugoslav comrades-in-arms and "American espionage."[13] The purge was directed against former home Communists, "Spaniards," and "Westerners." Stalin's classical method of "amalgam" was used in putting into the dock seven men with completely different backgrounds, among them the lifelong Communist Rajk, the Social Democrat Justus, General Palffy, the former professional officer and one of the few genuine resistance fighters, and Dr. Szonyi, the leader of the wartime Communist exiles in Switzerland.

The Rajk trial was the first and greatest show trial in Eastern Europe, and its Hungarian architects—Rakosi, Farkas, and secret police chief Peter—were all Jews. Of Rajk's six co-defendants, three were also Jews: Paul Justus, Tibor Szonyi, and Andras Szalai; a Social Democrat, a "Westerner," and a home Communist. They were arrested not because of their origin but because they fitted the roles in the "scenario." It was at the Rajk trial however that "Zionism" was first injected into the accusations. Szalai "confessed" that he had been a member of the "Trotskyite-Zionist group," while Szonyi "admitted" that he had spied "together with Zionist agents" for the American intelligence service in Switzerland. Though only a side issue at the time, the theme of a "world-wide Zionist conspiracy" appeared in the first show trial in Budapest—that is, more than three years before Prague and Moscow.[14]

Needless to say, Rakosi and his associates were for obvious reasons even more eager than the leaders of the other satellites to destroy the Zionist organizations in the wake of the Soviet policy switch in September 1948. Nowhere perhaps was there a crueler irony in the fate of Jews than in Hungary. Rakosi and the other "court Jews" were running the country as Moscow's agents and were seen by the population as Jewish stooges of a hated foreign oppressor. At the same time, nowhere else were the Jews so heavily represented in the liberal and free professions. Before the war about half of the doctors and lawyers, more than a third of the white-collar workers in industry, trade, and banking, and almost one third of the journalists were Jews.[15] The Nazi genocide campaign changed the situation since only some 140,000 Jews remained alive of the 725,000 who were registered in 1941 as residents in enlarged Hungary. The Jewish share in the total population fell from 5 per cent to 1.6 per cent, but the last occupational statistics, dating back to the end of 1945, showed that 45 per cent of the gainfully employed Jews were independent businessmen in industry and commerce, or belonged to the liberal professions.[16]

Thus the nationalization of small-scale businesses, retail trade outlets, and the artisans and the suppression of private legal and medical professions hit the Jews much more than their percentage share in the total population would indicate. When in 1951 the Rakosi regime began to deport expropriated "capitalists" and other "unproductive" elements among the remnants of the former urban middle class from Budapest and other cities to the distant villages, it was estimated (though never confirmed by official figures) that Jews accounted for about one third of the several tens of thousands of deportees.[17] It must be added that all this was part of the general terror under which the total number of political prisoners, including the inmates of internment camps and the people deported from urban centers, reached 150,000 or about 1.5 per cent of the population.[18] The former Jewish entrepreneurs and merchants suffered with the former landed gentry and Catholic priests. They were not hit as Jews, but as "alien" or "unreliable" elements. Because of the occupational structure they were disproportionately represented among the victims, as well as among the tormentors.

As we have seen in both Poland and Czechoslovakia, there is no direct relationship between political anti-Semitism and the virulence or absence of anti-Jewish prejudices. It depends rather on the ruling elite. The composition of the top leadership in Hungary at the height of the terror explains the seemingly contradictory attitude of many middle-class Jewish victims who hated the regime yet trembled that its collapse, as in 1919, would spark off anti-Jewish violence. The Communist Politburo (after the purge of Rajk and the former Social Democrats) had thirteen members, seven of whom were Jews. At the Party Congress in February 1951 it was increased to seventeen members with the number of the Jews remaining unchanged. The key Secretariat consisted of eight members, half of them Jews, while of the seventy-one Central Committee members, at least sixteen were of Jewish origin.[19]

Within two months, the rest of the home Communists were arrested, including Janos Kadar, deputy Secretary General; Gyula Kallai, the Foreign Minister; Geza Losonczy, secretary of state at the Ministry of Culture; and Ferenc Donath, chief of Rakosi's secretariat. Sandor Zold, the Minister of Interior (and along with Kadar a Polituburo member), killed his family and committed suicide. Neither Rajk nor Kadar ever represented anything even remotely comparable to a "Hungarian way to socialism." They had been as enthusiastic and as ruthless in the destruction of the non-Communist political forces and in the persecution of the Roman Catholic Church as their tormentors. In short, they were victims and not politicians with ideas of their own. Nevertheless their liquidation meant the disappearance of the last prominent home Communists.

While the waves of terror engulfed all whom Rakosi regarded as real, potential, or imagined opponents, the idolatry of the dictator reached fantastic proportions. It can be safely said that apart from Stalin no other Communist leader became in a matter of a few years such a legendary figure, so feted, flattered, and feared as Matyas Rakosi.[20] Textbooks, biographies, and innumerable articles wove legends about his life. Thus it turned out that not Bela Kun ("a base traitor") but he, the then humble deputy Commissar for Trade, had been the real leader of the Communist Revolution in 1919.

Everywhere in the Soviet orbit there were purges and executions. But the implementation of the general Soviet line was always influenced to a very considerable degree by the personality of the individual at the top. Psychological and not sociological interpretations are more important than is commonly thought in a society "so organized that the will of one man, or a small group, is the most powerful of the political and social forces."[21] This is not the place to go into an investigation of Rakosi's personality. But it is evident that the extra measure of hatred he accumulated during his sixteen years in prison during the prime of his life may have made him an especially vicious victor. His cunning ruthlessness and inhuman mercilessness were perhaps more responsible than anything else for the fact that the scope of the purges (especially within the ruling elite) surpassed that in every other Communist-ruled country in Eastern Europe. And Rakosi was a Jew.

At the same time this ugly little man with a gnomelike appearance was also the most notorious anti-Semite when it suited his convenience. Faced with Stalin's anti-Semitic frenzy in 1952, which led to the fall of Slansky in Prague, Pauker in Bucharest, and culminated in the "Doctors' Plot," Rakosi hastened to save his own skin by arresting and jettisoning his Jewish subordinates. Anticipating Stalin's planned blow against Soviet Secret Police Chief Beria, Rakosi ordered the arrest of the "Hungarian Beria," his closest colleague in keeping the terror machine in motion, Gabor Peter, and several of his high officials at the security police. The purge was directed not only against the former purgers, whose fall no one regretted, but also against Jews in general. The roll call of arrested Jews in December 1952 and January 1953 ranged from Dr. Stoeckler, the Communist-sponsored leader of the Jewish community, to scores of Jewish doctors, from Jewish home Communists such as Istvan Szirmai, the president of the Hungarian Radio, to Jewish journalists and executives. As always, the wave led to the arrests of other "unreliable elements," both Jews and non-Jews.

There are no statistics about the number of the victims. The author, who was arrested because of his Social Democratic past and for having been a disciple of Paul Justus[22] (perhaps also for being of Jewish origin), remembers that the scale of the purge went well beyond even the considerable "capacity" of the large investigating prison in Budapest. Cells for two inmates had, for example, at one point seven "guests." Three had to sleep sideways on each of the two bunks, taking clockwise shifts in the seventh place—on the concrete floor between the bunks. Later in a large "communal" cell, over fifty prisoners were forced to share fifteen benches. Stalin's death initially made our situation even worse. As one of the basic tenets of Stalinism claims that crisis situations demand increased vigilance, scores of totally unpolitical persons were taken into custody for having "grinned" or made "cynical remarks" on hearing that the "great leader of mankind" was dead.

While about one hundred thousand people were suffering under inhuman conditions and without any contact with their families in internment camps, the country was preparing for "elections." On May 10, 1953, the election eve, a huge mass meeting in Parliament Square in Budapest greeted "with cheers of wild enthusiasm and storms of applause the first candidate of the Hungarian people: Comrade Matyas Rakosi." The leader warned the nation: "Let us be vigilant in every field of the People's Democracy and let us act ruthlessly against those who want to sabotage the building of our happy future! Our People's Democracy must ceaselessly watch for conspiracies, for sabotage, and for espionage . . ."[23]

Only six weeks later the "wise father of the Hungarian people" was summoned to Moscow and accused of having driven Hungary to the verge of an economic catastrophe. The leadership in the Kremlin accused Rakosi of carrying out the very policy it had ordered and approved. "They will chase you out with pitchforks," Khrushchev snapped. Rakosi was accompanied, as the Russians had specified, by his two closest collaborators from the notorious "foursome," Erno Gero and Mihaly Farkas; the non-Communist head of state, Istvan Dobi, a nonentity; and Imre Nagy, Politburo member and deputy Premier.

Behind the sudden reversal of the Soviet attitude toward Moscow's obedient stooge lay the East Berlin uprising of a few days earlier, the riots in Czechoslovakia and demonstrations in Hungary. The Soviet leaders were afraid that unless there were radical and immediate changes the people in Hungary (and elsewhere) might at any moment turn against their leaders. A package of economic and political concessions was subsequently carried out —on the orders of Stalin's frightened successors—throughout the entire Soviet orbit.

What perhaps astounded the Hungarians more than anything else was the unprecedented grossness of the criticism of Rakosi, which revealed an anti-Semitism expressed in no uncertain terms. Beria (arrested almost immediately after the session of the Presidium) was particularly ruthless in debunking Rakosi's cult of personality: "Listen to me, Rakosi. We know that there have been in Hungary, apart from its own rulers, Turkish sultans, Austrian emperors, Tartar khans, and Polish princes. But, as far as we know, Hungary has never had a Jewish king. Apparently, this is what you have become. Well, you can be sure that we won't allow it."[24]

Various accounts agree that the Jewish Question, though a side issue, played an important part in the criticism. It had been a great mistake, the Russians declared, that in Hungary, where anti-Semitism had strong roots, all four leaders of the Party should be Jews. It was decided then and there that Rakosi should renounce his post as Premier but remain Party leader in order to mend his ways and correct his mistakes. The Soviet Presidium also resolved that two members of the "Rakosi quartet," Farkas and Revai, would have to give up their posts. Finally, they named Imre Nagy as new Premier and authorized him to draw up a new government program to alleviate the difficult internal situation.*

* The meeting in the Kremlin illuminated the scope and nature of Soviet control. As Tibor Meray dryly remarked in his book on the October uprising: "Some might find it strange that the Premier of Hungary should be

The Moscow meeting and subsequent changes in the Party and state leadership set in motion the dynamic forces that led to the October Revolution of 1956. Henceforth the Party and state apparatus was torn and ultimately paralyzed by an institutional conflict between the two heads of the new dual leadership, the Party leader responsible for the Stalinist terror and the Premier with a new reformist program. The single chain of command was split, with fateful repercussions.

Imre Nagy was chosen to succeed Rakosi as Premier for three main reasons: first, because he too was a Muscovite; second, because he was not a Jew; and third, because he had not been involved in the worst terrorist acts of the Rakosi regime. In fact, he had been the one prominent Communist politician who in 1948 had opposed the policy of forced collectivization of agriculture and as a result had been excluded from the Politburo for several years. Even after his comeback in 1951, he did not belong to the dominant group. Whatever his weaknesses as a tactician and politician, Nagy has gone down in Hungarian history as a man of absolute integrity. His famous "June program" in 1953 abandoned forced industrialization and collectivization, endorsed raising the standard of living, and above all opened the prison doors, dissolved the internment camps, and allowed the return of those banned from the capital.

The question of rehabilitations became the most explosive issue, for the release of many falsely accused Communists* had

named in Moscow, but to those participating in this conference such an action seemed quite natural." Three years later, it was again on the "advice" of the Soviet comrades that Rakosi was dismissed as First Secretary. Moscow's emissary, Presidium member A. Mikoyan, participated at both the Politburo meeting and the crucial Central Committee plenum (July 17–18, 1956). When Valeria Benke, then president of the Hungarian Radio, informed the senior editors about the details of Rakosi's fall, one of them asked her: "Didn't you find it odd, Comrade Benke, that the Central Committee session was held in Comrade Mikoyan's presence?" She replied: "I had not even thought about that!" In other words, the fact that the most crucial decisions affecting the Party were made by the Soviet Presidium seemed perfectly natural to those ruling Hungary.

* The Communists comprised of course only a minority of those in prisons and camps. Yet under the conditions of a single-party dictatorship, it is al-

to be carried out with the concurrence of the very persons who had been responsible for their imprisonment. Twenty months of power struggles and sordid intrigues followed between the Rakosi group and Nagy's reformists, with the majority veering from one side to the other, trimming its sails according to the prevailing wind in Moscow. The shifts in the battle for power in the Kremlin, especially the fall of Malenkov in early February 1955, enabled Rakosi to take revenge on his rival. In April the same Central Committee that only five months earlier had criticized Rakosi's leftist deviation as the principal danger now with the same unanimity expelled Imre Nagy from the Politburo and the Central Committee for his "rightist deviation." Next day Nagy was dismissed as Premier, and seven months later he was expelled from the Party.

But Rakosi's victory proved brief. He had been able to outmaneuver and crush Nagy, but he could not survive the result of the Soviet-Yugoslav rapprochement—the rising tide of external and internal demands for Rajk's rehabilitation. A master tactician, he made only one political blunder in his long career: he not only ordered the killing of his victims as had Stalin and other satellite leaders, he also claimed personal credit for the purge. In a speech after the Rajk trial he boasted that he had spent sleepless nights until he himself unraveled the threads of the conspiracy. This was to prove fatal.

Though Gabor Peter, the dreaded secret police chief, was sentenced to life imprisonment at a secret trial in March 1954, Rakosi could not avoid blame and claim like his colleagues in neighboring countries that all the evil came from the "Beria gang" and its agents. He tried of course to do precisely this, but his earlier revelations proved a deadly weapon against him. His erstwhile blind

---

ways the fight for and against the rehabilitation of the purged Communists, in other words the settling of scores within the ruling elite, that sets the centrifugal forces in motion. This is why the reappraisal of the trial of Rajk in Hungary, of Kostov in Bulgaria, of Gomulka in Poland, and of Slansky in Czechoslovakia invariably served as the most important igniting sparks for changes that ultimately affected the fate of non-Communist victims and the population at large.

disciples underwent a profound moral and emotional crisis and became his fiercest opponents when the innocence of the purge victims was admitted by the Party. Old militants who had passed long years in prison now aligned themselves with Nagy. Writers and journalists, artists and scientists (all Party members) wanted to reform the system.

But the Jewish Question played no role in the power battles of 1955–56. True, Rakosi and some of his closest associates, like his successor Erno Gero, were Jews. But so were a large number of the falsely accused Communists and left-wing Social Democrats. The same could be said of many close friends and advisers of Imre Nagy.

When, after the increasingly rebellious discussion evenings organized by the Petofi Circle and the Poznan riots, Rakosi drew up a list of four hundred oppositionists who would have to be arrested, he included scores of Jewish writers and journalists. It was common knowledge that among the driving spirits of the reform movement were such prominent writers and journalists of Jewish descent as Tibor Dery, Gyula Hay, Miklos Gimes, Zoltan Zelk, and Gyorgy Lukacs, the greatest living Marxist scholar in the Communist world. It was these people who first raised the banner of Hungary's patriotic and liberal traditions, evoked the spirit of 1848, demanded the rehabilitation of Imre Nagy, and defied Rakosi.

Thus we find the same diversity of views and actions among politically or culturally active Hungarians of Jewish descent as among the rest of the ruling class and its opponents. But the majority of the Jewish community, like bulk of the population, watched the unfolding drama from the wings. The same plurality of views was evident during and after the Revolution itself. There was at no point any faction or grouping in the upper and middle echelons of the Party that resorted to anti-Semitic innuendo.

It was above all the unity of the intellectuals and the youth against the common enemy—the terror system and Soviet domination—that nipped in the bud even the faintest sign of anti-Semitism during the October uprising, at any rate in the capital. Some Jews were killed by the bullets of insurgents or fell victims to mob justice, but this happened not because they were Jews but because they were secret police officers or functionaries. Many more participated in the revolutionary committees and workers' councils, some fell in the fighting against the Soviet troops, and scores of Jews were among those arrested and sentenced to long prison terms after the crushing of the uprising.

Following the installation of Janos Kadar's "Revolutionary Workers' and Peasants' Government" the official propaganda nevertheless referred in a White Book to "Anti-Semitism and Anti-Jewish Violence During the Hungarian Counterrevolution."[25] After relating eight or ten alleged anti-Semitic excesses in the provinces, the chapter concludes with the statement: "It is the opinion of the Jewish leaders . . . that if the counterrevolution had not been put down within a comparatively short time, it might have spelt death for Hungarian Jewry . . ."

This widely quoted statement, like the White Book itself, served to discredit the Hungarian Revolution. This author, whose apartment was situated in the very heart of the uprising, the Killian barracks area, can confirm from personal experience that there were no anti-Semitic excesses or actions of any kind in Budapest. It speaks for itself that none of the alleged anti-Jewish outrages related in the White Book refer to the capital and its environs. An astute foreign observer not incorrectly regarded the absence of anti-Semitic outbursts as "one of the great surprises, almost the miracle" of the October uprising.[26]

It is doubtful however whether, as he speculates, the Rakosi regime's anti-Semitism in 1952–53 was the chief reason for this phenomenon. The participation of Jewish intellectuals as a spearhead of the rebellion and the impressive unity of the entire nation were incomparably more important factors in staving off the danger of anti-Semitic atrocities. Yet it is perhaps appropriate to sound a note of caution. The unity was a coalition of disparate forces ranging from reformist Communists or democratic socialists to extreme right-wing elements. It should not be forgotten that within a few days Hungary turned full circle from a disintegrating terror system to the re-establishment of a multiparty system. And on the eve of the Soviet intervention the dynamics of the revolutionary tide were beginning to escape all control from above; Nagy and his allies were being more and more driven by—instead of directing—the elementary forces from below. There is no point in speculating what would have filled the vacuum of power had the Russians not struck on November 4, 1956.

A substantial segment of the Jewish community sensed danger, and those living in the provinces either left the country among the first refugees or moved to the capital. I am talking here not about the reformers or Stalinists of Jewish origin but about the politically uncommitted Jews who had no reason to regret the collapse of a system that had destroyed private commerce and the free professions. At the height of the fighting I encountered several Jewish friends or acquaintances gripped by an almost desperate fear that, with restraint going by the board and the central authority crumbling, an explosion of accumulated anti-Jewish resentment might follow. Nothing of the kind in fact happened, but their fears may well have been justified. The uprising lasted only thirteen days, and the tragic cases of lynch justice against reformist "liberal" Communists such as Imre Mezo, the progressive secretary of the Budapest Party committee, and enlisted militiamen guarding the Party offices were ominous straws in the wind. This is not to say that the Russians "saved Jewry from certain death," but to warn that it would be unwise and unrealistic to identify the absence of pogroms in thirteen days with a miraculous disappearance of deeply rooted traditional anti-Semitism and its explosive potential in a chaotic period.

In any case, rightly or wrongly, many former middle-class Jews instinctively preferred *any* order rather than the opening of *all* safety valves as the best protection against the danger of having to pay the price for the crimes of the Jewish Muscovites. Needless to say this consideration was uppermost in the minds of those Jewish functionaries and old militants who rallied immediately around the shaky Kadar regime. No less than eighteen to twenty thousand Jews, 10 per cent of the refugee total, left the country after the crushing of the October revolt. There is of course no way of knowing how many acted from the same motives as tens of thousands of fellow Hungarians and how many were also influenced to some extent by the fear of anti-Semitism. There is no information available about the occupational structure of the hundred thousand or so Jews[27] who remained in the country. As they constitute a religious denomination and not a national minority, as no personal documents or census forms ever put the question of religious faith, no one can estimate exactly even the number of Jews, let alone their distribution by age, sex, or occupation.

What matters is the political role played by Jews, and in this respect there is astounding diversity, which reflects the complete assimilation of Hungarian Jews. Nothing in Hungary, particularly the Jewish Question, can be understood outside the context of the trauma of the 1956 revolt. The presence of a disproportionate number of Jews among the Stalinists and among the driving spirits of the "Hungarian October" led almost automatically to a numerical reduction of the Jewish element in the top echelons of the Kadar regime. But, contrary to some Western assumptions,[28] this had nothing to do with a Polish-type "aryanization." The thaw and the drama of 1956 split the ruling elite into three main groups: Stalinists (the minority), reformists, and centrists. None of these was a closely knit faction, and each consisted of different wings.

The uprising and its aftermath produced rapid shifts and bewildering changes between and within the various groups which cannot be reduced to a simple pattern. All of the chief figures in the Party, which had been split from top to bottom, shifted their positions from day to day, swept along by the stream of circumstance. Men who had been thrown into prison by Rakosi in 1949–51 and often shared the same prison cells, or the young leaders of the Petofi Circle became bitter opponents in a matter of days and subsequently appeared in the roles of victims or victors. Of the four main defendants in the secret Kadar trial in 1951, two, Janos Kadar and Gyula Kallai, emerged as the leaders of the regime installed by Soviet troops in November 1956. Two others, Ferenc Donath and Geza Losonczy, were arrested and tried by their old comrades-in-arms and fellow cell-inmates after the Soviet intervention. Of the seven members of the committee that after the dissolution of the Hungarian Workers' Party was entrusted with forming a new Party, called the Hungarian Socialist Workers' Party, two were killed (Nagy and Losonczy), two were imprisoned (Donath and Sandor Kopacsi), and two (Gyorgy Lukacs and Zoltan Szanto) were deported to Rumania. Kadar, their companion in the task of reorganizing the Communist Party, became the country's supreme leader. Nothing could illustrate better the paradoxical changes produced by Kadar's efforts to heal the wounds of 1956 than that these two veterans of the movement, Lukacs and Szanto, both People's Commissars in 1919, were in the late 1960s readmitted to the Party and received the highest Government decoration on the occasion of the fiftieth anniversary of the short-lived Communist Soviet Republic.

In the settling of accounts between those who remained faithful to and those who betrayed the common cause, Jews were on both sides of the barricades and none of the new warring groupings could be labeled as "national" or "alien," "Hungarian" or "Jewish."

The climax of the period of revenge was reached on June 17, 1958, with the announcement of the verdict against the nine leaders of the October insurrection and the execution of Imre Nagy and three of his companions. Two of the nine defendants were of Jewish origin; one, Miklos Gimes, perhaps the most erudite journalist in postwar Hungary, was executed on the morning of June 16 together with Nagy, General Maleter, and Jozsef Szilagyi.[29] But there were also Jews intimately connected with the campaign of repression, like Ervin Hollos, one of the leaders of the new political police (and formerly member of the bureau organizing the rebellious Petofi Circle!), Geza Revesz, Minister of Defense in the Kadar government, and Antal Apro, Deputy Premier and Politburo member.

In short, the Jewish origin of a given politician or intellectual had nothing to do with his respective political posture. The background and attitude of the Communists of Jewish origin who rose to the top of the hierarchy under Kadar were also strikingly different. The first temporary Politburo included only one Jew—Apro, a home Communist, who retained his membership in the Politburo during virtually the entire Rakosi era. By 1966 the eleven-strong supreme Party body elected by the Ninth Party Congress included two more Jews: Dezso Nemes and Istvan Szirmai. While the former was a Muscovite and inveterate dogmatist, the latter was a moderate centrist and one of the architects of Kadar's "new course."*

Since 1959 there has been a gradual but considerable change in the psychological climate of Hungary, which has affected the Jewish community positively. The religious community operates the only rabbinical seminary in the Communist world, a Jewish high school, a library and museum (in Theodor Herzl's birthplace), eleven kosher butcher shops, a factory producing unlimited quantities of matzoh, an orphanage, and a home for old people. Its biweekly has a circulation of sixty-five hundred, and in Budapest alone, where the overwhelming majority of Jews live, there are thirty synagogues. Though the Communist-dominated "National Bureau of Hungarian Israelites" broke off official contacts with the World Jewish Congress in 1960 (because its "use as an instrument of Cold War and anti-Soviet policies"), since 1963 and even after the Six Day War, its leaders as well as many rabbis have made official lecture tours and missions to the United States, Britain, and other West European countries.

The Jewish community as a whole has profited from the tolerant policy with regard to private initiative, while writers, journalists, artists, and scientists cannot complain of any discrimination. There is no ceiling to their advancement in government service of any kind. The rate of intermarriage is very high among intellectuals and officials. Emigration to Israel has been minimal. Those who chose to use a tourist trip to the West for defection did so like their Catholic or Protestant compatriots, out of personal motives and not as Jews fleeing from prejudice.

All this does not mean that there is no popular or traditional anti-Semitism in Hungary. Though the disappearance of the hated "court Jews"—Rakosi, Gero, Farkas, Peter, etc.—may have made it less virulent, there is still widespread anti-Semitism of varying in-

* Since this chapter was written, Szirmai died.

tensity. In contrast to all other Communist countries, the official press from time to time admits this, writing about "the relics of the past," particularly in schools. Hungary is the only Communist-ruled country (to the knowledge of this author) that has allowed even timid attempts at such sociological investigations. Thus *Valosag,* a Budapest social-cultural monthly, in April 1967 concluded that "in villages where there are no Jews, anti-Semitism seems to be less of a burning issue than in the cities." Yet a poll of the inhabitants of three villages revealed that 13 per cent would not "willingly accept" a Jew as a neighbor, 16.3 per cent would not like to have a Jewish friend, and 36.3 per cent would not accept a Jewish spouse.[30] Nevertheless references to anti-Semitism are generally made only within an overview of national and religious prejudices.

In the course of heated debates in 1967 about "healthy patriotism" and "antisocialist nationalism," a leading cultural spokesman stated candidly in *Nepszabadsag,* the central Party organ: "I do not know why anti-Semitism seems to be an unbecoming topic with us. Everybody knows it exists, yet it is avoided . . . This present anti-Semitism persists mainly in the way that its 'practitioners' keep in evidence who is a Jew and who is not. But even this is intolerable, this internal discrimination, this quiet and sly pro memoria . . ."[31]

As far as political or official anti-Semitism goes, the Kadar regime passed two crucial tests with flying colors. The first was the Six Day War and its aftermath. Diplomatic relations were broken off with Israel on June 12, and the general line faithfully followed the shifts of Soviet policy. But at no point did the strong current of anti-Israeli propaganda sweep across the line that separates it from anti-Zionism, let alone from anti-Semitism. As everywhere in Eastern Europe, the Israeli victory, seen as a crushing defeat for the Russians, was extremely popular. Consequently the Hungarian leadership had to cope with the same embarrassing popular response as did the other regimes (except Rumania).

Here again however Kadar depended on persuasion and conciliation rather than on unbridled aggressiveness or anti-Semitic innuendo. Within two weeks, five members of the Politburo dealt with the Middle East conflict. They spelled out what became the official approach: the problem has to be judged on a principled class basis and not emotionally.[32] It was soon evident that many of those who fervently supported the official line did it for the "wrong" reasons, like an unidentified man who during the fighting asked a little boy to send a wire on his behalf to the Egyptian Embassy in Budapest. The telegram expressed the hope that "what Hitler started will be finished by the Arabs." There were some people "who inquired cynically whether it is now permitted or whether it is now mandatory to abuse the Jews."[33] The Politburo member Gyula Kallai, while commending the population for its "political maturity," referred in a public speech to those who "tried to exploit events for anti-Semitic incitement" and to those who "because of their relatives did not understand our firm stand against the Israeli aggression."[34] Occasionally the warnings against anti-Semitism were combined with a rejection of philo-Semitic views. But in rereading the entire propaganda barrage this author did not find a single reference to "Zionists" in Hungary.

In a basic policy speech held at the Communist youth congress in June 1967,[35] Kadar himself referred to the Middle East crisis. It is instructive to compare his tolerant approach with Gomulka's outbursts against the "Zionist fifth column" a few days earlier. After reiterating several times Israel's right to existence and recalling the persecution of Jews and the killing of "a great number of Jewish people," Kadar declared: "The Communist stand in this question has never been uncertain or controversial. We always rejected racial theories and fought without reservation and with all our might during World War II against racial discrimination, persecution of Jews, and the barbarism of Hitler fascism. We fought and are fighting racial discrimination and atrocities wherever and whenever encountered . . . This is one side of the question."

The other side of the question, Kadar proceeded to explain, is the fact that "during the past decades many Jewish people emigrated to Israel, also from Hungary, and became Israeli citizens.

Family and emotional relations can blur clear thinking. It is understandable that one's political attitude is disturbed if a brother or another relative of his lives in the country that committed the aggression. But the stand in foreign policy must also be based on principles."

Following this gesture (unprecedented in Eastern Europe), the Hungarian leader illustrated by the example of Hungarian family relations in the United States and West Germany that "serious problems would arise if we did not take a principled attitude. Where would we end in politics if we did not condemn consistently the imperialist policy and the Vietnam aggression perpetrated by American ruling circles because several tens of thousands of Hungarian citizens have family relations in the United States?" After referring to Hungarians in West Germany, Kadar turned to Israel: "And where would we get if we would not condemn Israel's undoubtedly illegal war moves as imperialist aggression because a few thousand people have fathers, children, or brothers in Israel? . . . And the people, the working people of Israel, will fare well if they oppose their own government's imperialist aggression and seek peace, friendship, and coexistence with Arab people. Thus we are against the imperialist policy and not against the Jewish people, nor against the State of Israel."

The Hungarian press published articles against Israeli expansion,[36] but the tone remained moderate and no reference was made to the "Zionists," nor were any of the venomous Soviet, Polish, or East German attacks reprinted.

The second test came with regard to the "March events" and the subsequent anti-Zionist witch-hunt in Poland. Hungarian liberalization had not progressed far enough that anyone could have publicly condemned what was going on in a "fraternal" country as the Czech and Yugoslav intellectuals did. But the leadership made its views unmistakably known through the tested device of almost completely ignoring the anti-Zionist aspects of the turmoil in Poland.[37] It was only after the July 1968 plenum of the Polish Central Committee, which signaled the end of the most violent phase, that Hungarian papers published Kliszko's and Gomulka's speeches minimizing the importance of a "Zionist" danger.

On balance, and especially in contrast to the "hard line" blowing throughout the rest of the Soviet orbit, Hungary is undoubtedly a haven of relaxation. And for reasons rooted in the contradictory Jewish role in politics, the absence of factional fighting, the limited liberalization of a regime with a shaky claim to legitimacy and the personality of its supreme leader, it has also become an island of security for the fully assimilated Jewry that is equal not only in theory but in practice.

Barring dramatic shifts at the top or spectacular failures at home and major upheavals abroad, Hungary is unlikely to produce or import political anti-Semitism in the foreseeable future.

## 2. THE SURPRISE OF RUMANIA

It is hardly an exaggeration to say that Rumania was the most anti-Semitic country in prewar Europe.

Hannah Arendt

If Soviet Jewry could achieve a status analogous with the co-religionists in Rumania, we would be very happy.

Rabbi Nussbaum of Hollywood

Rumania is the only country in the Communist world whose Jews have lost no sleep over what effect the June war might have on their lives.

*The New York Times*

When Nicolae Ceausescu in March 1965 at the age of forty-seven succeeded the dead dictator Gheorghiu-Dej as First Secretary of the Communist Party, a high Hungarian official in Budapest told the author that the new Party leader was "anti-Soviet, anti-Hungarian, and anti-Semitic—in that order." His flamboyant appeals to national sentiments initially seemed to confirm these warnings. Yet this same man, who in the meantime has become Rumania's supreme ruler, refused to sign the joint statement condemning "Israeli aggression" issued by a Communist summit meeting in Moscow on June 9, 1967, and stayed away altogether from the similar conference of Soviet and East European leaders in Budapest one month later. Alone among the East European states (including even Yugoslavia) Rumania continued to maintain diplomatic relations with Israel.

Rumania's initially almost imperceptible but in sum sensational emancipation from Russian domination in the 1960s has had beneficial effects on the position of the Jewish community. The Jews not only enjoy the same freedom of worship and facilities for cultural self-expression as their co-religionists in neighboring Hungary; they alone in the Communist world have been allowed since 1965 to have close relations with the World Jewish Congress and outside Jewish communities. In 1967 the Joint was invited by the Rumanian Government to resume its welfare activities. In view of the official Soviet-sponsored myth that the Joint is an espionage agency, this was an action of some political significance.

It would of course be highly naïve to imagine that the Six Day War or a genuine change of heart overnight made philo-Semites of the Communist leaders who as late as 1959 were still staging secret trials against Jews accused of "Zionist propaganda."[38] Rumania's "go-it-alone" moves during the Middle East conflict were merely part of the daring and imaginative foreign policy that, perfectly timed and brilliantly executed, has since 1963 defied Soviet domination on a number of key issues and attained for this small, isolated Balkan country a startling degree of genuine independence. To put it bluntly, Rumania broke with its Warsaw Pact allies in taking a neutral stance in the Israeli-Arab conflict (as it did in the case of the German Question, the Sino-Soviet rift, and the invasion of Czechoslovakia), not because of a change of heart but because of a change of interests.

Nationalism, or rather the defense of national individuality, has been all along the basis of the Rumanian bid for independence under extremely adverse geographic conditions. Deep-rooted traditions of a powerful nationalism and an equally profound aversion to Russia, the hereditary foe—both the products of a series of humiliating injustices—have enabled the once weakest ruling Communist Party in Eastern Europe to exploit the changes in the Communist world and in the international situation, to challenge Soviet domination and to set itself up as a champion of national interests. Nowhere in Eastern Europe are the sense of nationhood and the spirit of national identity, the glories of an ancient past and a cultural heritage so deliberately and conspicuously fostered and promoted by a Communist ruling group as in Rumania.*

What stunned observers however was the fact that this conscious appeal to national sentiments did not lead, as, for example, in Russia under Stalin or in Poland in 1968, to an upsurge of anti-Jewish (or "anti-Zionist") discrimination. On the contrary, Rumanian Jews have so far been beneficiaries and not casualties of the "new course" which has rallied the population around an indigenous Communist leadership. The reasons for the surprising impact of new patriotic fervor on Rumanian Jewry must be sought partly in Rumanian history and traditions.

In her controversial study *Eichmann in Jerusalem,* Hannah Arendt flatly stated: ". . . in Rumania even the SS were taken aback, and occasionally frightened, by the horrors of old-fashioned, spontaneous pogroms on a gigantic scale; they often intervened to save Jews from butchery, so that the killing could be done in what, according to them, was a civilized way. It is hardly an exaggeration to say that Rumania was the most anti-Semitic country in prewar Europe."[39] Her sweeping judgment was sharply rejected and described as an "egregious misconstruction" by the former Jewish liberal member of the prewar Rumanian Parliament, A. Berkowitz. Having been interned by Marshal Antonescu during World War II and subsequently kept in prison for seven years by the Communist regime, Berkowitz managed to emigrate in the 1960s and published his rejoinder in an American magazine.[40] So there is no reason to doubt his sincerity when he states: "The anti-Semitic movement was the exclusive preoccupation of a small segment of the student youth. Not even under Antonescu or during German occupation were Jews subjected to the degree of oppression and suffering perpetrated upon them by the Nazis in Hun-

* For a detailed analysis of Rumanian nationalism and bid for independence see the author's *Eagles in Cobwebs—Nationalism and Communism in the Balkans* (New York, 1969), pp. 262–350.

gary, Yugoslavia, Greece, and elsewhere. There were grave excesses, but excesses of this sort were isolated cases rather than systematic measures and cannot be attributed to the Rumanian people as a whole."

Whose reasoning is correct, Arendt's that the Rumanians were "the most anti-Semitic" nation in Europe, or Berkowitz's reply that "the great peasant mass accounting for 75 per cent of the population has never held or demonstrated anti-Semitic prejudices"? The paradox is that both are in some respects right; at the same time both can be challenged.

Ever since the reappearance of the Rumanians, who consider themselves descendants of the Romanized Dacians, as state-builders in the late nineteenth century after a "thousand years of mysterious silence,"[41] Rumania's overriding aims have been the unification of Moldavia and Wallachia, the two principalities under Turkish rule, and the establishment of Great Rumania, including the disputed provinces of Transylvania and Bukovina (which were part of Austro-Hungary) and Bessarabia (which was part of Russia). The misfortune of the Jews was that their massive immigration from Galicia and Russia coincided with the crucial final phases of the Rumanians' centuries-old fight for survival and unification.

The size and rate of the Jewish immigration during the nineteenth century has been a hotly disputed issue between anti-Semitic and liberal historians, and the data, particularly for the first half of the century, are imperfect and unreliable. In the words of R. W. Seton-Watson, the foremost Western chronicler of Rumanian history, "it appears certain that at the beginning of the nineteenth century there were only about two thousand Jewish families in Moldavia, hardly any in Wallachia."[42] While Seton-Watson accepted the Rumanian view that the Jews "invaded" the country only in the second half of the century, Jewish scholars can point to evidence that Jews were living in the two principalities in the late Middle Ages.[43] The fact remains however that in 1860 the number of Jews was estimated at 160,000 and had jumped to

260,000 by the end of the century, representing almost 5 per cent of the total population.

In Moldavia, Bukovina, and Bessarabia, Jews accounted for one third to one half of the urban population. "Forbidden to settle in the countryside since the 1830s, barred from almost all professions, and classified and treated as foreigners, the Jews were forced by circumstances just as much as by inclination or training to fit into an occupational pattern in which trade predominated . . . In contrast to the successful Jewish land contractors, bankers, and merchants, the larger part of the Jewish population led a miserable existence as artisans and intermediaries between the boyars and their contractors and the peasantry."[44] From the 1870s onward, small-town Jewish tavernkeepers, moneylenders, and go-betweens were the most conspicuous links in the exploitation of the peasants and had to bear the brunt of peasant unrest. The great peasant uprising in Moldavia in the spring of 1907 began with the plundering of Jewish homes before its fury was vented upon the feudal ruling class.

While in neighboring Hungary, Jews sat in Parliament and later even in the Government, the first constitution of the united principalities in 1866 made it illegal for Jews to acquire Rumanian citizenship. When the Old Kingdom* in 1878 became a sovereign state, the Treaty of Berlin stipulated that Jews should be recognized as Rumanian nationals enjoying full civil and political rights. The Rumanians however skillfully circumvented this obligation, and it was only in 1919 that the Government yielded to the pressure of the Allies and paid the price of emancipating the Jews to facilitate the birth of Greater Rumania.

Rumania emerged from World War I with more than double its prewar territory and population. While the Old Kingdom had an almost completely Rumanian population, Greater Rumania was a conglomeration of widely disparate provinces, with non-Rumanians accounting for one fourth of the total population. The acquisition of Transylvania, Bessarabia, and Bukovina brought

* The term "Old Kingdom" refers to Rumania before World War I and excludes Transylvania, Bessarabia, and Bukovina.

almost a half million more Jews. The number reached 756,000 in 1930 and an estimated 800,000 (4.2 per cent of the total population) by the eve of World War II.[45]

The tensions that dominated the entire interwar period arose mainly from complex minority problems and fears of possible encroachments on territorial integrity from the open or covert revisionist claims of neighboring Soviet Russia, Hungary, and Bulgaria. It is often overlooked that the Rumanian Jewish community, the third largest in Europe, also consisted of groups with totally different degrees of assimilation and cultural backgrounds. There were some three hundred thousand Bessarabian and Bukovinian Jews whose mother tongue (97 per cent and 80 per cent respectively) was Yiddish and whose culture was dominated by German or Russian influences. The 190,000 Jews in Transylvania on the other hand had been emancipated six decades earlier than their co-religionists in the Old Kingdom and were overwhelmingly Hungarian in language and culture.

These differences were reflected in the Rumanian attitude toward those Jews suspected of pro-Russian or pro-Hungarian sympathies and those of the Old Kingdom whom King Carol I had called "half-Rumanians." By 1930, 80 per cent of the Jews in Wallachia had Rumanian as their mother tongue (the rest Yiddish), and in Moldavia 40 per cent were Rumanian in language and culture.[46]

Rampant political and economic nationalism, the repercussions of the Great Depression, and the spread of pro-Nazi tendencies bred an increasingly anti-Semitic atmosphere that began to hit all categories of Jewry. In 1937–38, 120,000 Jews were stripped of their citizenship, and such rabid anti-Semitic movements as the Iron Guard and the so-called League of Christian National Defense won the support of almost one fourth of the voters.

Rumania is a unique example of a country whose pro-German Government under Marshal Antonescu was the first to embark on a large-scale massacre of the Jews, yet which in the end saved a higher proportion of Jews than any other German satellite. Both Arendt's sweeping anti-Rumanian generalizations and Berkowitz's equally wholesale defense of Rumania's honor overlook this basic contradiction. After their entry into the war on the side of Nazi Germany, the Rumanian troops committed unparalleled anti-Semitic atrocities in reconquered Bessarabia and occupied Russia*—but the Jews in old Rumania survived the war virtually intact. The Jewry in rump Rumania (after the dismemberment in 1940) suffered less than in any other Central and East European country. The hundred thousand Bucharest Jews, for example, were not required to wear the yellow badge nor subjected to movement restrictions, and no Jews from the territories of the Old Kingdom were shipped to the extermination camps in Poland.

This contrast in the treatment of different segments of the Jewish community cannot be explained merely in terms of Rumanian opportunism as the Soviet Army drew nearer the borders, although it is true that Marshal Antonescu, after killing two thirds of the Bessarabian and Bukovinian Jews, suddenly stopped the massacres in mid-1942 and was even planning to allow their emigration—at $1300 a head. The Rumanians' legendary flair for corruption also enabled many Jews to buy relief from persecution.[47] Yet all this cannot obscure the fact that while the Hungarian, Slovak, Croat, and Greek Jews were deported wholesale, the Jews of Rumania proper were protected from the worst. Their survival cannot of course mitigate the responsibility or the killing of the "enemy" Jews, but at the same time we should not forget that the Government of "the most anti-Semitic country in prewar Europe" deliberately saved its "own" Jews from genocide.

* The contested region of Bessarabia and Northern Bukovina (which had never belonged to Russia) were occupied by Soviet troops, in accordance with the secret protocols of the Hitler-Stalin pact of August 1939, in June 1940. Soon afterward Rumania also had to cede Northern Transylvania to Hungary and Southern Dobruja to Bulgaria. One year later, in June 1941, Rumanian troops joined the German Army in the invasion of the Soviet Union and recaptured Bessarabia and Northern Bukovina in four weeks. They even occupied ten thousand square miles of Russian territory. At the end of World War II, Rumania, by its last-minute break with Germany, managed to regain Transylvania from Hungary but had to accept the final loss of Bessarabia and Northern Bukovina, which were duly reabsorbed by Soviet Russia.

The fate of the Transylvanian Jewry vividly illustrates how misleading labels can be. The Hungarian-speaking Jews in Northern Transylvania, accused not without reason by the interwar Rumanian Government of sympathy for Hungarian irredentism, were killed by their fellow Hungarians when the Vienna Award of the Axis Powers allotted their territory to Hungary. Out of some 150,000 Jews, over 120,000 perished. But some 40,000 who remained in Southern Transylvania under Rumanian sovereignty survived. And it was Rumanian peasants who helped Jews to escape from Northern Transylvania into Rumania.[48] After World War II, Rumania (without Bessarabia and Bukovina) had a Jewish community numbering 428,000 people, only slightly less than had been recorded within the same borders before the war, and more than half of Greater Rumania's total Jewish population. Almost four out of every five Jews in the new territories annexed after World War I were killed. The figure cited above represented the Jewish community of old Rumania and what remained (about 100,000) of the 457,000 Jews of Bessarabia, Bukovina, and Transylvania.[49]

Thus the Rumanians simultaneously saved and killed Jews, protected their "own" and massacred "foreign" Jews. By the cruel standards of the Holocaust, the Rumanians' record was incomparably better than that of the Hungarians, Croats, or Slovaks. At least a partial explanation of this may be found in what the Jewish historian Baron noted about medieval Europe: the status of the Jews was most favorable in states of multiple nationality and most unfavorable in homogeneous national states. Between the two extremes were states that revealed some of the intolerance of the national state but lacked its decisiveness and simultaneity of action.[50]

After the Communist takeover, Rumanian Jews found themselves in much the same position as Jews in the other Soviet satellites. But because of the relatively large number of Jews and the strength of the various Zionist organizations, which claimed a membership of 100,000,[51] the twin issues of Zionism and emigration to Israel played a more important role in Rumania than elsewhere in Eastern Europe. By the end of 1951 about 120,000 (perhaps even as many as 160,000)[52] Rumanian Jews had found their way to Israel. With the policy change in Moscow, the Jewish community was brought under firm Communist control; Zionist parties and clubs were banned and about two hundred Zionist leaders subsequently arrested.[53]

As everywhere, the Jewish Communist leaders were second to none in pressing the destruction of the Jewish and Zionist organizations. And as everywhere, Jews were not only victims but also rulers under the new order. As pointed out earlier, the Rumanian Communist Party since its founding in 1921 had been dominated by Jews, Hungarians, Bulgarians, and Ukrainians. It was founded by the Bulgarian-born Christian Rakovsky and a Russian-born Jew, Mikhail Cass (or Katz), who later, under the name of Constantin Dobrogeanu-Gherea, became the only serious thinker Rumanian Communisn has so far produced. Between 1924 and 1944, two Secretary Generals of the underground Party were Hungarians (Elek Koblos and Stefan Foris), while two leaders (V. Holostenco and Boris Stefanov) were not even members of the Party, but belonged respectively to the Ukrainian branch of the Soviet Party and the Polish Party.

The new Party museum in Bucharest provides evidence of the preponderance of non-Rumanian elements in the Central Committees "elected" at the prewar Party congresses. Even excluding those who had Rumanianized names, the first nine-member Central Committee in 1922 included at least two Hungarians, two Jews, and one Bulgarian; Hungarians, Jews, and Bulgarians (and the Hungarians were often Jewish) accounted for half of the leadership in 1928 and 1931.[54] The clandestine Communist movement on the fringe of political life was run mainly by the Foreign Buro in Moscow, which was subordinate to the Comintern. And, as Secretary General Nicolae Ceausescu bluntly stated in his speech marking the Party's forty-fifth anniversary in 1966, the Comintern "appointed leadership cadres, including Secretaries General, from among people abroad who did not know the Rumanian people's life." Moreover, the orders from Moscow in-

stucted the Party "to fight for the breaking away from Rumania
of certain territories inhabited by an overwhelming majority of
Rumanians . . . and in fact promoted the dismemberment of the
national state and the breakup of the Rumanian people."[55]

This made it inevitable that Communism, despite the great social
discontent in the country, appealed only to minority groups. There
were, of course, also home-grown Communists among ethnic Rumanians whose leader, Lucretiu Patrascanu, was involved in the
preparations leading to King Michael's coup in August 1944.
Others like Gheorghiu-Dej and his future associates, including
Ceausescu, were serving long prison terms when the Soviet Army
was approaching Rumania.

The real leaders of the Party and the architects of the Communist takeover were, as usual, the "Muscovites" who returned to the
country in September 1944 with the Red Army. The hard core of
the Soviet-trained Communists was led by Ana Pauker, the daughter of a Jewish rabbi, whose upper middle-class husband, Marcel
Pauker, had been one of the founders of the movement and a
high Comintern functionary (later killed during Stalin's Great
Purge).[56] Her principal collaborators were Vasile Luca, a Hungarian from Transylvania, and Teohari Georgescu, an ethnic Rumanian. It was she and not the nominal leader, Gheorghiu-Dej,
who ranked as the most powerful figure after 1945. When General
Radescu, the Premier in February 1945, on the eve of the Communist seizure of power called Pauker and Luca "hyenas and foreigners without a God and a country," he only voiced what most
Rumanians felt about Moscow's agents.

The removal of the Pauker trio in May 1952 was undoubtedly
a landmark in the Rumanianization of the top leadership. Pauker,
Deputy Premier, Foreign Minister and Secretary of the Central
Committee, and her two friends in charge of the economy and the
secret police had been the supreme rulers of postwar Rumania.
It was only after their fall that Gheorghiu-Dej and his group, the
"home" Communists, assumed real control of the Party and state
apparatus. Pauker and her friends, accused of "opportunist right-
wing deviations," were thrown to the wolves as scapegoats for the

economic difficulties and popular discontent following the currency reform. While the question of whether the purge was primarily due to Soviet pressure or to the dynamics of an internal struggle for power is still a matter for conjecture, the final decision—at the height of Stalin's power—could have been made only in Moscow.

Though the charge of Zionism did not figure among the accusations against the fallen leaders, Pauker's removal fitted the general pattern of the replacement of Soviet-trained Jewish Communists by less unpopular native leaders.* Furthermore, she herself was personally vulnerable since her father had lived in Israel and she also maintained contacts with her brothers living in the West.[57] Seen against the background of the Slansky affair and the directing role of the Kremlin, Pauker's Jewish origin must have been an important contributary cause to the ascendancy of a native Rumanian but unquestionably orthodox Communist like Gheorghiu-Dej.

In contrast to Czechoslovakia, however, the purge did not have an overtly anti-Semitic character. Another Moscow-trained functionary, Iosif Chisinevschi, a Bessarabian Jew, was promoted to full membership in the Politburo, and Pauker's successor as Foreign Minister, Simion Bughici, was also of Jewish origin. But the changes in personnel brought no loosening of the tight Soviet grip on the country.

The second important landmark in the postwar history of the Rumanian Party was the purge of two powerful Politburo members, Miron Constantinescu† and Iosif Chisinevschi, in June 1957. Though this involved the fall of the last remaining top Jewish leader, the accusations against them and the manner of their removal was once again free from any overt taint of anti-Semitism. They were accused of both "left" and "right" deviation, of past abuses and "anarchistic-petit bourgeois" tendencies, but not of

---

* Of the three fallen leaders, Pauker and Georgescu were never tried. Pauker died in 1960. Georgescu's Party membership was restored in the 1960s and he is now the director of a large printing plant in Bucharest. Only Luca was sentenced, at a secret trial, to death in 1954, commuted later to life imprisonment. He died in prison. The Supreme Court annulled the sentence against Luca in September 1968.

† During the past few years he has made a significant come-back and is currently member of the party's Executive Committee.

"Zionism." (This would admittedly have been difficult since Constantinescu was a genuine "home" Communist and a reformer, while Chisinevschi ranked as a Muscovite hard-liner.) Whatever the reasons for lumping together these two men of totally different backgrounds, the purge revealed Gheorghiu-Dej's consummate skill as a tactician and made him the absolute ruler of the country.

It was however only after the withdrawal of the Soviet troops in 1958 and in the wake of the Twenty-second Soviet Party Congress in 1961, that the long forgotten Pauker affair became a political factor of prime importance. At the Central Committee plenum in November–December 1961, Gheorghiu-Dej coped easily with the repercussions of Khrushchev's second de-Stalinization campaign. The Party leader, who since March 1961 had also been President of the republic, asserted that he had been a helpless prisoner of the Pauker group and, by purging them, had restored "collective leadership." In fact, if not in so many words, he claimed that he had been the first to de-Stalinize—and that during the height of Stalinism.

The real political significance of the meeting lay in the fact that it made the first major attempt to identify the Party with the Rumanian people. The factional fighting was presented by speaker after speaker as a battle between the "alien elements" who had "usurped" the dominant positions after World War II, and "native" Communists. Ceausescu, the rising star in the hierarchy, referred to the long struggle between the various Muscovite leaders and those "comrades who risked arrest and execution, who suffered the burden of prison and concentration camps (in Rumania) . . . who fought with international brigades against Franco in Spain or in France against the German occupation." It was the exiles in Moscow who after their return had propagated the cult of Stalin, enjoyed the sympathy of Molotov's "anti-Party" group in belittling and disapproving the exploits of the home Communists, including the August 1944 coup, and "opposed and hindered the promotion of those activists who were connected with the working class and the people."[58]

This nationalistic rewriting of Party history with its veiled anti-

Soviet overtones was a covert declaration of independence addressed to the initiate among the by then almost nine hundred thousand Party members.[59] The plenum, whose significance was overlooked at the time, marked the beginning of the coordinated efforts to free the Party from the stigma of being "un-Rumanian" and to project it as the torchbearer of what from 1963 onward has become an exuberantly national course. Even a cursory review of the Rumanian search for autonomy would go beyond the scope of this survey. Suffice it to say that the "Rumanianization" of the Party and state apparatus was one of the most important factors that enabled a regime with the weakest indigenous roots of any Communist Party to capture the sentiment of the country and to win genuine popular support in its dispute with its erstwhile protector and master.

The nationalization of policies and personnel could not fail to reduce the strength of the "alien elements"—Hungarians, Bulgarians, and Jews—who were disproportionately represented in the ranks of the Moscow-trained emigrants. Yet the national revival and the increasingly daring moves toward national emancipation have not been accompanied by any deliberate abetting of latent anti-Semitic resentment.

There appear to have been at least three main factors responsible for the surprising phenomenon that rampant nationalism has so far helped rather than harmed the status of the Jewish community in Rumania. First, the Jewish Communists and former Socialists were heavily represented among the survivors of the eight hundred Rumanian fighters in the Spanish Civil War and in the French resistance movement during World War II.[60] Thus they were invariably hit by the repercussions of the Soviet-sponsored purges against the "Spaniards" and "Westerners." As in neighboring Hungary, the Jews were both rulers and victims under the single-party dictatorship and did not represent a closely knit group. At the trial of the nationalist leader Lucretiu Patrascanu in April 1954, several Jewish intellectuals were also sentenced to life imprisonment, while it is now claimed that in addition to Gheorghiu-Dej and the then Minister of Interior Alexandru

Draghici, the Jewish secretary of the Central Committee, Chisinev-sçhi, was primarily responsible for the frame-up.[61] When at the 1961 plenum, such Jewish old-timers as Gheorghe Stoica and Gaston Marin attacked Pauker and the other fallen leaders for terrorizing the veterans of the Spanish Civil War and the French resistance, and thanked Gheorghiu-Dej for "protecting" them, they may well have spoken the truth.[62]

Neither the purge of the Pauker group nor the fall from grace of Chisinevschi in 1957 was used by Gheorghiu-Dej to unleash an anti-Semitic campaign on the Czechoslovak pattern. Chisinev-schi's successor as chief of the key Agitation-Propaganda Department was another Bessarabian Jew, Leonte Rautu, who became an alternate member of the Politburo at the end of 1955. Out of the ninety-six full members and alternates elected at the 1955 Party Congress, fifteen were of Jewish origin.[63]

Whatever Ceausescu's "personal" feelings toward the Jews may be, his accession to the Party leadership in March 1965 paved the way for a rehabilitation of Patrascanu and many other disgraced functionaries. In building up his power base the young leader, who in less than three years also took over the post of President of the State Council, relied not only on younger functionaries closely associated with him, but also on the assistance of those Party veterans who had been the victims of Gheorghiu-Dej and his Old Guard. The settling of scores led once again to a reinterpretation of postwar Party history. At the 1961 plenum of the Central Committee, Gheorghiu-Dej saddled the "Pauker group" with the responsibility for the horrors of Stalinism. Seven years later another plenum in April 1968 shattered the sacred myth that "we do not have to rehabilitate anyone post mortem." Now it was the turn of the dead dictator and his Minister of Interior, Alexandru Draghici, to be blamed for the murder of Patrascanu and other excesses.[64]

The power struggles connected with the rehabilitations lasted for two and a half years. The man who headed the four-member spe-cial investigating commission was the Jewish Party veteran Gheorghe Stoica. He and other old-timers, including several Jews, lent a helping hand to Ceausescu in raising the issue of past repressions. The hunt for the guilty was—as always—a pretext for the settling of political scores. After all, Ceausescu himself owed his meteoric rise in the Party hierarchy between 1952 and 1955, as well as his later ascendancy, to the fact that he had been a favorite of the late dictator. Nevertheless it was the senior members of the old Politburo, still in the saddle, against whom the rehabilitation drive was directed. In April 1968, Draghici was stripped of all his functions. By the end of the year, three further influential members of the Old Guard had retired, and at the Tenth Party Congress in August 1969 Ceausescu eliminated Gheorghiu-Dej's two closest associates and his erstwhile rivals for the top position, Chivu Stoica (former Premier, later head of state) and Gheorghe Apostol (First Secretary of the Party in 1954–55).[85]

Thus the issue of rehabilitations served as the single most important lever to oust the majority of the former Politburo. As none of these men was Jewish, the issue of anti-Semitism played no role in the fierce power struggle. The April plenum rehabilitated posthumously nineteen prominent functionaries who perished in Stalin's purges in the Soviet Union. At least eight of them were Jewish and two Hungarian, and the list included even Marcel Pauker, who as recently as 1961 had been denounced by Ceausescu himself as the evil spirit of prewar Rumanian Communism.[66]

In short, the purgers and the purged of the past, Gheorghiu-Dej and the Pauker couple, Luca and Georgescu, now rank as men who committed "serious errors" or "grave excesses" but were not traitors and in some cases had "undeniable merits." This consensus, reflected also in the exhibits in the lavish Party museum in Bucharest, is characteristic of the prudent and cautious manner in which the present leaders "master the past" without undermining the legitimacy of their own power.

The supreme policy-making bodies are now dominated by men of the "second generation" fully committed to Ceausescu and those members of the Old Guard who aligned themselves with him at an early date. The nine-member Standing Presidium elected at the last congress includes no Jews (or Hungarians). The Executive Committee that serves as a "connecting link" between the Presidium and the mammoth Central Committee (165 members and 120 alternates) has three Jews (and one Hungarian) among the twenty-one full members.[67] The reshuffles represent the concentration of power in the hands of Ceausescu and his close associates, not a deliberate policy of "Aryanization." It is true that since 1965 a handful of Jewish ministers, including the former Planning Chief and Deputy Premier, Gaston Marin, have been demoted or dismissed. This writer however is hesitant to share the view of those diplomats in the Rumanian capital who attribute their personal setbacks mainly to anti-Jewish prejudices.[68] In any case, the overall record of the last four years does not seem to indicate any tendency toward political anti-Semitism and official discrimination.

The second and more important factor that explains the absence of anti-Semitic undertones in the appeals to national sentiments is the character of Rumanian nationalism. What may be described as the process of national reaffirmation is, in Rumania as elsewhere in Eastern Europe, basically a defensive nationalism. The defense of national individuality and the aspiration to real, not purely formal independence is primarily an anti-Soviet nationalism—as long at any rate as the balance of power and fundamental Soviet policies remain unchanged.

At the same time Rumania's national course is not the result of an unchecked eruption of pressures from below. The Rumanian challenge to Soviet hegemony has been launched and, thus far, controlled from above. Furthermore, the national revival has not stimulated any kind of parochial isolation from the great forces of our time. On the contrary, Rumania—as indeed so often in the past—once again looks westward for economic ties and cultural inspiration. The dynamics of nationalism involve serious risks and can create crisis situations both within and between the East European countries. But in the case of nations that are fighting for their right not to be ruled by an outside great power, the stirrings of national sentiments cannot possibly be identified with reactionary causes. In Rumania, nationalism is an ally of democracy and the basis of an outward-looking foreign policy.

In a sense, the Rumanian developments provide a historic parallel with the Kingdom of Naples in the sixteenth century. The treatment of Jews in the Kingdom "illustrated how its anti-Jewish xenophobia could be overshadowed by the larger fear of seeing its own autonomous evolution submerged by the Spanish imperial power . . ."[69] Similarly, anti-Semitism in Rumania is not really a live issue; it has been overshadowed and superseded by the "larger fear" of the rapacious Russian neighbor. If there is a national problem within Rumania, it is the delicate issue of the large Hungarian minority associated with another, neighboring country, and not related to the Jewish Question. The deliberate policy of "Rumanianization" is loaded with political dynamite primarily against Russia and may pose a covert threat to the national identity of the Hungarians, but at no point has it been tainted by any trace of official anti-Semitism.

Finally, Rumanian policy toward the Jews was intimately connected with the question of exit visas to Israel. As its Jewish community was the largest in postwar Eastern Europe, and the vast majority longed to go to Israel, the question of emigration was a live issue, much more than in Hungary or other East European countries. A considerable part of Rumanian Jewry, perhaps as much as one third of the survivors, had left by 1951.[70] For the next seven years virtually no exit permits were issued. As in Hungary, many Jews were engulfed in the deportation in 1951–52 of "unproductive" elements to remote places in the Black Sea region. It was an indication of the unrest and embitterment in the Jewish community that even after Stalin's death in 1954 scores of Zionist leaders were sentenced to long prison terms at secret trials.[71] They were released only during the period of the relative thaw after the Twentieth Soviet Party Congress in 1956.

The number of Jews in Rumania has long been a matter of dispute. At the census in February 1956, 146,264 persons claimed Jewish nationality and about one fourth of them (34,000) gave Yiddish as their mother tongue. It is generally agreed that thousands of Jews avoided registering as such for fear of persecution or professional setbacks. The estimates about the real number of Jews in 1959–60 ranged from 200,000 to 250,000.[72] When the Rumanian authorities in September 1958 suddenly decided to grant exit visas to Israel, Western sources reported that over a hundred thousand Jews had registered for emigration.[73] After about twenty thousand had left, Arab protests and, evidently, Soviet pressure forced the Rumanians to stop issuing further exit permits. On February 25, 1959, the Rumanian Government issued a statement accusing "Israeli and imperialist circles of unleashing a diversionist campaign trumpeting abroad the crude invention that there was a mass migration of Jews to Israel." It denied any suggestion of a "mass migration," assured the Arab nations of Rumanian sympathy, deplored the fact that they had been led astray by a slanderous campaign, and accused the Israeli Embassy in Bucharest of spreading Zionist slogans among Rumanian Jews.[74]

It is still not clear whether the sudden decision to allow the departure of Jews was an independent Rumanian initiative or the result of an agreement with Moscow.[75] What mattered was the equally sudden deterioration of the position of the Jews. Especially those fourteen thousand persons who had already renounced their citizenship and disposed of their property on the eve of emigration found themselves in a desperate situation. Many of them had been dismissed from their jobs as soon as they made their applications. Many remained restless since families had been split, with some members already in Israel and the rest trapped in Rumania. The regime replied with a mixture of propaganda barrage and a wave of arrests. Dozens of Jews were arrested and tried in 1959 on charges of espionage and treason. Within eighteen months three Israeli diplomats were expelled because of "abuse of diplomatic privileges."[76]

The halt of emigration was partly the result of the noisy publicity with which both the Israeli Government and certain Jewish organizations abroad surrounded the departure of the first trainloads of Rumanian Jews. This in turn was eagerly exploited by Arab propaganda, which published wildly exaggerated data about the number of Rumanian immigrants arriving in Israel. As subsequent developments illustrated, the Rumanians had intended to carry out the operation quietly and furtively. At the same time they must have been disconcerted, if not shocked, by the unexpectedly large number of those who registered to go. The large-scale departure of trained Jewish personnel may also have had adverse effects on the Rumanian economy.

The emigration of the Jews was allowed for fairly obvious reasons: it helped to provide jobs and flats for the new middle class, to make the population more homogeneous and to broaden the domestic basis of an unpopular regime. The pressure for emigration also convinced the Rumanian leaders that most of the applicants were not willing or able to assimilate and that their loyalty to the regime was bound to remain in doubt. The resumption of the emigration in 1961 was part of the move to promote the domestic consolidation of the regime on the eve of an open friction with Moscow.

Nevertheless the Rumanians learned from the lessons of the "scandal" in early 1959. Jewish families were granted exit permits provided they gave as their destination any country other than Israel. While most of them proceeded there from Vienna, the Rumanians could in good faith assure the Arab governments that they were not encouraging emigration to Israel. As all sides concerned were more discreet than in 1959, a considerable number of Jews was allowed to leave the country in the early 1960s: almost 12,000 departed in 1961, over 5000 in 1962, 7000 in 1963, 9000 in 1964, and 1400 in 1965. In all, between 1960 and 1965, about 35,000 Jews left the country quietly and unobtrusively without causing any diplomatic troubles with the "Arab friends."[77]

At the same time, the pressure on the Jewish community was lifted and those arrested in 1959 were released by the end of 1960. As no comprehensive statistics have ever been published about the Jews emigrating to Israel and the West since 1958, there are different estimates about the size of the present Jewish community. The semiofficial figure repeatedly announced by the Chief Rabbi,

Dr. Moses Rosen, is that there are seventy-five Jewish communities and a total Jewish population of "approximately 100,000."[78] The real number is certainly higher, perhaps by 15 to 20 per cent. As, however, there are about 300,000 citizens of Rumanian origin in Israel, the estimates of 200,000 or more Jews still living in Rumania appear to be excessively high.[79]

Since 1960, and especially after 1965, the situation of the Jews has steadily improved. There is total freedom of religion, with 150 synagogues and temples open. It is the lack of rabbis, administrators and worshipers and not any kind of restriction that is responsible for the religious decline among the Jews. The state maintains a Yiddish Theater and allows the Jewish community to publish a fortnightly newspaper in Hebrew, Yiddish, and Rumanian, the only periodical of its kind in Eastern Europe. Since the Joint was allowed to resume its activities in 1967, about forty-five hundred aged persons receive a monthly allowance in addition to their state pensions, and eighty-five hundred persons benefit from a twice yearly distribution of clothing. There are also twelve kosher restaurants and canteens supplying needy families with free meals.[80]

The Rumanian regime since 1959 has not only abstained from the usual Communist attacks against "Zionism," but also allowed the resumption of close contacts between the Jewish community and international Jewish organizations abroad. Chief Rabbi Rosen is a member of the Council of the World Jewish Congress and frequently visits Western Europe, North America, and Israel. At the same time he has been able to welcome in Rumania a great number of distinguished foreign Jewish visitors. The Government made the celebrations marking the twentieth anniversary of Rosen's appointment as Chief Rabbi in July 1968 a glittering state affair. Headed by the Orthodox Patriarch Justinian, representatives of thirteen religious denominations, as well as a great number of Jewish guests from abroad led by Israeli Chief Rabbi Yitzhak Nissim, participated in the ceremonies. In 1966 the Rumanian leadership had already made an unprecedented gesture when it allowed the shipping of some two thousand Torah scrolls to Israel. All this clearly represents a qualitative change in official policy toward Rumanian Jewry. As in so many other fields, one has the impression that whatever contributes to national prestige, and particularly to the Rumanian nation's image abroad, is permissible so long as it does not impair the absolute power of the Party. There is no doubt that this tolerant attitude has reaped handsome dividends in Jewish good will toward Rumania. The status of the Rumanian Jewry has, not without reason, been contrasted with the plight of co-religionists in the Soviet Union.[81]

The steadily improving position of the Rumanian Jews must also be seen in the context of the changing relations between Rumania and Israel. In accord with its increasingly independent foreign policy, Rumania actually began to prepare the ground for a more balanced Middle East policy toward the end of 1965, when its representatives at the meeting of the Communist-sponsored World Federation of Trade Unions abstained in the vote on an anti-Israeli motion. It was however a meeting between Israeli Foreign Minister Abba Eban and his Rumanian colleague, Corneliu Manescu, in New York in October 1966 that gave the green light for the intensification of economic contacts.

A new chapter was opened in April 1967 by the visit of Israeli Finance Minister Shapir who signed a trade agreement providing a substantial increase by 1970. The two sides also agreed on technical-scientific cooperation and set up a mixed economic commission. But the political implications of the change in Rumanian policy became evident only in the period preceding the Six Day War when, in contrast to the other Communist countries, the Rumanian mass media took a moderate line of noninterference. As in the case of the Sino-Soviet conflict, the Rumanian leadership perceived the underlying trends correctly and showed a profound appreciation of the implications of new military technology and its effects upon international politics.

The vindication of the neutral policy constituted the most publicized victory of Rumania's independent course. When the East European leaders, including even Marshal Tito, gathered in Moscow on June 9, 1967, Secretary General Ceausescu and Premier Maurer refused to sign the joint statement condemning "Israeli aggression." Instead, the Rumanian Central Committee and Government issued next day a joint statement expressing "profound anxiety" about the hostilities, speaking out for the withdrawal of Israeli and all other troops to within the limits of frontiers, but also for direct negotiations to settle the controversial problems. Subsequently, the Rumanian press took a clear stand against outside interference and for a negotiated settlement based on the observance of the legitimate interests of the people concerned.[82] Rumania did not break off diplomatic relations with Israel, and its representatives did not participate at the second summit meeting of the Soviet and East European leaders held in Budapest on July 10, 1967.

The Rumanian position, spelled out in a moderate and masterful speech by Premier Maurer at the UN General Assembly, was an act of remarkable audacity. It tremendously enhanced Rumania's prestige in the world. A special session of the Rumanian Parliament, convened July 24–26, 1967, underlined the popular backing for Rumania's independent moves on the Middle East conflict and the German Question. In his speech, Ceausescu openly criticized Arab saber rattling: "We wish honestly to tell our Arab friends that we do not understand and do not share the position of those circles that speak in favor of the liquidation of the state of Israel. We do not wish to give advice to anybody, but the lessons of history show that no people can achieve their national and social aspirations against the right to existence of another people."

During the following two years, Rumanian diplomacy performed the unique feat of maintaining good relations with both sides, of dispatching delegations to the Arab countries offering shipments of badly needed wheat as a gift, and of sending Chief Rabbi Rosen to Israel bringing as a gift of the Rumanian Government a further three thousand Torah scrolls "although the Jewish communities in the United States were willing to purchase them for two million dollars . . ."[83] In December 1967 Foreign Trade Minister Ciora arrived for the first session of the mixed commission in Israel, the first East European official of ministerial rank ever to visit Israel. During his visit and the return visit of Israeli Minister of

Commerce, Zeev Sharef, a number of ambitious agreements covering the establishment of joint industrial enterprises in Rumania, three-corner deals on foreign markets, and direct air links were concluded. From ministers and scientists to soccer teams, the exchanges of visits continued at all levels. Trade between the two countries jumped from five million dollars in 1966 to eleven million dollars in 1967 and doubled again to twenty-one million dollars in the following year. In 1969 it reached over thirty million dollars.[84]

The presence of an estimated three hundred thousand people of Rumanian origin in Israel contributes to the attraction of the country as a promising market for Rumanian products. Thousands of Israeli tourists visited Rumania in 1969, and the establishment of regular flights Tel Aviv–Bucharest–New York will give a powerful boost to the Rumanian tourist industry. In sum, Rumania reaped tangible benefits because its policy in the Middle East, as indeed everywhere else, was guided by calculated self-interest.[85]

Having said all this, one must sound a note of caution in regard to the position of Rumanian Jews. Rumanian leaders repeatedly stress the full equality of all citizens without regard to ethnic origin and religious faith. Theoretically the Jews are complete equals, but not always in practice. They cannot complain of any genuine persecution—though many of them tend to see anti-Jewish discrimination where there is none. Yet one has the feeling after many visits to the country that they are faced with an invisible but often very definite ceiling to their advancement in the civil service, the academic and cultural worlds. Most, if not all, of them seem to belong to the category of "deputies"—deputy directors, deputy chairmen of commissions, deputy editors, etc., one peg below the top position. There are, of course, significant exceptions— deputy Premiers, ministers, ambassadors, and so on, but the frequent visitor somehow always leaves with the impression that the Rumanians of "Mosaic faith" do not feel as at ease in Rumania as in neighboring Hungary. On the other hand this atmospheric difference may well be due primarily to historic factors, such as the different degrees of assimilation and the heritage of traditional anti-Semitism.

Nevertheless, in terms of past Rumanian policies toward the Jews, there have been startling and previously unthinkable changes, which in one way or another have affected every single Jew, both those who subsequently emigrated and those who have stayed in their country. Rumania is an illustration of the fact that nationalism cannot be automatically and always identified with anti-Semitism. Rumania's self-assertive, nationally motivated foreign policy, repeatedly defying Soviet pressure, from the outset began to produce very noticeable changes in the position of the Jews, as indeed in the psychological and political climate of the entire country. Whatever the degree of latent anti-Semitism may be, Rumania during the 1960s demonstrated to the world that real national interests can induce the Communist rulers of "the most anti-Semitic country in prewar Europe" to break with both domestic "anti-Zionism" and an aggressively anti-Israeli line in foreign policy. A combination of special factors have combined to create a special security for a Jewish minority that only a decade ago was experiencing the worst persecution in Eastern Europe.

# NOTES

(The material in this book for the most recent period is based on primary sources: Soviet and East European publications or information collected during the author's trips to the area. All data on details of the "anti-Zionist" purge in Poland, if not otherwise specified, was gathered from interviews with some forty Poles, including several former high Party and state officials who in 1968–69 left their country and whose statements the author checked and counterchecked. Books, not only read but also used in the preparation of this study, are cited directly in the footnotes.)

PART ONE
COMMUNISM AND THE JEWS

1. Hannah Arendt, *The Origins of Totalitarianism*, 2d ed. enl. (New York, 1962), p. 3.
2. Z. Bauman, "The End of Polish Jewry—a Sociological Review," *Bulletin on Soviet and East European Jewish Affairs*, London, January 1969.
3. Arendt, p. 5.
4. Bauman.
5. *Jewish Observer*, London, March 1959.
6. *Komsomolskaya Pravda*, Moscow, February 6, 1969; *Sovietskaya Rossiya*, March 14, 1969; T. K. Kichko in Radio Kiev Domestic Service, April 9, 1969. See also *Krasnaya Zvezda*, August 17, 1968.
7. *Krasnaya Zvezda*.
8. Vilem Hejl, "A Solution, Once and for All," *Zitrek*, Prague, March 19, 1969.
9. Earl Raab, "The Black Revolution and the Jewish Question," *Commentary*, New York, January 1969, p. 23.
10. For details see R. Conquest, *Power and Policy in the U.S.S.R.* (London, 1962), pp. 172 and 438–39.
11. Ibid., pp. 163–64.
12. Khrushchev's secret speech in February 1956. Ibid., p. 437.
13. Isaac Deutscher, *Stalin*, rev. ed. (London, 1968), pp. 611–12.
14. Conquest, pp. 206–8.
15. George Lichtheim, "Socialism and the Jews," *Dissent*, New York, July–August 1968, pp. 315–16.

352

16. See for an analysis of the mechanism of the purge Z. K. Brzezinski, *The Permanent Purge* (Cambridge, Mass., 1956), pp. 12–37.

17. Arendt, p. 363.

18. Ibid., pp. 423–24.

19. Brzezinski, p. 168. The term "artificial revolution" is from Michel Tatu's *Power in the Kremlin* (London, 1969).

20. Arendt, p. 362.

21. See Norman Cohn, *Warrant for Genocide* (New York, 1967), and J. S. Curtiss, *The Protocols of Zion* (New York, 1942).

22. Cohn.

23. *Komsomolskaya Pravda*, October 4, 1967.

24. See *Jews in Eastern Europe*, London, March 1968, pp. 7–13.

25. From his novel *The Age of Longing*.

26. Arendt, p. 362.

27. Ibid., p. 4.

28. G. F. Kennan, *Memoirs, 1925–1950* (New York, 1967), p. 367.

29. Prewar statistics from *The Jews in the Soviet Satellites* (Syracuse, 1953). Same source for 1945 figures. Figures for 1968 partly from official spokesmen of the Jewish communities (in Hungary, Rumania, and Yugoslavia), Jewish periodicals from Bulgaria and Poland. The figure for Czechoslovakia is a rough estimate based on information from several Jewish organizations in Prague, Bratislava, and Vienna.

30. Estimated from Jewish organizations, diplomatic sources, and Jewish emigrants and refugees.

31. S. W. Baron, *A Social and Religious History of the Jews*, 2d ed. rev. & enl., Vol. XI (New York, 1967), p. 145.

32. *The Trail of the Dinosaur* (London, 1955), pp. 106–41.

33. Isaac Deutscher, *The Non-Jewish Jew and Other Essays* (London, 1968), pp. 21–41.

34. Figures from confidential but unimpeachable sources.

35. See preceding note.

36. Arendt, p. 3.

37. J. L. Talmon, *The Unique and the Universal* (London, 1965), p. 122.

38. Deutscher, *Non-Jewish Jew*, p. 86.

39. Jean-Paul Sartre, *Réflexions sur la question juive* (Paris, 1954).

40. Erno Laszlo, "Hungarian Jewish Settlements and Demography," in *Studies Hungarian-Jewish*, ed. R. K. Brabham (New York, 1966). See also Peter Meyer, Introduction in *Jews in the Soviet Satellites*, (Syracuse, 1953), p. 7.

41. R. L. Buell, *Poland: Key to Europe* (New York, 1939), p. 92. For details see S. M. Dubnow, *History of the Jews in Russia and Poland*, 3 vols. (Philadelphia, 1916–20).

42. Baron, XI, p. 281.

43. Arthur Hertzberg, *The French Enlightenment and the Jews* (New York, 1968), p. 33.

44. Baron, XI, p. 110.

45. Arendt, p. 29.

46. Nicholas Spulber, "Development, Entrepreneurship, and Discrimina-

tion: a Comparative Analysis," in his *The State and Economic Development in Eastern Europe* (New York, 1966), pp. 89–152.

47. Arendt, pp. 23–28.

48. Meyer, p. 8.

49. Hugh Seton-Watson, *Eastern Europe Between the Wars 1918–1941* (Cambridge, 1945), p. 268.

50. It was Heinrich Heine who commented on Ludwig Boerne's conversion as an attempt to obtain "an entrance ticket to European civilization."

51. Deutscher, *Non-Jewish Jew*, p. 54.

52. *Studies Hungarian-Jewish*, p. 172. See also Meyer, p. 18.

53. Arendt, p. 28.

54. J. L. Talmon, "Israel Among the Nations," *Commentary*, June 1968, p. 36.

55. Deutscher, *Non-Jewish Jew*, pp. 66–67. For Zionist strength see also B. D. Weinryb, "Poland," in *Jews in the Soviet Satellites*, pp. 217–21.

56. Deutscher, *Non-Jewish Jew*, p. 97.

57. Hertzberg, op. cit., J. L. Talmon, *Political Messianism: The Romantic Phase* (New York, 1961), and the studies of Léon Poliakov and Edmund Silberner. For a concise and excellent essay on the problems see George Lichtheim's "Socialism and the Jews" in *Dissent*, July–August 1968.

58. Ibid., p. 316.

59. *The Trail of Dinosaur*, p. 48.

60. Talmon, *The Unique and the Universal*, pp. 84–85.

61. Leonard Schapiro, *The Communist Party of the Soviet Union* (London, 1960), p. 22.

62. Deutscher, *Non-Jewish Jew*, p. 64. See also Schapiro, pp. 47–50. A. B. Ulam, *The Bolsheviks* (New York, 1968), pp. 190–91.

63. Lenin, "Critical Remarks on the National Question" (1913), *Collected Works* (Sochineniya), 4th ed. (Moscow), Vol. 20, pp. 3–37. See also his lecture on the 1905 Revolution delivered on January 1922 in Zurich. English translation in *Selected Works* (London, 1936), Vol. 3, pp. 1–19. For Lenin's high appreciation of Jewish revolutionaries (as confided to his sister Anna) see Ulam, p. 190.

64. Stalin, *Collected Works* (Moscow, 1946), Vol. 2, pp. 50–51.

65. See particularly R. V. Burks, *The Dynamics of Communism in Eastern Europe* (Princeton, 1961); John A. Armstrong, *The Soviet Bureaucratic Elite* (New York, 1959); H. D. Lasswell and D. Lerner, eds., *World Revolutionary Elites* (Cambridge, Mass., 1966).

66. Deutscher, *Non-Jewish Jew*, pp. 55 and 68–69.

67. Arendt, p. 14.

68. Schapiro, pp. 349–50. No figures are available for the Jewish share of total membership. For an estimate of "perhaps 1.5 to 1.7 per cent in 1965" see T. H. Rigby, *Communist Party Membership in the USSR* (Princeton, 1969), p. 387.

69. Hitler's *Tischgespräche* (Bonn, 1951), p. 119.

70. Talmon, "Israel Among the Nations," p. 36. For the most up-to-date report on Soviet Jewry see *The Unredeemed: Anti-Semitism in the Soviet*

354

*Union*, ed. R. I. Ruben (Chicago, 1968). Elie Wiesel's *The Jews of Silence* (New York, 1966) is a moving account. See also for the historical background S. Schwarz, *Jews in the Soviet Union* (Syracuse, 1951).

71. For Jewish percentage among prewar members see *Polytika*, Warsaw, November 29, 1958; Andrzej Werblan, "Contribution to the Genesis of the Conflict" in *Miesiecznik Literacki*, Warsaw, June 1968. For prewar Communist membership, T. Daniszewski in *Nowe Drogi*, Warsaw, November–December 1948, p. 148. See also Burks, p. 160, quoting J. A. Regula's probably exaggerated estimates about half of the members being Jewish in 1931.

72. Arpad Szelpal, *Les 133 Jours de Bela Kun* (Paris, 1959), p. 235. Though all sources agree about the major role of Jews, some of the figures are highly speculative and unsubstantiated. Thus Werner Sombart (*Der proletarische Sozialismus, II* (Jena, 1924), pp. 298–300 flatly states that of 203 higher officials in the Kun government, 161 were Jewish. But this was mainly based on the "personal knowledge" of a Hungarian undergraduate's essay written for Sombart's seminar. The rest of his documentation relies on the hastily compiled and violently anti-Semitic collection of studies published by the Hungarian right-wing politician Gusztav Gratz immediately after the victory of the counterrevolution. See *A bolsevizmus Magyarországon* (Budapest, 1921).

73. M. K. Dziewanowski, *The Communist Party of Poland* (Cambridge, Mass., 1959), p. 92.

74. Burks, p. 161.

75. Ibid., p. 187.

76. Ibid., p. 188.

77. Ibid., pp. 73–85.

78. A. Ságvári, *Tömegmozgalmak és politikai küzdelmek Budapesten, 1945–47* (Budapest, 1964), p. 92.

79. Burks, pp. 73–74.

80. Baron, pp. 182 and 189.

81. H. Seton-Watson, pp. 21–22.

82. Arendt, p. 40.

83. This figure is no more than a rough estimate based on the prewar membership and the known and likely share of Jews.

84. See for details the reports on the war crimes trials in Frankfurt in August 1968, in the *Neue Zürcher Zeitung*, Zurich, August 10 and 21, 1968.

85. Figures mainly from Albert Vajs, "Jevreji u novoj Jugoslaviji," in *Jevrejski Almanah*, Belgrade, 1954, pp. 5–47. See also pp. 91–96.

86. Deutscher, *Non-Jewish Jew*, p. 88. Quoted in a slightly different form in Talmon's "Israel among the Nations," p. 36.

87. Deutscher, *Non-Jewish Jew*, p. 37.

88. Ibid., pp. 88–89.

89. H. Seton-Watson, p. 295.

90. Meyer, p. 45.

91. Author's personal impressions in Hungarian prisons. For the rampant anti-Semitism in Stalinist Czechoslovakia's prisons see Artur London, *L'aveu* [Confession] (Paris, 1968), especially pp. 217–18 and 401–2.

92. Z. K. Brzezinski, *The Soviet Bloc* (New York, 1961), p. 86; Burks, pp. 49–53. See also P. Lendvai, *Eagles in Cobwebs—Nationalism and Communism in the Balkans* (New York, 1969), pp. 65–67, 213–22, and 287–88.
93. His speech at the December 1961 plenum, published in *Scinteia*, Bucharest, December 13, 1961.
94. Brzezinski, *Soviet Bloc*, p. 97.
95. *Válasz*, Budapest, VIII, 10–11, pp. 865–71. Quoted by E. Duschinsky, "Hungary," in *The Jews in the Soviet Satellites*, p. 438.
96. Ibid.
97. T. Aczel and T. Meray, *The Revolt of the Mind* (London, 1960), p. 37.
98. Ibid., pp. 38–40.
99. Ibid., p. 44.
100. Meyer, p. 42.
101. Aczel-Meray, pp. 7–15.
102. F. Fejtö, *Les Juifs et l'Antisémitisme dans les Pays Communistes* (Paris, 1960), p. 85.
103. Brzezinski, *The Permanent Purge*, p. 246.
104. Arendt, pp. 105–6.
105. Ibid.
106. Talmon, *The Unique and the Universal*, p. 66.
107. Arendt, p. 8.
108. Sartre, pp. 81 and 108.
109. Arendt, p. 28.
110. Quoted by Walter Laqueur in *Commentary*, July 1967, p. 84.
111. Baron, p. 192.

PART TWO

NIGHTMARE IN POLAND

1. *Prawo i Zycie*, Warsaw, March 24, 1968.
2. See specifically for this line of reasoning Prime Minister Cyrankiewicz's speech in Parliament on April 10, 1968. Text in *Trybuna Ludu*, April 11, and an extensive English summary in *Polish Perspectives*, Warsaw, May 1968, and Andrzej Werblan, "Contribution to the Genesis of the Conflict," *Miesiecznik Literacki*, Warsaw, June 1968.
3. This official version was compiled from a number of basically similar speeches and articles by Gomulka, Cyrankiewicz, Moczar, Kepa, Kakol, Soluba, as well as from articles in *Trybuna Ludu*, March 11, 12, 14, and 26; *Slowo Powszechne*, March 11; and *Kurier Polski*, March 12, about the "March events" and the "instigators." For details see also notes below.
4. Bauman (see Part One, n. 2).
5. *Polityka*, Warsaw, January 11, 1969.
6. Deutscher, *Stalin*, p. 612.
7. Tatu, p. 117.
8. For details about the number of arrested, released, and expelled students see Gomulka's speech on March 19 cited in *Trybuna Ludu*, March 20, 1968,

Cyrankiewicz in Parliament, *Trybuna Ludu*, April 11, 1968, Minister of Higher Education Jablonski's article *Nowe Drogi*, Warsaw, May 1968, *Trybuna Ludu*, June 27, 1968, and Radio Warsaw, November 8, 1968. For a good summary of the student demonstrations and their extent see H. Lauen, "Die Märzunruhen in Polen und ihre Folgen" [The March Riots in Poland and Their Aftermath], *Osteuropa*, Stuttgart, January 1969.

9. For details see "Polish Writers Meeting," *Survey*, London, July 1968.

10. Bauman.

11. *Trybuna Ludu*, March 17, 1968.

12. Radio Free Europe, Polish Situation Report/31, April 23, 1968.

13. Cited in *The Observer*, London, June 16, 1968.

14. Two articles by Ryszard Gontarz in *Walka Mlodych*, October 28, 1968, and *Prawo i Zycie*, November 17, 1968, both containing strong and overt anti-Semitic overtones. For the change of line reporting on the trials with hardly any allusion to Zionism see *Prawo i Zycie*, February 9 and 23, 1969, *Zycie Warszawy*, January 17, 1969.

15. R. Hilberg, *The Destruction of the European Jews* (Chicago, 1961), p. 8.

16. Warsaw Television, April 5, 1968.

17. *Trybuna Ludu*, April 3, 1968.

18. Alexander Solzhenitsyn, *The First Circle* (London, 1968), p. 454–55.

19. *Trybuna Ludu*, March 15, 1968.

20. *Trybuna Ludu*, March 18, 1968.

21. *Trybuna Ludu*, April 11, 1968, as quoted in *Jews in Eastern Europe*, January 1969.

22. Hilberg, p. 654. For a comparison see Moczar's speech on May 4, 1968, at the meeting of the ZBOWiD leadership, cited in *Trybuna Ludu*, May 5, 1968, about "the slanderous accusations against Poland mainly conducted by Americans of Jewish origin through television, radio, and press and slanderous publications managed by American Zionist organizations." Also his speech during the election campaign in 1969 cited in *Zolnierz Wolnosci*, June 1, 1969, quoted after a Reuter dispatch: "And yet it would be quite natural if precisely Israel were to influence all press concerns and publishing houses in the world belonging to Jews or under their control—such as the New York *Times*, the Washington *Post, Life*, as well as radio and television centers—to begin acting and writing and speaking the truth about the Hitlerite murderers."

23. Cited after *Trybuna Mazowiecka*, Warsaw, April 1968.

24. *Express*, Vienna, April 3, 1968.

25. Wladyslaw Kmitowski, *Syjonizm, jego geneza, charakter polityczny i antypolskie oblicze*, Lodz, Polska Zjednoczona Partia Robotnicza Lodzki Osrodek Propagandy Partyjnej, Kwiecien, 1968g. (do uzytku wewnentznego) [*Zionism, Its Origins, Political Character, and Anti-Polish Countenance*, Lodz, Polish United Workers' Party, Lodz Party Propaganda Center, April 1968 (for internal use)], pp. 25–26.

26. Radio Warsaw, March 14, and *Trybuna Ludu* (milder version), March 15, 1968.

27. See Kakol's article, *Prawo i Zycie*, April 7, 1968.

28. As part of the family at the time of this writing is still in Warsaw, no names can be revealed.

29. Isaac Deutscher, *Heretics and Renegades* (London, 1955), pp. 201–2.

30. Tatu, p. 176.

31. Kakol, *Prawo i Zycie*, March 24, 1968.

32. *Slowo Powszechne*, March 16, 1968.

33. *Trybuna Ludu*, March 20, 1968. For English summary see *Polish Perspectives*, April 1968.

34. K. A. Jelenski, "White Eagle Today and Yesterday," *Survey*, January–March 1961, pp. 12–25.

35. For an excellent survey about anti-Semitism in 1956 see Czeslaw Milosz, "Anti-Semitism in Poland," *Problems of Communism*, Washington, May–June 1956.

36. S. Segal, *The New Poland and the Jews* (New York, 1938), pp. 88–90, also Buell, pp. 208–313, and H. Seton-Watson, pp. 157–71.

37. See A. R. Johnson, "Poland: The End of the Post-October Era," *Survey*, July 1968.

38. Radio Warsaw, March 21, 1968, and *Trybuna Ludu*, March 22, 1968. The Party paper, as usual, published somewhat milder versions of the speeches, specifically omitting Kozdra's references to "Jews" and also the roll call of "Zionist" politicians and intellectuals.

39. *Vjesnik*, Zagreb, April 6, 1968.

40. *Prawo i Zycie*, April 7, 1968.

41. Ibid.

42. Segal, pp. 108–9.

43. March 31, 1968.

44. *Trybuna Ludu*, March 17, 22, 25, and 26, 1968.

45. Simon Wiesenthal, "Jew-baiting in Poland: A Documentation About Prewar Fascists and Nazi Collaborators and Their Unity of Action with Anti-Semites from the Ranks of the Communist Party of Poland" (mimeographed), Vienna, 1969. The list contains forty-eight names of prominent politicians, writers, and journalists and its data have been confirmed by numerous Poles and well-informed sources. In the opinion of this author, however, the inclusion of the writer Jerzy Putrament among the prewar fascists and Nazi collaborators is incorrect since he was already in 1941 a well-known Communist intellectual and prominent member of the so-called "Wilno group." Thus whatever Putrament may have done as a freshman at the university, in a very difficult period he became a fighter against Nazism. He may be a consummate opportunist—but has never been for any length of time a fascist.

46. Segal, p. 90.

47. *Politika*, Belgrade, December 2, 1968.

48. Segal, p. 88.

49. *Zolnierz Wolnosci*, April 3 and 4, 1968.

50. J. Burgin, *Przeglad Kulturalny*, February 13, 1957.

51. A censored version was published in *Trybuna Ludu*, July 10, 1968.

358

52. Figure published by the Institute of Strategic Studies, London.

53. His speech on July 31, 1967, at the celebration marking the anniversary of the Warsaw Rising.

54. In the weekly broadcast "The Voice of ZBOWiD" on Warsaw Radio, July 17, 1967.

55. *Zolnierz Wolnosci*, March 25, 1968.

56. Reported in *Arbeiter Zeitung*, Vienna, January 19, 1969, and also confirmed by arrivals from Poland.

57. Cited in *Frankfurter Allgemeine Zeitung* by its Warsaw correspondent, April 25, 1968.

58. Buell, pp. 310–13.

59. Aside from the anti-Semitic party pamphlets, most of the data, if not otherwise specified, stems from A. Grabowska's "Lodzki marzec" [March in Lodz] from the Polish monthly *Kultura*, Paris, May 1969. (Not to be confused with the Warsaw weekly.)

60. See n. 25 for title of pamphlet. All quotes are from the original pamphlets, a few copies of which reached the West.

61. For details of the "Dayan story" see *Kultura*, Paris, May 1969.

62. Quoted without exact publication date in *Jews in Eastern Europe*, January 1969, p. 26.

63. Reported by UPI from Warsaw, April 30, 1968.

64. Quoted, without date, in *Kultura*, Paris, May 1969.

65. Related by L. Szulczynski, *Die Zeit*, Hamburg, April 18, 1969.

66. *Zycie Literackie*, Cracow, April 3, 1966.

67. For postwar aid by the Joint see B. D. Weinryb, "Poland," in *Jews in the Soviet Satellites*, p. 290. For relief from 1957 to 1967 see *Jews in Eastern Europe*, October 1959, and interview with L. Horwitz, Director General of the Joint, *L'Arche*, Paris, February 26–March 25, 1969, pp. 47–49.

68. Weinryb, pp. 290–98.

69. *The Times*, London, February 7, 1969.

70. "A Personal Testimony," a document smuggled out of Poland in September 1968 and published in *Jews in Eastern Europe*, January 1969, pp. 56–71. The document quotes *Poglady*, May 15–31, 1968, *Argumenty*, April 16, 1968. Quote about "Zionists among brown-shirted thugs" from Z. Soluba, "Zionism—Political Subversion," *Trybuna Ludu*, April 21, 1968.

71. "Documents From Hell" in *Tygodnik Kulturalny*, April 28, 1968. See also *Kurier Lubelski*, April 22, 1968, and *Slowo Powszechne*, May 31, 1968. Quoted in *Jews in Eastern Europe*, January 1969.

72. Z. Lakomski, "Political Kidnapers," *Trybuna Ludu*, April 5, 1968.

73. Bauman.

74. *Trybuna Ludu,* April 19, 1968.

75. *Politika*, Belgrade, December 17, 1968. See also *Vjesnik*, Zagreb, November 16, 1968.

76. Raab, p. 26.

77. Reported by AP from Warsaw on October 17, 1968. For expulsions from the basic organization in downtown Warsaw see *Zycie Warszawy*, October 8, 1968, and for victims of the first four weeks of the witch-hunt in

the capital, Warsaw secretary Kepa cited in *Trybuna Ludu,* April 19, 1968.

78. Weinryb, pp. 274–75.

79. *Zycie Literackie,* ibid.

80. Bauman, ibid.

81. An extensive summary of Kliszko's speech in *Nowe Drogi,* August 1968. All speeches (of course censored) in *Trybuna Ludu,* April 9–13, 1968.

82. Official statement released on June 10, 1969, by PAP, the Polish news agency. Details from unimpeachable but confidential Jewish sources.

83. Hilberg, pp. 90–105.

84. Moczar's interview with PAP on April 12, published in *Trybuna Ludu* on April 13–15, 1968. Rakowski was saved by Gomulka and, albeit only barely, managed to retain his position.

85. *Trybuna Ludu,* July 13, 1968.

86. Cited in *Glos Olsztynski,* July 25, 1968.

87. *Trybuna Ludu,* July 11, 1968.

88. Bauman.

89. Hilberg, p. 318.

90. Radio Warsaw, April 18, 1968.

91. A. M. Rosenthal, Warsaw: "They Knew What They Did," *New York Times Magazine,* quoted in *NYT* International Edition, October 23, 1965.

92. Raab, p. 30.

93. Rosenthal.

94. *Prawo i Zycie,* April 10, 1966.

95. *Forum,* June 12, 1966, and *Prawo i Zycie,* December 4, 1966.

96. T. Walichnowski, *Israel A NRF* (Israel and the German Federal Republic), Warsaw, 1967, pp. 193–96. See also *Slowo Powszechne,* November 14, 1967, and February 2, 1968.

97. *Slowo Powszechne,* February 2, 1968.

98. *Polityka,* Warsaw, November 11, 1967. The very first attack was actually launched by W. Machejek, the editor of *Zycie Literackie,* Cracow, on August 6, 1967.

99. *Prawo i Zycie,* March 24, 1968. See also *Trybuna Ludu,* March 18, April 3, 7, and 25, 1968.

100. Radio Warsaw, April 5, 1968, cited in Lauen, "Die Märzunruhen und ihre Folgen" (II), *Osteuropa,* February 1969.

101. *Trybuna Ludu,* May 23, 25, and 26, 1968.

102. Wiesenthal (see n. 45 above).

103. Hilberg, p. 146.

104. *Polityka,* March 30, 1968, speaks about "several thousand," Cyrankiewicz on April 10 in Parliament mentions "many thousands," Pilichowski's Commission for the Investigation of Hitlerite Crimes on April 24 puts the number of Jews saved by Poles at "over 100,000" and *Glos Olsztynski,* April 8, 1968, refers to "several hundreds of thousands." At the height of the "anti-Zionist" campaign a book was hastily brought out by the Jewish historian Szymon Datner, *The Grove of the Just: a Page From the History of Assistance to the Jews in Occupied Poland* (Warsaw, 1968). It investigated 105 cases of execution of Poles for helping Jews. In all, 343 Poles and 248

Jews were killed. Cited in a review by A. Horodynski in *Polish Perspectives*, April 1969. But the point of the matter is that survival cannot be identified with "having been saved" by the Poles. To start with, in Poland itself at the time of the liberation there were about 50,000 survivors. The estimates ranging up to 100,000 were challenged already in 1945–46. For details see Weinryb, pp. 239–43. But the greater part of the survivors remained alive in the camps either through the hàsty retreat of the Nazis or through successfully disguising their identity. A smaller group comprised those who had been in hiding, or those who had fought as Partisans. As to how many of these had forged identification papers provided by the underground or bought by themselves, how many survived through help or bribery, there is no way of knowing. In Warsaw there were 200 Jews when the Red Army arrived, in Lublin 50, and in Lodz 870—out of over three quarters of a million Jews before the start of the genocide. These are the facts which no rewriting of history can alter.

105. *Zolnierz Wolnosci*, April 12, 1968.

106. *Trybuna Ludu*, April 25, 1968.

107. Ibid., April 24, 1968.

108. *Prawo i Zycie*, March 24, April 7 and 21, 1968.

109. For Martula see *Trybuna Ludu*, February 4, 1969. Case of Szapiro reported by Poles to the author.

110. Z. Soluba, "Zionism—Political subversion," *Trybuna Ludu*, April 21, 1968.

111. *Glos Olsztynski*, April 8, 1968. See also Moczar's speech at ZBOWiD meeting cited in *Trybuna Ludu*, May 5, 1968, Walichnowski in *Glos Szczecinski*, March 15, 1968, K. Sidor's commentary on Warsaw Radio, June 4, 1968, for an earlier "survey" of Zionist-German collusion since "Herzl linked the Zionist movement with the propaganda, diplomacy, and military and political intelligence of Kaiser Wilhelm's Germany," *Zolnierz Wolnosci*, July 8, 1967.

112. Neither Israel nor Poland has ever published the text of the note. For a good summary of Israeli-Polish relations see *Frankfurter Allgemeine Zeitung*, June 7, 1967.

113. *Trybuna Ludu*, May 5, 1968.

114. PAP dispatch from The Hague about the press conference staged by Pilichowski in June 1968, cited in *Jews in Eastern Europe*, January 1969.

115. *Trybuna Ludu*, April 13–15, 1968. See also *Trybuna Mazowiecka*, April 11, 1968, *Sztandar Ludu*, Lublin, April 17, 1968.

116. *Volksstimme* and *Arbeiter Zeitung*, Vienna, both April 18, 1968.

117. Soluba (see n. 110, above).

118. Wiesenthal.

119. Segal, pp. 108–9. For speech in Parliament see *Slowo Powszechne*, April 12, 1968. Also three sharp articles representing Moczar's line in *Slowo Powszechne*, March 11, 16, and April 9, 1968.

120. Private information of the author. See also Wiesenthal.

121. *Survey*, July 1968, pp. 107–8. See also *Trybuna Ludu*, March 27, 1968.

122. *Briefe an Freunde* [Letters to Friends], ed. B. Kautsky (Hamburg,

1950), pp. 48–49. The most comprehensive biography of Rosa Luxemburg is Peter Nettl, *Rosa Luxemburg* (London, 1966).

123. Lenin, *Collected Works* (Sochineniya), 4th ed. (Moscow), Vol. 33, pp. 194–95. Lenin's appraisal of Rosa Luxemburg was in connection with the posthumous publication of her short treatise on the Russian Revolution, written in prison in 1918 and published in 1922 by her close associate and leader of the German Communist Party, Paul Levi, after the latter had split with his comrades and the Comintern over the abortive Putsch attempt in March 1921 in Germany. See also Rosa Luxemburg, *The Russian Revolution; and, Leninism or Marxism?* (University of Michigan Press, 1961).

124. Deutscher, *Non-Jewish Jew*, p. 33.

125. Cited in *Zukunft*, Vienna, March 1969, p. 1.

126. Deutscher, *Non-Jewish Jew*, pp. 26–27 and 33–34.

127. For details see Dziewanowski, pp. 22–40; Nettl, Chs. I–IV; Schapiro, pp. 21–22 and 148–49; Ulam, pp. 292, 301–2, 496–97.

128. H. Seton-Watson, pp. 156–71. See also Jelenski (see n. 34).

129. Seton-Watson; Weinryb, pp. 207–10; Segal.

130. For a detailed discussion see Dziewanowski, pp. 120–39. See for an interesting analysis of the "May error" and the factional battles Isaac Deutscher, "La Tragédie du Communisme Polonais Entre Les Deux Guerres" [The Tragedy of Polish Communism Between the Two Wars], *Les Temps Modernes*, Paris, March 1958, pp. 1632–77.

131. Lenin's speech of May 12, 1917, at the Seventh All-Russian Conference of the Bolshevik Party in Petrograd, cited in Dziewanowski, pp. 65–66.

132. See the programmatic article by Andrzej Werblan, "Contribution to the Genesis of the Conflict," *Miesiecznik Literacki*, Warsaw, June 1968.

133. Ibid. As the KPP was outlawed during the entire interwar period, there are no lists of the Central Committee members available. But prewar members estimate that in the 1930s after the takeover by Lenski's "minority," the proportion of the Jews in the top and medium echelons was in the region of 50 per cent. The central editorial board in charge of propaganda in the mid-1930s for instance consisted of five members—two Ukrainians, two Jews, and one Pole. Professor Bauman, who spent the war in the Soviet Union, estimated that Jews at one point accounted for 60 to 70 per cent of the top and medium-level functionaries.

134. R. Conquest, *The Great Terror* (London, 1968), p. 434.

135. Dziewanowski, p. 150.

136. Conquest, *Great Terror*, pp. 433–36.

137. Ibid. See also Dziewanowski, pp. 149–54. Eighteen years later the Party was rehabilitated since the charges "had been faked by a gang of saboteurs and provocateurs whose real role was only brought to light after Beria was unmasked . . ." The communique, published on February 19, 1956, in *Trybuna Ludu* was signed by the delegates of the Parties of the Soviet Union, Italy, Bulgaria, Finland, and Poland. The statement did not explain however why the Party was dissolved and who those provocateurs were. For the English text see P. E. Zinner, ed., *National Communism and Popular Revolt in Eastern Europe* (New York, 1956), pp. 37–39.

362

138. *Soviet Peace Policy, Four Speeches* by V. Molotov (London, 1941), p. 101, quoted in Dziewanowski, p. 158. Even before the actual capitulation Molotov, the Soviet Premier, sent a message to the German ambassador in Moscow: "I have received your communication regarding the entry of German troops into Warsaw. Please convey my congratulations to the German Reich Government." (Nazi-Soviet Relations, 1939–1941. Documents from the Archives of the German Foreign Office, U.S. Department of State, 1948, p. 89.)

139. Z. K. Brzezinski, *The Soviet Bloc*, p. 9.

140. T. Bor-Komorowski, *The Secret Army* (London, 1951), pp. 121–22.

141. While all official and private sources agree on this fact, the dissensions within the PPR as indeed the entire prewar Party history are described in the official Party records, in personal remembrances of Gomulka, Jozwiak (Witold), and other participants always according to the given Party line. In other words the documents published prior to 1956 give the Stalinist and "antinationalist" version, those in the 1960s the equally embellished Gomulka legends. For a summary see Dziewanowski, pp. 161–81, and H. Stehle, *Nachbar Polen* [Neighbor Poland], enl. new ed. (Frankfurt, 1968), pp. 37–49. The author received valuable information about this period from two former "Muscovites" and one ranking member of the home underground.

142. Bor-Komorowski, p. 242, and other documents released by the Government in exile, cited by Dziewanowski, p. 180. The weakness of the Communist Partisans was confirmed by the three sources (mentioned in the preceding note) in conversations with the author.

143. Dziewanowski, pp. 177–81.

144. S. Korbonski, *W Imieniu Kremla* (Paris, 1956), pp. 268, 290; *Po Prostu*, Warsaw, October 14, 1956; *Polityka*, February 15, 1958; cited in Brzezinski, p. 8.

145. Jelenski.

146. Weinryb, pp. 239–43, p. 266. These figures or rather estimates refer to the Jews who remained in Poland between 1945–48.

147. Buell, pp. 310–13.

148. Weinryb, pp. 252–53.

149. Ibid., p. 249.

150. Cited in Segal, p. 88.

151. Weinryb, pp. 249–52.

152. Dziewanowski, pp. 212–13. See also A. B. Ulam, *Titoism and the Cominform* (Cambridge, Mass., 1952), p. 188.

153. Stehle, pp. 49–51, quoting a Gomulka speech held on May 27, 1945, but first published only twenty-two years later!

154. J. Swiatlo, "Behind the Scenes of the State Security and the Party," Radio Free Europe leaflet, 1954. Colonel Swiatlo's assertions (after his defection in December 1953) were essentially confirmed by J. Berman, the Politburo member in charge of security affairs at the 1956 October Central Committee Plenum. *Nowe Drogi*, October 1956.

155. Brzezinski, p. 119.

156. Ibid., pp. 96–97. The relative weakness of the Polish Party could not

have been decisive since the Hungarians were equally weak. A partial explanation may be found in the different personalities of the Polish Bierut and the Hungarian Rakosi, the first being a "moderate," the second a bloodthirsty, fanatical Stalinist.

157. Ibid., p. 125. For over-all losses see J. Wszelaki, *Communist Economic Strategy: The Role of East Central Europe* (Washington, 1959), pp. 68–77.

158. See the excellent treatise on the factional battle between March and October 1956 in Brzezinski, pp. 236–65. For the importance of the Jewish Question and the Pulawska and Natolin factions see W. Jedlicki's provocative piece "Jews and Boors," *Kultura*, Paris, December 1962.

159. Jedlicki.

160. J. Siekierska, *Nowe Drogi*, June 1956. For desecrations see *Trybuna Ludu*, June 9, 1956, also *Sztandar Mlodych*, May 8, 1958; for intimidation *Po Prostu*, January 6, 1957, *Przeglad Kulturalny*, April 4, 1957. For calculated plan of Stalinists, *Po Prostu*, January 6, 1957, and *Przeglad Kulturalny*, February 7, 1957.

161. Reported by *Po Prostu*, January 6, 1957. Ochab's experience reported by Jelenski, "Antisémitisme et déstalinisation en Pologne," *Evidences*, Paris, August–September 1956, cited in Fejtö, p. 71.

The author, staying over a month in Poland in January 1957, vividly remembers his astonishment at seeing the importance attached by his Polish friends to the fight against anti-Semitism. Many non-Jewish intellectuals went on cross-country tours lecturing about anti-Semitism as a demagogic device of the pro-Soviet Stalinists. It was this lecture campaign that in addition to the mass media thwarted the attempts of the Natolinists.

162. Gomulka's speech at the national conference of Party activists on November 4, 1956. Here quoted after Brzezinski, p. 248.

163. *Trybuna Ludu*, October 25, 1956. For English text see Zinner, pp. 239–57.

164. Brzezinski, pp. 333–39.

165. Jedlicki.

166. This was strikingly evident in a comparison of his pre-1949 speeches (that is before his fall) and his post-October 1956 statements on certain key issues. See Brzezinski, pp. 333–39.

167. *Borba*, Belgrade, October 8, 1968. *Vjesnik u Srijedu*, Zagreb, April 24, 1968, referred to an estimated surplus of a half million employees. As the entire economy is geared to faulty price and investment signals, there are no reliable estimates available.

168. Segal, pp. 108–9. See also for Piasecki's career L. Blit, *The Eastern Pretender* (London, 1965); A. Bromke, "From Falanga to Pax," *Survey*, December 1961; Stehle, pp. 176–85; A. Korab, "Piasecki and the Polish Communists," *Problems of Communism*, Washington, November–December 1957. For Piasecki's old and "new" political ideas see B. Piasecki, *Duch Czasow Nowych a Ruch Mlodych* [The Spirit of the New Era and the Youth Movement] (Warsaw, 1935), and *Zagadnienia Istotne* [Fundamental Problems] (Warsaw, 1954). For an analysis of his maneuvering during the 1968

crisis see Radio Free Europe Research Analysis, "PAX and the Polish Leadership Crisis," August 1, 1968.

169. Latest figures from Stehle, p. 178. Piasecki's commercial empire in 1956 had a larger turnover than all other private industry in Poland combined—300 million zlotys. Ten years later the gross profit alone was 222 million, after taxes 93 million zlotys. According to the tourist rate of exchange (24 zlotys to the dollar) Piasecki's enterprises yielded the equivalent of four million dollars! Even if one takes the real (that is black-market) rate of 100 zlotys for one dollar, the PAX group has ample funds to finance its propaganda and press, and to win the favor of a number of people ranging from underpaid bureaucrats to selected foreign correspondents.

170. *Trybuna Ludu,* April 13–15, 1968.

171. April 20, 1968.

172. See specifically his speeches, *Trybuna Ludu,* May 5, 1968, January 17, 1969, *Zolnierz Wolnosci,* June 1, 1969, all sharply attacking Israel, Zionism, and U.S. mass media under Zionist influence as well as Israeli-West German collusion. His speech in the election campaign (see n. 22) however was published in a toned-down version in the central press with the exception of *Zolnierz Wolnosci,* the Army paper.

173. Author's private information from an unimpeachable Polish source. Gomulka merely crossed out the names of three Jewish functionaries (L. Kasman, R. Werfel, and S. Daniszewski).

174. *Trybuna Ludu,* July 12, 1968.

175. H. Szafranski, Warsaw voivodship secretary on October 28, 1968, referring to demands "at many Party meetings."

PART THREE
CZECHOSLOVAKIA: HOW TO MANUFACTURE ZIONISTS

1. *Rude Pravo,* Prague, November 28, 1951.

2. A "verbatim transcript" was published—of course after appropriate editing in February 1953 in Prague. *Rude Pravo* printed every day what purported to be the "authentic" version. I used for the quotes from the prosecutor's summing up and the testimonies the English translation, as published in P. Meyer, "Czechoslovakia," in *Jews in the Soviet Satellites,* pp. 166–91.

3. Klement Gottwald at the National Party Conference, *Rude Pravo,* December 17, 1952, here quoted after J. Slanska, *Rapport sur mon mari* [Report About My Husband] (Paris, 1969), p. 46.

4. *Rude Pravo,* November 24 and 25, 1951. Quoted in Meyer, p. 187. In contrast to the reports at the time of the trial, which took for granted that the relatives had been forced to sign these letters, Artur London's memoirs, published sixteen years later, reveal that his French-born wife wrote to the President of the court and to Gottwald of her own free will without having been told to, let alone forced, by anyone. Her denunciation of her husband as well as her application to divorce him show the horrifying result of being

conditioned as a lifelong Communist to believe the Party rather than her husband. The explanations provided by Mrs. London many years later shed light on her motives and the general atmosphere, but nevertheless fail to explain her behavior in full. In contrast to her allegation now, her letter was not truncated and distorted but except for one brief sentence was published unchanged in the Party paper. See Artur London, *L'aveu*, pp. 327–56.

5. G. F. Kennan, *From Prague After Munich* (Princeton, 1968), pp. 42–57.

6. Meyer, p. 153.

7. K. Kaplan, "Thoughts About the Political Trials," in *Nova Mysl*, Prague, the theoretical monthly of the Party, August 1968. Two preceding parts of this extensive essay were published in *Nova Mysl*, June and July 1968. This book-sized study is the most candid inquiry about the purges ever published in a Communist country, even including Yugoslavia, for the Yugoslavs did attack Stalin but kept silent about such cases as the criminal proceedings against Djilas. The author is a social scientist and was elected at the height of the reform movement as a member of the Party Control Commission. Probably due to his revelations about the extent of Soviet involvement, he was dismissed from the Control Commission and according to Radio Prague, March 21, 1970, is to be expelled from the Party. See also the full text of the "Report of the Commission of the Central Committee of the Czechoslovak Communist. Party About the Political Trials and Rehabilitations, 1949–1968," in *Das unterdrückte Dossier* [The Suppressed File], ed. Jiri Pelikan (Vienna, 1970).

8. Kaplan.

9. Slansky's hitherto unpublished report at the conference of regional secretaries on December 8, 1949, quoted by Kaplan.

10. Ibid.

11. Ibid.

12. For Kopriva's revelations see *Vecerni Praha*, May 7, 1968; for Bacilek, *Smena*, Bratislava, April 28, 1968.

13. Kaplan.

14. Ibid. See also Kopriva and Bacilek.

15. Ibid. For details of Slansky's arrest and the fate of his family see J. Slanska, pp. 135–203.

16. Kaplan.

17. Conquest, *The Great Terror*, p. 45.

18. E. Loebl, D. Pokorny, *Die Revolution rehabilitiert ihre Kinder—Hinter den Kulissen des Slansky-Prozesses* [The revolution rehabilitates its children —Behind the scenes of the Slansky Trial] (Vienna, 1968). See also London, pp. 327–56.

19. London, p. 35.

20. Ibid., pp. 217–18, 345. See for the virulent anti-Semitism of the guards and the physical assaults on Jewish prisoners, pp. 401–3.

21. Ibid., p. 345.

22. Loebl, pp. 34–35.

23. *Mlada Fronta*, Prague, March 30, 1968.

24. Kaplan.

366

25. T. Draper, *Israel and World Politics* (New York, 1968), p. 29.

26. For the evolving version see Novotny's speech at the National Party Conference on June 11, 1956, at the Central Committee meeting on November 15, 1961, speech published in *Rude Pravo*, November 21, his report to the Party Congress in December 1962. For the hitherto unpublished minutes of the Presidium meeting from 1954 onward and the letters of prison inmates to the Party leaders see Kaplan.

27. V. Benes, "Czechoslovakia" in *East European Government and Politics* (New York, 1966), p. 71.

28. Kaplan.

29. Draper, pp. 7–8. For friendly relations with Israel in 1948 see Meyer, pp. 127–33.

30. See particularly Novotny's speech on June 11, 1967, in Lidice marking the twenty-fifth anniversary of the razing of the village by the Nazis in reprisal for the assassination of Heydrich. For anti-Israeli articles see especially *Rude Pravo*, June 6, 15, and 26, July 18, 1967; *Pravda*, Bratislava, June 18.

31. *Literarni Noviny*, Prague, August 4, 1967.

32. Revealed by Ladislav Mnacko in his declaration on leaving the country, published in *Frankfurter Allgemeine Zeitung*, August 11, 1967. See details about placards carried by Arab students published one year later by *Prace*, Prague, June 8, 1968.

33. For details of the protests and the clashes at the writers' congress see *Reden zum IV. Kongress des Tschechoslowakischen Schriftstellerverbandes, Prag, Juni 1967* [Speeches at the IV Congress of the Czechoslovak Writers' Union, Prague, June 1967] Frankfurt, 1968), P. Kohout, *Aus dem Tagebuch eines Konterrevolutionärs* [From the Diary of a Counterrevolutionary] (Luzern, 1969), pp. 202–22. See also A. Lustig's open letter to the Slovak poet L. Novomesky, in *Literarni Listy*, Prague, May 23, 1968.

34. Lustig.

35. Kohout's speech, quoted after *Reden zum IV. Kongress*, pp. 20–22.

36. Commentary by Radio Bratislava, June 22, 1967. See also *Pravda*, Bratislava, June 18, 1967, *Uj Szo*, Bratislava, July 1, 1967, and *Rude Pravo*, July 18, 1967.

37. Mnacko.

38. For an excellent summing up see R. H. Estabrook's article in the Washington *Post*, October 29, 1967, reprinted in *The Unredeemed: Anti-Semitism in the Soviet Union*, ed. R. I. Rubin (Chicago, 1968), pp. 196–206.

39. See *Jews in Eastern Europe*, May 1968, pp. 25–29 and *Arbeiter Zeitung*, Vienna, March 17, 1968.

40. Professor E. Goldstuecker, *Literarni Listy*, March 1, 1968.

41. See Prague Radio commentator Vera Stovickova, April 30, 1968, *Prace*, June 8, 1968, *Student*, Prague, May 29, June 26, 1968, and Mnacko's interview with *Slobodne Slovo*, Prague, July 5, 1968.

42. *Student*, May 29, 1968.

43. Ibid., June 26, 1968, AP dispatch from Prague, June 21, 1968.

44. *Kulturny Zivot*, Bratislava, March 14 and May 24, 1968; *Slobodne Slovo*, July 5, 1968.

45. For invitation to Polish professors and Lustig's open letter see *Literarni Listy*, April 4, 1968. For a summary of protest actions see Agence France Press dispatch in *Le Monde*, Paris, April 10, 1968; for first covert official criticism see *Rude Pravo*, April 10, 1968.

46. *Prace*, May 4, 1968.

47. CTK agency from Prague, May 24, 1969. For student rally see New York *Times*, May 4, 1968.

48. For Party rallies see New York *Times*, May 12, 1968. For press criticism see *Trybuna Ludu*, May 4, and May 9, 1968, *Zolnierz Wolnosci*, May 21, 1968.

49. *Kultura*, Warsaw, June 23, 1968.

50. Printed in *Reporter*, Prague, October 23, 1968. See also Kohout, pp. 50–55.

51. Kohout.

52. *Prace*, May 5, 1968.

53. Ibid., June 9, 1968.

54. The forged letter was dated May 21, 1968. The Documentation Center in Vienna released it coupled with Wiesenthal's protest on June 20, 1968. See also *Der Ausweg*, Vienna, September 1968, and *Le Monde*, September 18, 1968.

55. For statement by the Federation of Anti-Fascist Resistance Fighters, see CTK, June 28, 1968; see also open letter by Dr. Jiri Dolezal against anti-Semitism in *Rude Pravo*, July 1, 1968. Professor B. Spacek suggested that Party statutes should state that "any expression of racial discrimination and anti-Semitism is incompatible with membership," *Rude Pravo*, July 16, 1968.

56. See Sik's letter published in *Slobodne Slovo* and *Mlada Fronta*, March 25, and *Reporter*, Prague, March 27, 1969. Some sources maintain Sik is half-Jewish despite his denials. See *The Use of Anti-Semitism Against Czechoslovakia*, published by the Institute of Jewish Affairs (London, 1968), pp. 4 and 13, and *The Jerusalem Post*, September 16, 1969.

57. *Vecerni Praha*, July 6, 1968.

58. *Izvestia*, August 22, 1968. See also the Soviet publication *About the Events in Czechoslovakia* (Moscow, 1968). This so-called White Book was also published in Czech, English, German, French, and other languages. The three persons mentioned earlier remained "the agents of an international Zionist organization" but the name of the "Joint" was omitted, p. 72. None of them is Jewish, according to *The Use of Anti-Semitism Against Czechoslovakia*.

59. For details see *Le Monde*, September 12, 1968, *The Times*, London, September 13, 1968. Bertrand Russell's letter about the Soviet plan of Zionist show trials and his appeal to socialists and Communists "throughout the world resolutely to oppose these Soviet demands for scapegoats," *Times*, September 16, 1968. See also *International Herald Tribune*, Paris, October 24, 1968, and P. Tigrid's account of the Moscow negotiations in *Le Monde*, March 25, 1969.

60. *Trybuna Ludu*, August 25, 1968.

368

61. Warsaw Television, August 26, 1968; *Chlopska Droge*, August 30, 1968; *Zolnierz Wolnosci*, August 31, 1968; *Trybuna Ludu*, September 2, 1968.
62. *Pravda Ukrainy*, Kiev, August 28, 1968.
63. For Radio "Vltava," see also *Neue Zürcher Zeitung*, September 7, 1968, and Radio Free Europe Research Report, Munich, November 11, 1968.
64. *Neues Deutschland*, East Berlin, August 31, 1968.
65. Vienna, September 6, 1968.
66. *Volksstimme*, Vienna, September 3, 1968.
67. B. Utitz in *Politika*, Prague, October 17, 1968.
68. *Volksstimme*, September 4, 1968.
69. Ibid., September 5, 1968; *Le Monde*, September 6, 1968.
70. Interview with Hajek in *Reporter*, Prague, October 23, 1968.
71. *Rude Pravo*, October 12, 1968. Even after his fall, in his first speech, Dubcek publicly condemned anti-Semitism on May 18, 1969, in the city of Terezin (Theresienstadt), the site of a former Nazi concentration camp, New York *Times*, May 19, 1969.
72. The vicious anti-Semitic attack under the headline "Schwejk's Meeting with Dr. Kriegel" was published by *Zpravy* on November 2. The Presidium of Parliament dealt with Kriegel's complaint on November 28 and "resolutely condemned the article" and asked the Government to stop the distribution of *Zpravy* since it was incompatible with the Czechoslovak laws. *Uj Szo*, Bratislava, November 29, 1968.
73. Quoted by Radio Prague commentator P. Pithart on March 23, 1969.
74. November 2, 1968.
75. *Reporter*, Prague, February 27, 1969. The meeting was held on January 22, 1969.
76. TASS international service in English, March 6, 1969.
77. *Neues Deutschland* reported sterilization story December 4, 1968. Moscow Radio's broadcast (without date) condemned by Israeli Minister of Information Galili on July 16, 1969. Same source for Moscow's picking up the Bormann "story." About Nazi officers see Moscow Radio's home service on March 25, 1969, quoted in *Jews in Eastern Europe*, July 1969, p. 45. For original Polish source for Nazi Army advisers see n. 54 in Part Two on Poland; for Mrs. Meir "hiding Bormann," see *Glos Robotniczy*, May 12, 1968.
78. April 19, 1969.
79. See n. 56.
80. See n. 73.
81. *Belarus*, August 1968, quoted in *Jews in Eastern Europe*, July 1969, pp. 37–39.
82. Husak's speech at the CKD factory in Prague on May 31, 1969.
83. There was already in April 1968 an open split between the progressive Slovak intellectuals who regarded democratization as the primary task, and such nationalists and Husak followers as V. Mihalic, the chairman of the Slovak Writers' Union, M. Valek, a poet and present Minister of Culture in Slovakia, and Ladislav Novomesky, who was imprisoned together with Husak. The latter, one of the greatest Czechoslovak poets, published in *Rude*

*Pravo* of May 12, 1968, an attack on Lustig's "passionately pro-Israeli and pro-Zionist declarations" on Prague Television. His complaint that the Czech writers had "a whole pleiad of excellent experts on Israel" but few champions of the Slovak cause, revealed a streak of covert anti-Semitic bias. Lustig replied in the literary weekly (May 23, 1968). His rejoinder reminded Novomesky that at the time of the Middle East conflicts hundreds of thousands of words were hurled against Israel and no one was allowed to talk about the topic. At that time Novomesky kept his alleged concern for the Jews for himself, remained silent during ten months of lying about Israel and broke his silence only to attack Lustig. This incident deserves therefore a certain attention because Novomesky is Husak's closest friend, member of the Slovak Party Presidium, and his article reflected the thinking of Slovak nationalists.

84. *Pravda*, Bratislava, May 28, 1969.

85. His speech was not published officially, but reported by the DPA, the West German news agency, on June 5, 1969, and an extensive summary was published in the German weekly *Der Spiegel*, Hamburg, July 14, 1969.

86. His speech was held at the plenary meeting of the Central Committee of the Slovak Communist Party and published in *Pravda*, Bratislava, June 10, 1969. An even more disturbing statement reminiscent of the Stalinist trials was made by Colonel B. Molnar, a leading secret police official in an interview (*Svoboda*, Prague, December 9, 1969) tracing the "Zionist excesses" in 1967–68 back to World War II when Goldstuecker and Eugen Loebl (former Deputy Foreign Trade Minister, sentenced to life imprisonment at the Slansky trial) set up "Zionist cells" in London. Since Dubcek's fall a spate of articles has been published in *Rude Pravo* and other Party papers about "Zionism and anti-Semitism" and "Zionism in the service of imperialism." See for particularly venomous accusations *Pravda*, Bratislava, January 4, 1970, *Rude Pravo*, April 10, 1970, and the serialization of a new book, *Zionism and Anti-Semitism* in July 1970.

87. Vienna, June 13, 1969.

88. V. Hejl, "A Solution, Once and for All" in *Zitrek*, March 19, 1969.

89. The Jewish community's monthly *Vestnik Zidovskych Nabozenskych Obci v Ceskoslovensku*, Prague, May 1969, referred to a decision by "a congress of delegates" on April 20. See also *The Times*, London, May 7, 1969. A moving appeal for contacts with world Jewry, permission to celebrate "at long last" the Jewish millennium with extensive foreign participation and for religious instruction of the youth was issued by the Jewish community in Bohemia and published in *Literarni Listy*, May 30, 1968.

90. A. Charim, *Die Toten Gemeinden* [The Dead Communities] (Vienna, 1966).

370

1. As François Fejtö aptly put it (p. 91), "the grandfathers were capitalists, the sons liberals, and the grandchildren professed socialist ideas." Hungary had Jewish members of Parliament less than two decades after the first Jewish M.P. was elected to the House of Commons in Britain; and the Government in World War I already included a Jewish Minister of Justice. In addition to a number of important industrialists and bankers, the Jewish community produced outstanding Hungarian writers, editors, publishers, painters, composers, as well as eminent doctors and scientists. Out of the gainfully employed Jews, numbering 189,700 in 1930 (in Trianon, Hungary), 38.4 per cent were independent businessmen or engaged in liberal professions while 27.8 per cent were white-collar employees in commerce, industry, and cultural life. For details see Duschinsky, "Hungary," in *The Jews in the Soviet Satellites*, pp. 374–76.

2. Oszkar Jaszi: *Magyar Kalvaria, Magyar Feltamadas* [Hungarian Calvary, Hungarian Resurrection] (Vienna, 1920), p. 121.

3. The industrial labor force initially consisted mainly of Germans and Slavs while its leadership was dominated by German influence and Jewish intellectuals. Jews were not only prominent among the Communists in 1918–19 (see Part One, n. 72) but also among their moderate Social Democratic opponents, such as the brilliant intellectual Zsigmond Kunfi and many others.

4. See Mihaly Korom, "A nacibarat es revizios kulpolitika vegsö kovetkezmenyei: Magyarorszag reszvetele a masodik vilaghaboruban" [The Final Results of the Pro-Nazi and Revisionist Foreign Policy; Hungary's Participation in World War II], in *A magyar nacionalizmus kialakulasa es tortenete* [Evolution and History of the Hungarian Nationalism] (Budapest, 1964), pp. 441–62.

5. For details see *A magyar forradalmi munkasmozgalom tortenete 1–2* (The history of the Hungarian Revolutionary Workers' Movement, Vols. 1–2), Budapest, 1966–67.

6. Ibid., Vol. 2, pp. 34–36 and 62–67. Estimates of Jewish share in leading bodies here and later based on author's personal knowledge and tend to err, if anything, on the side of caution.

7. Conquest, *Great Terror*, pp. 431–32. For Kun's fate and a tendentious account of the factional fighting between Kun and Landler (both Jews) see also Kun Belane, *Kun Bela* (Budapest, 1966).

8. List of Central Committee in Agnes Sagvari, *Tomegmozgalmak es politikai kuzdelmek Budapesten, 1945–1947* [Mass Movements and Political Struggles in Budapest, 1945–1947] (Budapest, 1964), p. 130. Number of Jews based on author's personal knowledge.

9. Sagvari, pp. 86, 92, 130, 262, and 302–4.

10. Quoted in Duschinsky, p. 421.

11. Sandor Nogradi, *Uj tortenet kezdodott* [A New History Began] (Buda-

pest, 1966), p. 92. The author omits to mention that the victims were Jews but also refers (p. 32) to former fascist party members among young workers who wanted to join the Communists. Though whitewashing his own opportunistic past, this leading figure of postwar history provides illuminating insights into the mentality of the Muscovites and the confusion reigning in the Party leadership between 1953 and 1956.

12. Vincent Savarius (Bela Szasz) involved in the Rajk affair mentions a figure of two hundred and twenty in his interesting memoirs, *Minden kenyszer nelkul* [Without Any Coercion] (Brussels, 1963), p. 264.

13. The author heard in 1955–56 frequent but unsubstantiated rumors that Stalin, Beria, and Rakosi hesitated for some time in choosing between Rajk and Imre Nagy (some say even Kadar) as the principal victim of the frame-up. Professor Aladar Mod, who published an intriguing but contradictory attempt to analyze the Rajk affair in the May 1969 issue of the literary journal *Kortars*, Budapest, confirmed for the first time in print that "Rakosi and his advisers" (there is no reference to the Russians in the lengthy piece) had in mind "several variations" concerning the person of the chief defendant. See also the open letter written by Rajk's widow in the June 1969 issue.

14. The emphasis was however primarily on the "Titoist-imperialist" angle. The author and most of his friends at the time paid no attention to the few sentences about "Zionism."

15. See Duschinsky, pp. 376–77, also I. Cohen, "The Jews in Hungary," *Contemporary Review*, London, November 1939, quoted by Hilberg.

16. Ibid., p. 400. See also *Hungarian-Jewish Studies* (New York, 1966), p. 421 and passim.

17. See Fejtö, p. 94, and Duschinsky, pp. 471–80. Fejtö gives no source for the estimated share of 30 per cent while Duschinsky refers to Hungarian organizations and newspapers abroad as well as to Western press reports. The author can only confirm that the number of Jews deported from the capital was certainly high and none of the deportees was shipped to the Soviet Union as some reports quoted by Duschinsky suggested at the time.

18. F. A. Vali, *Rift and Revolt in Hungary* (Cambridge, Mass., 1961), p. 64. This figure is also an estimate, but it was generally agreed that the number of internees in camps reached about a hundred thousand. See also Savarius, p. 296.

19. For list of members see *Szabad Nep*, Budapest, March 3, 1951. Proportion of Jews based on author's personal knowledge.

20. For a brilliant profile of Rakosi and the climate of those years see Aczel-Meray, especially pp. 162–83.

21. Conquest, *Great Terror*, p. 63.

22. Paul Justus (died in 1968), poet, writer, and translator of Marxist and literary classics was undoubtedly the most eminent and original thinker of the Hungarian Social Democratic movement, and leader of its left wing. Many of the purge victims and some of the high functionaries of the present regime participated at one time or another at his seminars. He was sentenced to life imprisonment at the Rajk trial and spent over five years in prison. The Kadar group offered him a ministerial post but Justus retired from active

politics and devoted his last years to the translation of Shakespeare's sonnets.

23. *Szabad Nep*, May 11, 1953.

24. Aczel-Meray, pp. 159–60; T. Meray, *Thirteen Days That Shook the Kremlin* (New York, 1959), pp. 3–9. See also for the Soviet warnings (but without the anti-Semitic outbursts) Imre Nagy, *On Communism: In Defense of the New Course* (New York, 1957), pp. 66, 250.

25. *The Counterrevolutionary Forces in the October Events in Hungary, Vol. IV* (Budapest, 1957), pp. 67–75.

26. Fejtö, p. 88.

27. This is the official figure which since 1960 has always been mentioned by the leaders of the Jewish community. As there were about 140,000 survivors, the published figures about emigration to Israel (10,000 in 1947–48 and 2000 in 1949–51) and the number of refugees after October 1956 (18,-000 to 20,000) seem to indicate that the figure of 100,000 cannot be very much off the mark. For emigration to Israel see Duschinsky, pp. 458–64. But there are no reliable statistics whatsoever and the great majority of Hungarian Jews appear to have withdrawn altogether from participation in religious life.

28. Fejtö, p. 98.

29. Geza Losonczy, who would have been the second-ranking defendant, died during the investigation according to the communique about the trial. No time or place of his death was given. One of the most brilliant and honest intellectuals, Losonczy, a prewar Communist, had contracted tuberculosis in Horthy's jails. He suffered from a new bout of serious lung condition during the three years he had to spend in prison under the Rakosi regime. Already in ailing health, Losonczy could not survive the long months of prison interrogation. He died at the age of forty.

30. The degree of prejudices was less pronounced against the Protestants (over 70 per cent of the Hungarians are Catholic): as neighbor 9.5 per cent, as friend 8.6 per cent, and as spouse 23.8 per cent. The author stressed the fact that the opinion about the gypsies was "much more shocking and discomforting" than with regard to the Jews (with rejection ranging from 64 per cent to 77 per cent) . . . For another report on racial prejudices among eleven- to fourteen-year-old high school students see a teacher's article in *Tarsadalmi Szemle*, Budapest, March 1967. The author noted that she "has encountered cases of anti-Semitism somewhat more often but in less brutal form than statements made against gypsies." See also for popular resistance and indifference to the massacres perpetrated by Hungarian troops in occupied Yugoslavia a poll among five hundred viewers of the film *Cold Days*, in *Valosag*, Budapest, December 1966.

31. Imre Dobozy, one of the (non-Jewish) leaders of the Writers' Union in *Nepszabadsag*, Budapest, February 5, 1967.

32. See Politburo member Z. Komocsin's television interview, text published in *Nepszabadsag*, June 15, 1967; editorial calling for "vigilance, unity, and discipline," *Nepszabadsag*, June 17, 1967; Apro's speech, ibid.; Sandor Gaspar, then Trade Union Chairman and Politburo member, *Nepszabadsag*,

June 29, 1967. For a more balanced approach, ibid., July 26, 1967, that is after the UN Assembly's session.

33. Related in a Radio Budapest commentary on June 20, 1967.

34. *Nepszabadsag*, June 16, 1967.

35. Quoted after *Nepszabadsag*, July 2, 1967.

36. Two series of articles written by the editor of *Nepszabadsag*, J. Gosztonyi, in January 1968 and January 1969 respectively. The paper's former correspondent in East Berlin published a seven-piece series about "The Curious Alliance of Bonn-Tel Aviv," June 15–22, 1968.

37. At the beginning of the campaign, M. Ovari, Central Committee member, in a lecture about nationalism stressed with special emphasis that regardless of his opposition to a political line "a Communist cannot be an anti-Semite . . . he cannot be a prisoner of racial prejudices," *Nepszabadsag*, March 14, 1968. The only reference to the "anti-Zionist" campaign was twenty-four lines in a lengthy piece about Poland, *Nepszabadsag*, March 26, 1968. The foreign political weekly *Magyarorszag*, when asked by readers for "information about Polish events," republished on March 31, 1968 (that is almost two weeks later) Gomulka's speech (of March 19) on two pages without any commentary whatsoever. Reports about expulsions from the party in Warsaw omitted any reference to the "Zionist" issue, *Nepszabadsag*, April 6 and 20, 1968.

38. For details see *The Times*, London, November 3, 1959; *Jewish Chronicle*, London, October 30, 1959; *Jews in Eastern Europe*, November 1959.

39. Hannah Arendt, *Eichmann in Jerusalem* (London, 1963), p. 172.

40. *East Europe*, New York, November 1963.

41. R. W. Seton-Watson, *A History of the Roumanians* (Cambridge, 1934), p. 192.

42. Ibid., p. 347.

43. Nicolas Sylvain, "Rumania" in *The Jews in the Soviet Satellites*, pp. 494–95. See also Spulber, p. 99. For population figures, ibid., pp. 142–45.

44. Spulber.

45. Sylvain, pp. 493–502. Same source, based on official census figures, gives details about the cultural patterns in the various Jewish communities. For Transylvanian Jews, see *Hungarian-Jewish Studies*, pp. 172–212.

46. Sylvain.

47. Hilberg, pp. 485–509.

48. *Hungarian-Jewish Studies*.

49. Sylvain, pp. 516–17.

50. Baron, p. 199.

51. Sylvain, p. 536.

52. Sylvain (p. 531) refers to 40,000 Jews who in 1947 legally or illegally departed from Rumania, and later (p. 549) quotes the Statistical Bulletin of Israel about the immigration of about 120,000 Rumanian Jews between 1948 and 1951. It is not clear whether the latter figure includes the early arrivals before the establishment of the State of Israel. A publication of the Jewish Agency about twenty years of immigration, states that between May 15, 1948, and 1951 one third (118,940) of Rumanian Jewry came to

Israel (*The Jerusalem Post*, July 28, 1969). As however the number of Jews in postwar Rumania was 428,000, the immigrants could not have amounted to one third of the total. The estimate is probably based on a figure of 345,-000, published in the spring of 1948 by the Jewish Democratic Committee in Bucharest, the correctness of which is disputed by Sylvain, pp. 540 and 556.

53. Sylvain, pp. 532–40; *The Times*, London, November 3, 1959. See also R. L. Wolff, *The Balkans in Our Time* (Cambridge, Mass., 1956), pp. 460–61.

54. Data based on notes made by the author on two visits to the museum in 1967.

55. *Scinteia*, Bucharest, May 9, 1966.

56. Ana Pauker allegedly denounced her own husband as a Trotskyite. See Wolff, p. 278, and D. J. Dallin, *Soviet Espionage* (New Haven, 1956), p. 100.

57. For details see Ghita Ionescu, *Communism in Rumania* (London, 1964), p. 214, and Wolff, p. 460. For a brief but interesting sketch of the personality of Ana Pauker and other Communist leaders as seen by a foreign observer during the battle for power see Elisabeth Barker, *Truce in the Balkans* (London, 1948), pp. 137–43.

58. Ceausescu's speech at the 1961 plenum, published in *Scinteia*, December 13, 1961.

59. See R. V. Burks, "Rumäniens nationale Abweichung" (Rumania's National Deviation), in *Osteuropa*, Stuttgart, May–June 1966.

60. See speech by Petre Borila at the 1961 plenum, *Scinteia*, December 13, 1961, and by Valter Roman at the Tenth Party Congress who referred to five hundred Rumanian participants in the Spanish Civil War and three hundred in the French World War II resistance movement. *Scinteia*, August 9, 1969.

61. For Patrascanu's co-defendants see Ionescu, pp. 165–66, and for Chisinevschi's responsibility see the Central Committee resolution "about the rehabilitation of some party functionaries," *Scinteia*, April 27, 1968. Chisinevschi died in 1964.

62. For speeches by Borila, Marin, Roman, and others, see *Scinteia*, December 7–19, 1961.

63. Radio Free Europe Research Department, The New Rumanian Central Committee, August 10, 1965 (Munich, mimeographed). Out of the 121 full and 79 alternate members elected at the Congress in August 1965, 12 were of Jewish origin according to the same source.

64. Central Committee resolution of April 1968, *Scinteia*, April 27, 1968.

65. Within four years, six of the nine Politburo members in power during Gheorghiu-Dej's lifetime and four out of the seven members of the Standing Presidium elected at the 1965 Congress were removed from political life.

66. Central Committee resolution (see n. 64).

67. They are Leonte Rautu, a Soviet-trained erstwhile Stalinist who despite his alleged unpopularity in the Party has so far survived all the reshuffles; Gheorghe Stoica, a veteran of the Spanish Civil War who during his exile in Moscow was among the Rumanian victims of Stalin's purges; and Petre Lupu, a professional Party functionary since World War II.

68. Marin lost his post as planning chief in the summer of 1965. Though he

was a favorite of Gheorghiu-Dej (like Ceausescu himself!), he has remained a member of the Government. Other ministers of Jewish origin removed in 1965 were Mihai Petre, Minister of Foreign Trade, and Mihail Florescu, Minister of Chemical Industries. The first has a minor job as deputy manager of an enterprise, while Florescu became a section chief of the Central Committee apparatus. As however planning, foreign trade and chemicals were repeatedly criticized as weak spots and as there were many other personnel changes, the Jewish origin of the three is unlikely to have played a decisive role. Marin and Florescu were re-elected as members of the Central Committee at the 1969 Congress.

69. Baron, p. 261.

70. See n. 51.

71. See Fejtö, p. 74.

72. The New York *Times*, January 27 and May 24, 1959, in dispatches from Bucharest referred to unofficial estimates of 250,000 and 200,000 to 250,000 respectively. *East Europe*, New York, March 1959, published a figure of 200,000 for 1957, based on data supplied by the World Jewish Congress; *Jewish Chronicle*, October 30, 1959, and some Jewish visitors to Rumania cited an estimated number of 180,000.

73. The New York *Times*, February 26, 1969.

74. Ibid. See also *Scinteia*, March 8, 1959.

75. See Fejtö, p. 77.

76. For diplomats see Tanjug dispatch (Belgrade-Bucharest), July 7, 1960. For predicament of Jews, the New York *Times*, May 24, 1959, and Radio Free Europe, *Situation Report*, Munich, December 24, 1959. For arrests and trials see n. 38.

77. Figures from unimpeachable Jewish sources in Vienna. Some sources claim that between September 1958 and 1960 not 20,000 but 45,000 to 50,-000 Jews left Rumania.

78. Information from the Federation of Jewish Communities in Bucharest transmitted in the spring of 1969 through courtesy of Rumanian Embassy in Vienna. Similar figures were given by Chief Rabbi Rosen on his visit to Britain and the United States at the end of 1966 as quoted in *Jews in Eastern Europe*, May 1967. At the beginning of the same year, however, at a press conference in London he put the Jewish community at "approximately 110,000," see *Jews in Eastern Europe*, June 1966.

79. For Rumanian Jews in Israel see *Le Monde*, January 24, 1968.

80. Information from the Federation of Jewish Communities and for the Joint welfare program, interview with Mr. Louis Horwitz in *L'Arche*, Paris, February 25, 1969. He indicated that a further seventy-five hundred elderly and needy persons would also receive monthly payments providing the organization's budget sufficed.

81. See statement by Rabbi Max Nussbaum at the session of the council of the World Jewish Congress and in an interview, *The Times*, London, July 12, 1968.

82. Joint statement on June 11 circulated as an official document at the United Nations. See also communique about Foreign Minister Manescu's

376

talks with Israeli and Egyptian ambassador and editorial, *Scinteia*, June 13, 1967. The line—Israeli withdrawal but recognition of each state within secure and recognized borders—was repeated in *Scinteia*, May 28, 1968.

83. *Le Monde*, January 24, 1968.

84. For latest trade figures see Reuters' dispatch from Tel Aviv, February 10, 1969, and *Neue Zürcher Zeitung*, March 5, 1969, in connection with Nicolae Giosan, the Rumanian Minister of Agriculture's visit to Israel (February 3–10, 1969). See also *The Jerusalem Post*, October 2, 1969.

85. Rumania and Israel decided on August 17, 1969, to raise their diplomatic relations to the ambassadorial level. As a result, Sudan and Syria broke off diplomatic relations with Rumania while Iraq and the United Arab Republic recalled their heads of mission. The Rumanian Government responded with protest notes and articles, accusing the four Arab states of interference in Rumania's internal affairs. Significantly, the Soviet and East European press reported the Arab reactions to the Rumanian move. In September the Arab League threatened to boycott Rumania economically. By the spring of 1970, however, the Rumanian diplomacy succeeded in improving relations with the Arab world.

# INDEX

388

| DATE DUE | | | |
|---|---|---|---|
| MAR 2 0 1994 | | | |
| APR 1 0 1994 | | | |
| | | | |
| | | | |
| | | | |
| | | | |
| | | | |
| | | | |
| | | | |
| | | | |
| | | | |
| | | | |
| | | | |